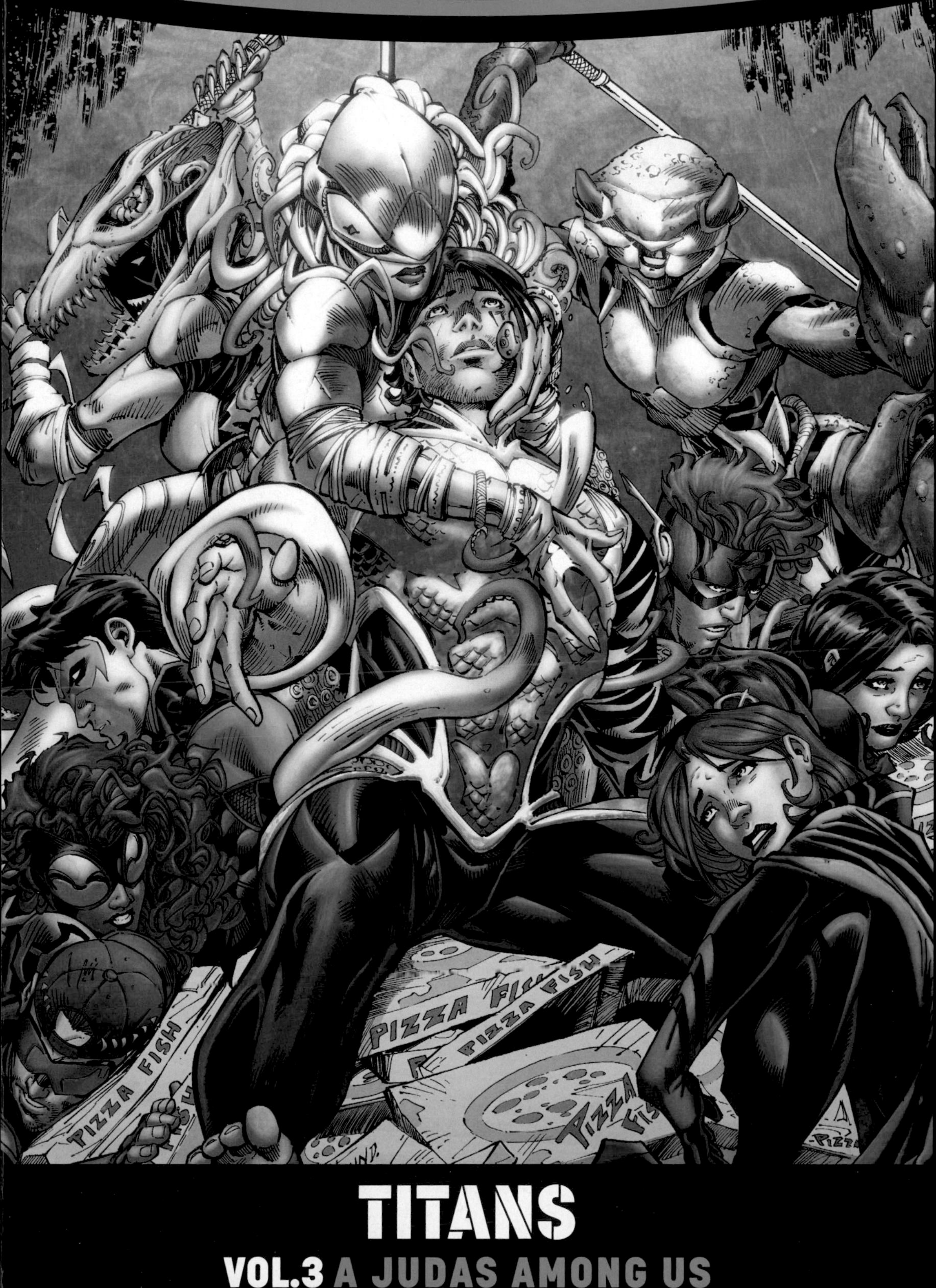
PIZZA FISH
PIZZA FISH
PIZZA FISH
PIZZA FISH

TITANS

VOL.3 A JUDAS AMONG US

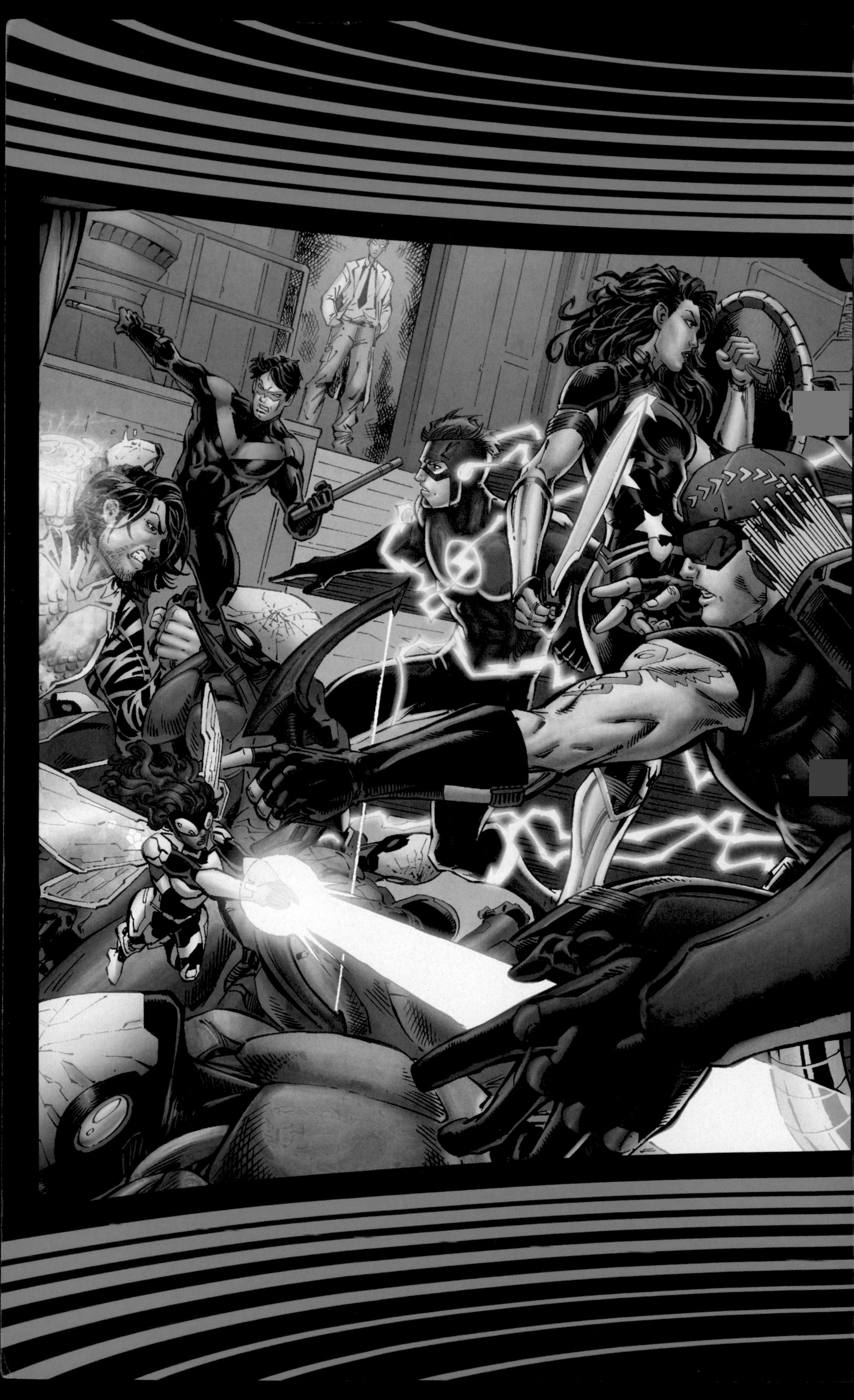

TITANS

VOL.3 A JUDAS AMONG US

DAN ABNETT
writer

BRETT BOOTH
KENNETH ROCAFORT * V KEN MARION * MINKYU JUNG
pencillers

NORM RAPMUND
MICK GRAY
inkers

ANDREW DALHOUSE
DAN BROWN * BLOND
colorists

JOSH REED * **TRAVIS LANHAM**
letterers

DAN MORA
collection cover artist

NIGHTWING created by **MARV WOLFMAN** and **GEORGE PÉREZ**

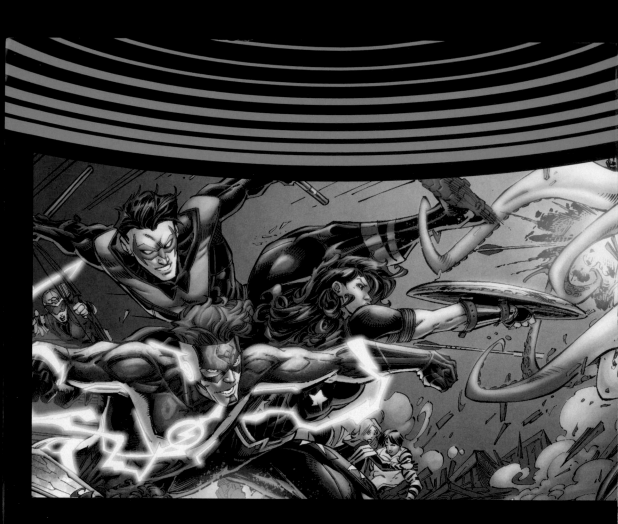

ALEX ANTONE Editor - Original Series * **BRITTANY HOLZHERR** Associate Editor - Original Series
DIEGO LOPEZ DAVE WIELGOSZ Assistant Editors - Original Series
JEB WOODARD Group Editor - Collected Editions * **ROBIN WILDMAN** Editor - Collected Edition
STEVE COOK Design Director - Books * **MONIQUE NARBONETA** Publication Design

BOB HARRAS Senior VP - Editor-in-Chief, DC Comics
PAT McCALLUM Executive Editor, DC Comics

DIANE NELSON President * **DAN DiDIO** Publisher * **JIM LEE** Publisher * **GEOFF JOHNS** President & Chief Creative Officer
AMIT DESAI Executive VP - Business & Marketing Strategy, Direct to Consumer & Global Franchise Management
SAM ADES Senior VP & General Manager, Digital Services * **BOBBIE CHASE** VP & Executive Editor, Young Reader & Talent Development
MARK CHIARELLO Senior VP - Art, Design & Collected Editions * **JOHN CUNNINGHAM** Senior VP - Sales & Trade Marketing
ANNE DePIES Senior VP - Business Strategy, Finance & Administration * **DON FALLETTI** VP - Manufacturing Operations
LAWRENCE GANEM VP - Editorial Administration & Talent Relations * **ALISON GILL** Senior VP - Manufacturing & Operations
HANK KANALZ Senior VP - Editorial Strategy & Administration * **JAY KOGAN** VP - Legal Affairs * **JACK MAHAN** VP - Business Affairs
NICK J. NAPOLITANO VP - Manufacturing Administration * **EDDIE SCANNELL** VP - Consumer Marketing
COURTNEY SIMMONS Senior VP - Publicity & Communications * **JIM (SKI) SOKOLOWSKI** VP - Comic Book Specialty Sales & Trade Marketing
NANCY SPEARS VP - Mass, Book, Digital Sales & Trade Marketing * **MICHELE R. WELLS** VP - Content Strategy

TITANS VOL. 3: A JUDAS AMONG US

DC Comics, 2900 West Alameda Ave., Burbank, CA 91505
Printed by LSC Communications, Kendallville, IN, USA. 1/12/18. First Printing.
ISBN: 978-1-4012-7759-8

Library of Congress Cataloging-in-Publication Data is available.

PEFC Certified
Printed on paper from sustainably managed forests, controlled sources
www.pefc.org
PEFC/29-31-337

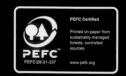

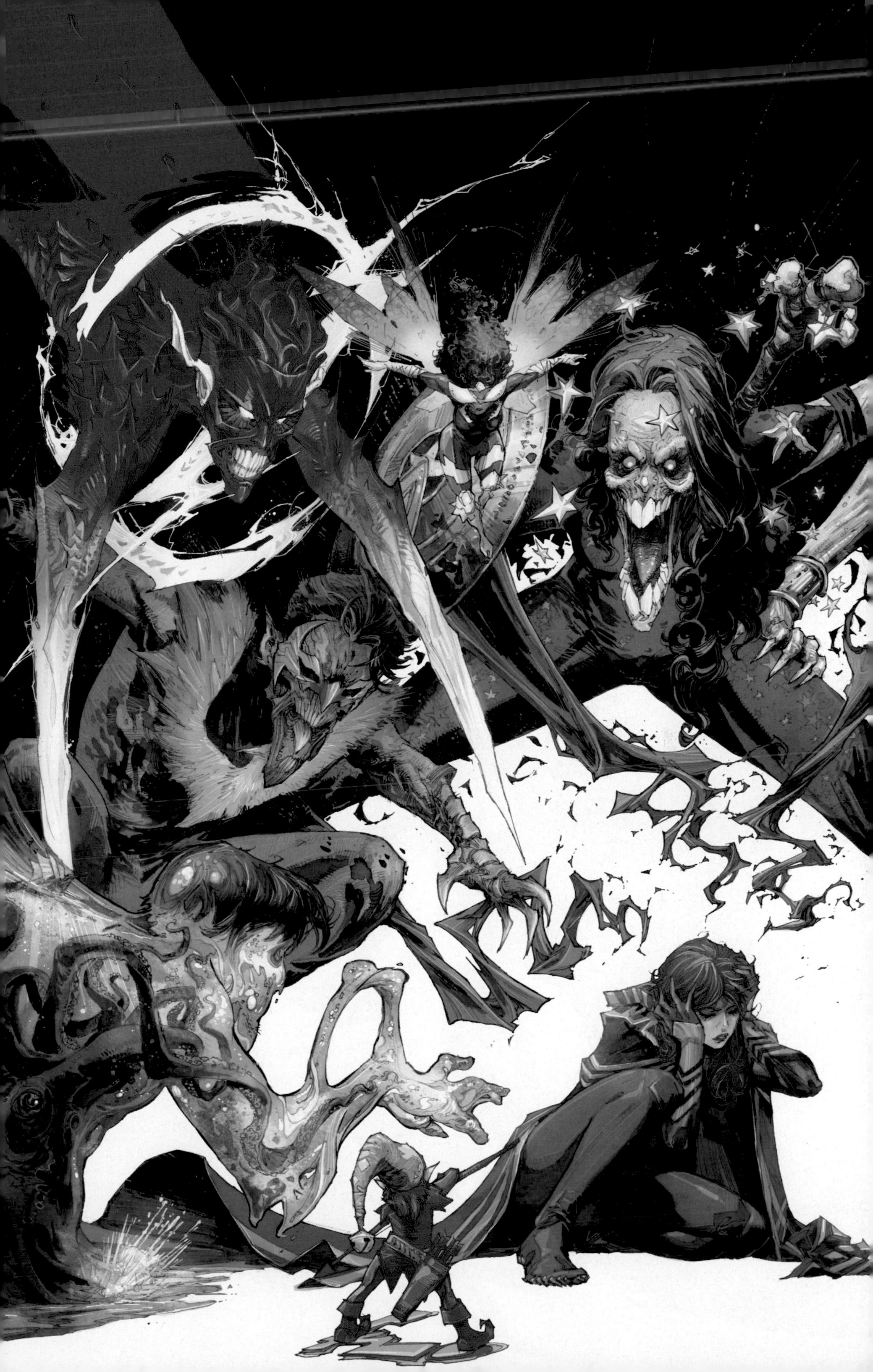

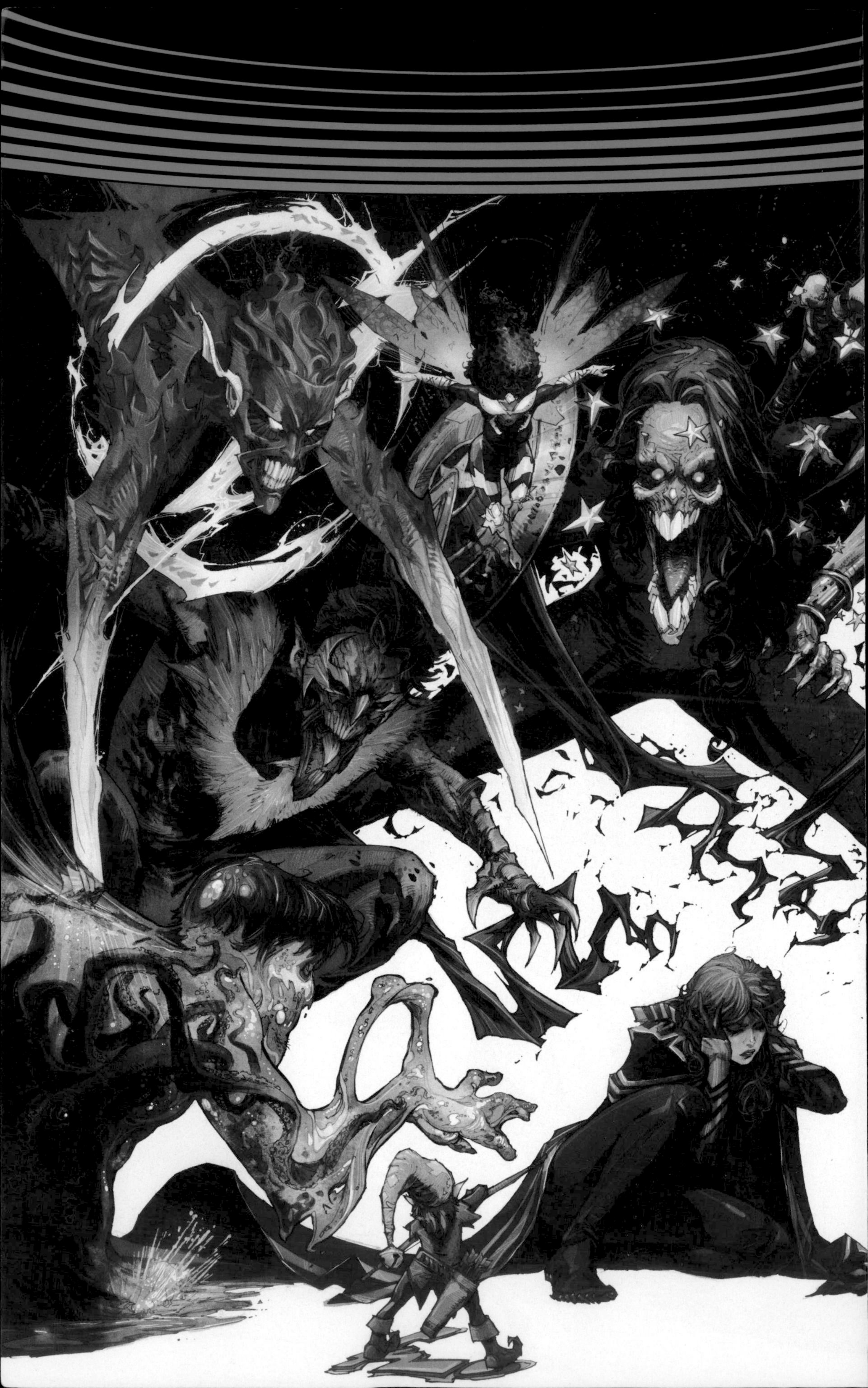

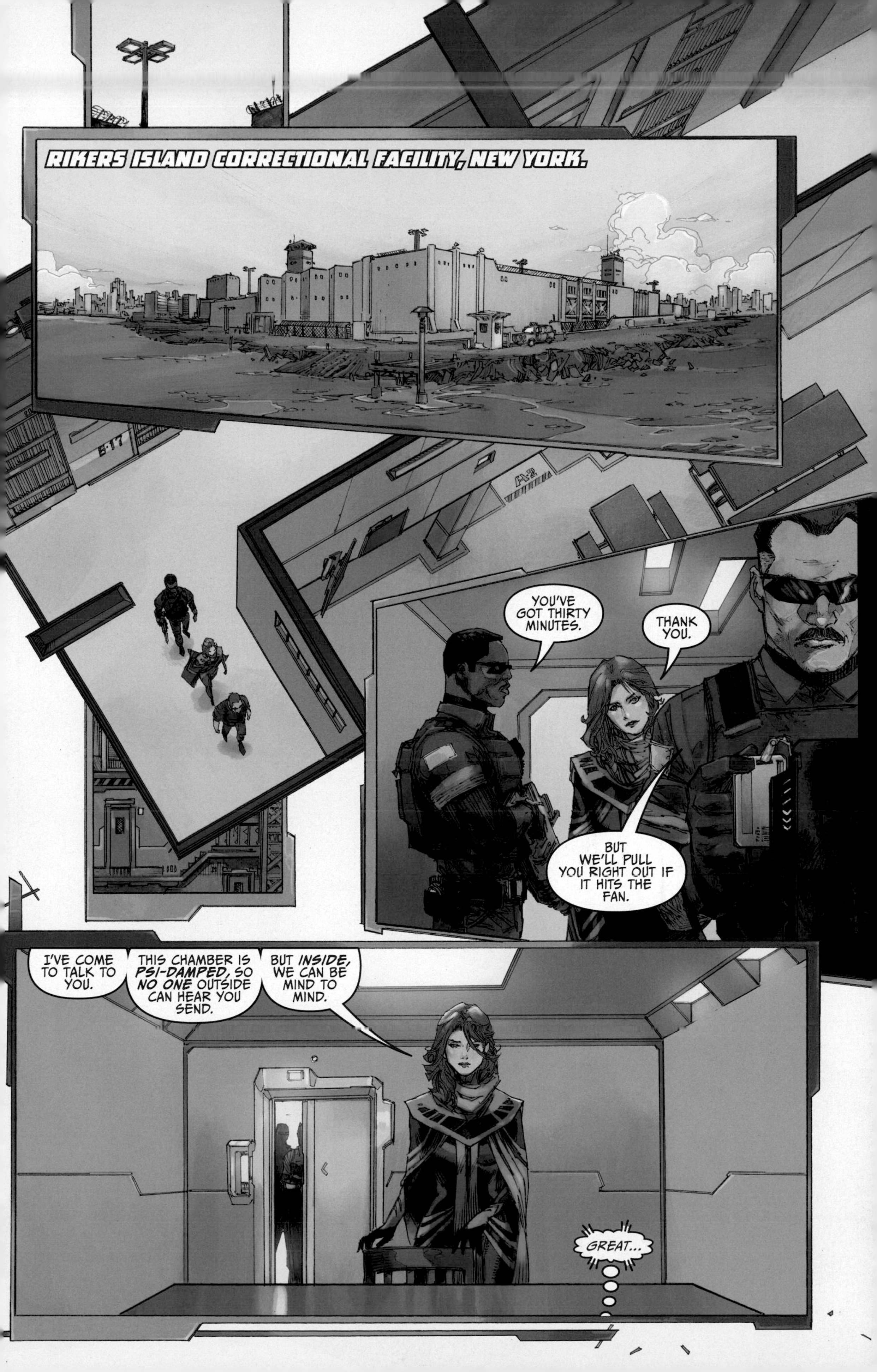

RIKERS ISLAND CORRECTIONAL FACILITY, NEW YORK.
YOU'VE GOT THIRTY MINUTES.
THANK YOU.
BUT WE'LL PULL YOU RIGHT OUT IF IT HITS THE FAN.
I'VE COME TO TALK TO YOU.
THIS CHAMBER IS *PSI-DAMPED*, SO *NO ONE* OUTSIDE CAN HEAR YOU SEND.
BUT *INSIDE*, WE CAN BE MIND TO MIND.
GREAT...

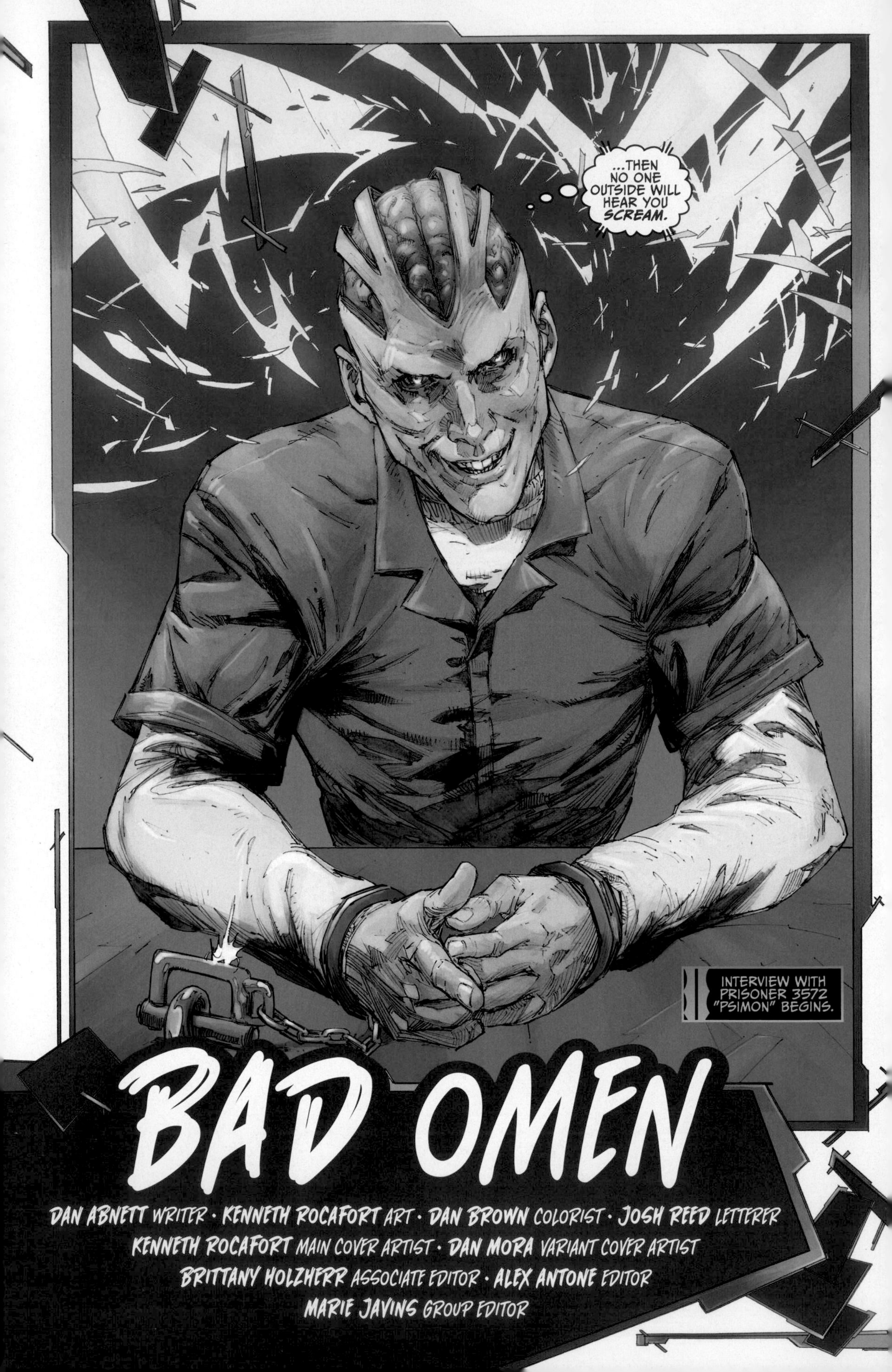
...THEN NO ONE OUTSIDE WILL HEAR YOU SCREAM.
INTERVIEW WITH PRISONER 3572 "PSIMON" BEGINS.
BAD OMEN
DAN ABNETT WRITER · KENNETH ROCAFORT ART · DAN BROWN COLORIST · JOSH REED LETTERER
KENNETH ROCAFORT MAIN COVER ARTIST · DAN MORA VARIANT COVER ARTIST
BRITTANY HOLZHERR ASSOCIATE EDITOR · ALEX ANTONE EDITOR
MARIE JAVINS GROUP EDITOR

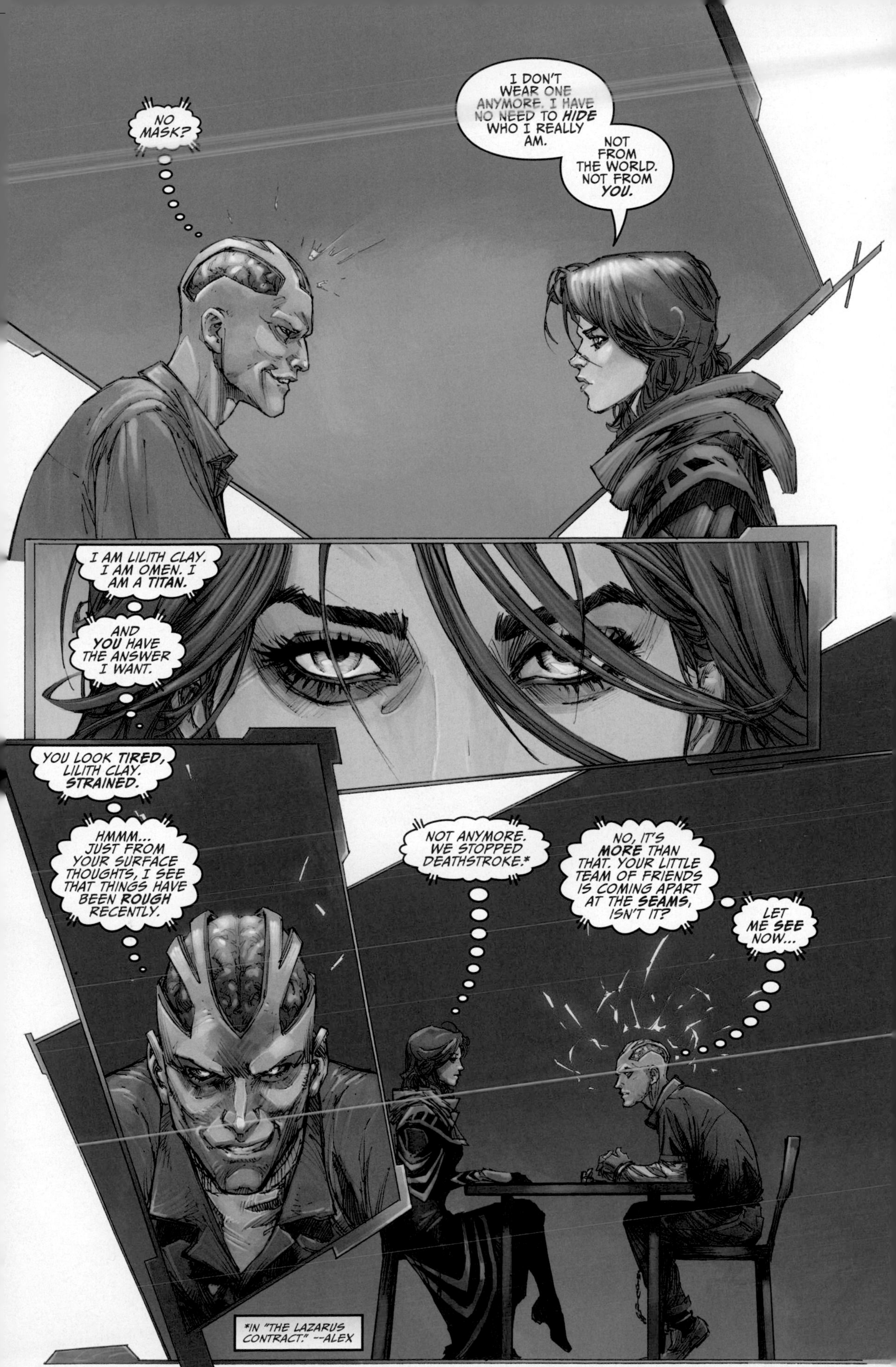
NO MASK?
I DON'T WEAR ONE ANYMORE. I HAVE NO NEED TO HIDE WHO I REALLY AM.
NOT FROM THE WORLD. NOT FROM YOU.
I AM LILITH CLAY. I AM OMEN. I AM A TITAN.
AND YOU HAVE THE ANSWER I WANT.
YOU LOOK TIRED, LILITH CLAY. STRAINED.
HMMM... JUST FROM YOUR SURFACE THOUGHTS, I SEE THAT THINGS HAVE BEEN ROUGH RECENTLY.
NOT ANYMORE. WE STOPPED DEATHSTROKE.*
NO, IT'S MORE THAN THAT. YOUR LITTLE TEAM OF FRIENDS IS COMING APART AT THE SEAMS, ISN'T IT?
LET ME SEE NOW...
*IN "THE LAZARUS CONTRACT." --ALEX

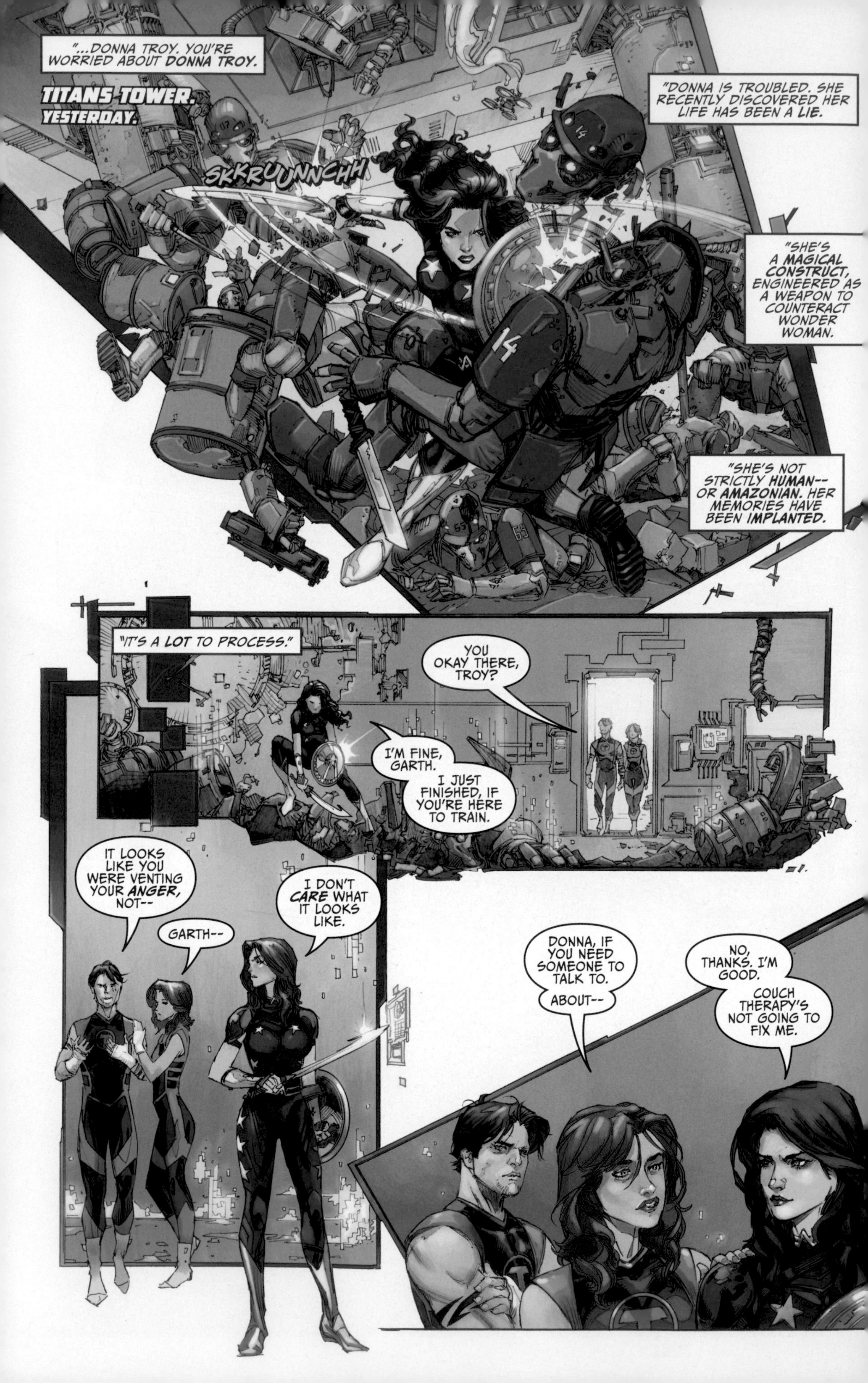
"...DONNA TROY. YOU'RE WORRIED ABOUT DONNA TROY.
TITANS TOWER. YESTERDAY.
"DONNA IS TROUBLED. SHE RECENTLY DISCOVERED HER LIFE HAS BEEN A LIE.
SKKRUUNNCHH
"SHE'S A MAGICAL CONSTRUCT, ENGINEERED AS A WEAPON TO COUNTERACT WONDER WOMAN.
"SHE'S NOT STRICTLY HUMAN-- OR AMAZONIAN. HER MEMORIES HAVE BEEN IMPLANTED.
"IT'S A LOT TO PROCESS."
YOU OKAY THERE, TROY?
I'M FINE, GARTH.
I JUST FINISHED, IF YOU'RE HERE TO TRAIN.
IT LOOKS LIKE YOU WERE VENTING YOUR ANGER, NOT--
GARTH--
I DON'T CARE WHAT IT LOOKS LIKE.
DONNA, IF YOU NEED SOMEONE TO TALK TO.
ABOUT--
NO, THANKS. I'M GOOD.
COUCH THERAPY'S NOT GOING TO FIX ME.

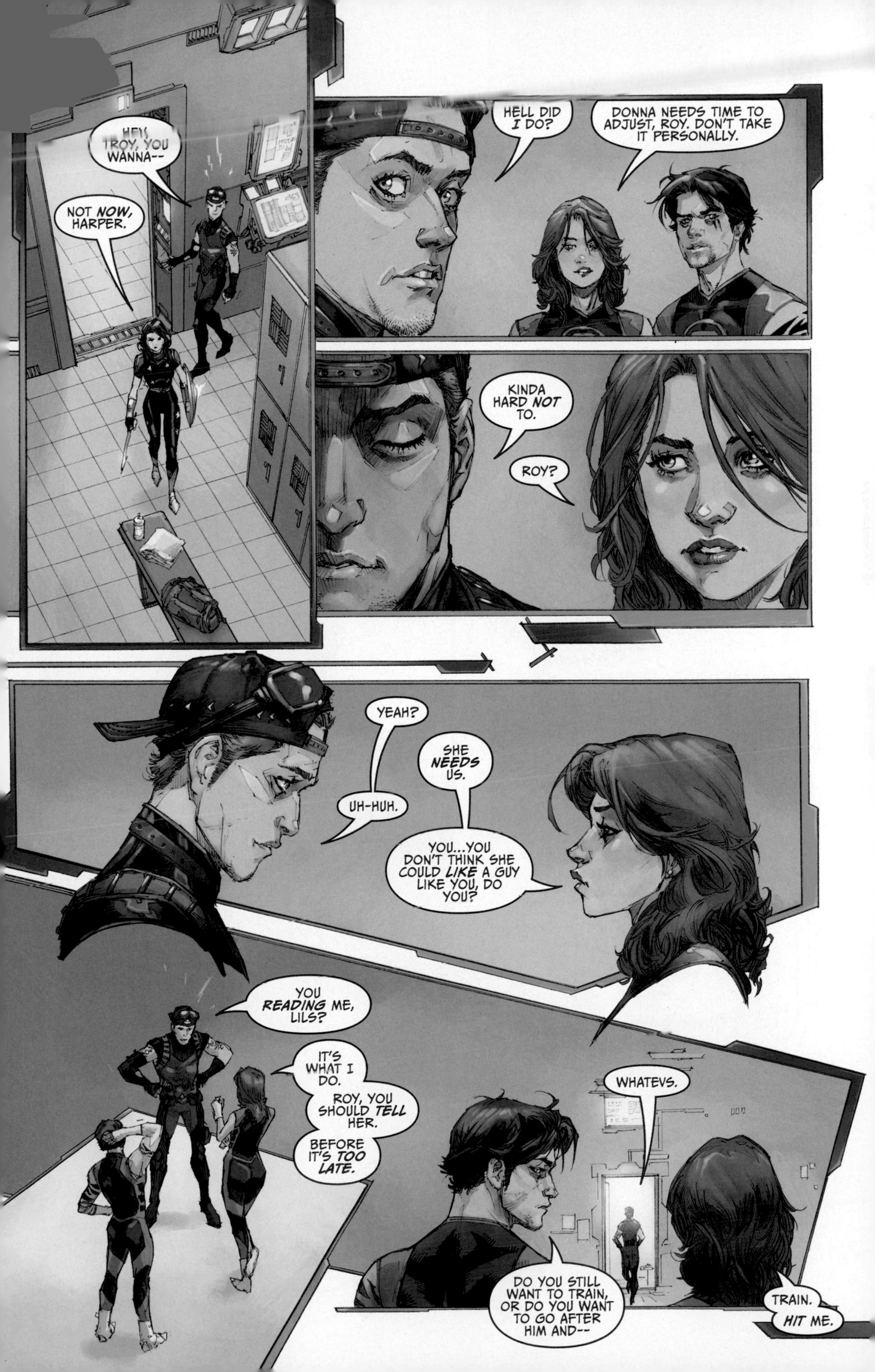
HEY, TROY, YOU WANNA--
NOT NOW, HARPER.
HELL DID I DO?
DONNA NEEDS TIME TO ADJUST, ROY. DON'T TAKE IT PERSONALLY.
KINDA HARD NOT TO.
ROY?
YEAH?
SHE NEEDS US.
UH-HUH.
YOU...YOU DON'T THINK SHE COULD LIKE A GUY LIKE YOU, DO YOU?
YOU READING ME, LILS?
IT'S WHAT I DO.
ROY, YOU SHOULD TELL HER.
BEFORE IT'S TOO LATE.
WHATEVS.
DO YOU STILL WANT TO TRAIN, OR DO YOU WANT TO GO AFTER HIM AND--
TRAIN.
HIT ME.

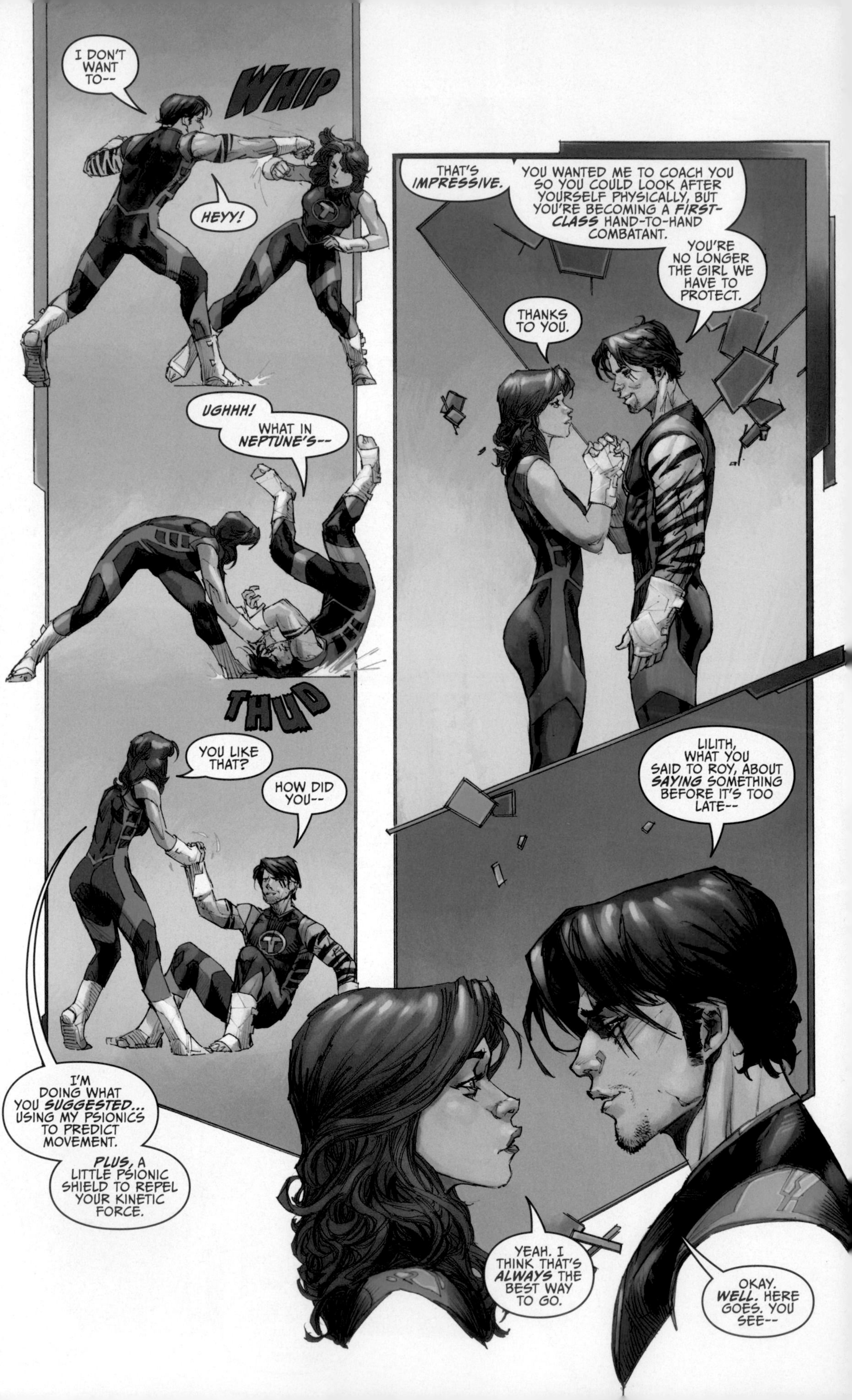
I DON'T WANT TO--
WHIP
HEYY!
UGHHH! WHAT IN NEPTUNE'S--
THUD
YOU LIKE THAT?
HOW DID YOU--
I'M DOING WHAT YOU SUGGESTED... USING MY PSIONICS TO PREDICT MOVEMENT.
PLUS, A LITTLE PSIONIC SHIELD TO REPEL YOUR KINETIC FORCE.
THAT'S IMPRESSIVE.
YOU WANTED ME TO COACH YOU SO YOU COULD LOOK AFTER YOURSELF PHYSICALLY, BUT YOU'RE BECOMING A FIRST-CLASS HAND-TO-HAND COMBATANT.
YOU'RE NO LONGER THE GIRL WE HAVE TO PROTECT.
THANKS TO YOU.
LILITH, WHAT YOU SAID TO ROY, ABOUT SAYING SOMETHING BEFORE IT'S TOO LATE--
YEAH. I THINK THAT'S ALWAYS THE BEST WAY TO GO.
OKAY. WELL. HERE GOES. YOU SEE--

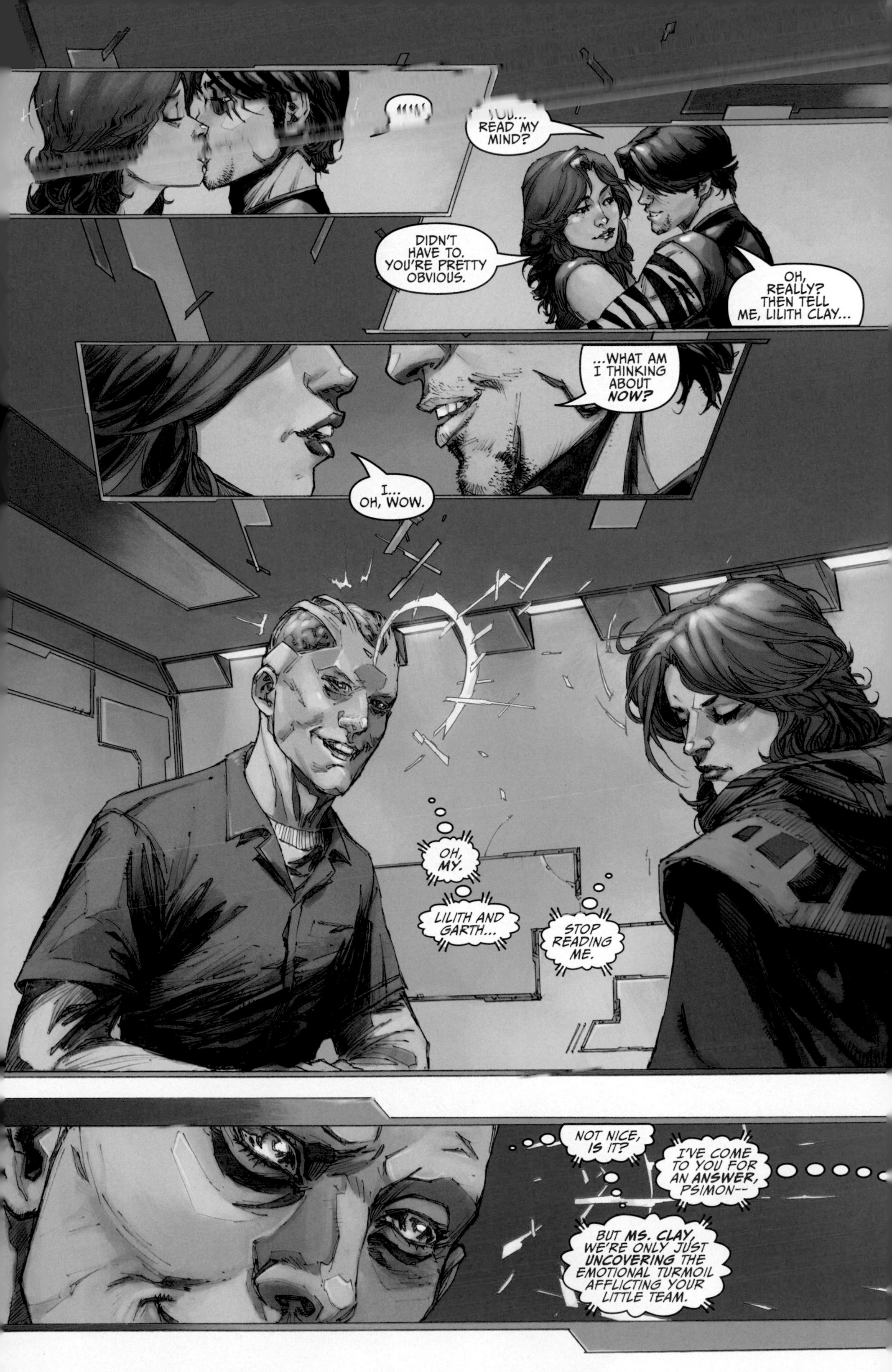
READ MY MIND?
DIDN'T HAVE TO. YOU'RE PRETTY OBVIOUS.
OH, REALLY? THEN TELL ME, LILITH CLAY...
...WHAT AM I THINKING ABOUT NOW?
I... OH, WOW.
OH, MY.
LILITH AND GARTH...
STOP READING ME.
NOT NICE, IS IT?
I'VE COME TO YOU FOR AN ANSWER, PSIMON--
BUT MS. CLAY, WE'RE ONLY JUST UNCOVERING THE EMOTIONAL TURMOIL AFFLICTING YOUR LITTLE TEAM.

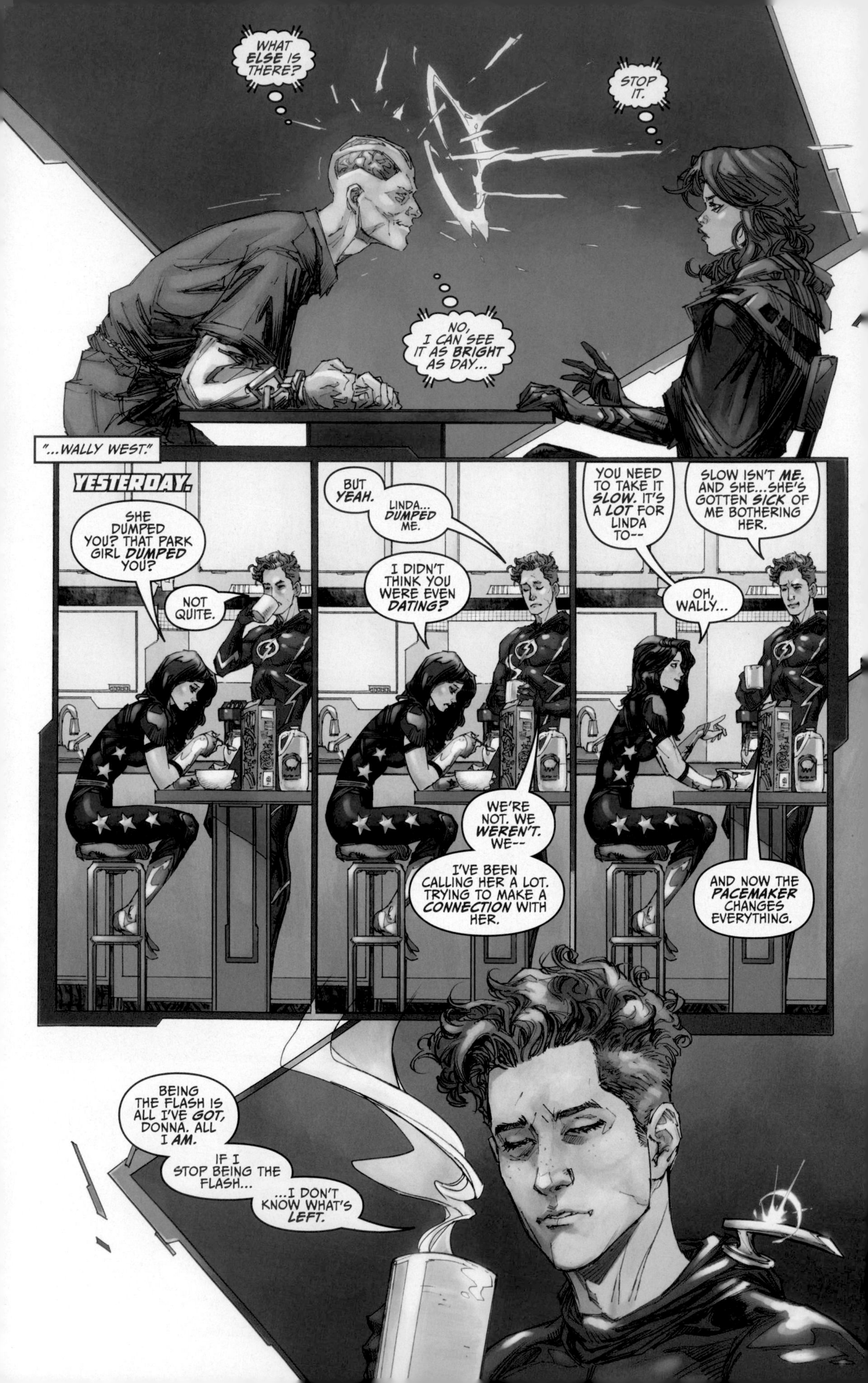
WHAT ELSE IS THERE?
STOP IT.
NO, I CAN SEE IT AS BRIGHT AS DAY...
"...WALLY WEST."
YESTERDAY.
SHE DUMPED YOU? THAT PARK GIRL DUMPED YOU?
NOT QUITE.
BUT YEAH.
LINDA... DUMPED ME.
I DIDN'T THINK YOU WERE EVEN DATING?
WE'RE NOT. WE WEREN'T. WE--
I'VE BEEN CALLING HER A LOT. TRYING TO MAKE A CONNECTION WITH HER.
YOU NEED TO TAKE IT SLOW. IT'S A LOT FOR LINDA TO--
SLOW ISN'T ME. AND SHE...SHE'S GOTTEN SICK OF ME BOTHERING HER.
OH, WALLY...
AND NOW THE PACEMAKER CHANGES EVERYTHING.
BEING THE FLASH IS ALL I'VE GOT, DONNA. ALL I AM.
IF I STOP BEING THE FLASH...
...I DON'T KNOW WHAT'S LEFT.

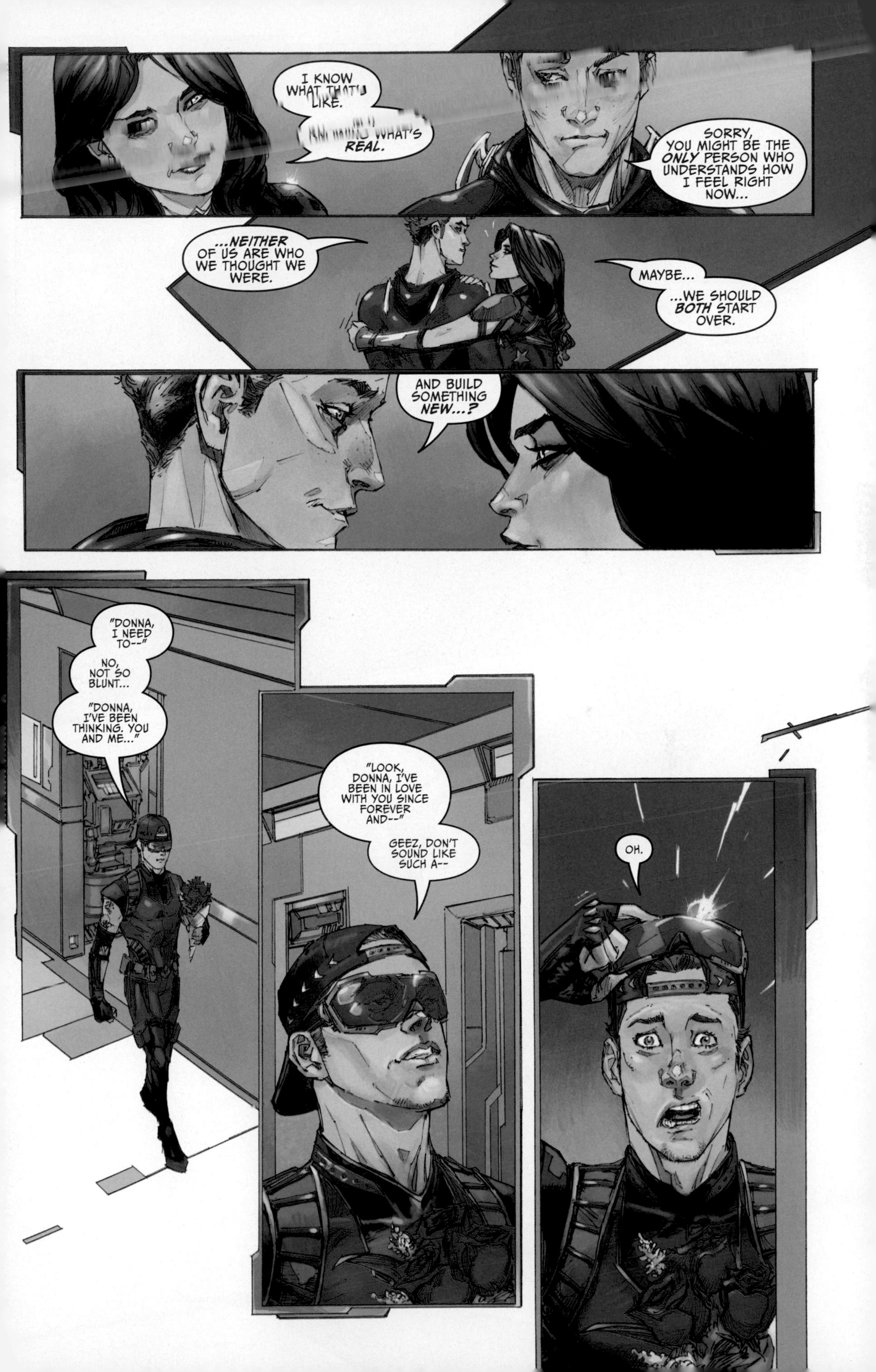

I KNOW WHAT THAT'S LIKE.
WHAT'S REAL.
SORRY, YOU MIGHT BE THE ONLY PERSON WHO UNDERSTANDS HOW I FEEL RIGHT NOW...
...NEITHER OF US ARE WHO WE THOUGHT WE WERE.
MAYBE...
...WE SHOULD BOTH START OVER.
AND BUILD SOMETHING NEW...?
"DONNA, I NEED TO--"
NO, NOT SO BLUNT...
"DONNA, I'VE BEEN THINKING. YOU AND ME..."
"LOOK, DONNA, I'VE BEEN IN LOVE WITH YOU SINCE FOREVER AND--"
GEEZ, DON'T SOUND LIKE SUCH A--
OH.

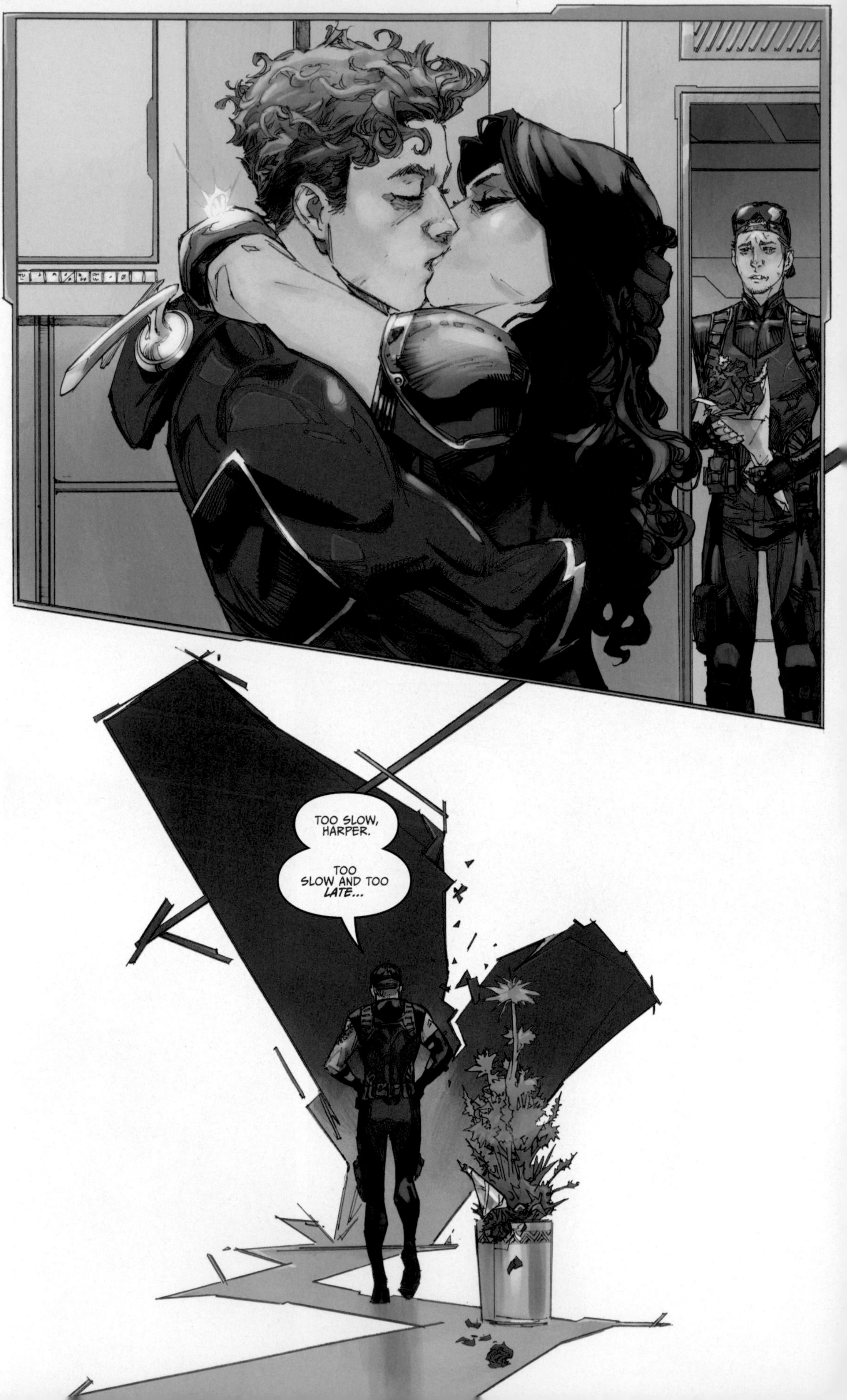
TOO SLOW, HARPER.
TOO SLOW AND TOO *LATE*...

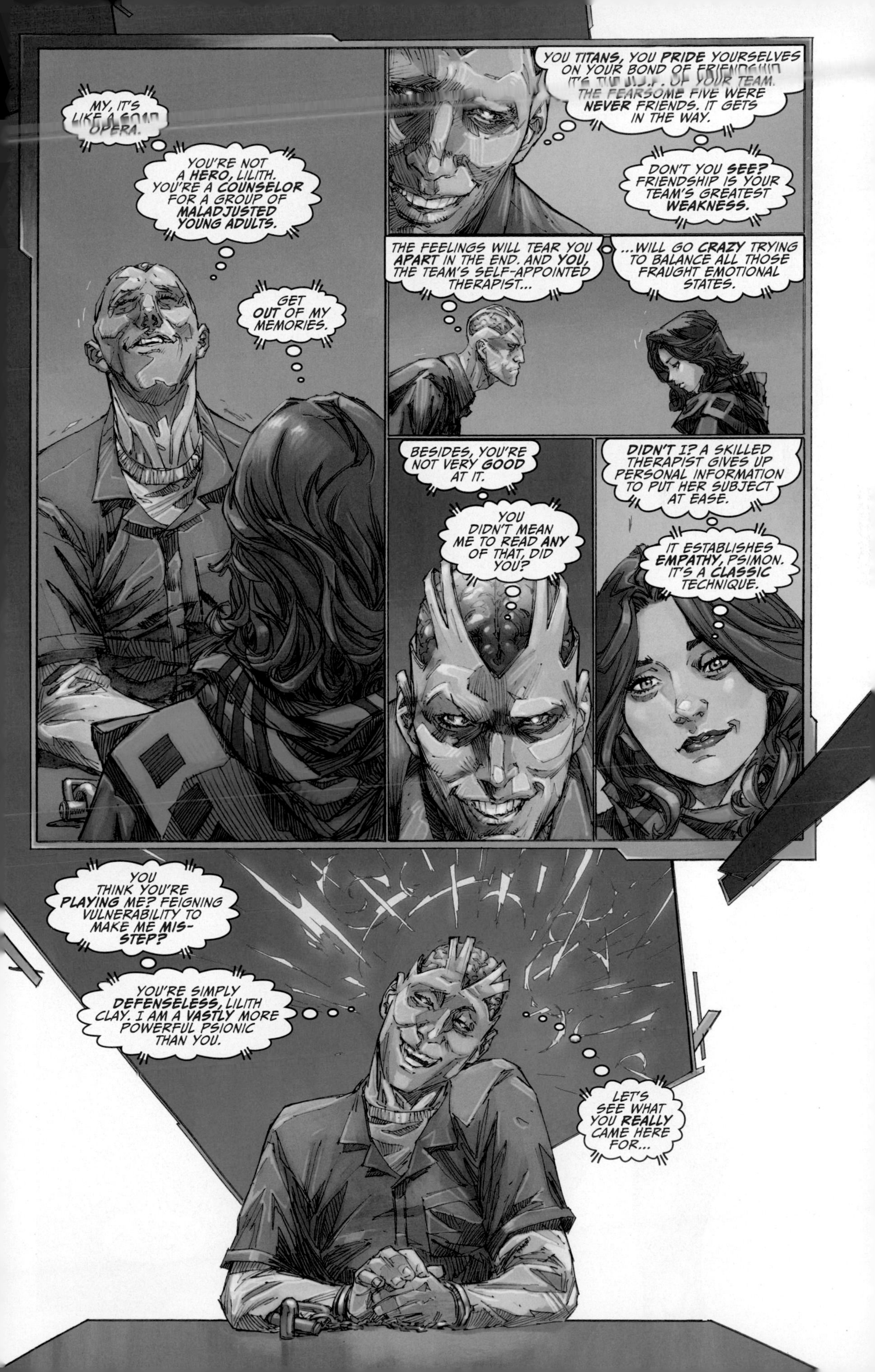
MY, IT'S LIKE A SOAP OPERA.
YOU'RE NOT A HERO, LILITH. YOU'RE A COUNSELOR FOR A GROUP OF MALADJUSTED YOUNG ADULTS.
GET OUT OF MY MEMORIES.
YOU TITANS, YOU PRIDE YOURSELVES ON YOUR BOND OF FRIENDSHIP. IT'S THE OF YOUR TEAM. THE FEARSOME FIVE WERE NEVER FRIENDS. IT GETS IN THE WAY.
DON'T YOU SEE? FRIENDSHIP IS YOUR TEAM'S GREATEST WEAKNESS.
THE FEELINGS WILL TEAR YOU APART IN THE END. AND YOU, THE TEAM'S SELF-APPOINTED THERAPIST...
...WILL GO CRAZY TRYING TO BALANCE ALL THOSE FRAUGHT EMOTIONAL STATES.
BESIDES, YOU'RE NOT VERY GOOD AT IT.
YOU DIDN'T MEAN ME TO READ ANY OF THAT, DID YOU?
DIDN'T I? A SKILLED THERAPIST GIVES UP PERSONAL INFORMATION TO PUT HER SUBJECT AT EASE.
IT ESTABLISHES EMPATHY, PSIMON. IT'S A CLASSIC TECHNIQUE.
YOU THINK YOU'RE PLAYING ME? FEIGNING VULNERABILITY TO MAKE ME MIS-STEP?
YOU'RE SIMPLY DEFENSELESS, LILITH CLAY. I AM A VASTLY MORE POWERFUL PSIONIC THAN YOU.
LET'S SEE WHAT YOU REALLY CAME HERE FOR...

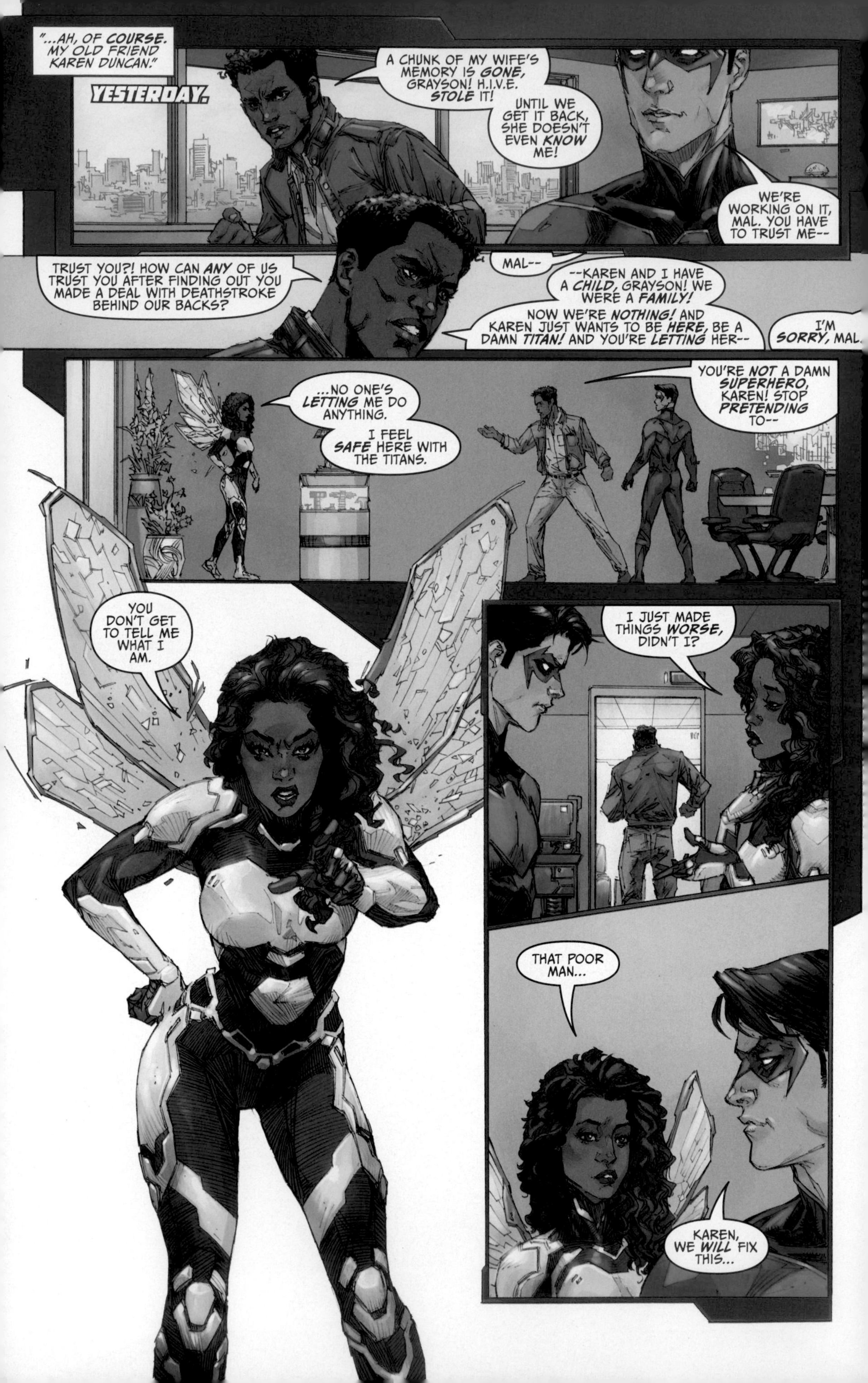
"...AH, OF COURSE. MY OLD FRIEND KAREN DUNCAN."
YESTERDAY.
A CHUNK OF MY WIFE'S MEMORY IS GONE, GRAYSON! H.I.V.E. STOLE IT!
UNTIL WE GET IT BACK, SHE DOESN'T EVEN KNOW ME!
WE'RE WORKING ON IT, MAL. YOU HAVE TO TRUST ME--
TRUST YOU?! HOW CAN ANY OF US TRUST YOU AFTER FINDING OUT YOU MADE A DEAL WITH DEATHSTROKE BEHIND OUR BACKS?
MAL--
--KAREN AND I HAVE A CHILD, GRAYSON! WE WERE A FAMILY!
NOW WE'RE NOTHING! AND KAREN JUST WANTS TO BE HERE, BE A DAMN TITAN! AND YOU'RE LETTING HER--
I'M SORRY, MAL.
...NO ONE'S LETTING ME DO ANYTHING.
I FEEL SAFE HERE WITH THE TITANS.
YOU'RE NOT A DAMN SUPERHERO, KAREN! STOP PRETENDING TO--
YOU DON'T GET TO TELL ME WHAT I AM.
I JUST MADE THINGS WORSE, DIDN'T I?
THAT POOR MAN...
KAREN, WE WILL FIX THIS...

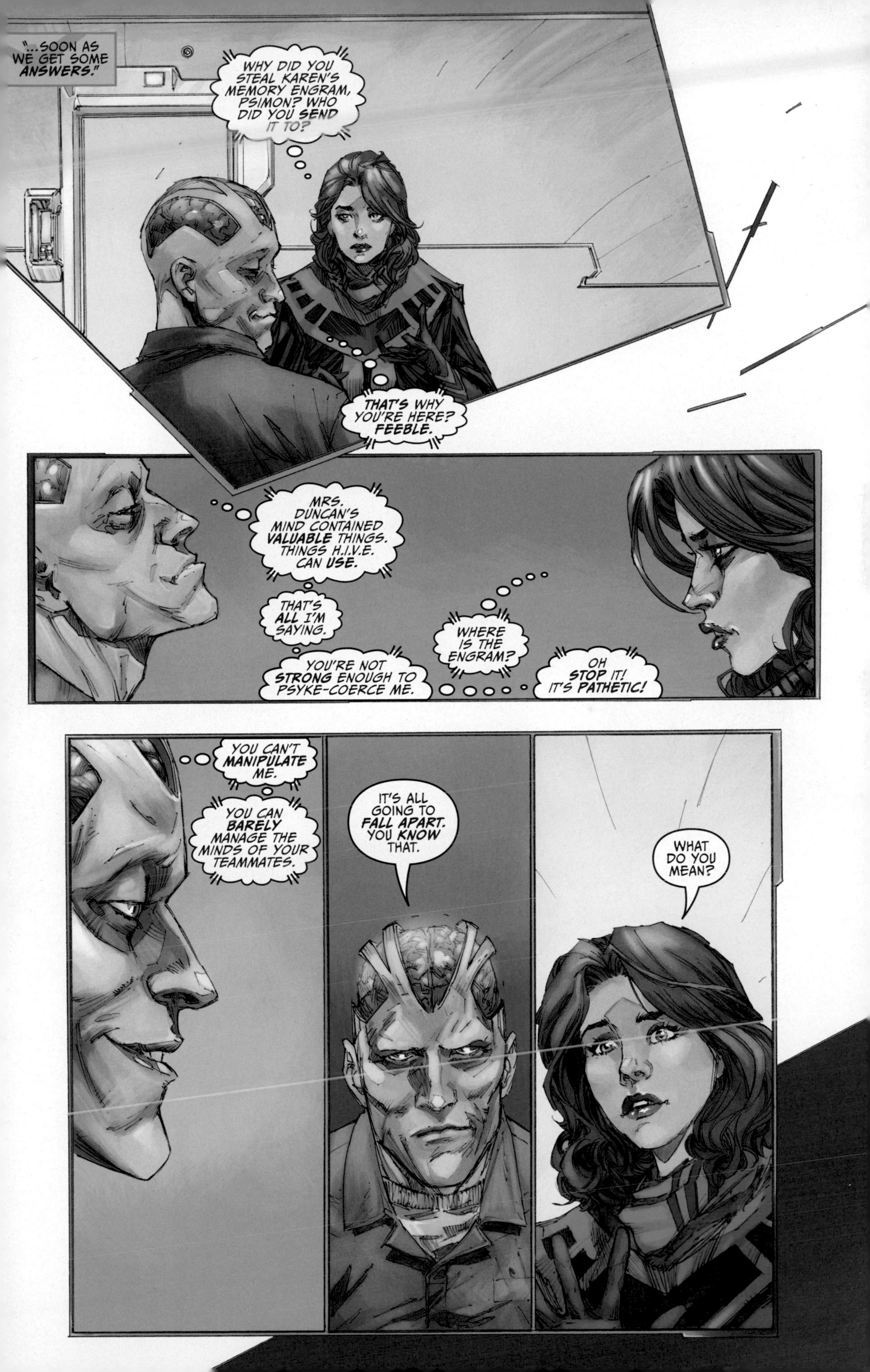
"...SOON AS WE GET SOME ANSWERS."
WHY DID YOU STEAL KAREN'S MEMORY ENGRAM, PSIMON? WHO DID YOU SEND IT TO?
THAT'S WHY YOU'RE HERE? FEEBLE.
MRS. DUNCAN'S MIND CONTAINED VALUABLE THINGS. THINGS H.I.V.E. CAN USE.
THAT'S ALL I'M SAYING.
WHERE IS THE ENGRAM?
YOU'RE NOT STRONG ENOUGH TO PSYKE-COERCE ME.
OH STOP IT! IT'S PATHETIC!
YOU CAN'T MANIPULATE ME.
YOU CAN BARELY MANAGE THE MINDS OF YOUR TEAMMATES.
IT'S ALL GOING TO FALL APART. YOU KNOW THAT.
WHAT DO YOU MEAN?

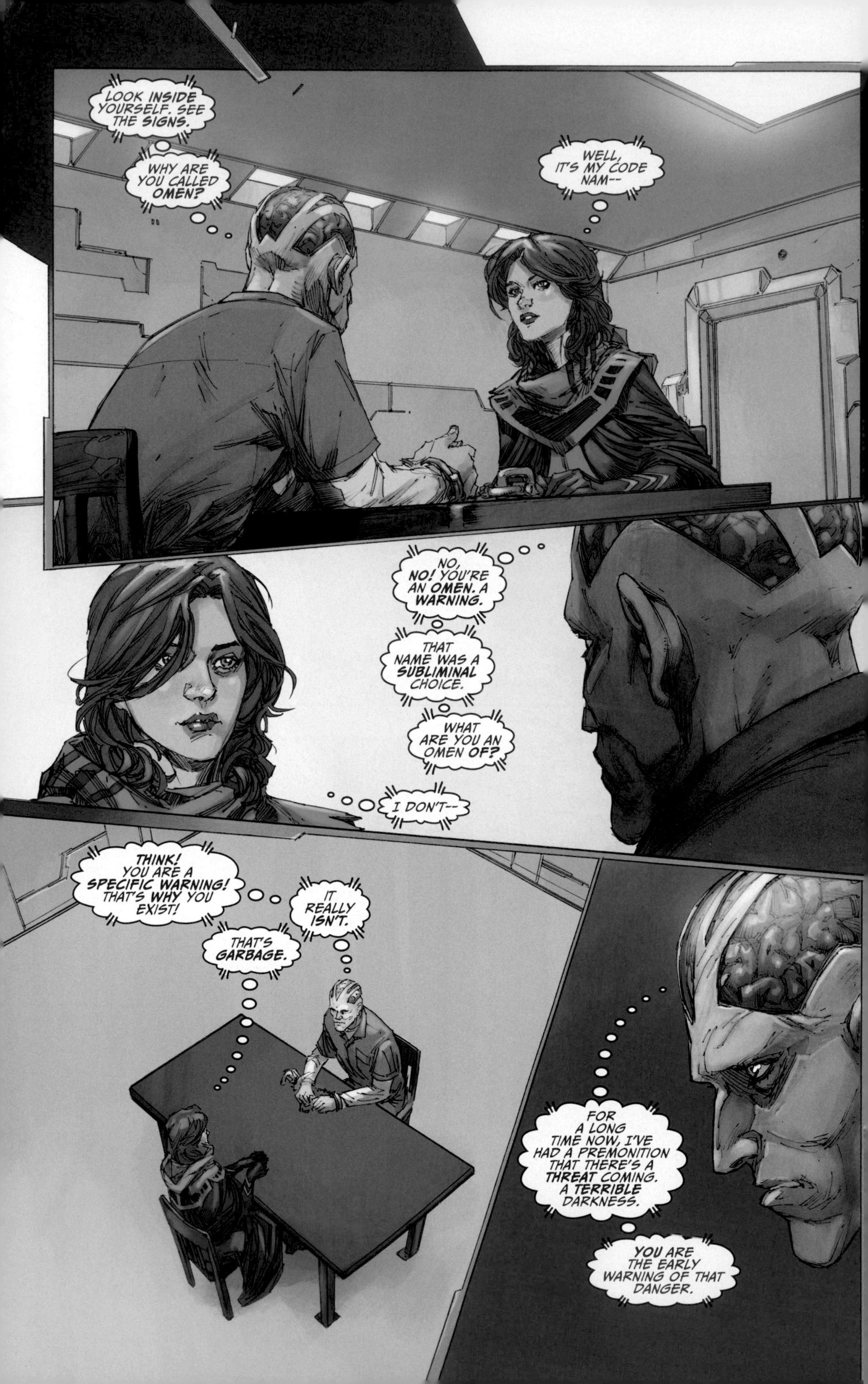
LOOK INSIDE YOURSELF. SEE THE SIGNS.
WHY ARE YOU CALLED OMEN?
WELL, IT'S MY CODE NAM--
NO, NO! YOU'RE AN OMEN. A WARNING.
THAT NAME WAS A SUBLIMINAL CHOICE.
WHAT ARE YOU AN OMEN OF?
I DON'T--
THINK! YOU ARE A SPECIFIC WARNING! THAT'S WHY YOU EXIST!
IT REALLY ISN'T.
THAT'S GARBAGE.
FOR A LONG TIME NOW, I'VE HAD A PREMONITION THAT THERE'S A THREAT COMING. A TERRIBLE DARKNESS.
YOU ARE THE EARLY WARNING OF THAT DANGER.

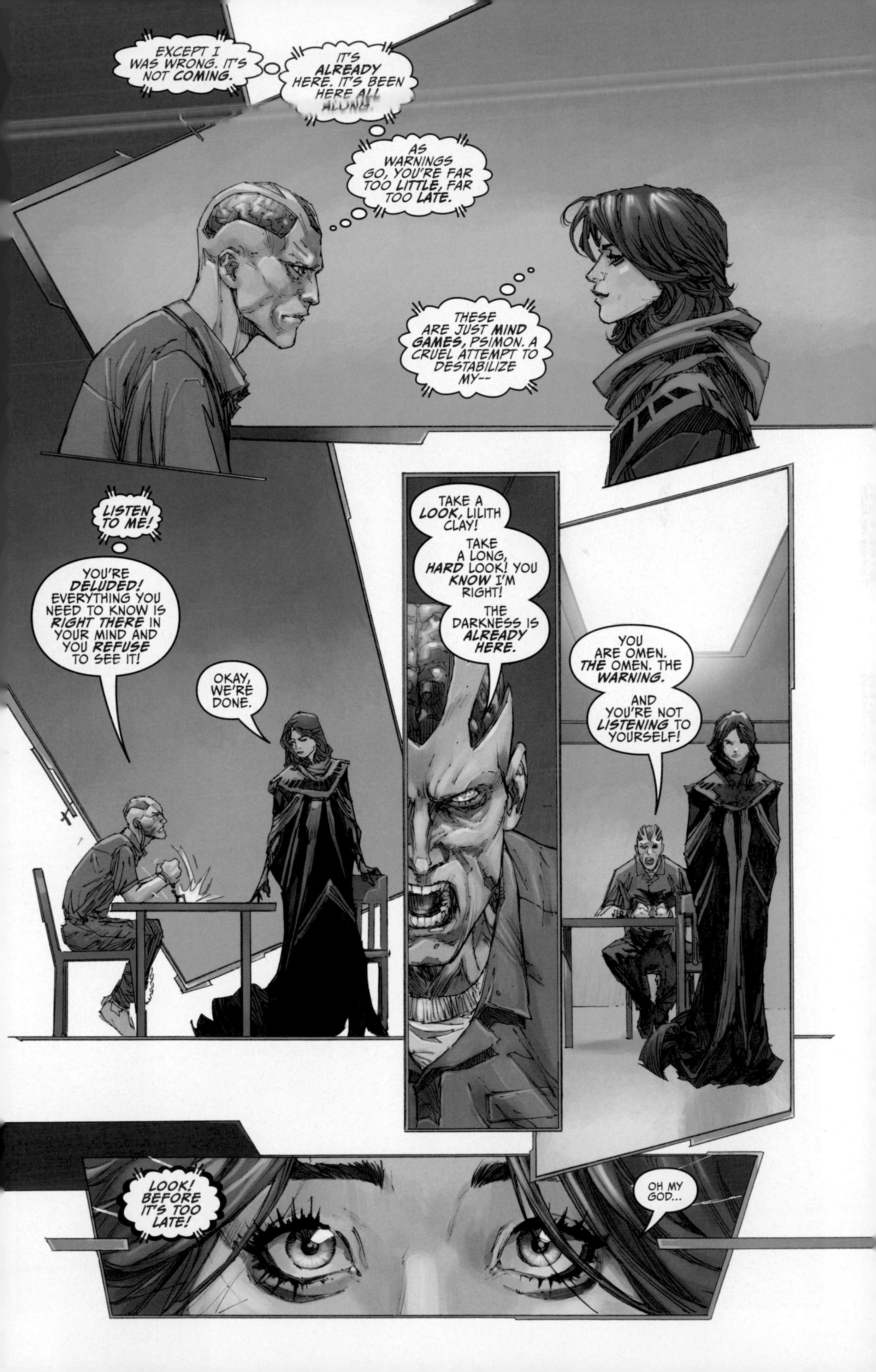
EXCEPT I WAS WRONG. IT'S NOT COMING.
IT'S ALREADY HERE. IT'S BEEN HERE ALL ALONG.
AS WARNINGS GO, YOU'RE FAR TOO LITTLE, FAR TOO LATE.
THESE ARE JUST MIND GAMES, PSIMON. A CRUEL ATTEMPT TO DESTABILIZE MY--
LISTEN TO ME!
YOU'RE DELUDED! EVERYTHING YOU NEED TO KNOW IS RIGHT THERE IN YOUR MIND AND YOU REFUSE TO SEE IT!
OKAY, WE'RE DONE.
TAKE A LOOK, LILITH CLAY!
TAKE A LONG, HARD LOOK! YOU KNOW I'M RIGHT!
THE DARKNESS IS ALREADY HERE.
YOU ARE OMEN. THE OMEN. THE WARNING.
AND YOU'RE NOT LISTENING TO YOURSELF!
LOOK! BEFORE IT'S TOO LATE!
OH MY GOD...

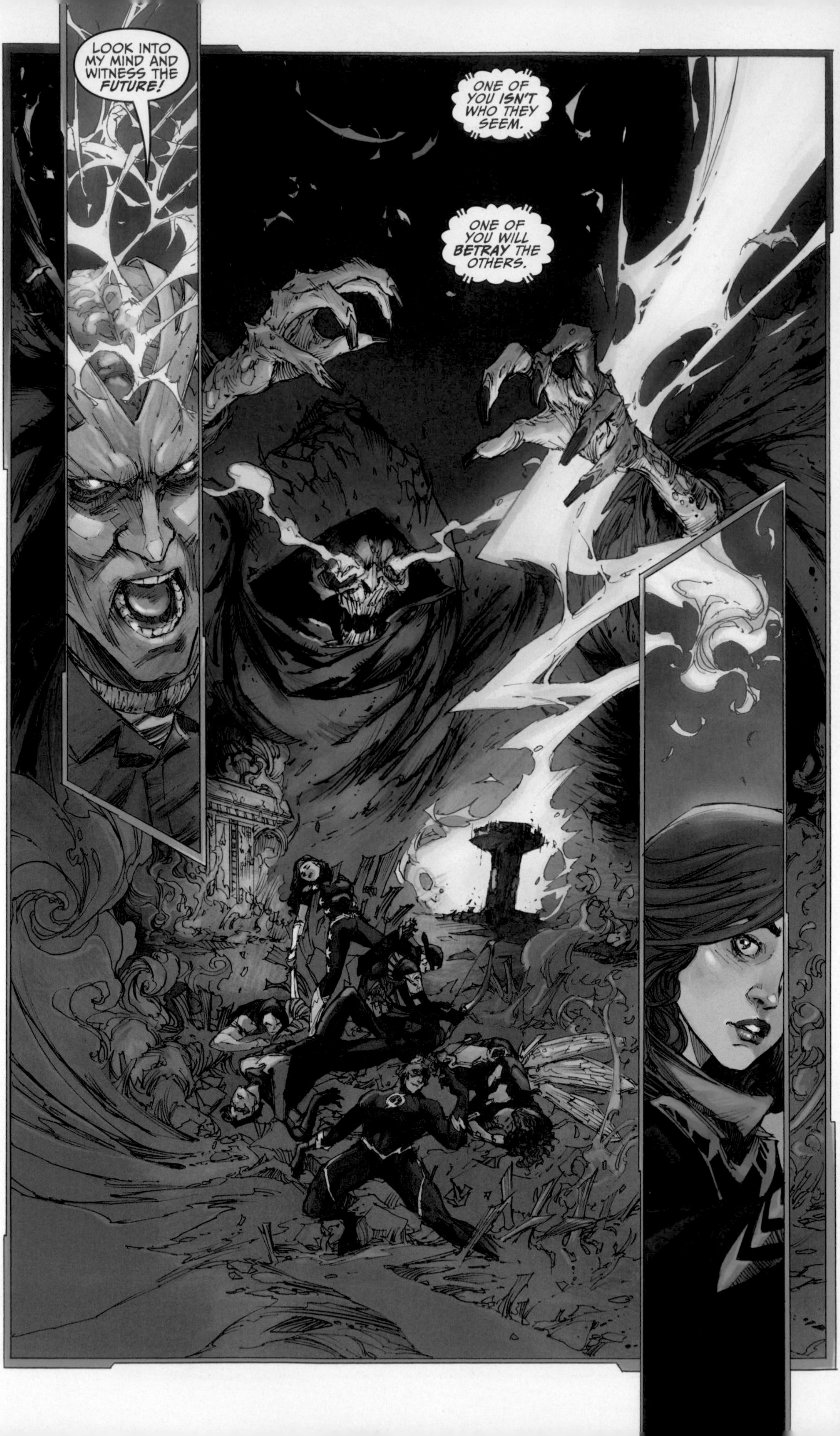
LOOK INTO MY MIND AND WITNESS THE FUTURE!
ONE OF YOU ISN'T WHO THEY SEEM.
ONE OF YOU WILL BETRAY THE OTHERS.

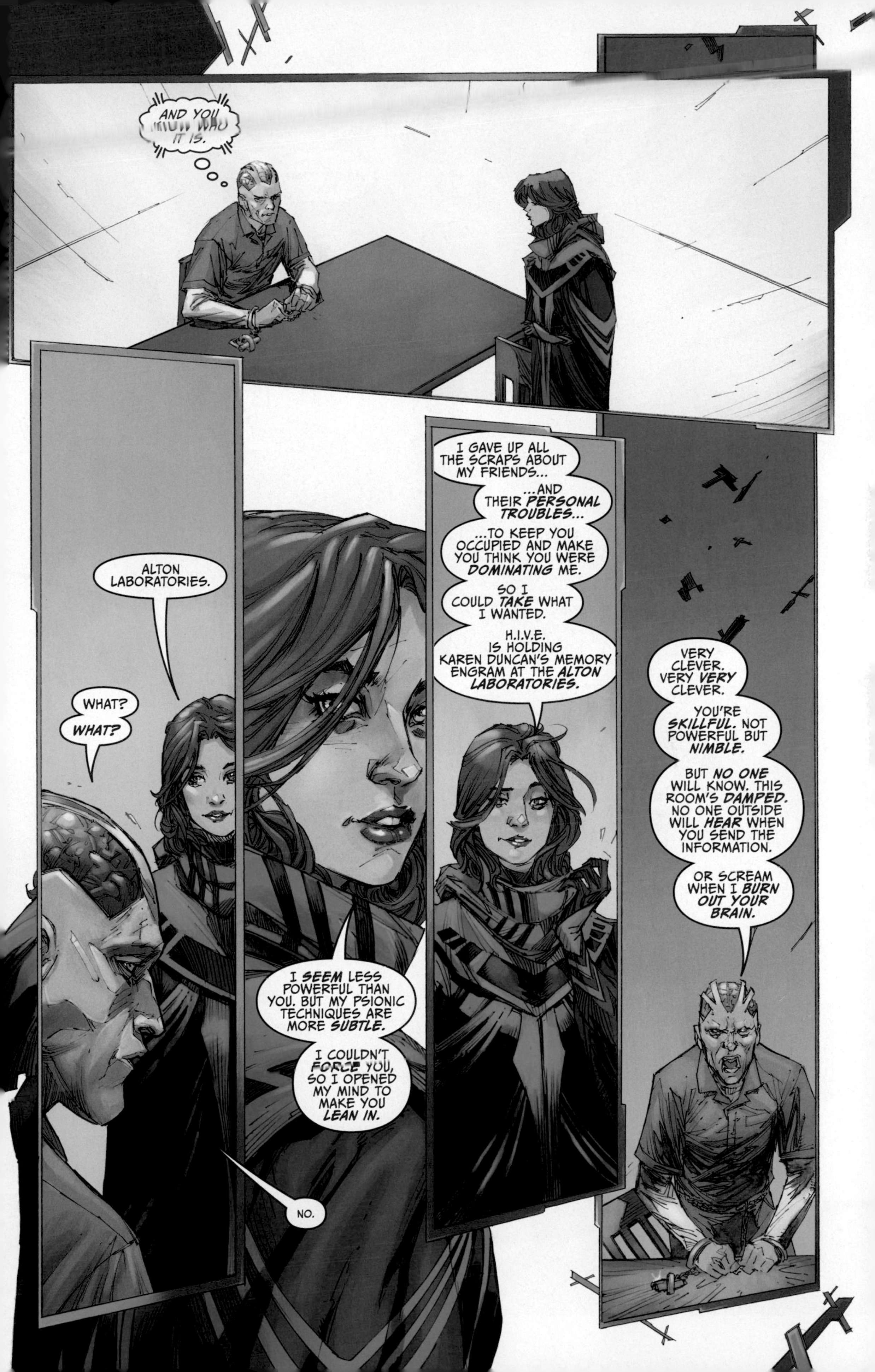
AND YOU IT IS.
ALTON LABORATORIES.
WHAT? WHAT?
I GAVE UP ALL THE SCRAPS ABOUT MY FRIENDS...
...AND THEIR PERSONAL TROUBLES...
...TO KEEP YOU OCCUPIED AND MAKE YOU THINK YOU WERE DOMINATING ME.
SO I COULD TAKE WHAT I WANTED.
H.I.V.E. IS HOLDING KAREN DUNCAN'S MEMORY ENGRAM AT THE ALTON LABORATORIES.
I SEEM LESS POWERFUL THAN YOU. BUT MY PSIONIC TECHNIQUES ARE MORE SUBTLE.
I COULDN'T FORCE YOU, SO I OPENED MY MIND TO MAKE YOU LEAN IN.
NO.
VERY CLEVER. VERY VERY CLEVER.
YOU'RE SKILLFUL. NOT POWERFUL BUT NIMBLE.
BUT NO ONE WILL KNOW. THIS ROOM'S DAMPED. NO ONE OUTSIDE WILL HEAR WHEN YOU SEND THE INFORMATION.
OR SCREAM WHEN I BURN OUT YOUR BRAIN.

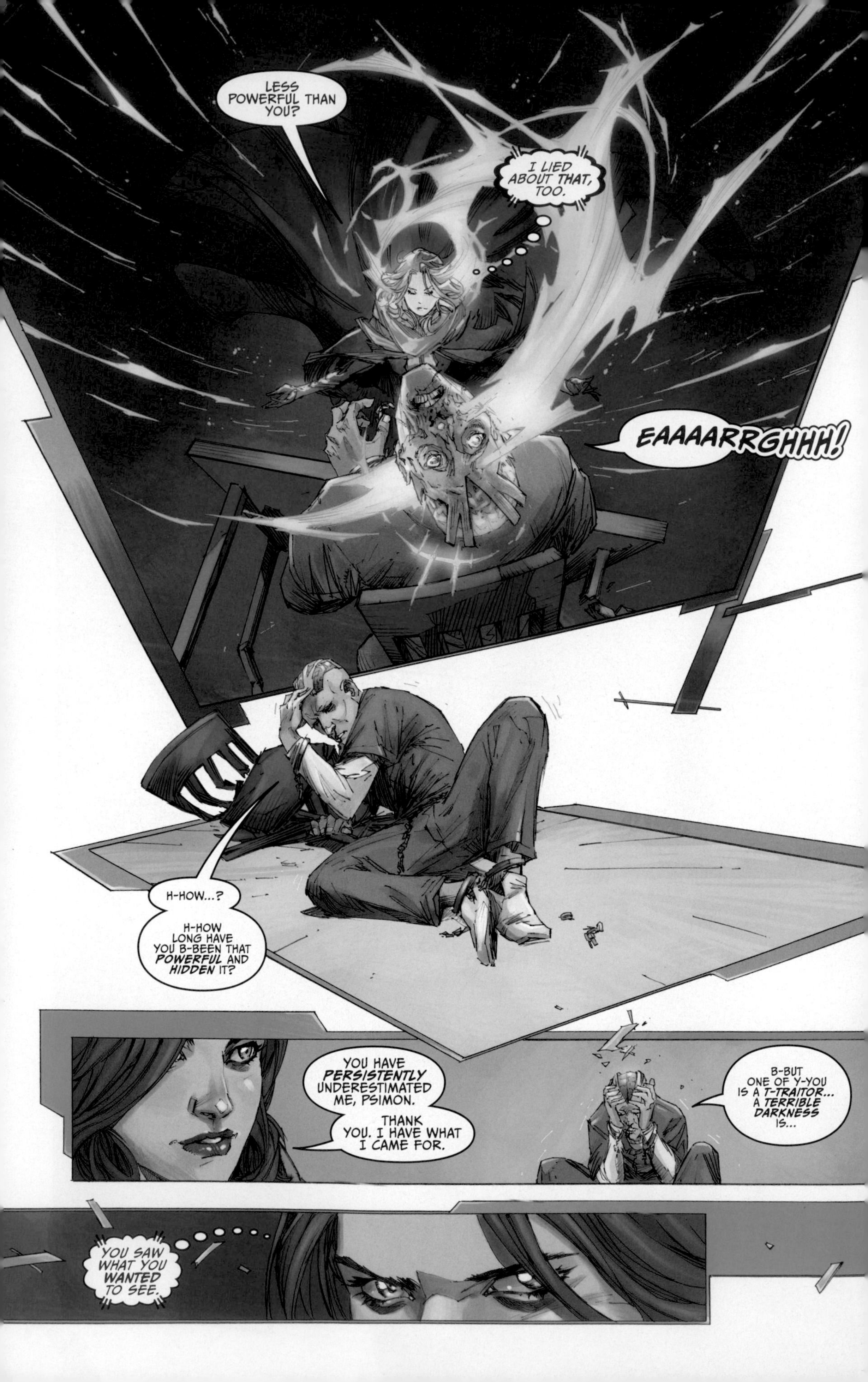

LESS POWERFUL THAN YOU?
I LIED ABOUT THAT, TOO.
EAAAARRGHHH!
H-HOW...?
H-HOW LONG HAVE YOU B-BEEN THAT POWERFUL AND HIDDEN IT?
YOU HAVE PERSISTENTLY UNDERESTIMATED ME, PSIMON.
THANK YOU. I HAVE WHAT I CAME FOR.
B-BUT ONE OF Y-YOU IS A T-TRAITOR... A TERRIBLE DARKNESS IS...
YOU SAW WHAT YOU WANTED TO SEE.

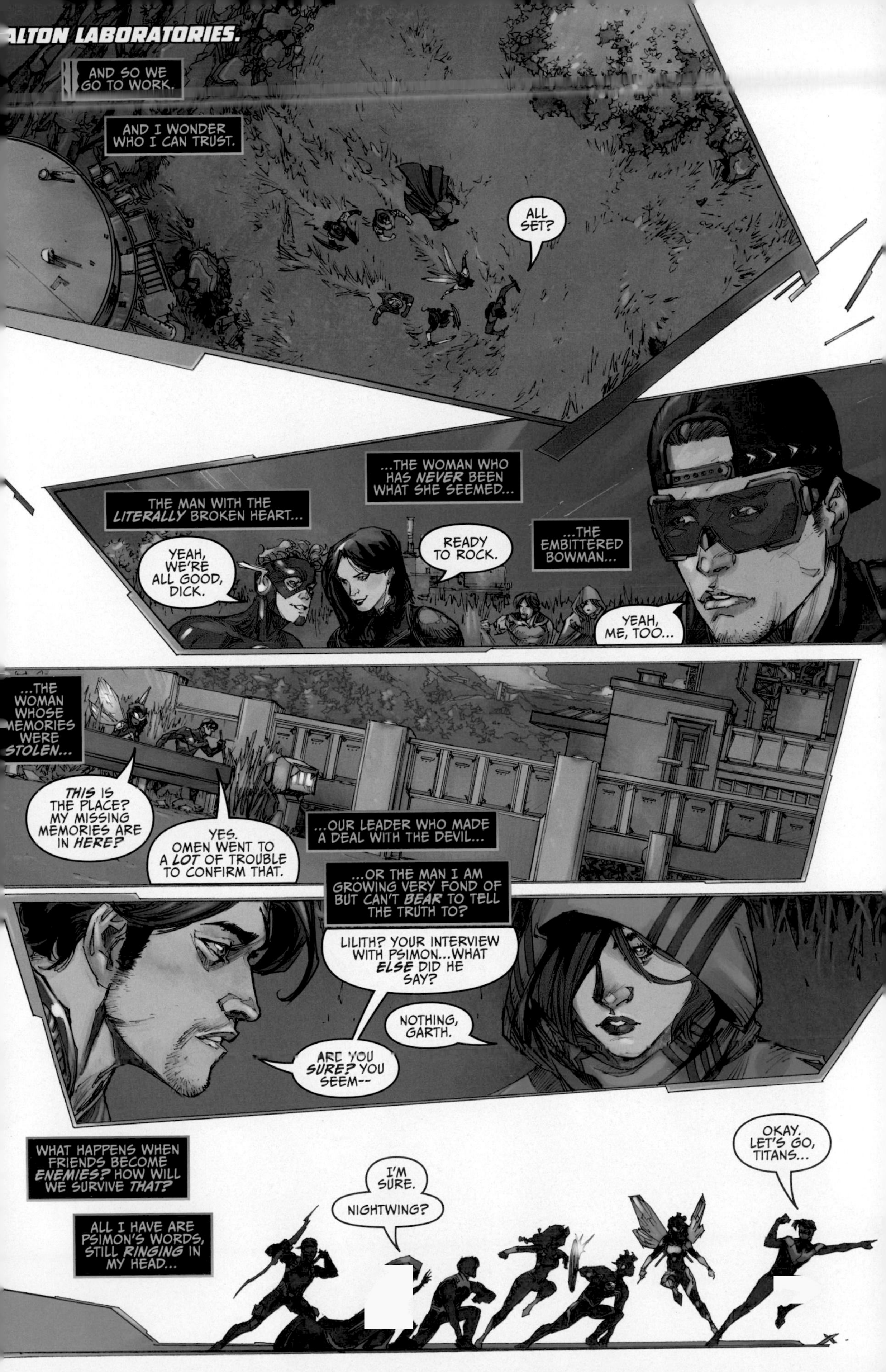
ALTON LABORATORIES.
AND SO WE GO TO WORK.
AND I WONDER WHO I CAN TRUST.
ALL SET?
THE MAN WITH THE LITERALLY BROKEN HEART...
YEAH, WE'RE ALL GOOD, DICK.
...THE WOMAN WHO HAS NEVER BEEN WHAT SHE SEEMED...
READY TO ROCK.
...THE EMBITTERED BOWMAN...
YEAH, ME, TOO...
...THE WOMAN WHOSE MEMORIES WERE STOLEN...
THIS IS THE PLACE? MY MISSING MEMORIES ARE IN HERE?
YES. OMEN WENT TO A LOT OF TROUBLE TO CONFIRM THAT.
...OUR LEADER WHO MADE A DEAL WITH THE DEVIL...
...OR THE MAN I AM GROWING VERY FOND OF BUT CAN'T BEAR TO TELL THE TRUTH TO?
LILITH? YOUR INTERVIEW WITH PSIMON...WHAT ELSE DID HE SAY?
NOTHING, GARTH.
ARE YOU SURE? YOU SEEM--
WHAT HAPPENS WHEN FRIENDS BECOME ENEMIES? HOW WILL WE SURVIVE THAT?
ALL I HAVE ARE PSIMON'S WORDS, STILL RINGING IN MY HEAD...
I'M SURE.
NIGHTWING?
OKAY. LET'S GO, TITANS...

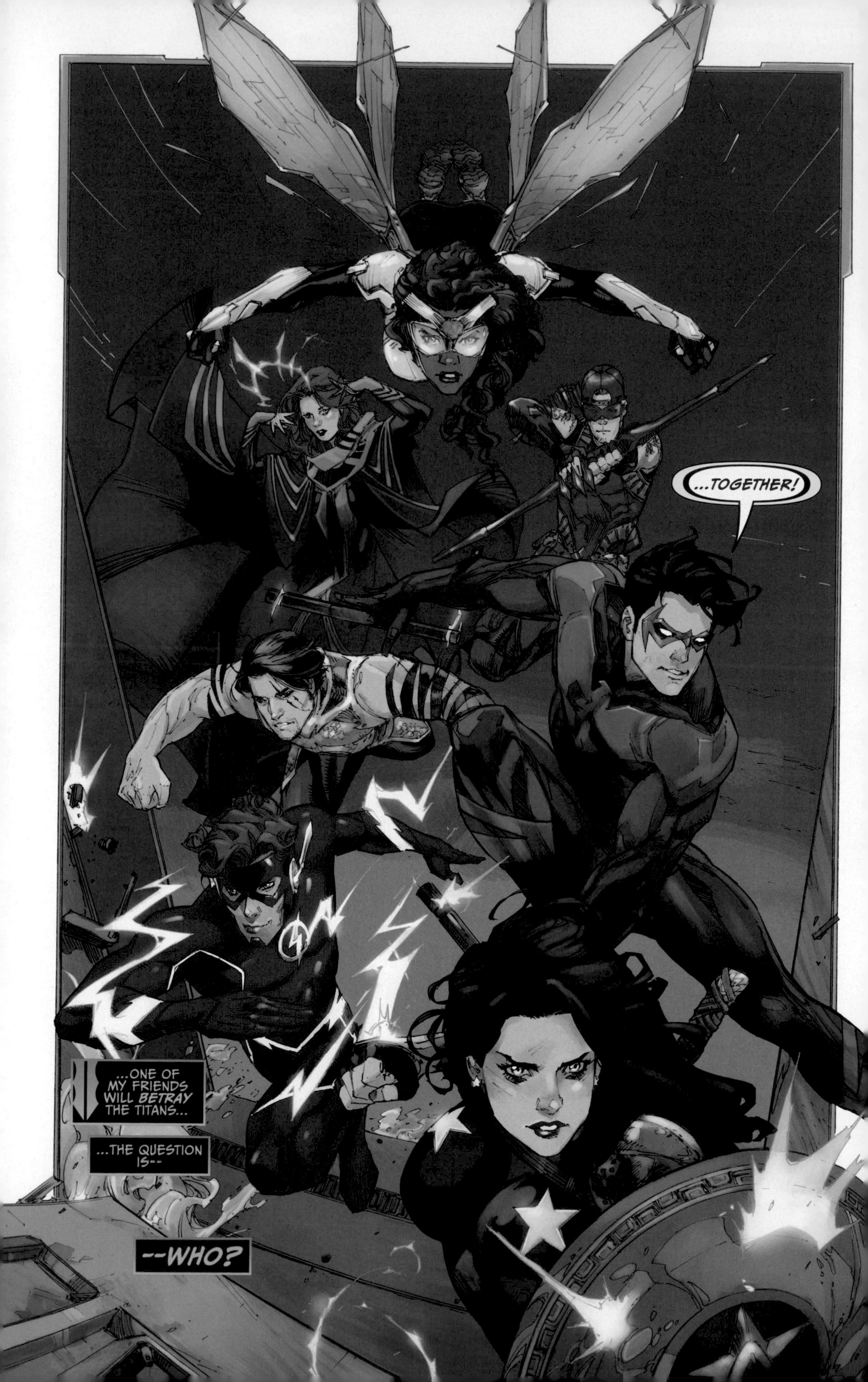
...TOGETHER!
...ONE OF MY FRIENDS WILL BETRAY THE TITANS...
...THE QUESTION IS--
--WHO?

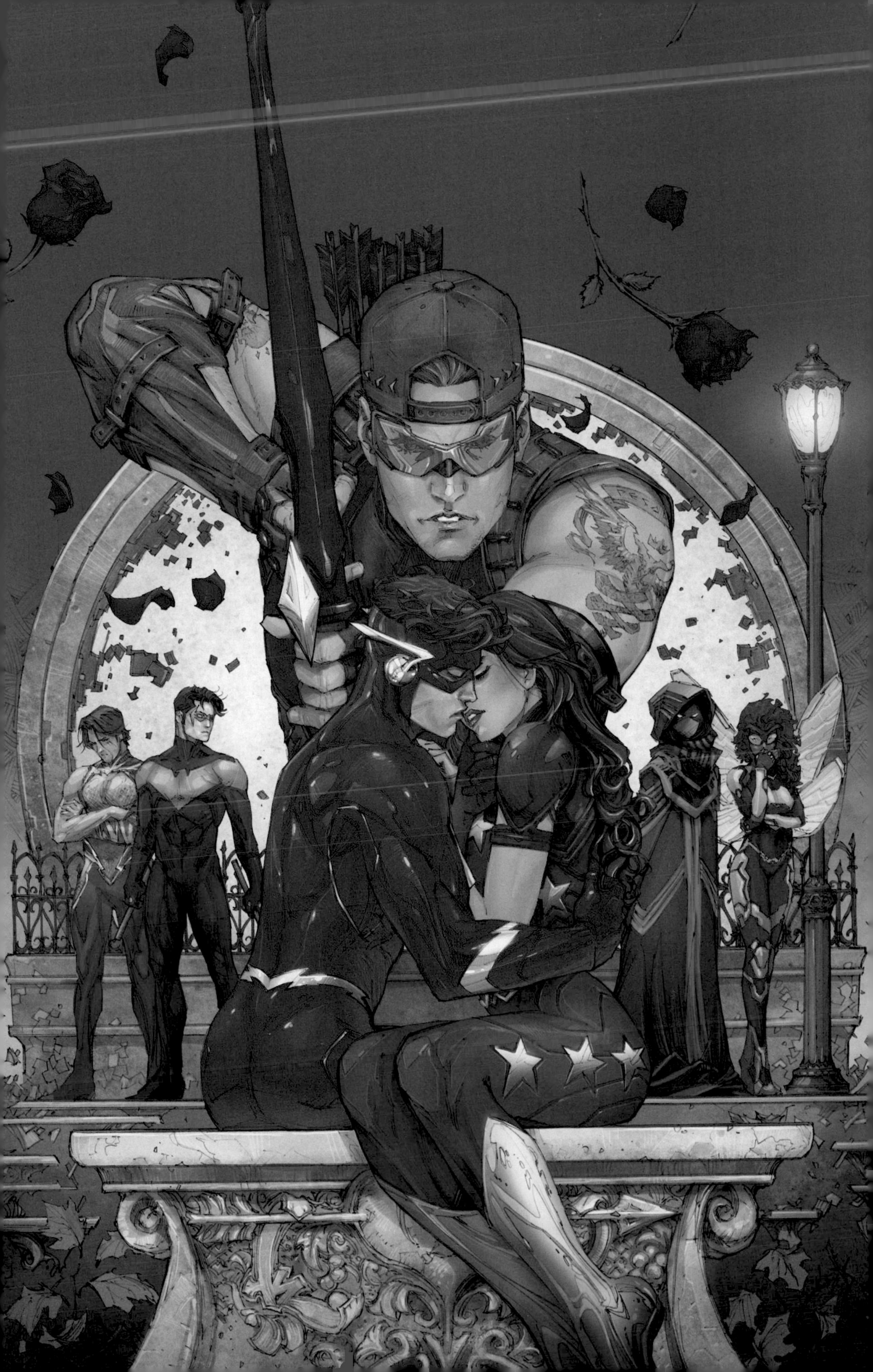

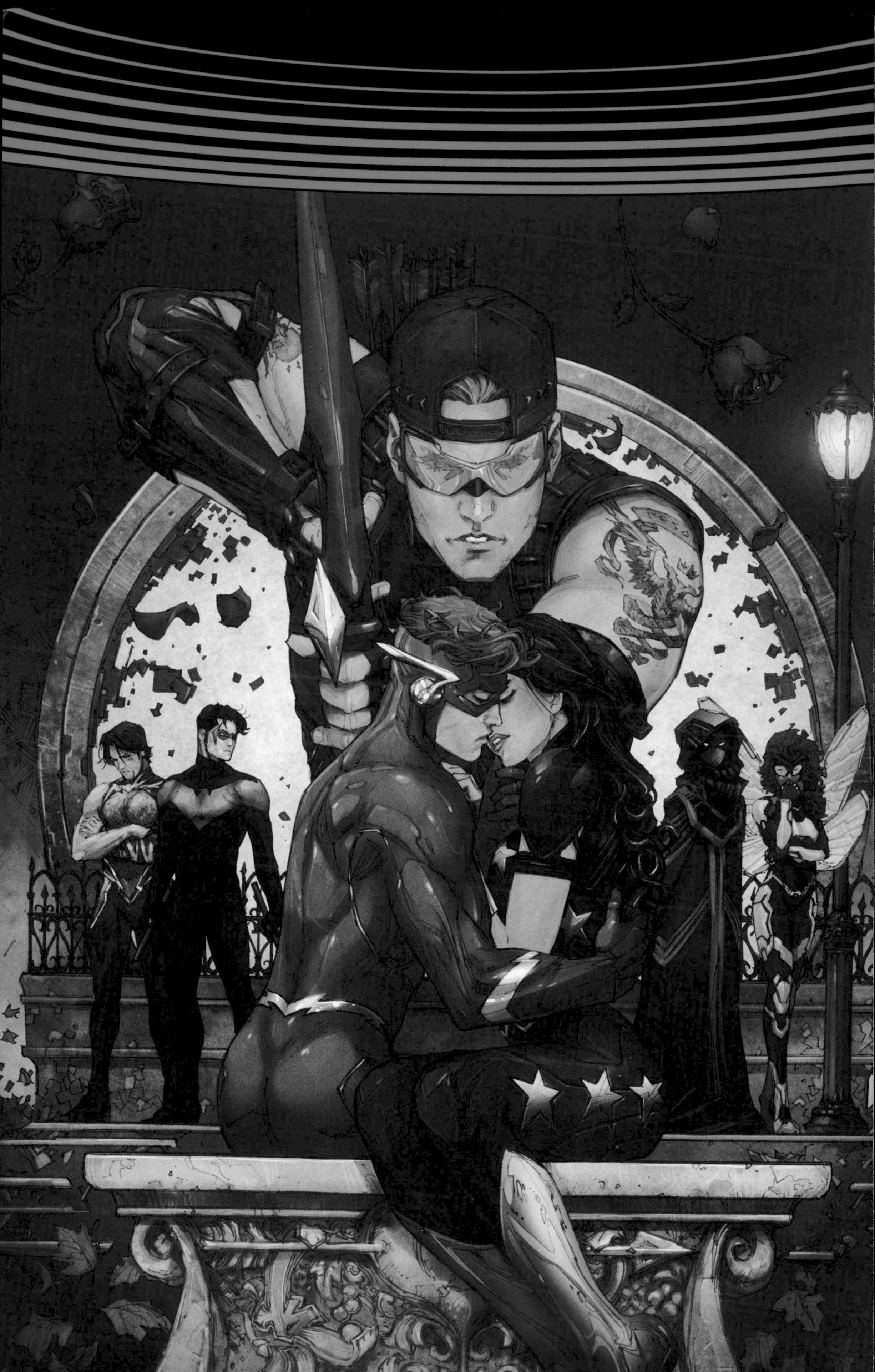

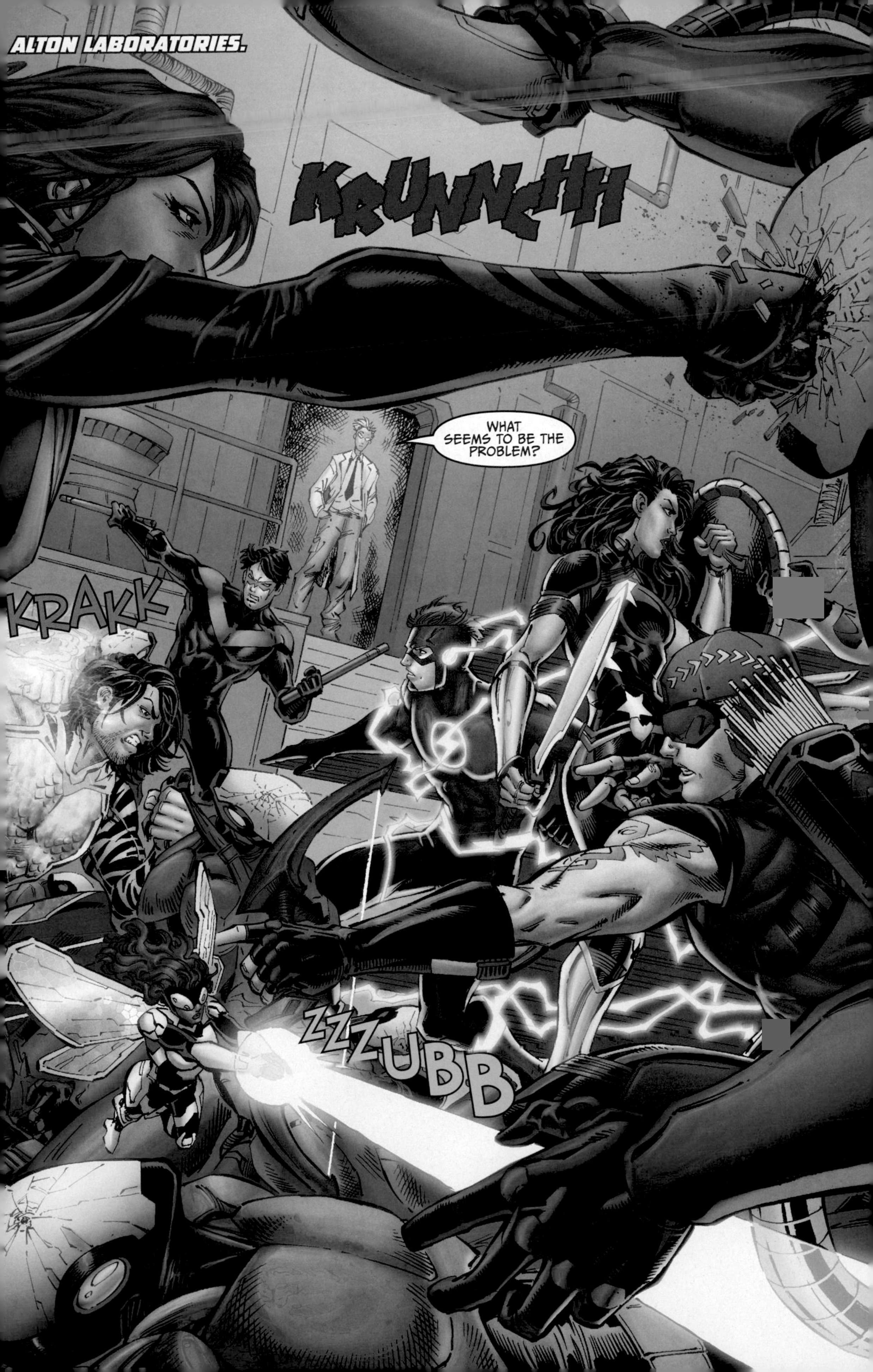
ALTON LABORATORIES.
KRUNNCHH
WHAT SEEMS TO BE THE PROBLEM?
KRAKK
ZZZUBB

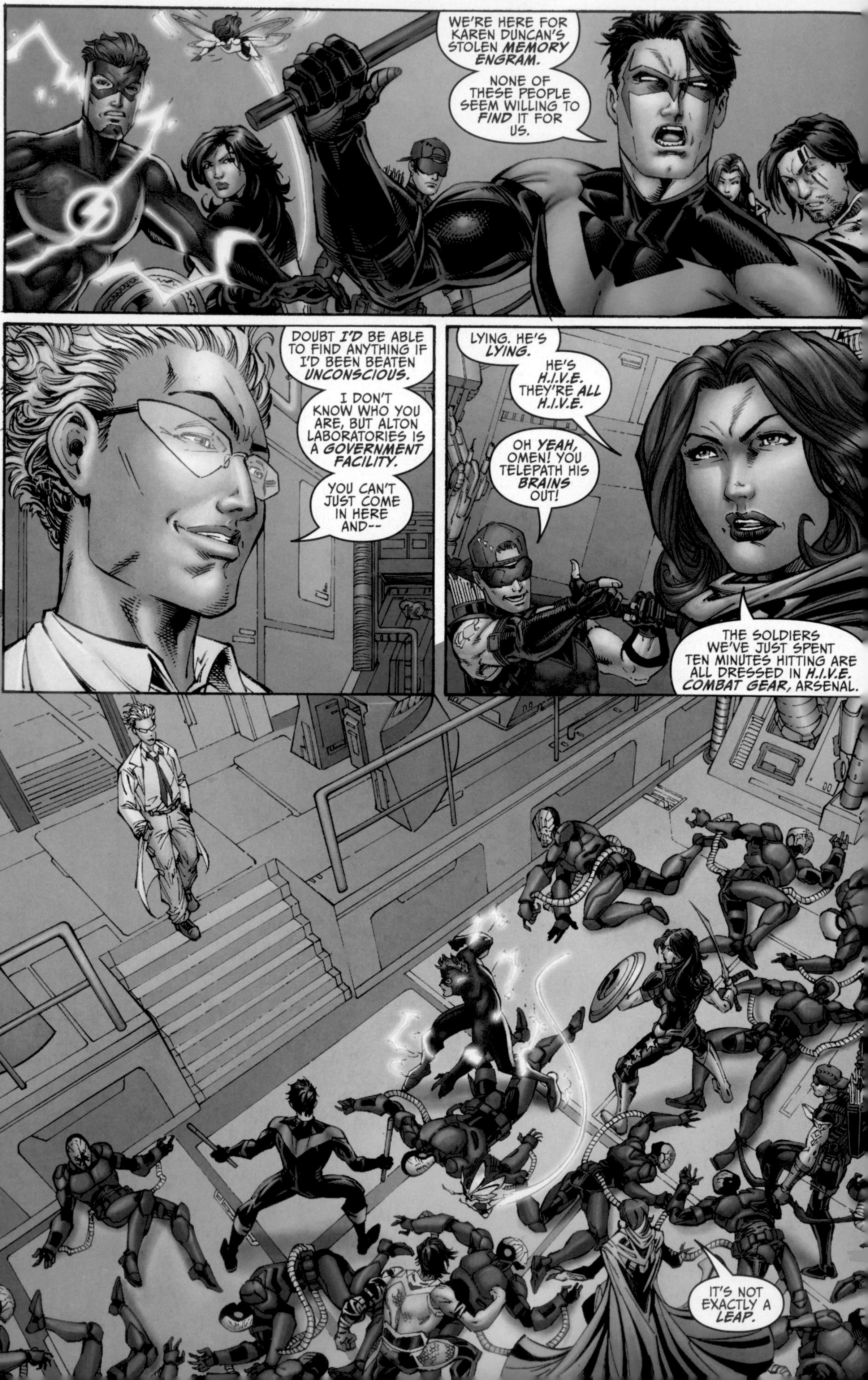
WE'RE HERE FOR KAREN DUNCAN'S STOLEN MEMORY ENGRAM.
NONE OF THESE PEOPLE SEEM WILLING TO FIND IT FOR US.
DOUBT I'D BE ABLE TO FIND ANYTHING IF I'D BEEN BEATEN UNCONSCIOUS.
I DON'T KNOW WHO YOU ARE, BUT ALTON LABORATORIES IS A GOVERNMENT FACILITY.
YOU CAN'T JUST COME IN HERE AND--
LYING. HE'S LYING.
HE'S H.I.V.E. THEY'RE ALL H.I.V.E.
OH YEAH, OMEN! YOU TELEPATH HIS BRAINS OUT!
THE SOLDIERS WE'VE JUST SPENT TEN MINUTES HITTING ARE ALL DRESSED IN H.I.V.E. COMBAT GEAR, ARSENAL.
IT'S NOT EXACTLY A LEAP.

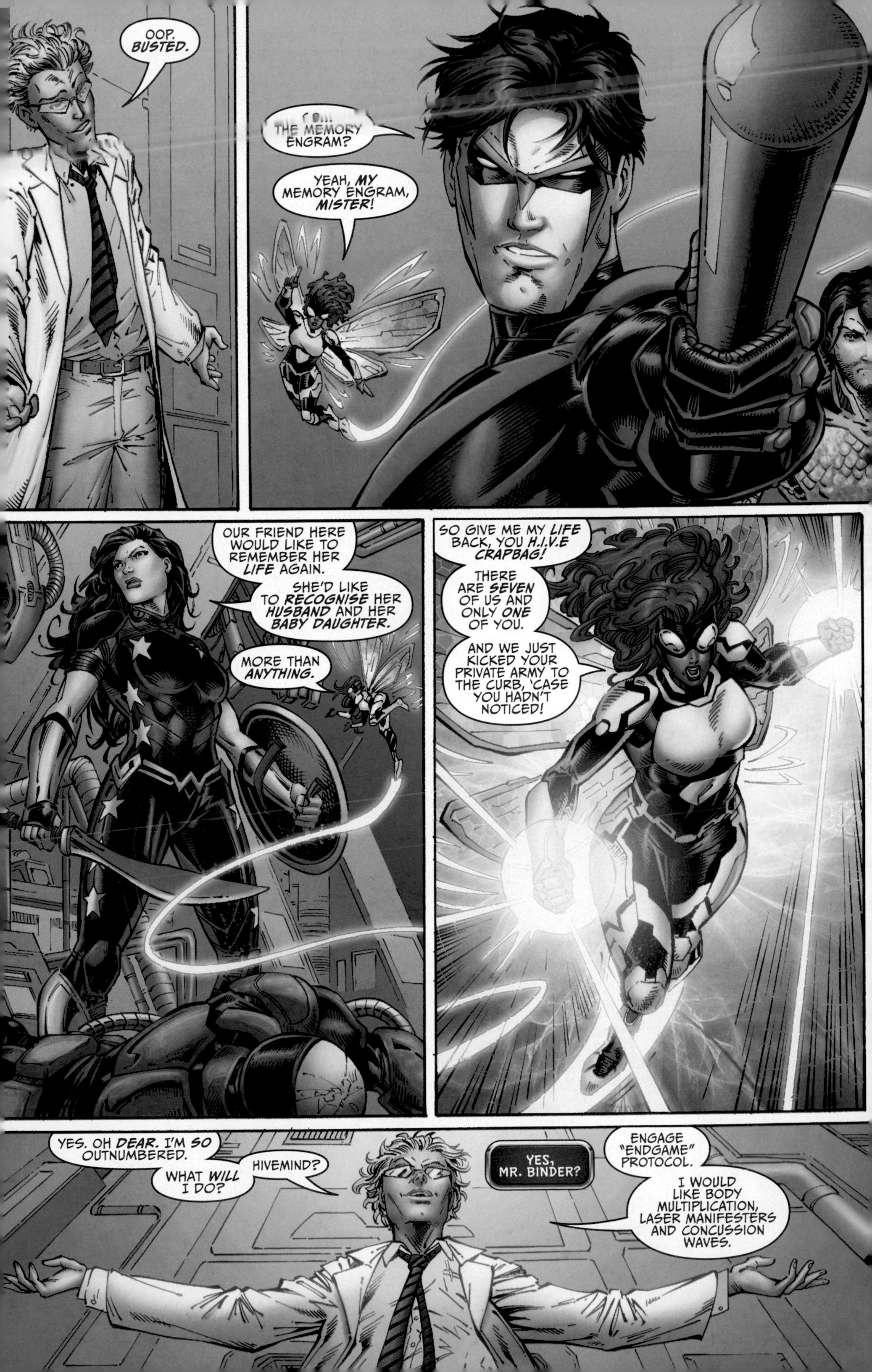
OOP. BUSTED.
THE MEMORY ENGRAM?
YEAH, MY MEMORY ENGRAM, MISTER!
OUR FRIEND HERE WOULD LIKE TO REMEMBER HER LIFE AGAIN.
SHE'D LIKE TO RECOGNISE HER HUSBAND AND HER BABY DAUGHTER.
MORE THAN ANYTHING.
SO GIVE ME MY LIFE BACK, YOU H.I.V.E CRAPBAG!
THERE ARE SEVEN OF US AND ONLY ONE OF YOU.
AND WE JUST KICKED YOUR PRIVATE ARMY TO THE CURB, 'CASE YOU HADN'T NOTICED!
YES. OH DEAR. I'M SO OUTNUMBERED.
WHAT WILL I DO?
HIVEMIND?
YES, MR. BINDER?
ENGAGE "ENDGAME" PROTOCOL.
I WOULD LIKE BODY MULTIPLICATION, LASER MANIFESTERS AND CONCUSSION WAVES.

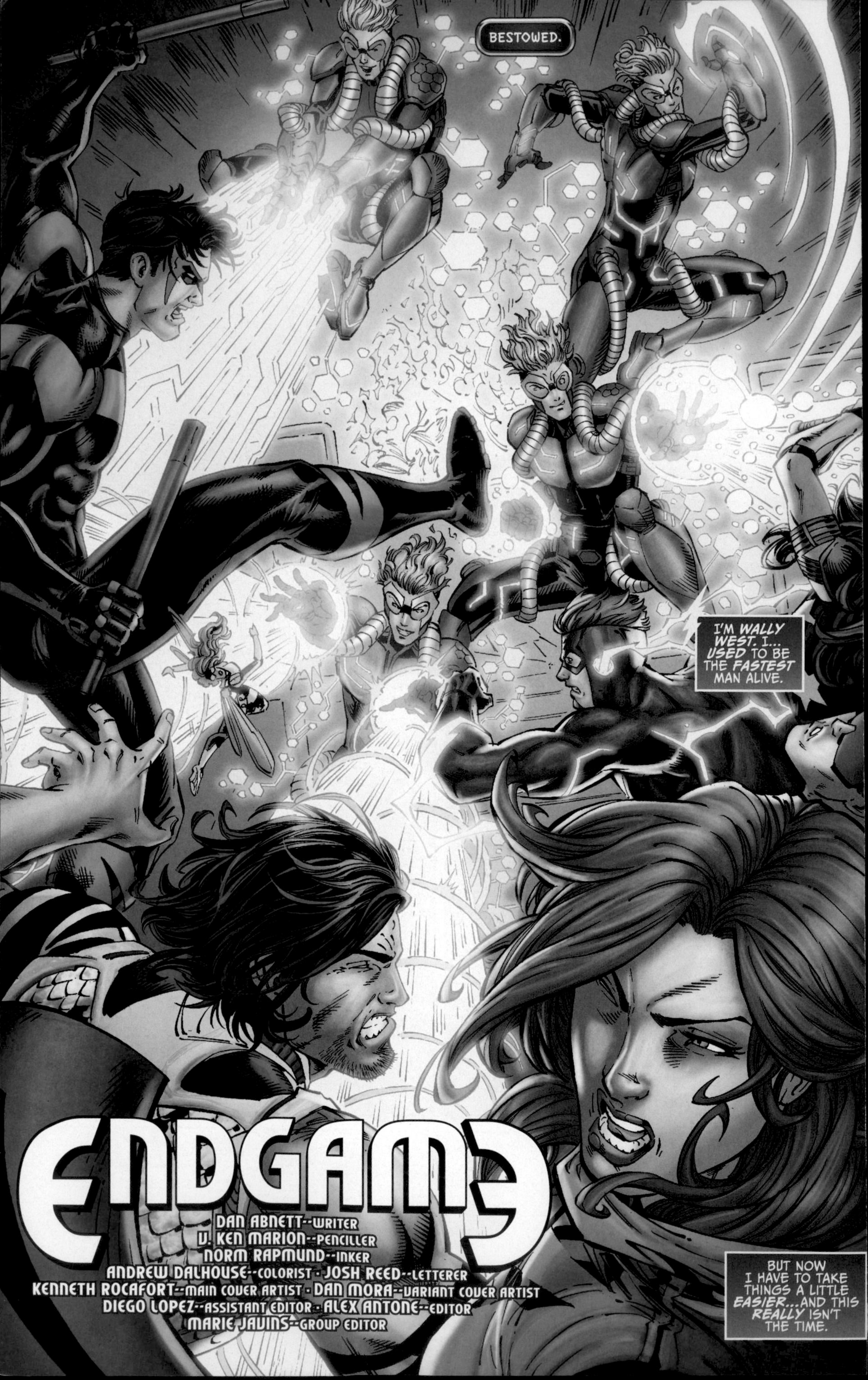
BESTOWED.
I'M WALLY WEST. I... USED TO BE THE FASTEST MAN ALIVE.
ENDGAME
DAN ABNETT--WRITER
V. KEN MARION--PENCILLER
NORM RAPMUND--INKER
ANDREW DALHOUSE--COLORIST · JOSH REED--LETTERER
KENNETH ROCAFORT--MAIN COVER ARTIST · DAN MORA--VARIANT COVER ARTIST
DIEGO LOPEZ--ASSISTANT EDITOR · ALEX ANTONE--EDITOR
MARIE JAVINS--GROUP EDITOR
BUT NOW I HAVE TO TAKE THINGS A LITTLE EASIER... AND THIS REALLY ISN'T THE TIME.

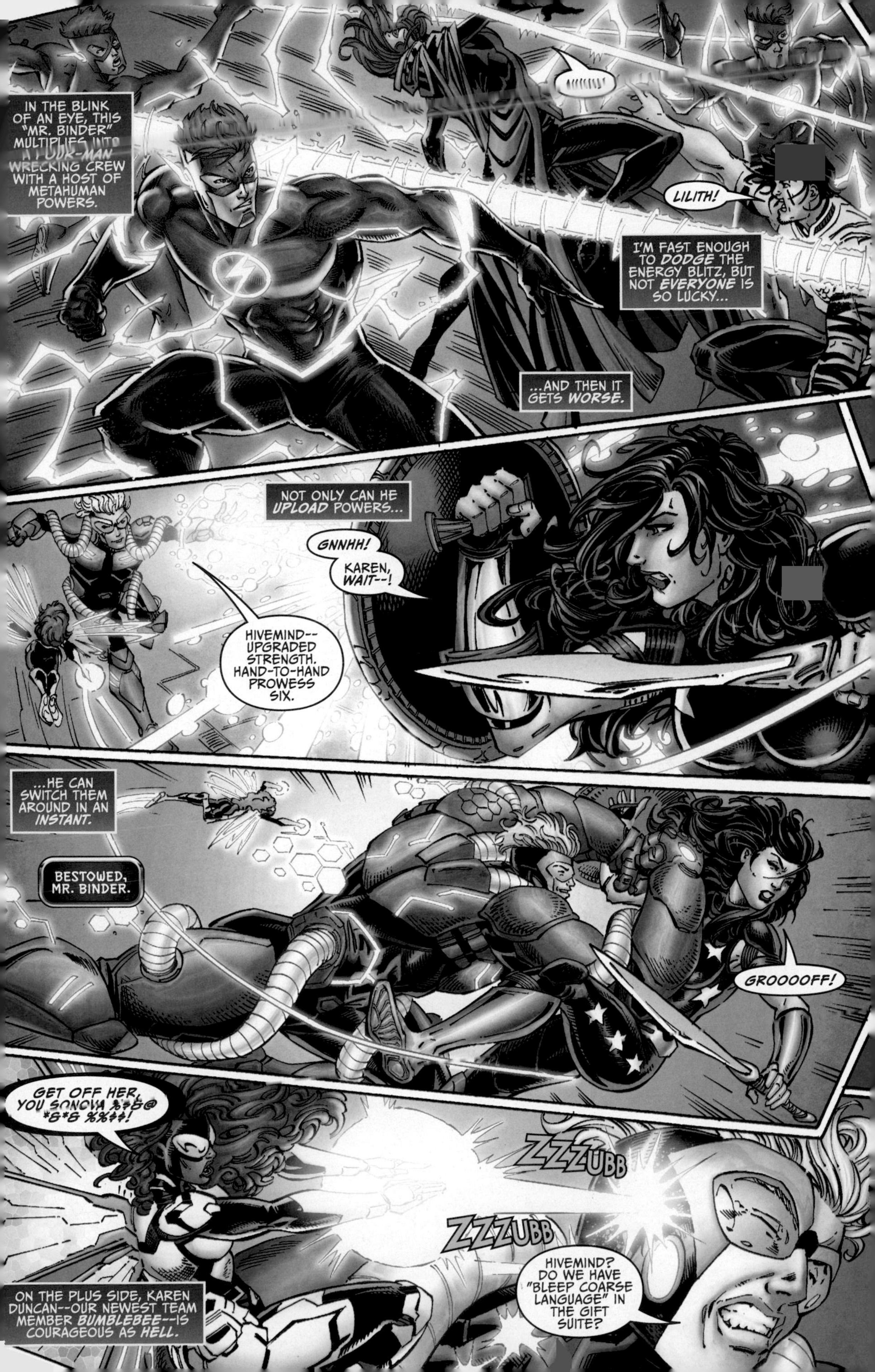
IN THE BLINK OF AN EYE, THIS "MR. BINDER" MULTIPLIES INTO A FOUR-MAN WRECKING CREW WITH A HOST OF METAHUMAN POWERS.
LILITH!
I'M FAST ENOUGH TO DODGE THE ENERGY BLITZ, BUT NOT EVERYONE IS SO LUCKY...
...AND THEN IT GETS WORSE.
NOT ONLY CAN HE UPLOAD POWERS...
GNNHH!
KAREN, WAIT--!
HIVEMIND-- UPGRADED STRENGTH. HAND-TO-HAND PROWESS SIX.
...HE CAN SWITCH THEM AROUND IN AN INSTANT.
BESTOWED, MR. BINDER.
GROOOOFF!
GET OFF HER, YOU SONOVA %$&@ *&*& %%$$!
ZZZUBB
ZZZUBB
ON THE PLUS SIDE, KAREN DUNCAN--OUR NEWEST TEAM MEMBER BUMBLEBEE--IS COURAGEOUS AS HELL.
HIVEMIND? DO WE HAVE "BLEEP COARSE LANGUAGE" IN THE GIFT SUITE?

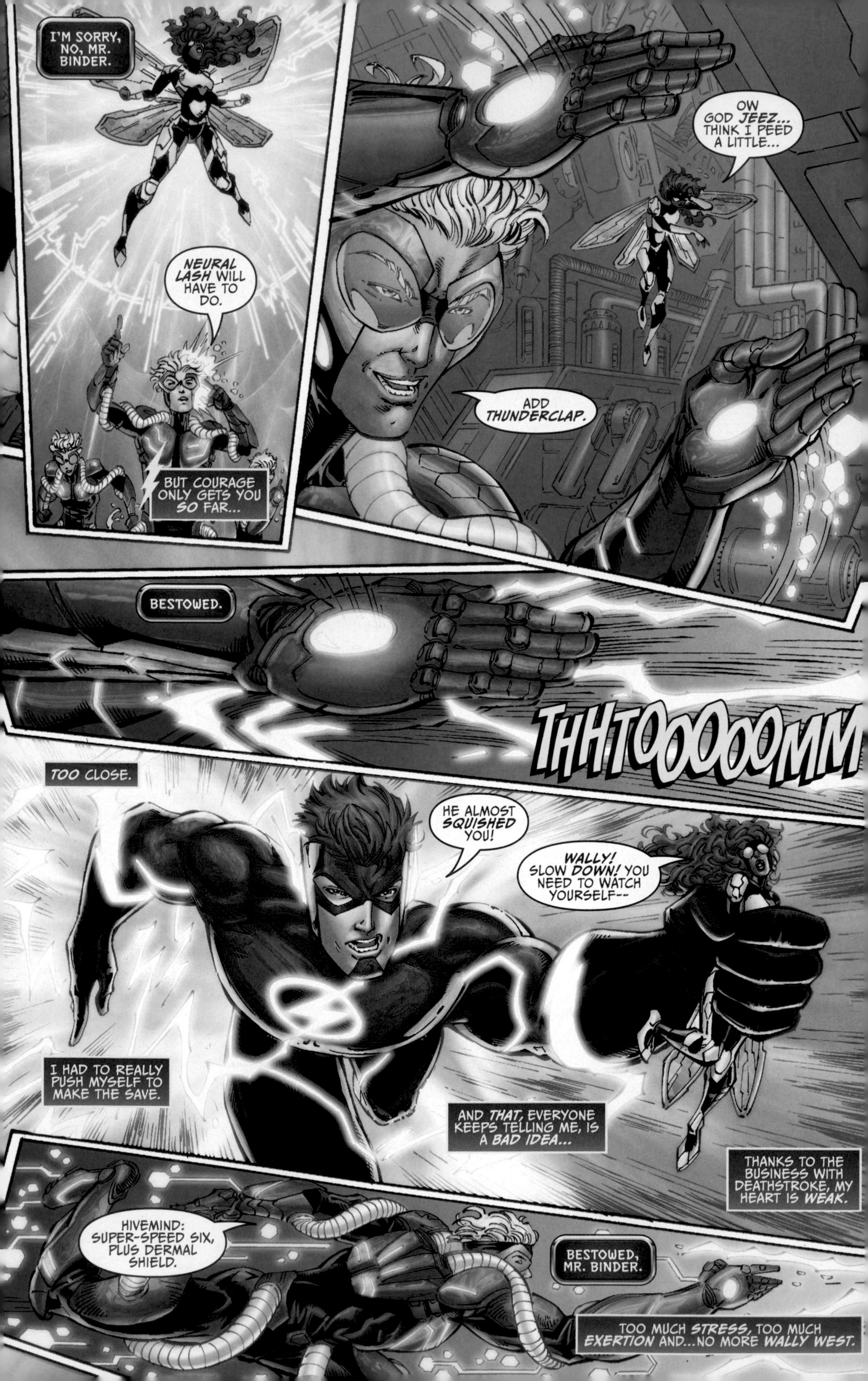
I'M SORRY, NO, MR. BINDER.
NEURAL LASH WILL HAVE TO DO.
BUT COURAGE ONLY GETS YOU SO FAR...
OW GOD JEEZ... THINK I PEED A LITTLE...
ADD THUNDERCLAP.
BESTOWED.
THHTOOOOOMM
TOO CLOSE.
HE ALMOST SQUISHED YOU!
WALLY! SLOW DOWN! YOU NEED TO WATCH YOURSELF--
I HAD TO REALLY PUSH MYSELF TO MAKE THE SAVE.
AND THAT, EVERYONE KEEPS TELLING ME, IS A BAD IDEA...
THANKS TO THE BUSINESS WITH DEATHSTROKE, MY HEART IS WEAK.
HIVEMIND: SUPER-SPEED SIX, PLUS DERMAL SHIELD.
BESTOWED, MR. BINDER.
TOO MUCH STRESS, TOO MUCH EXERTION AND...NO MORE WALLY WEST.

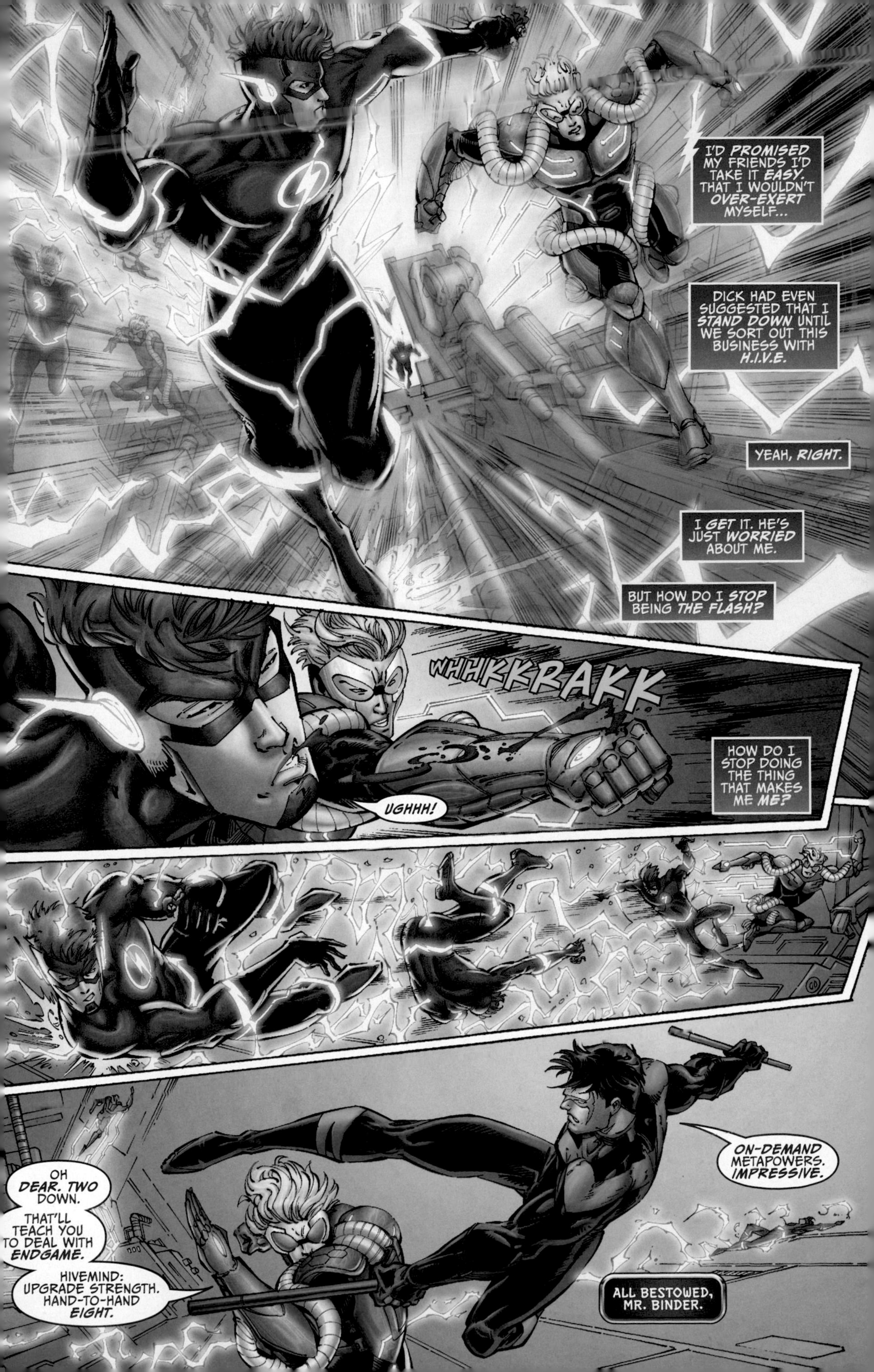
I'D PROMISED MY FRIENDS I'D TAKE IT EASY. THAT I WOULDN'T OVER-EXERT MYSELF...
DICK HAD EVEN SUGGESTED THAT I STAND DOWN UNTIL WE SORT OUT THIS BUSINESS WITH H.I.V.E.
YEAH, RIGHT.
I GET IT. HE'S JUST WORRIED ABOUT ME.
BUT HOW DO I STOP BEING THE FLASH?
WHHKKRAKK
HOW DO I STOP DOING THE THING THAT MAKES ME ME?
UGHHH!
ON-DEMAND METAPOWERS. IMPRESSIVE.
OH DEAR. TWO DOWN.
THAT'LL TEACH YOU TO DEAL WITH ENDGAME.
HIVEMIND: UPGRADE STRENGTH. HAND-TO-HAND EIGHT.
ALL BESTOWED, MR. BINDER.

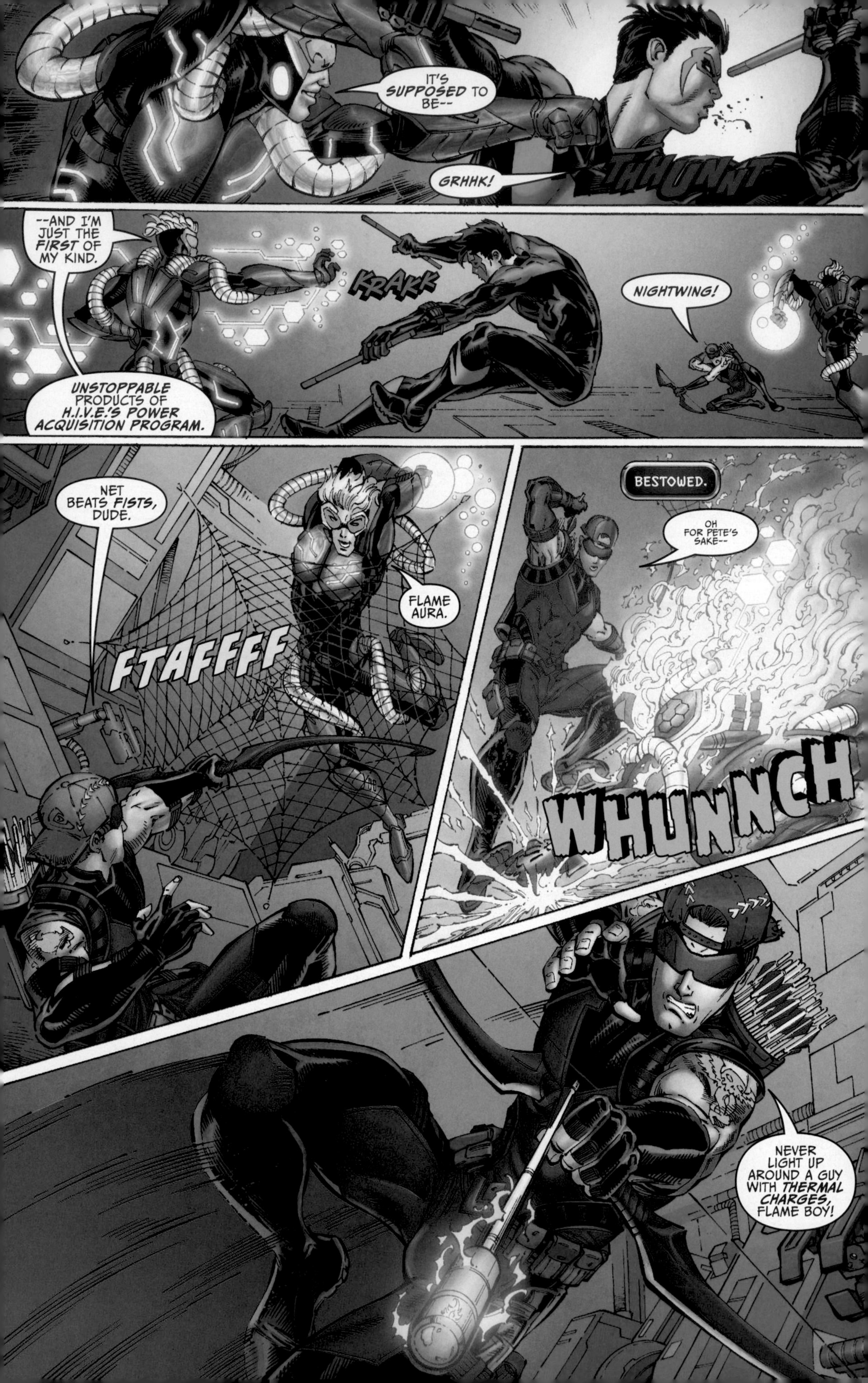
IT'S SUPPOSED TO BE--
GRHHK!
THHUNNT
--AND I'M JUST THE FIRST OF MY KIND.
KRAKK
NIGHTWING!
UNSTOPPABLE PRODUCTS OF H.I.V.E.'S POWER ACQUISITION PROGRAM.
NET BEATS FISTS, DUDE.
FTAFFFF
FLAME AURA.
BESTOWED.
OH FOR PETE'S SAKE--
WHUNNCH
NEVER LIGHT UP AROUND A GUY WITH THERMAL CHARGES, FLAME BOY!

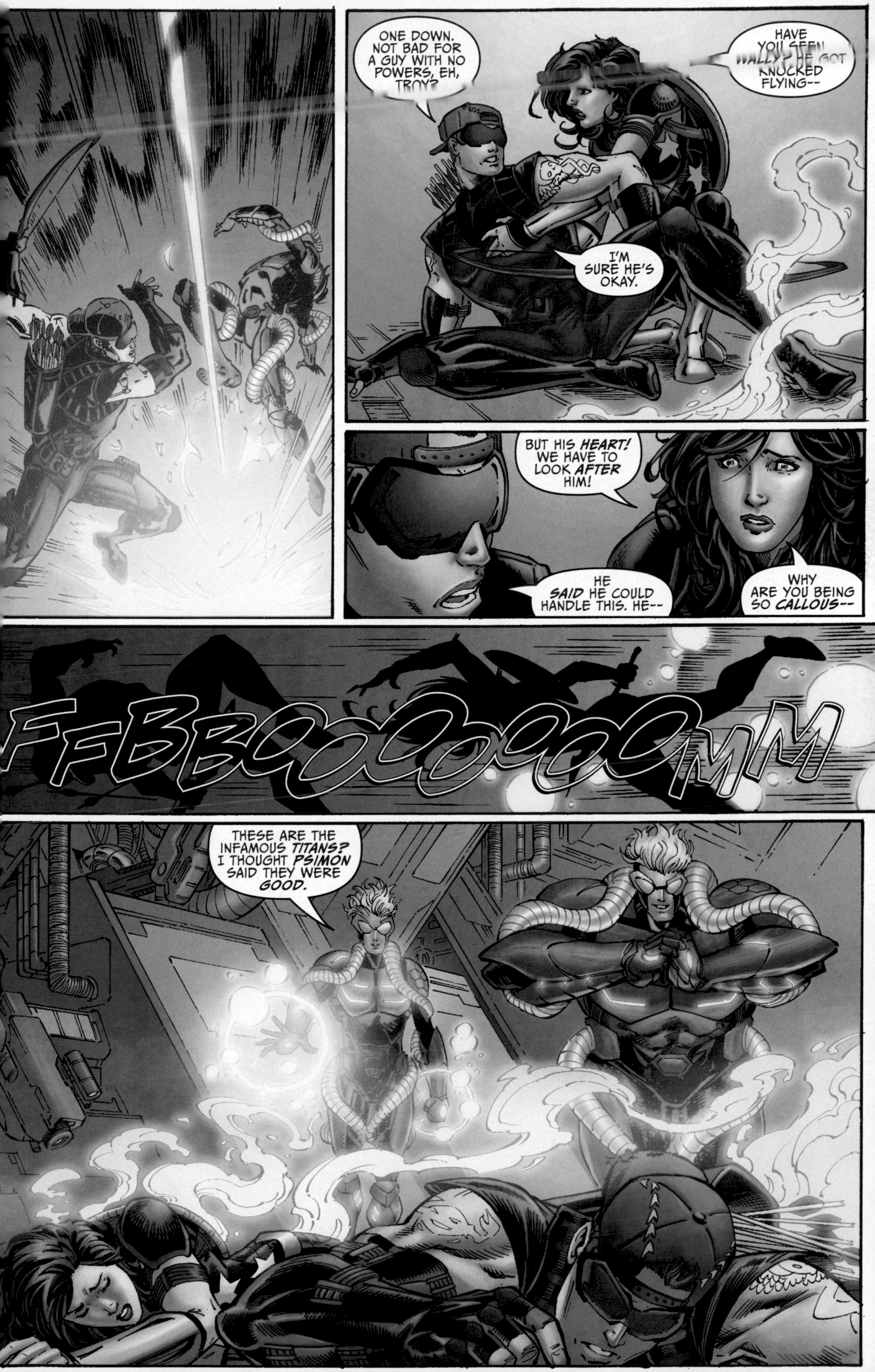
ONE DOWN. NOT BAD FOR A GUY WITH NO POWERS, EH, TROY?
HAVE YOU SEEN WALLY? HE GOT KNOCKED FLYING--
I'M SURE HE'S OKAY.
BUT HIS HEART! WE HAVE TO LOOK AFTER HIM!
HE SAID HE COULD HANDLE THIS. HE--
WHY ARE YOU BEING SO CALLOUS--
FFBBOOOOOOOMM
THESE ARE THE INFAMOUS TITANS? I THOUGHT PSIMON SAID THEY WERE GOOD.

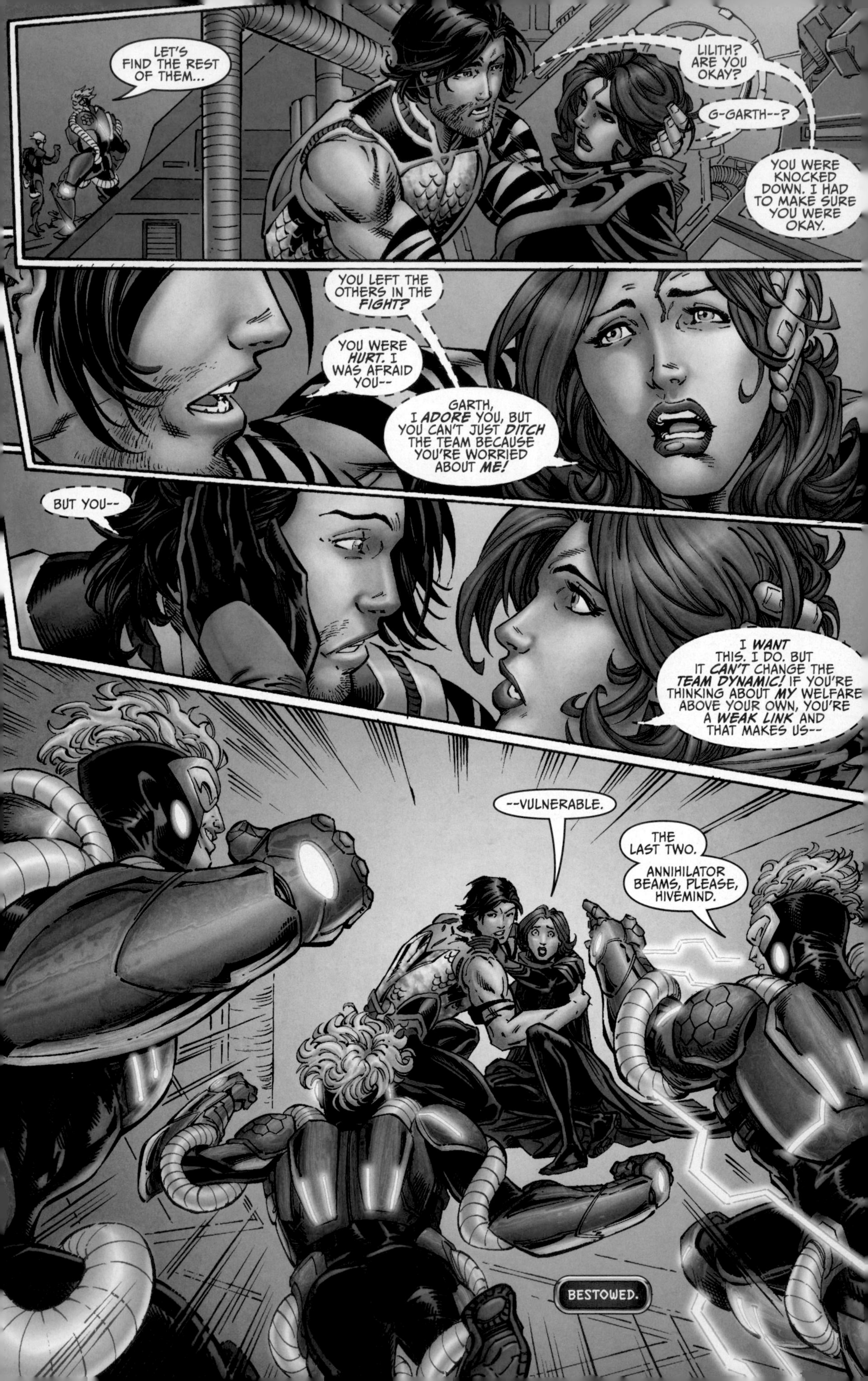
LET'S FIND THE REST OF THEM...
LILITH? ARE YOU OKAY?
G-GARTH--?
YOU WERE KNOCKED DOWN. I HAD TO MAKE SURE YOU WERE OKAY.
YOU LEFT THE OTHERS IN THE FIGHT?
YOU WERE HURT. I WAS AFRAID YOU--
GARTH, I ADORE YOU, BUT YOU CAN'T JUST DITCH THE TEAM BECAUSE YOU'RE WORRIED ABOUT ME!
BUT YOU--
I WANT THIS. I DO. BUT IT CAN'T CHANGE THE TEAM DYNAMIC! IF YOU'RE THINKING ABOUT MY WELFARE ABOVE YOUR OWN, YOU'RE A WEAK LINK AND THAT MAKES US--
--VULNERABLE.
THE LAST TWO.
ANNIHILATOR BEAMS, PLEASE, HIVEMIND.
BESTOWED.

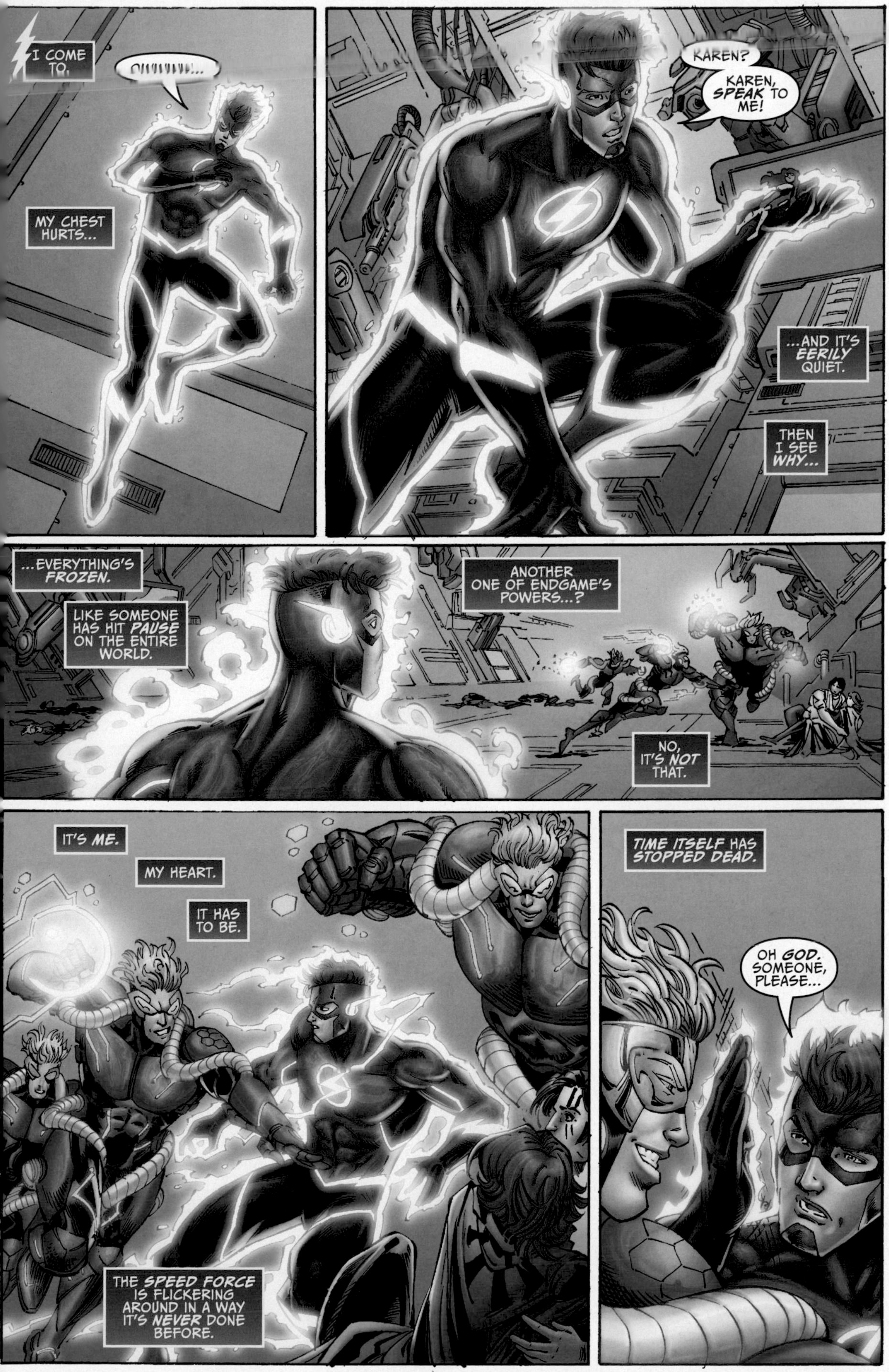
I COME TO.
UNNNNN...
MY CHEST HURTS...
KAREN?
KAREN, SPEAK TO ME!
...AND IT'S EERILY QUIET.
THEN I SEE WHY...
...EVERYTHING'S FROZEN.
LIKE SOMEONE HAS HIT PAUSE ON THE ENTIRE WORLD.
ANOTHER ONE OF ENDGAME'S POWERS...?
NO, IT'S NOT THAT.
IT'S ME.
MY HEART.
IT HAS TO BE.
THE SPEED FORCE IS FLICKERING AROUND IN A WAY IT'S NEVER DONE BEFORE.
TIME ITSELF HAS STOPPED DEAD.
OH GOD. SOMEONE, PLEASE...

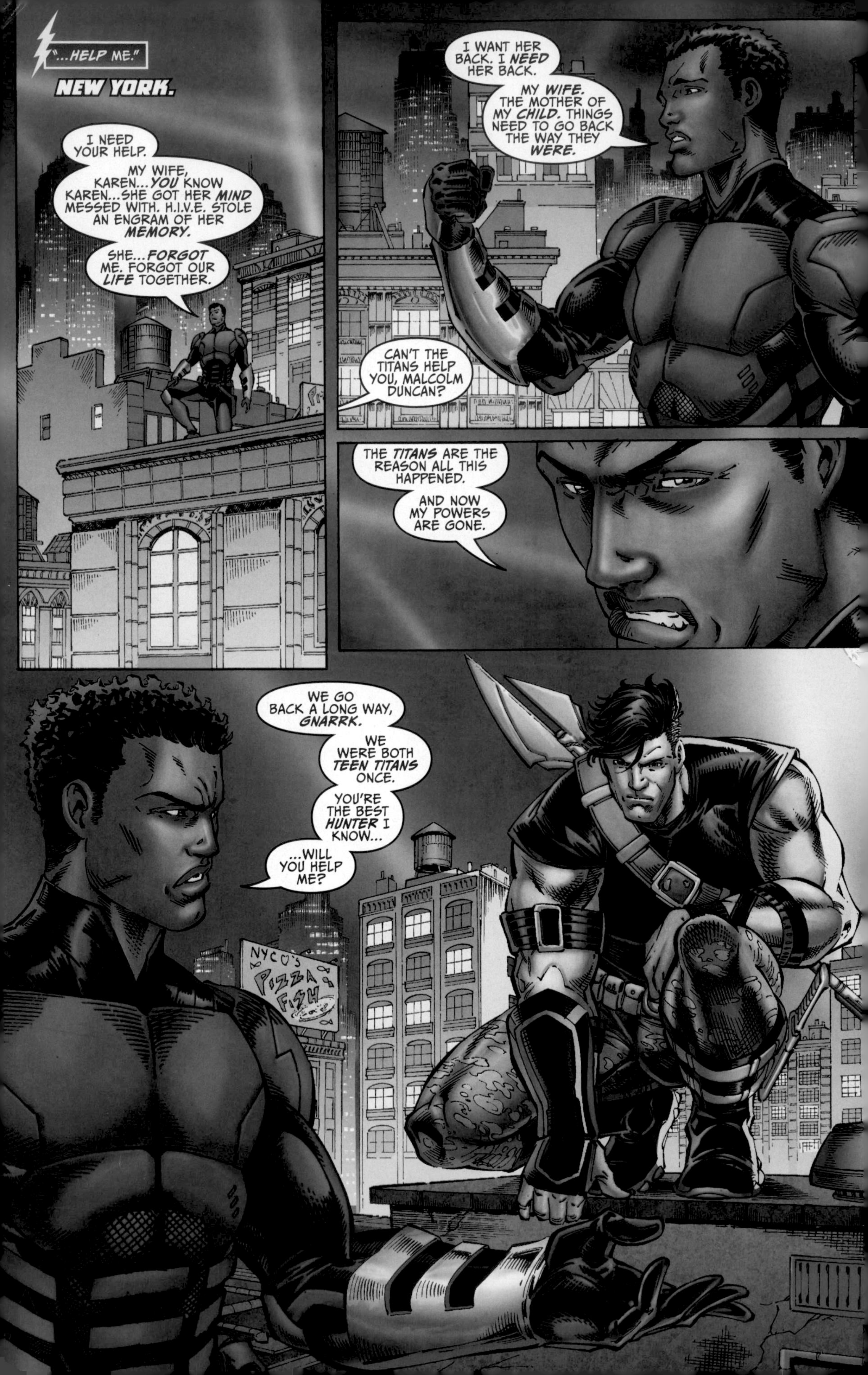
"...HELP ME."
NEW YORK.
I NEED YOUR HELP.
MY WIFE, KAREN...YOU KNOW KAREN...SHE GOT HER MIND MESSED WITH. H.I.V.E. STOLE AN ENGRAM OF HER MEMORY.
SHE...FORGOT ME. FORGOT OUR LIFE TOGETHER.
I WANT HER BACK. I NEED HER BACK.
MY WIFE. THE MOTHER OF MY CHILD. THINGS NEED TO GO BACK THE WAY THEY WERE.
CAN'T THE TITANS HELP YOU, MALCOLM DUNCAN?
THE TITANS ARE THE REASON ALL THIS HAPPENED.
AND NOW MY POWERS ARE GONE.
WE GO BACK A LONG WAY, GNARRK.
WE WERE BOTH TEEN TITANS ONCE.
YOU'RE THE BEST HUNTER I KNOW...
...WILL YOU HELP ME?
NYC'S PIZZA FISH

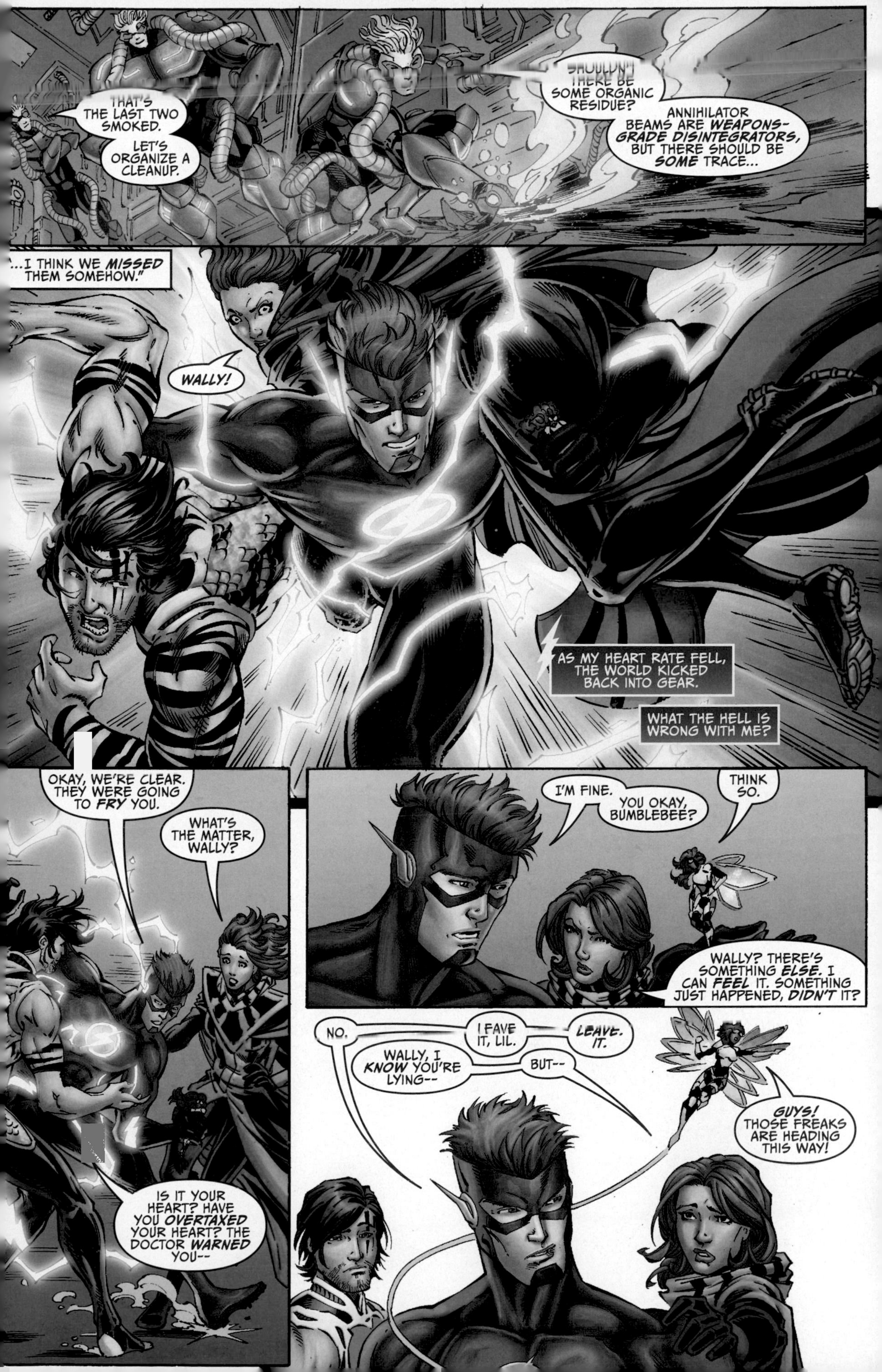

THAT'S THE LAST TWO SMOKED.
LET'S ORGANIZE A CLEANUP.
SHOULDN'T THERE BE SOME ORGANIC RESIDUE?
ANNIHILATOR BEAMS ARE *WEAPONS-GRADE DISINTEGRATORS*, BUT THERE SHOULD BE *SOME* TRACE...
"...I THINK WE *MISSED* THEM SOMEHOW."
WALLY!
AS MY HEART RATE FELL, THE WORLD KICKED BACK INTO GEAR.
WHAT THE HELL IS WRONG WITH ME?
OKAY, WE'RE CLEAR. THEY WERE GOING TO *FRY* YOU.
WHAT'S THE MATTER, WALLY?
IS IT YOUR HEART? HAVE YOU *OVERTAXED* YOUR HEART? THE DOCTOR *WARNED* YOU--
I'M FINE.
YOU OKAY, BUMBLEBEE?
THINK SO.
WALLY? THERE'S SOMETHING *ELSE*. I CAN *FEEL* IT. SOMETHING JUST HAPPENED, *DIDN'T* IT?
NO.
WALLY, I *KNOW* YOU'RE LYING--
LEAVE IT, LIL.
BUT--
LEAVE. IT.
GUYS! THOSE FREAKS ARE HEADING THIS WAY!

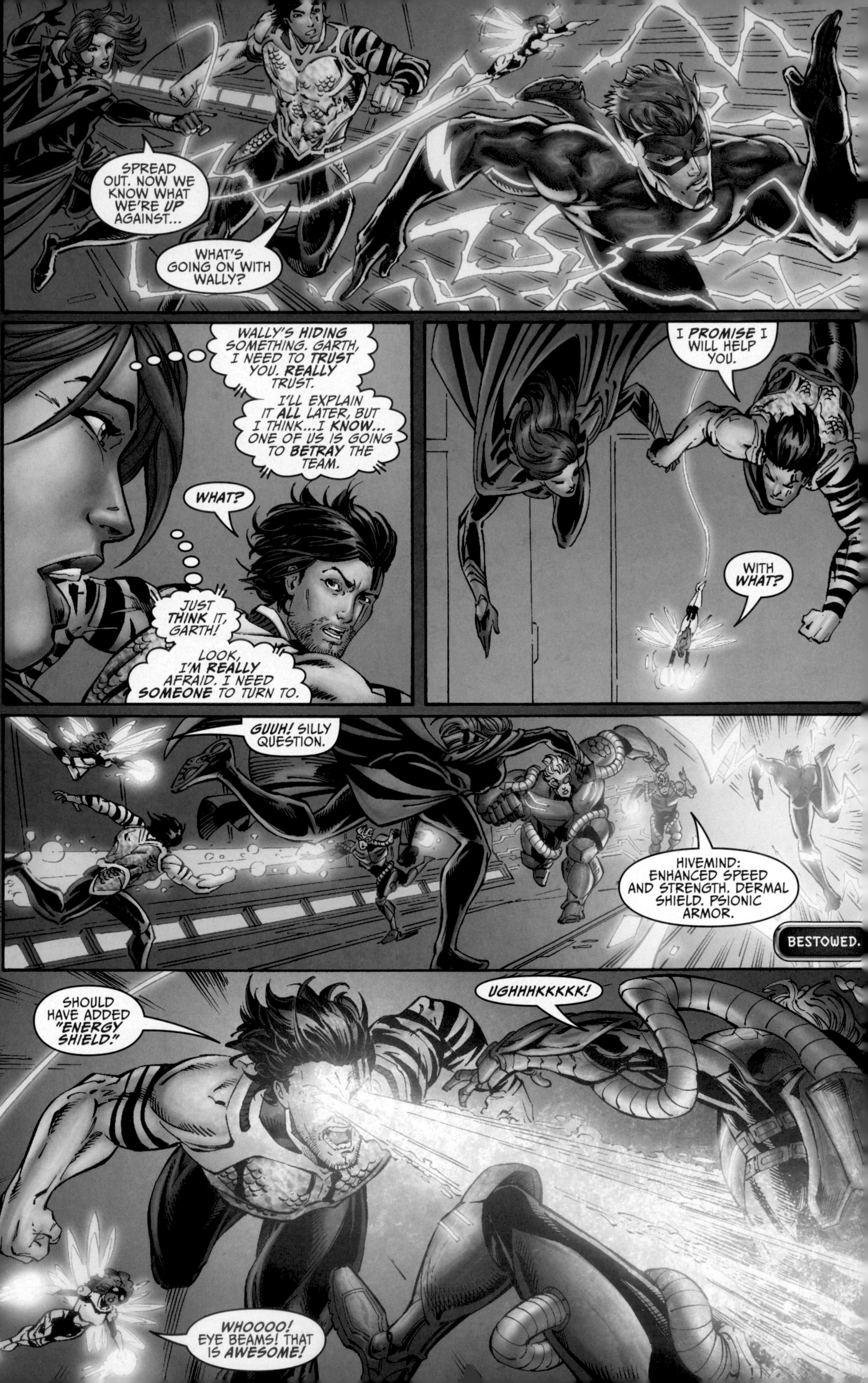
SPREAD OUT. NOW WE KNOW WHAT WE'RE UP AGAINST...
WHAT'S GOING ON WITH WALLY?
WALLY'S HIDING SOMETHING. GARTH, I NEED TO TRUST YOU. REALLY TRUST.
I'LL EXPLAIN IT ALL LATER, BUT I THINK...I KNOW... ONE OF US IS GOING TO BETRAY THE TEAM.
WHAT?
JUST THINK IT, GARTH!
LOOK, I'M REALLY AFRAID. I NEED SOMEONE TO TURN TO.
I PROMISE I WILL HELP YOU.
WITH WHAT?
GUUH! SILLY QUESTION.
HIVEMIND: ENHANCED SPEED AND STRENGTH. DERMAL SHIELD. PSIONIC ARMOR.
BESTOWED.
SHOULD HAVE ADDED "ENERGY SHIELD."
UGHHHKKKKK!
WHOOOO! EYE BEAMS! THAT IS AWESOME!

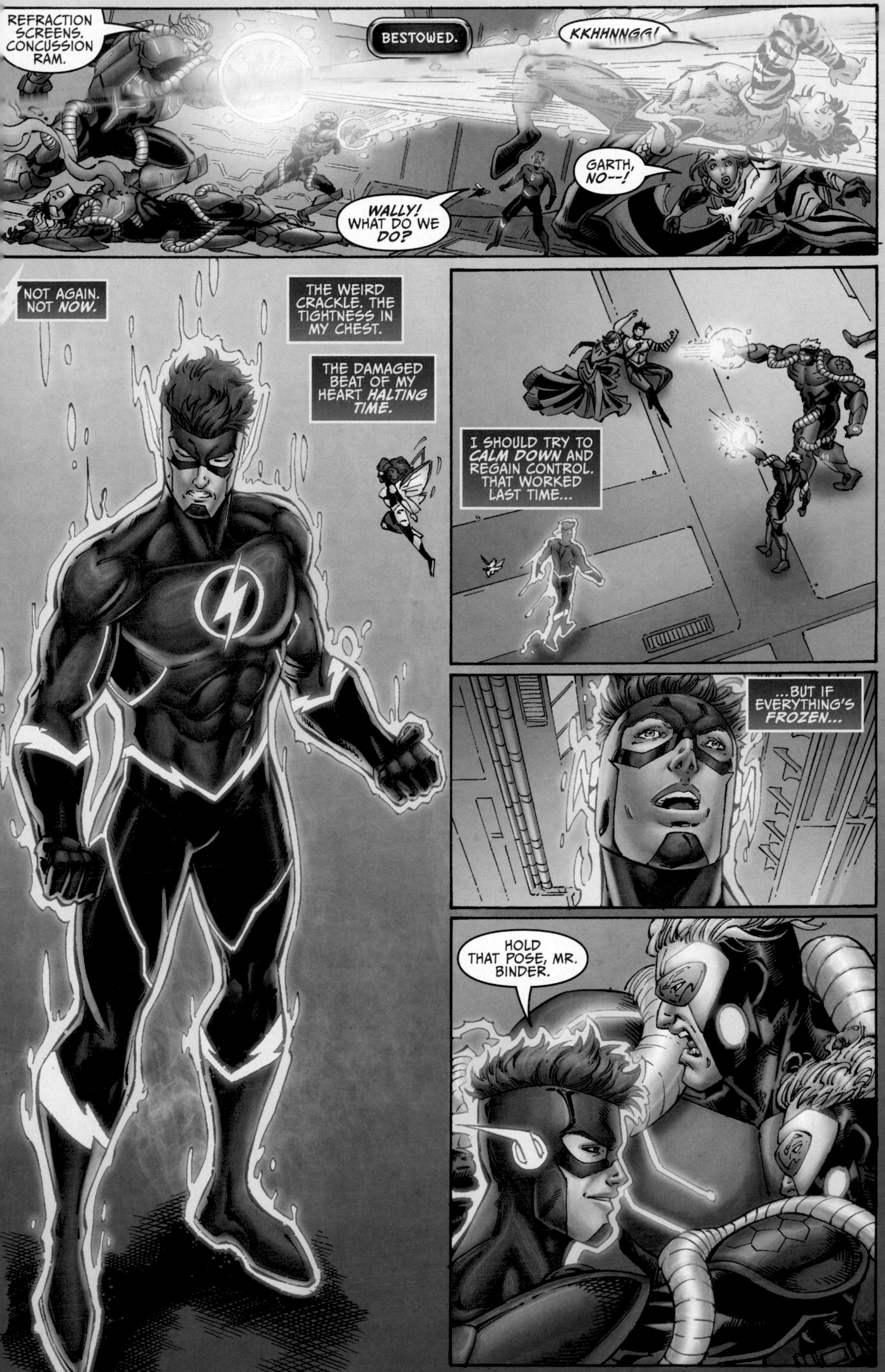
REFRACTION SCREENS. CONCUSSION RAM.
BESTOWED.
KKHHNNGG!
GARTH, NO--!
WALLY! WHAT DO WE DO?
NOT AGAIN. NOT NOW.
THE WEIRD CRACKLE. THE TIGHTNESS IN MY CHEST.
THE DAMAGED BEAT OF MY HEART HALTING TIME.
I SHOULD TRY TO CALM DOWN AND REGAIN CONTROL. THAT WORKED LAST TIME...
...BUT IF EVERYTHING'S FROZEN...
HOLD THAT POSE, MR. BINDER.

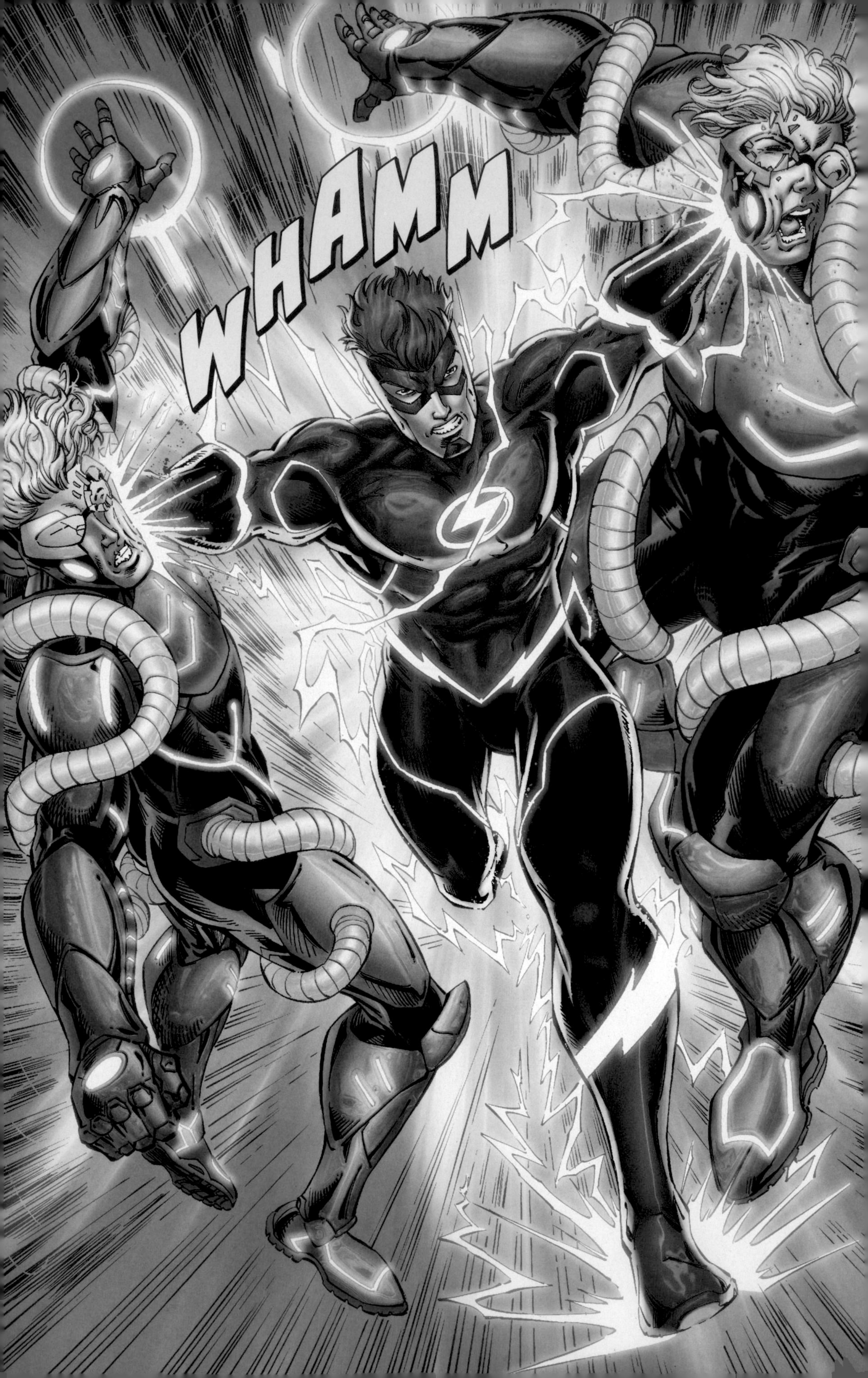
WHAMM

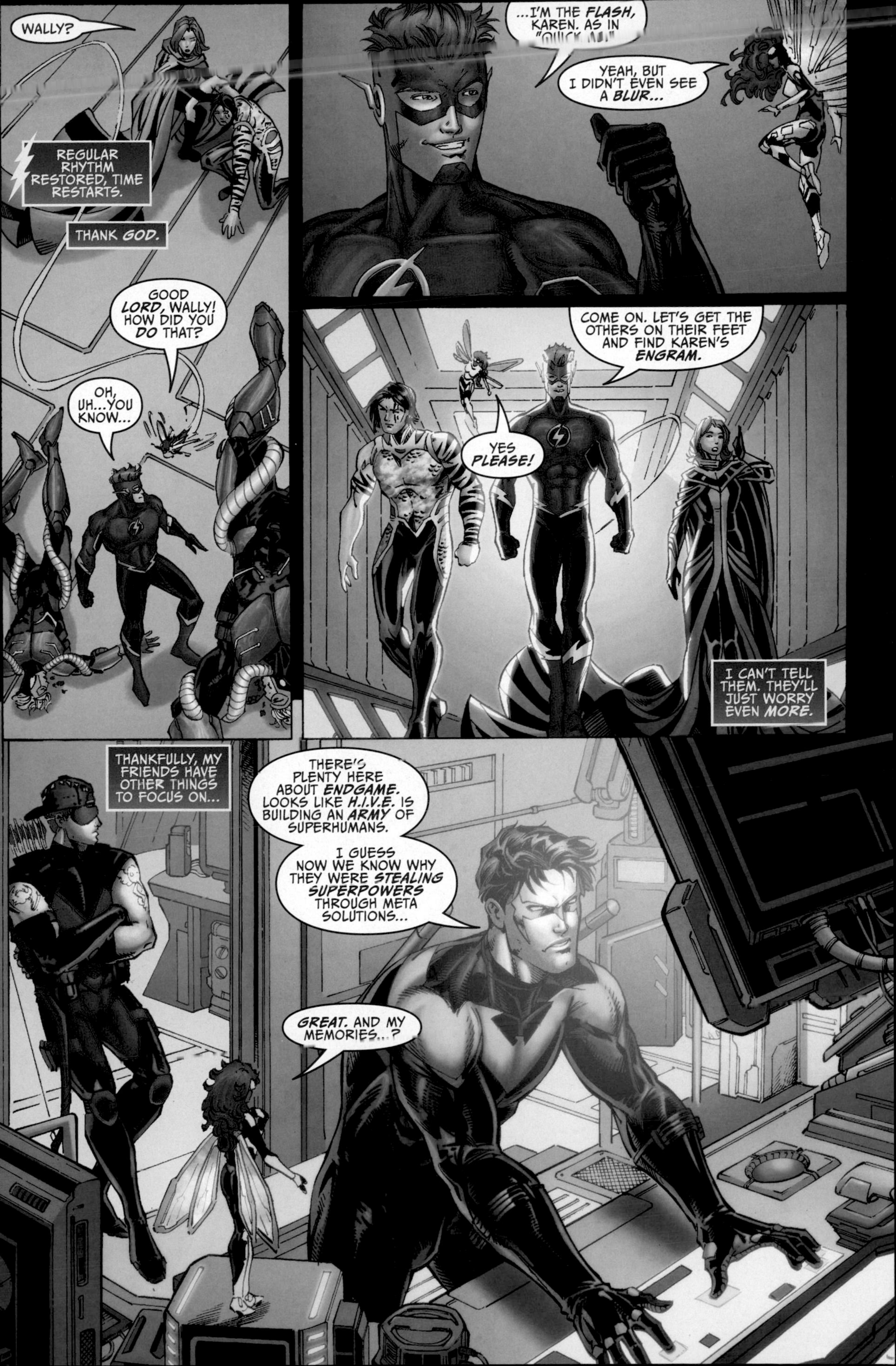
WALLY?
REGULAR RHYTHM RESTORED, TIME RESTARTS.
THANK GOD.
...I'M THE FLASH, KAREN. AS IN
YEAH, BUT I DIDN'T EVEN SEE A BLUR...
GOOD LORD, WALLY! HOW DID YOU DO THAT?
OH, UH...YOU KNOW...
COME ON. LET'S GET THE OTHERS ON THEIR FEET AND FIND KAREN'S ENGRAM.
YES PLEASE!
I CAN'T TELL THEM. THEY'LL JUST WORRY EVEN MORE.
THANKFULLY, MY FRIENDS HAVE OTHER THINGS TO FOCUS ON...
THERE'S PLENTY HERE ABOUT ENDGAME. LOOKS LIKE H.I.V.E. IS BUILDING AN ARMY OF SUPERHUMANS.
I GUESS NOW WE KNOW WHY THEY WERE STEALING SUPERPOWERS THROUGH META SOLUTIONS...
GREAT. AND MY MEMORIES...?

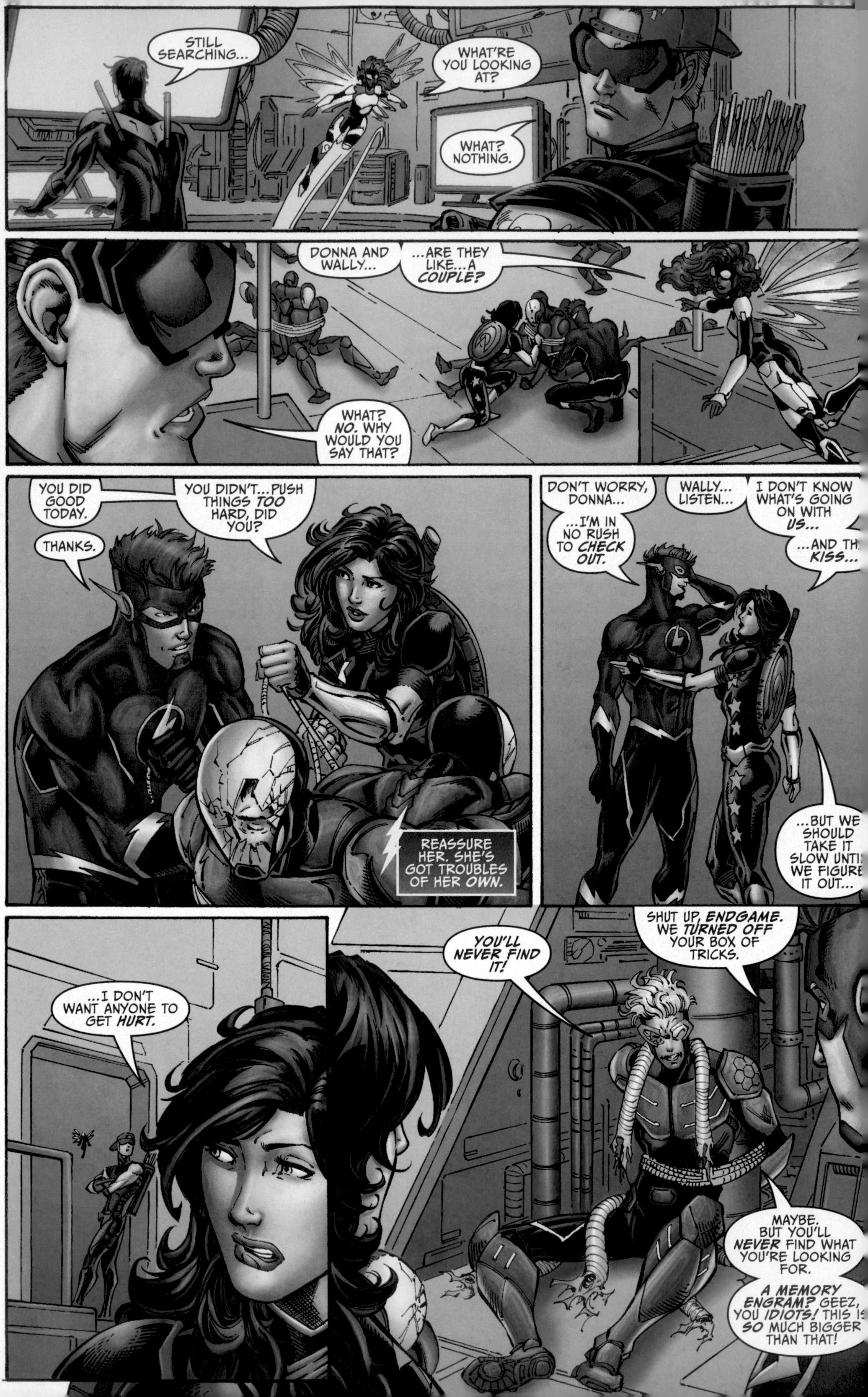
STILL SEARCHING...
WHAT'RE YOU LOOKING AT?
WHAT? NOTHING.
DONNA AND WALLY...
...ARE THEY LIKE...A *COUPLE?*
WHAT? *NO.* WHY WOULD YOU SAY THAT?
YOU DID GOOD TODAY.
THANKS.
YOU DIDN'T...PUSH THINGS *TOO* HARD, DID YOU?
REASSURE HER. SHE'S GOT TROUBLES OF HER *OWN.*
DON'T WORRY, DONNA...
...I'M IN NO RUSH TO *CHECK OUT.*
WALLY... LISTEN...
I DON'T KNOW WHAT'S GOING ON WITH *US...*
...BUT WE SHOULD TAKE IT SLOW UNTI WE FIGURE IT OUT...
...I DON'T WANT ANYONE TO GET *HURT.*
YOU'LL NEVER FIND IT!
SHUT UP, *ENDGAME.* WE *TURNED OFF* YOUR BOX OF TRICKS.
MAYBE. BUT YOU'LL *NEVER* FIND WHAT YOU'RE LOOKING FOR.
A MEMORY ENGRAM? GEEZ, YOU *IDIOTS!* THIS IS *SO* MUCH BIGGER THAN THAT!

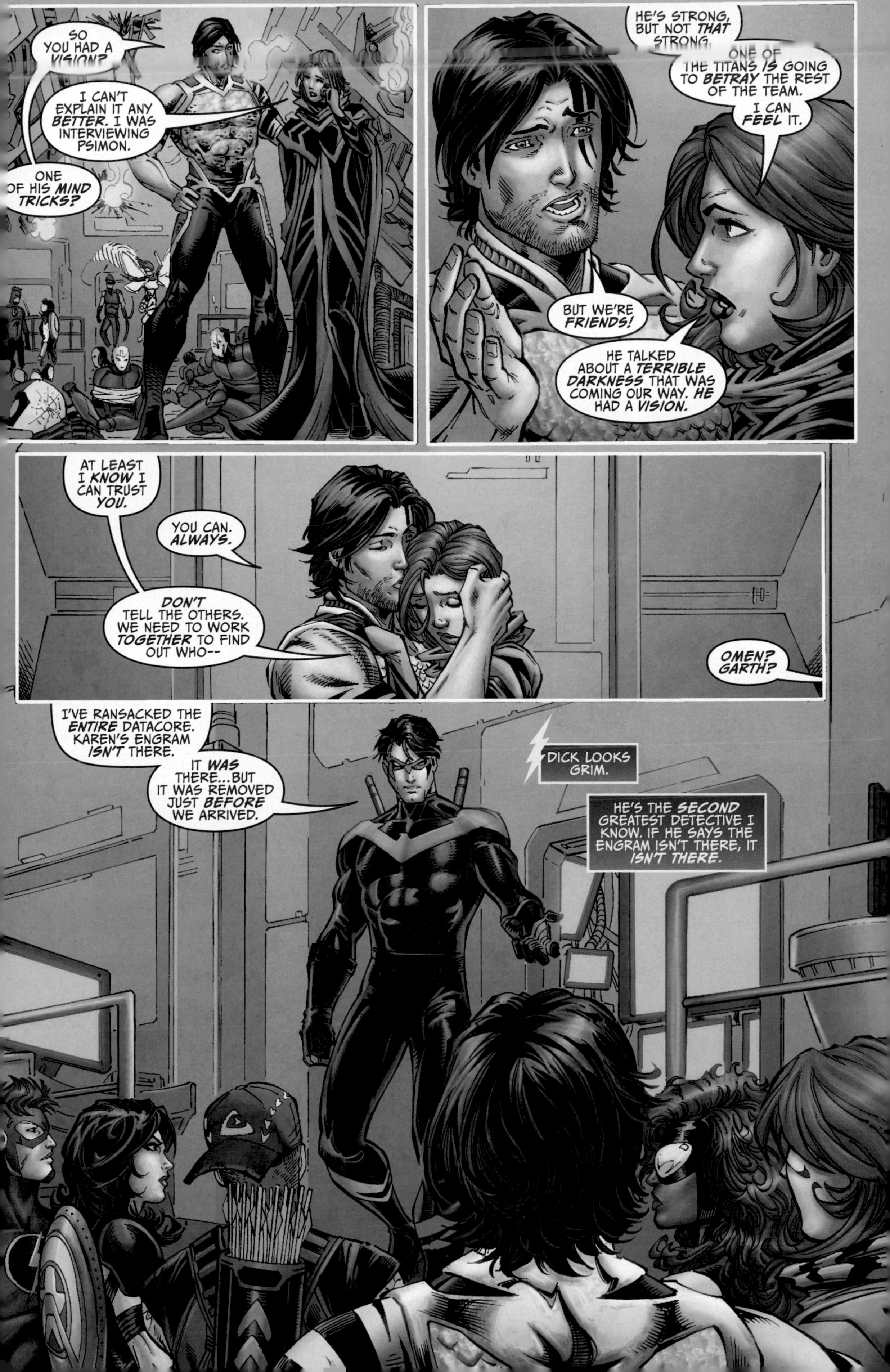
SO YOU HAD A VISION?
I CAN'T EXPLAIN IT ANY BETTER. I WAS INTERVIEWING PSIMON.
ONE OF HIS MIND TRICKS?
HE'S STRONG, BUT NOT THAT STRONG.
ONE OF THE TITANS IS GOING TO BETRAY THE REST OF THE TEAM.
I CAN FEEL IT.
BUT WE'RE FRIENDS!
HE TALKED ABOUT A TERRIBLE DARKNESS THAT WAS COMING OUR WAY. HE HAD A VISION.
AT LEAST I KNOW I CAN TRUST YOU.
YOU CAN. ALWAYS.
DON'T TELL THE OTHERS. WE NEED TO WORK TOGETHER TO FIND OUT WHO--
OMEN? GARTH?
I'VE RANSACKED THE ENTIRE DATACORE. KAREN'S ENGRAM ISN'T THERE.
IT WAS THERE...BUT IT WAS REMOVED JUST BEFORE WE ARRIVED.
DICK LOOKS GRIM.
HE'S THE SECOND GREATEST DETECTIVE I KNOW. IF HE SAYS THE ENGRAM ISN'T THERE, IT ISN'T THERE.

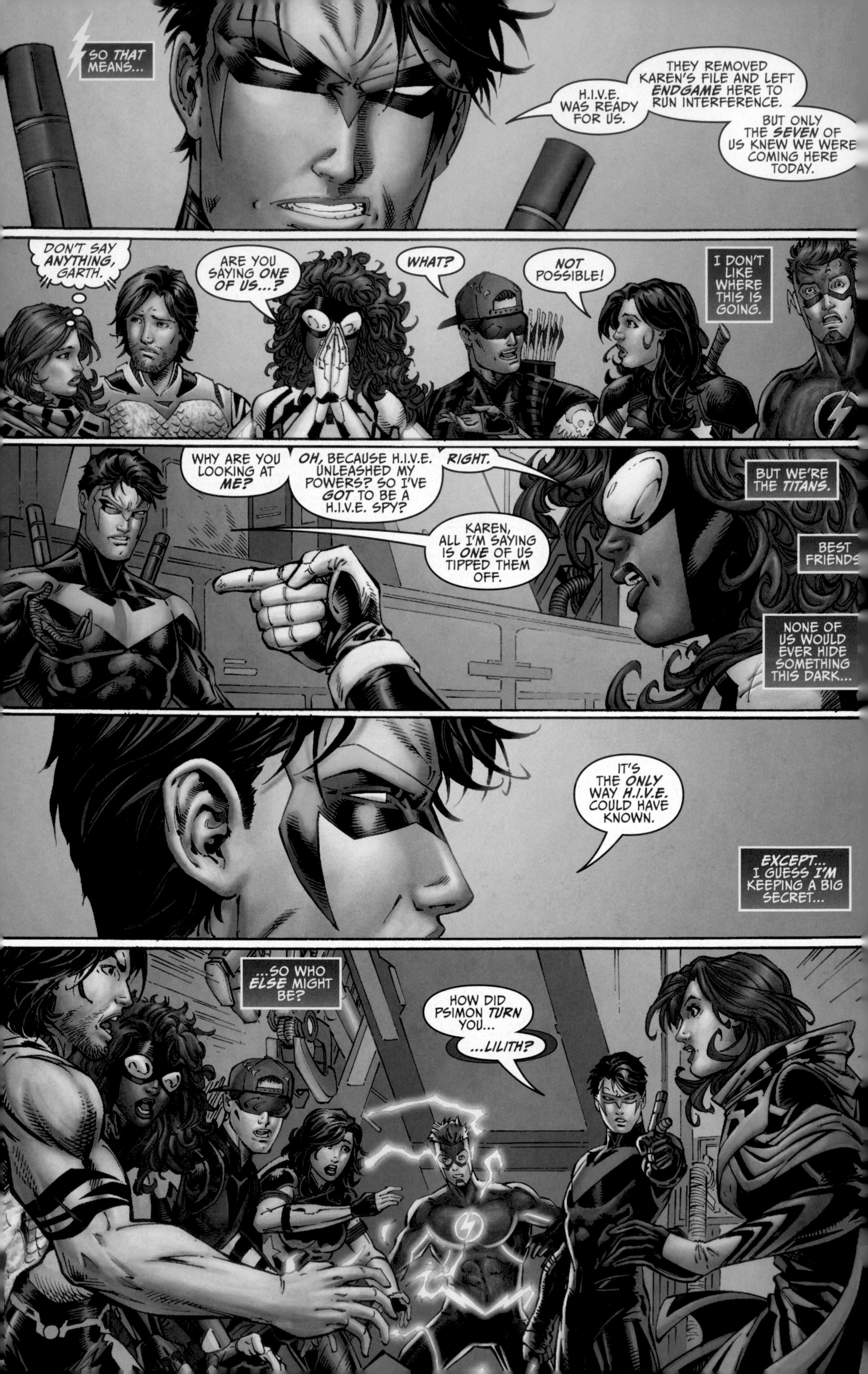

SO THAT MEANS...
H.I.V.E. WAS READY FOR US.
THEY REMOVED KAREN'S FILE AND LEFT ENDGAME HERE TO RUN INTERFERENCE.
BUT ONLY THE SEVEN OF US KNEW WE WERE COMING HERE TODAY.
DON'T SAY ANYTHING, GARTH.
ARE YOU SAYING ONE OF US...?
WHAT?
NOT POSSIBLE!
I DON'T LIKE WHERE THIS IS GOING.
WHY ARE YOU LOOKING AT ME?
OH, BECAUSE H.I.V.E. UNLEASHED MY POWERS? SO I'VE GOT TO BE A H.I.V.E. SPY?
RIGHT.
KAREN, ALL I'M SAYING IS ONE OF US TIPPED THEM OFF.
BUT WE'RE THE TITANS.
BEST FRIENDS
NONE OF US WOULD EVER HIDE SOMETHING THIS DARK...
IT'S THE ONLY WAY H.I.V.E. COULD HAVE KNOWN.
EXCEPT... I GUESS I'M KEEPING A BIG SECRET...
...SO WHO ELSE MIGHT BE?
HOW DID PSIMON TURN YOU...
...LILITH?

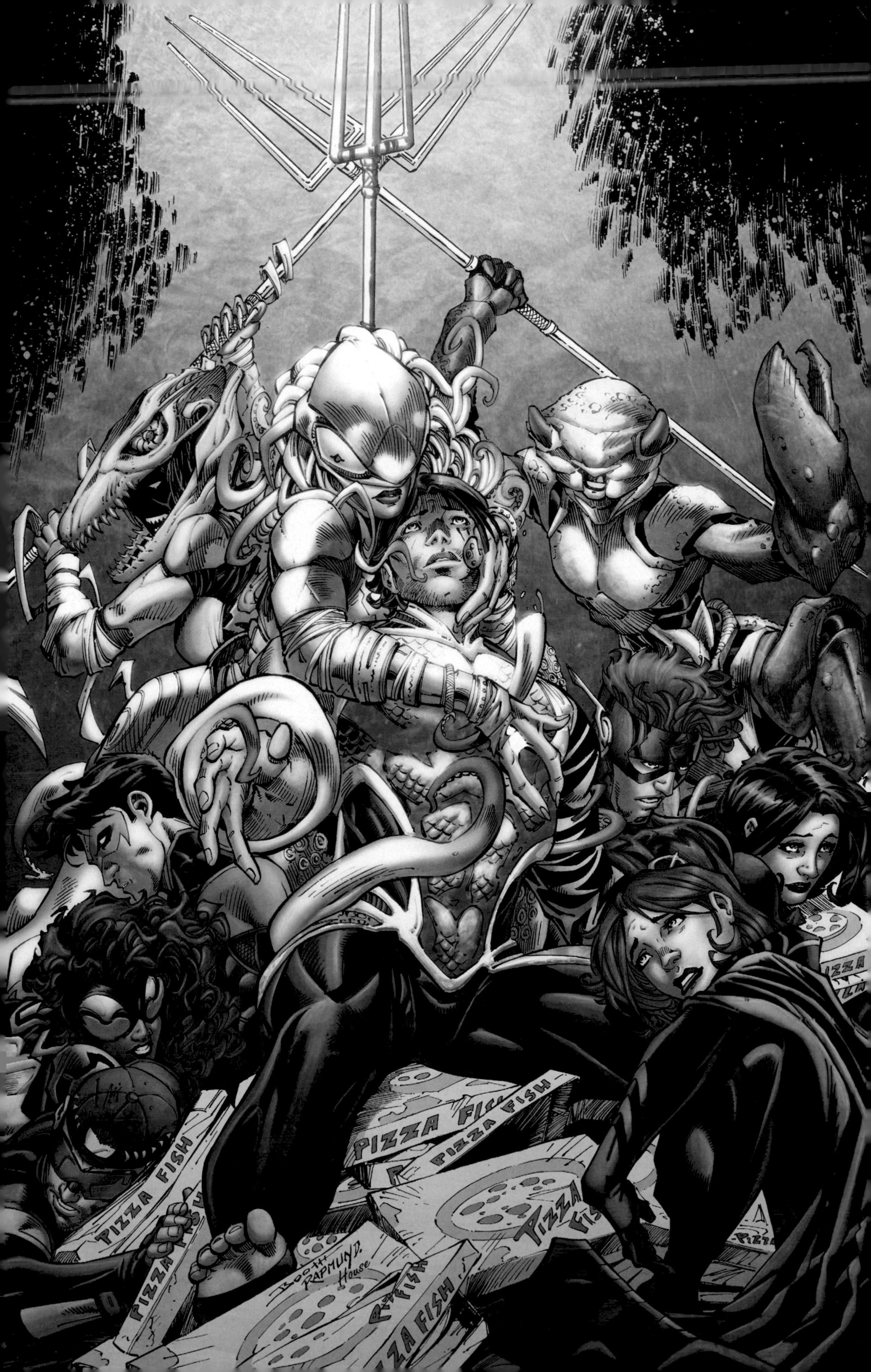
PIZZA FISH
PIZZA FISH
PIZZA FISH
PIZZA FISH
PIZZA FISH
PIZZA FISH

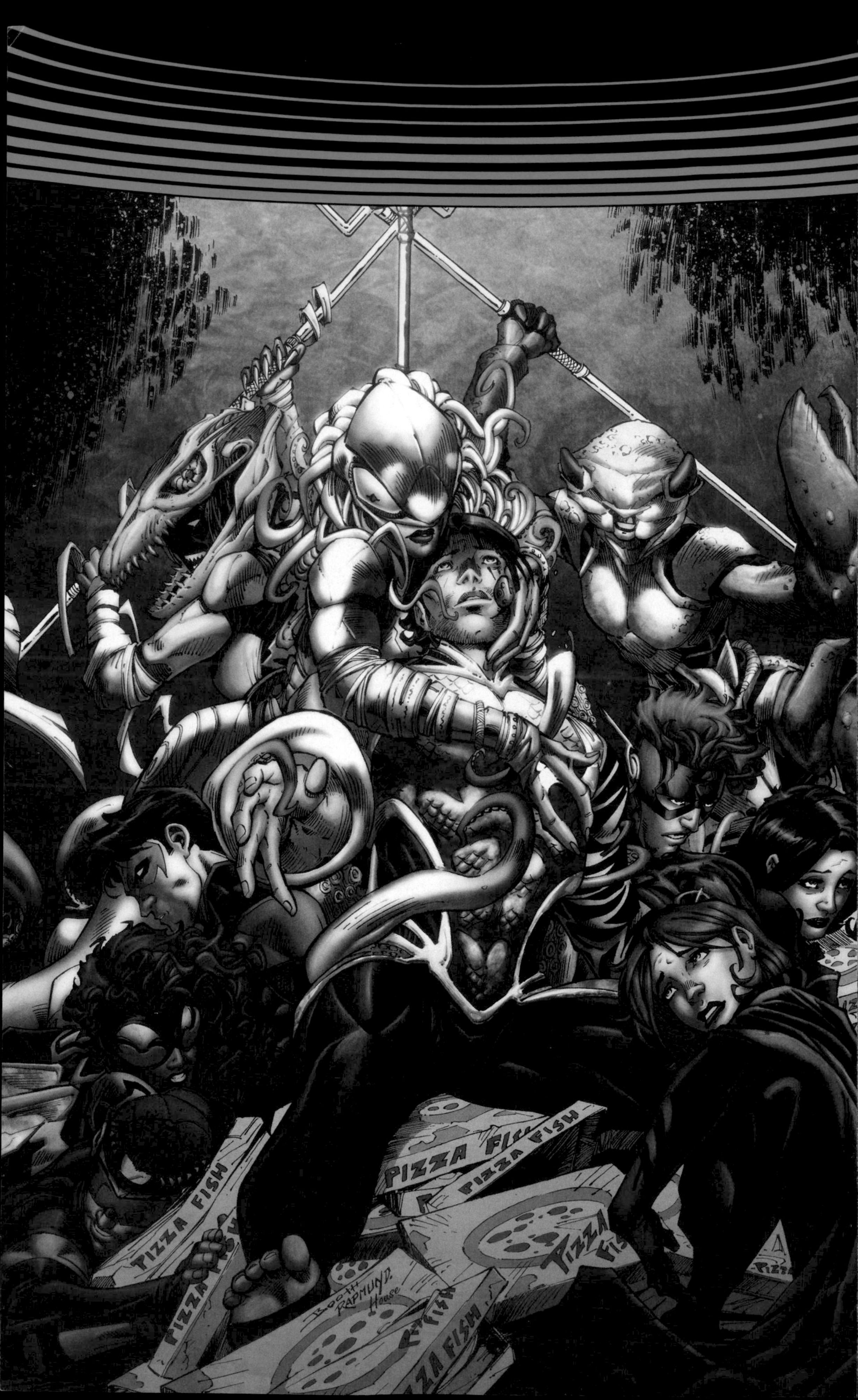
PIZZA FISH
PIZZA FISH
PIZZA FISH
PIZZA FISH
BOOTH
RAPMUND.
House
PIZZA FISH
PIZZA FISH

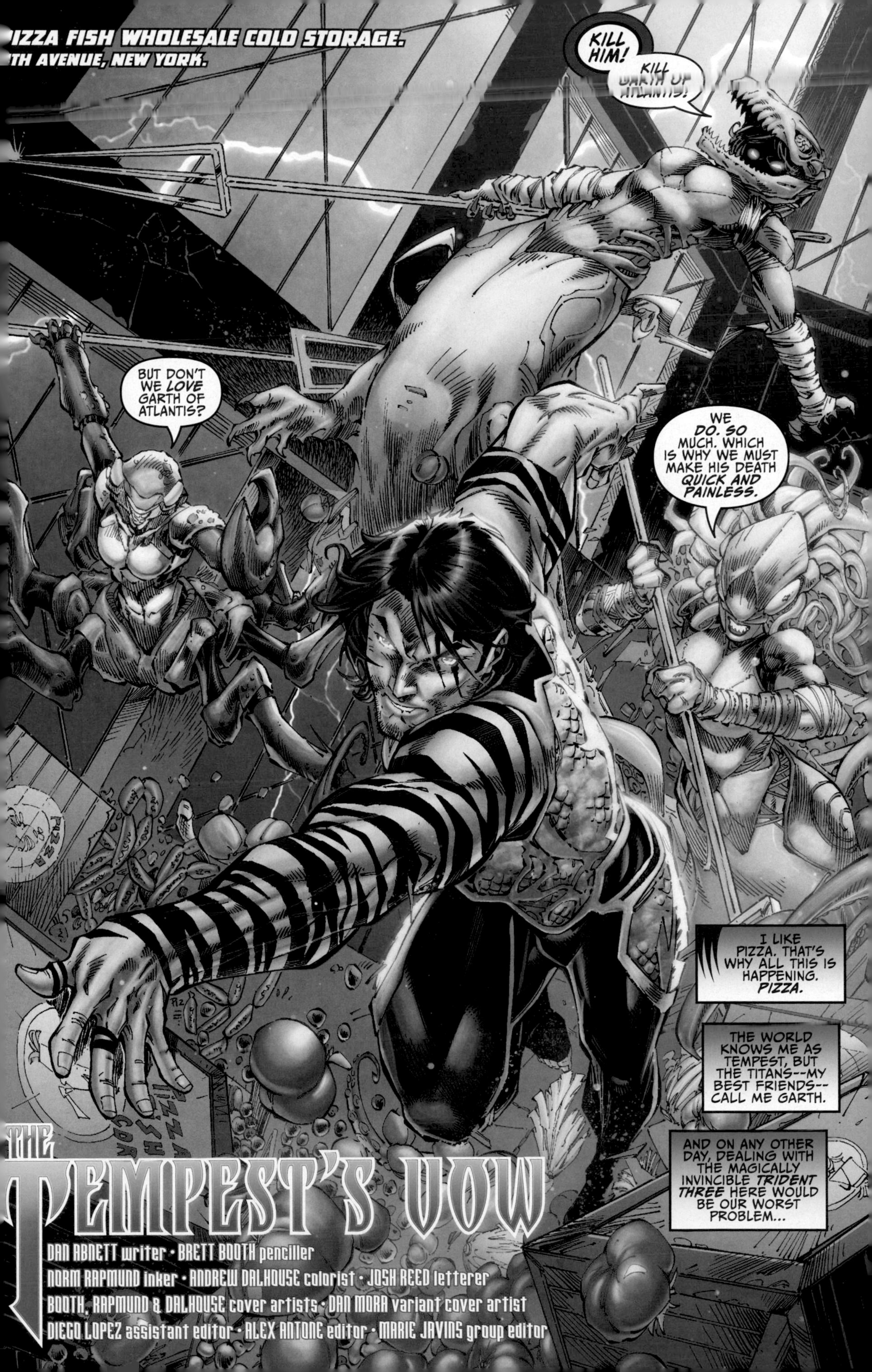
PIZZA FISH WHOLESALE COLD STORAGE.
TH AVENUE, NEW YORK.
KILL HIM!
KILL GARTH OF ATLANTIS!
BUT DON'T WE LOVE GARTH OF ATLANTIS?
WE DO. SO MUCH. WHICH IS WHY WE MUST MAKE HIS DEATH QUICK AND PAINLESS.
I LIKE PIZZA. THAT'S WHY ALL THIS IS HAPPENING. PIZZA.
THE WORLD KNOWS ME AS TEMPEST, BUT THE TITANS--MY BEST FRIENDS--CALL ME GARTH.
AND ON ANY OTHER DAY, DEALING WITH THE MAGICALLY INVINCIBLE TRIDENT THREE HERE WOULD BE OUR WORST PROBLEM...
THE TEMPEST'S VOW
DAN ABNETT writer • BRETT BOOTH penciller
NORM RAPMUND inker • ANDREW DALHOUSE colorist • JOSH REED letterer
BOOTH, RAPMUND & DALHOUSE cover artists • DAN MORA variant cover artist
DIEGO LOPEZ assistant editor • ALEX ANTONE editor • MARIE JAVINS group editor

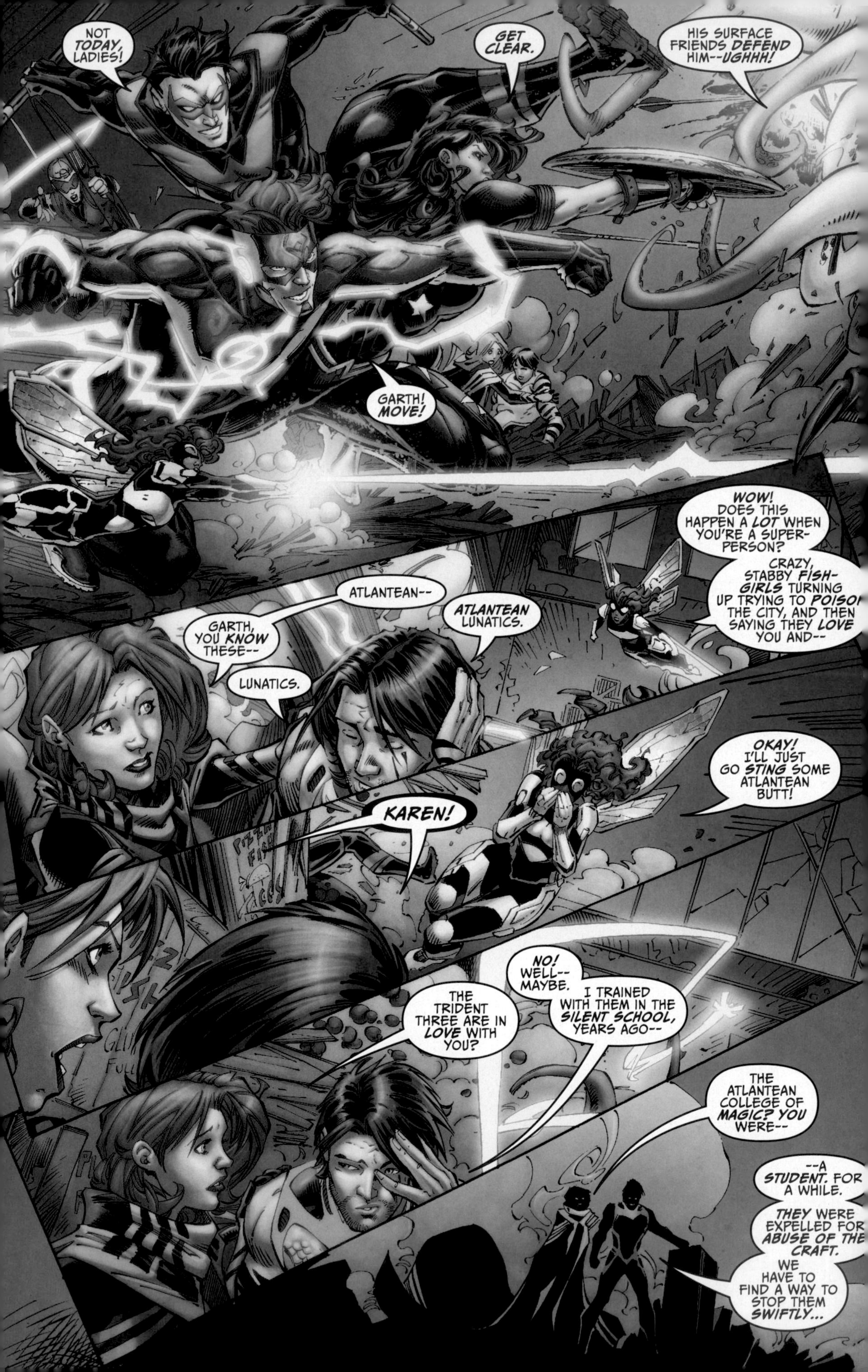
NOT TODAY, LADIES!
GET CLEAR.
HIS SURFACE FRIENDS DEFEND HIM--UGHHH!
GARTH! MOVE!
WOW! DOES THIS HAPPEN A LOT WHEN YOU'RE A SUPER-PERSON?
CRAZY, STABBY FISH-GIRLS TURNING UP TRYING TO POISON THE CITY, AND THEN SAYING THEY LOVE YOU AND--
ATLANTEAN--
GARTH, YOU KNOW THESE--
ATLANTEAN LUNATICS.
LUNATICS.
OKAY! I'LL JUST GO STING SOME ATLANTEAN BUTT!
KAREN!
THE TRIDENT THREE ARE IN LOVE WITH YOU?
NO! WELL-- MAYBE.
I TRAINED WITH THEM IN THE SILENT SCHOOL, YEARS AGO--
THE ATLANTEAN COLLEGE OF MAGIC? YOU WERE--
--A STUDENT. FOR A WHILE.
THEY WERE EXPELLED FOR ABUSE OF THE CRAFT.
WE HAVE TO FIND A WAY TO STOP THEM SWIFTLY...

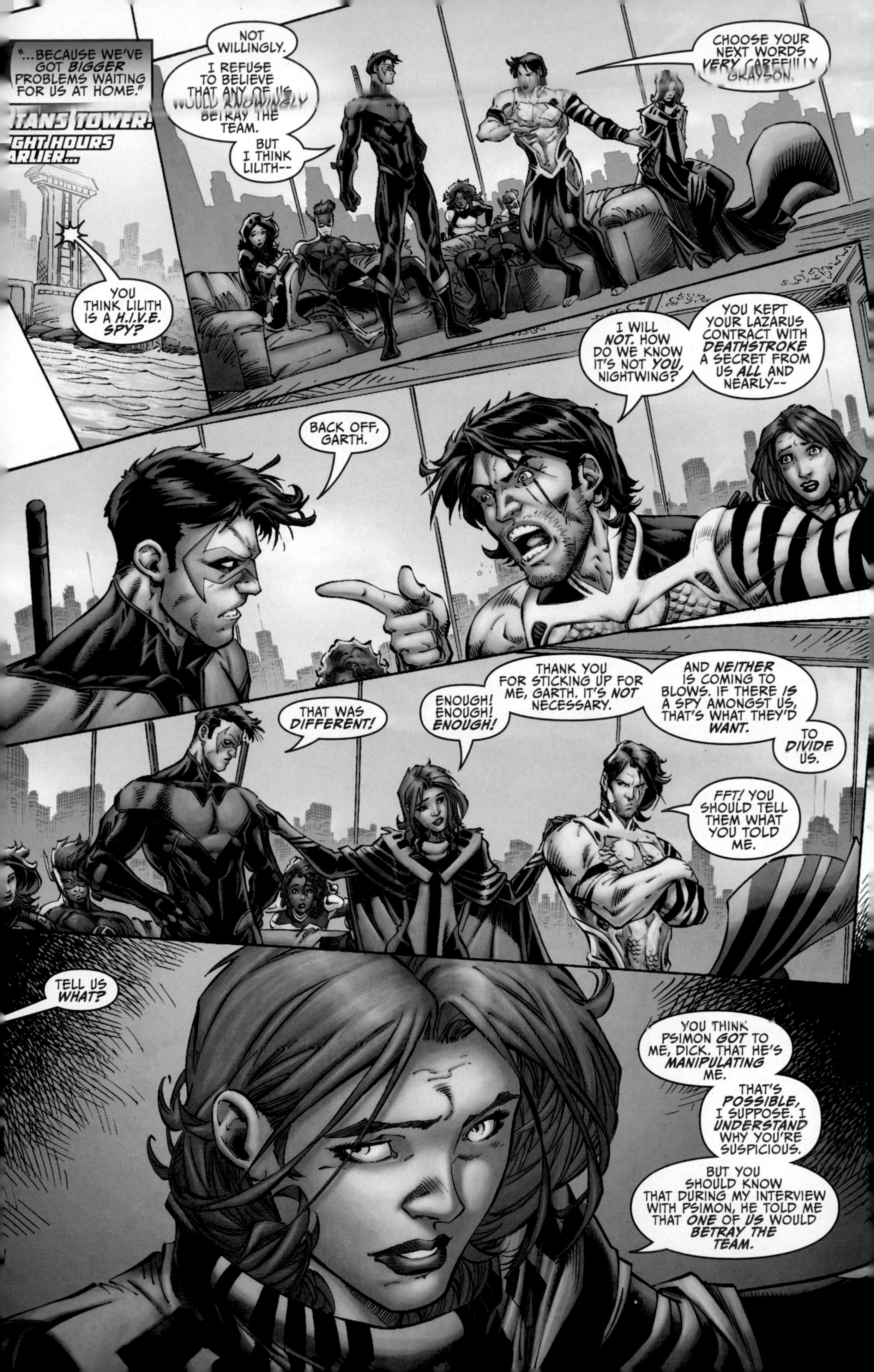
"...BECAUSE WE'VE GOT BIGGER PROBLEMS WAITING FOR US AT HOME."
TANS TOWER!
GHT HOURS
ARLIER...
YOU THINK LILITH IS A H.I.V.E. SPY?
NOT WILLINGLY.
I REFUSE TO BELIEVE THAT ANY OF US WOULD KNOWINGLY BETRAY THE TEAM.
BUT I THINK LILITH--
CHOOSE YOUR NEXT WORDS VERY CAREFULLY, GRAYSON.
I WILL NOT. HOW DO WE KNOW IT'S NOT YOU, NIGHTWING?
YOU KEPT YOUR LAZARUS CONTRACT WITH DEATHSTROKE A SECRET FROM US ALL AND NEARLY--
BACK OFF, GARTH.
THAT WAS DIFFERENT!
ENOUGH! ENOUGH! ENOUGH!
THANK YOU FOR STICKING UP FOR ME, GARTH. IT'S NOT NECESSARY.
AND NEITHER IS COMING TO BLOWS. IF THERE IS A SPY AMONGST US, THAT'S WHAT THEY'D WANT.
TO DIVIDE US.
FFT! YOU SHOULD TELL THEM WHAT YOU TOLD ME.
TELL US WHAT?
YOU THINK PSIMON GOT TO ME, DICK. THAT HE'S MANIPULATING ME.
THAT'S POSSIBLE, I SUPPOSE. I UNDERSTAND WHY YOU'RE SUSPICIOUS.
BUT YOU SHOULD KNOW THAT DURING MY INTERVIEW WITH PSIMON, HE TOLD ME THAT ONE OF US WOULD BETRAY THE TEAM.

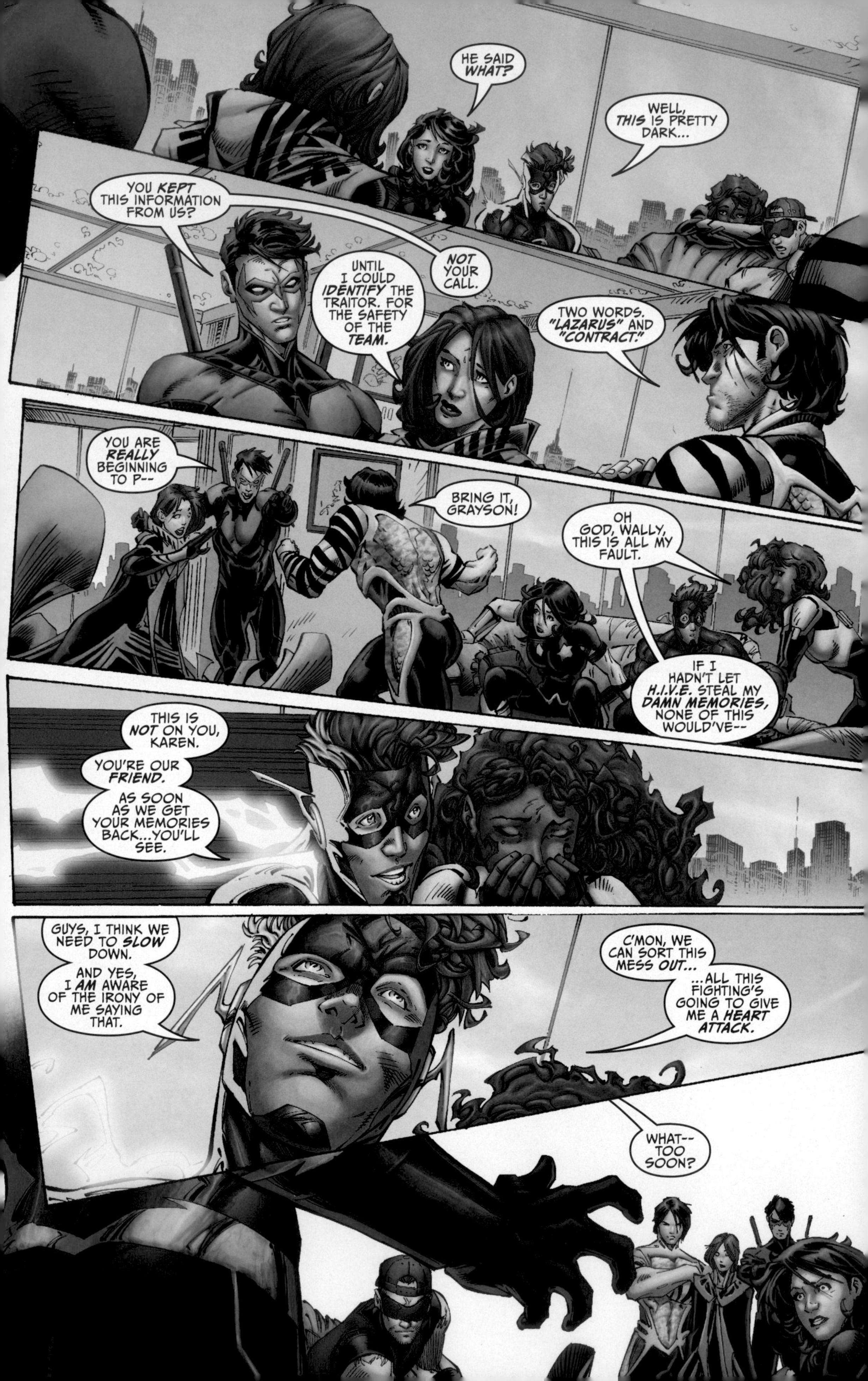
HE SAID WHAT?
WELL, THIS IS PRETTY DARK...
YOU KEPT THIS INFORMATION FROM US?
NOT YOUR CALL.
UNTIL I COULD IDENTIFY THE TRAITOR. FOR THE SAFETY OF THE TEAM.
TWO WORDS. "LAZARUS" AND "CONTRACT."
YOU ARE REALLY BEGINNING TO P--
BRING IT, GRAYSON!
OH GOD, WALLY, THIS IS ALL MY FAULT.
IF I HADN'T LET H.I.V.E. STEAL MY DAMN MEMORIES, NONE OF THIS WOULD'VE--
THIS IS NOT ON YOU, KAREN.
YOU'RE OUR FRIEND.
AS SOON AS WE GET YOUR MEMORIES BACK...YOU'LL SEE.
GUYS, I THINK WE NEED TO SLOW DOWN.
AND YES, I AM AWARE OF THE IRONY OF ME SAYING THAT.
C'MON, WE CAN SORT THIS MESS OUT...
...ALL THIS FIGHTING'S GOING TO GIVE ME A HEART ATTACK.
WHAT-- TOO SOON?

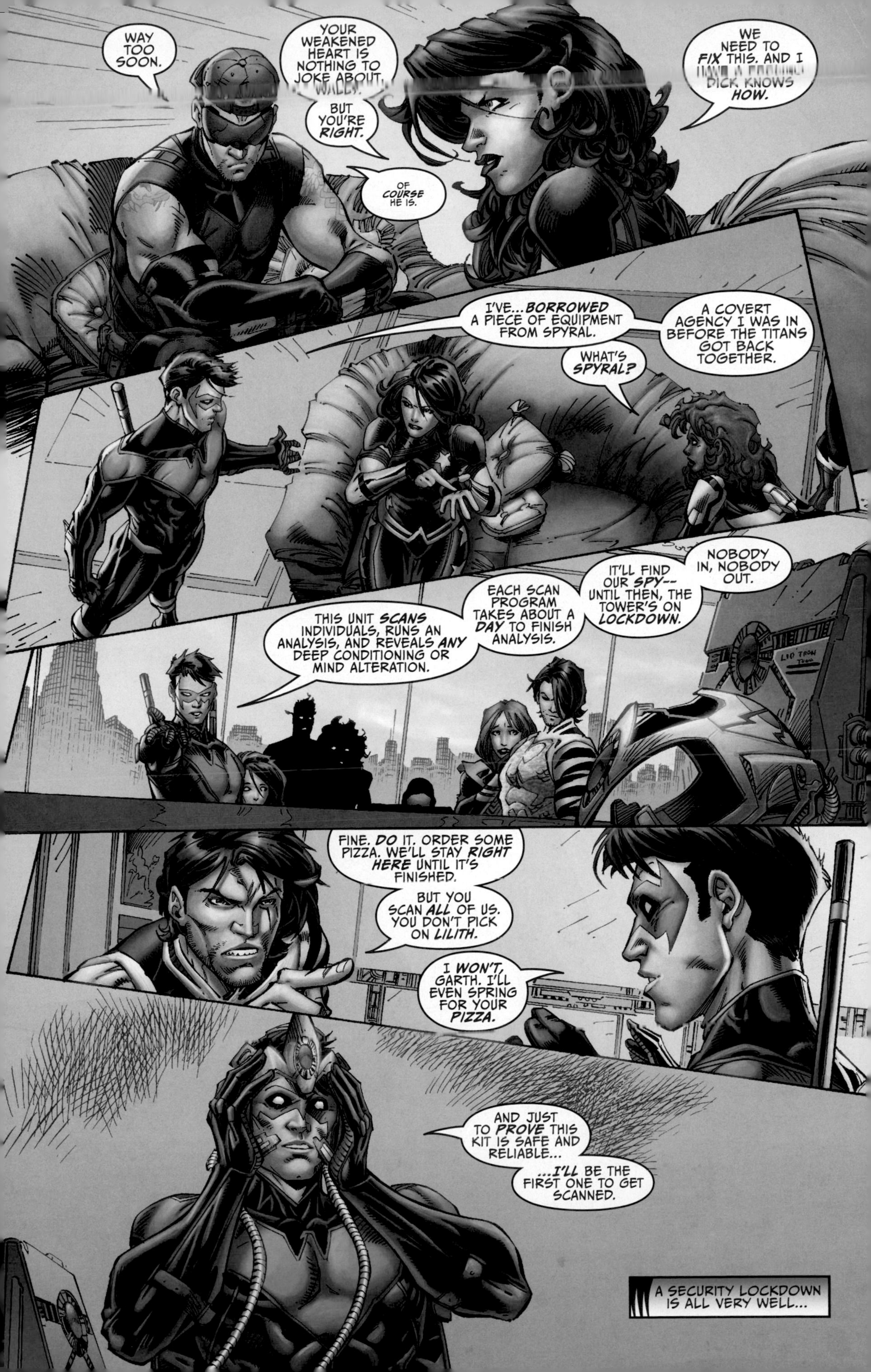

WAY TOO SOON.
YOUR WEAKENED HEART IS NOTHING TO JOKE ABOUT, WALLY.
BUT YOU'RE RIGHT.
OF COURSE HE IS.
WE NEED TO FIX THIS. AND I
DICK KNOWS HOW.
I'VE...BORROWED A PIECE OF EQUIPMENT FROM SPYRAL.
A COVERT AGENCY I WAS IN BEFORE THE TITANS GOT BACK TOGETHER.
WHAT'S SPYRAL?
THIS UNIT SCANS INDIVIDUALS, RUNS AN ANALYSIS, AND REVEALS ANY DEEP CONDITIONING OR MIND ALTERATION.
EACH SCAN PROGRAM TAKES ABOUT A DAY TO FINISH ANALYSIS.
IT'LL FIND OUR SPY-- UNTIL THEN, THE TOWER'S ON LOCKDOWN.
NOBODY IN, NOBODY OUT.
FINE. DO IT. ORDER SOME PIZZA. WE'LL STAY RIGHT HERE UNTIL IT'S FINISHED.
BUT YOU SCAN ALL OF US. YOU DON'T PICK ON LILITH.
I WON'T, GARTH. I'LL EVEN SPRING FOR YOUR PIZZA.
AND JUST TO PROVE THIS KIT IS SAFE AND RELIABLE...
...I'LL BE THE FIRST ONE TO GET SCANNED.
A SECURITY LOCKDOWN IS ALL VERY WELL...

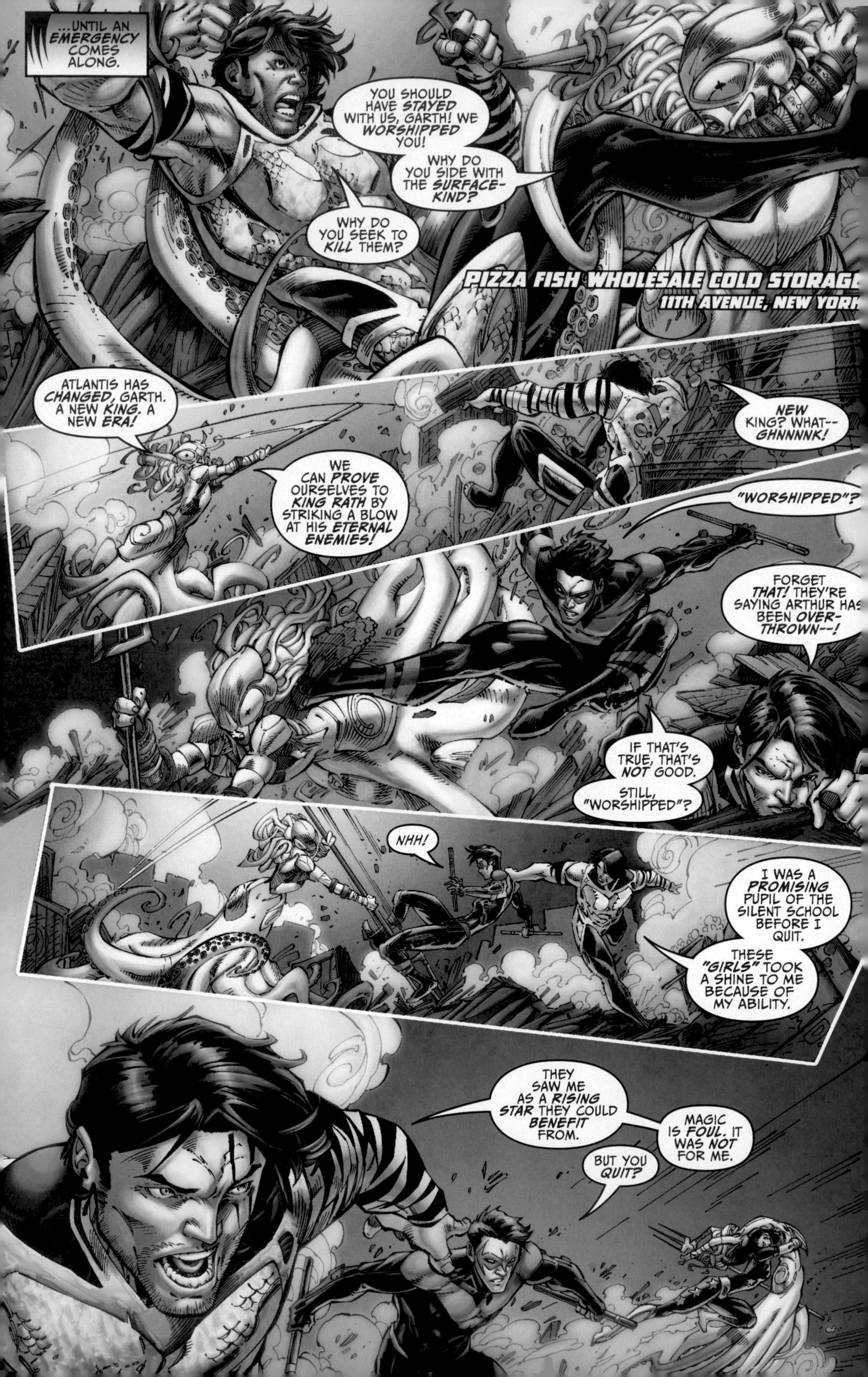
...UNTIL AN EMERGENCY COMES ALONG.
YOU SHOULD HAVE STAYED WITH US, GARTH! WE WORSHIPPED YOU!
WHY DO YOU SIDE WITH THE SURFACE-KIND?
WHY DO YOU SEEK TO KILL THEM?
PIZZA FISH WHOLESALE COLD STORAGE
11TH AVENUE, NEW YORK
ATLANTIS HAS CHANGED, GARTH. A NEW KING. A NEW ERA!
NEW KING? WHAT-- GHNNNNK!
WE CAN PROVE OURSELVES TO KING RATH BY STRIKING A BLOW AT HIS ETERNAL ENEMIES!
"WORSHIPPED"?
FORGET THAT! THEY'RE SAYING ARTHUR HAS BEEN OVER-THROWN--!
IF THAT'S TRUE, THAT'S NOT GOOD.
STILL, "WORSHIPPED"?
NHH!
I WAS A PROMISING PUPIL OF THE SILENT SCHOOL BEFORE I QUIT.
THESE "GIRLS" TOOK A SHINE TO ME BECAUSE OF MY ABILITY.
THEY SAW ME AS A RISING STAR THEY COULD BENEFIT FROM.
BUT YOU QUIT?
MAGIC IS FOUL. IT WAS NOT FOR ME.

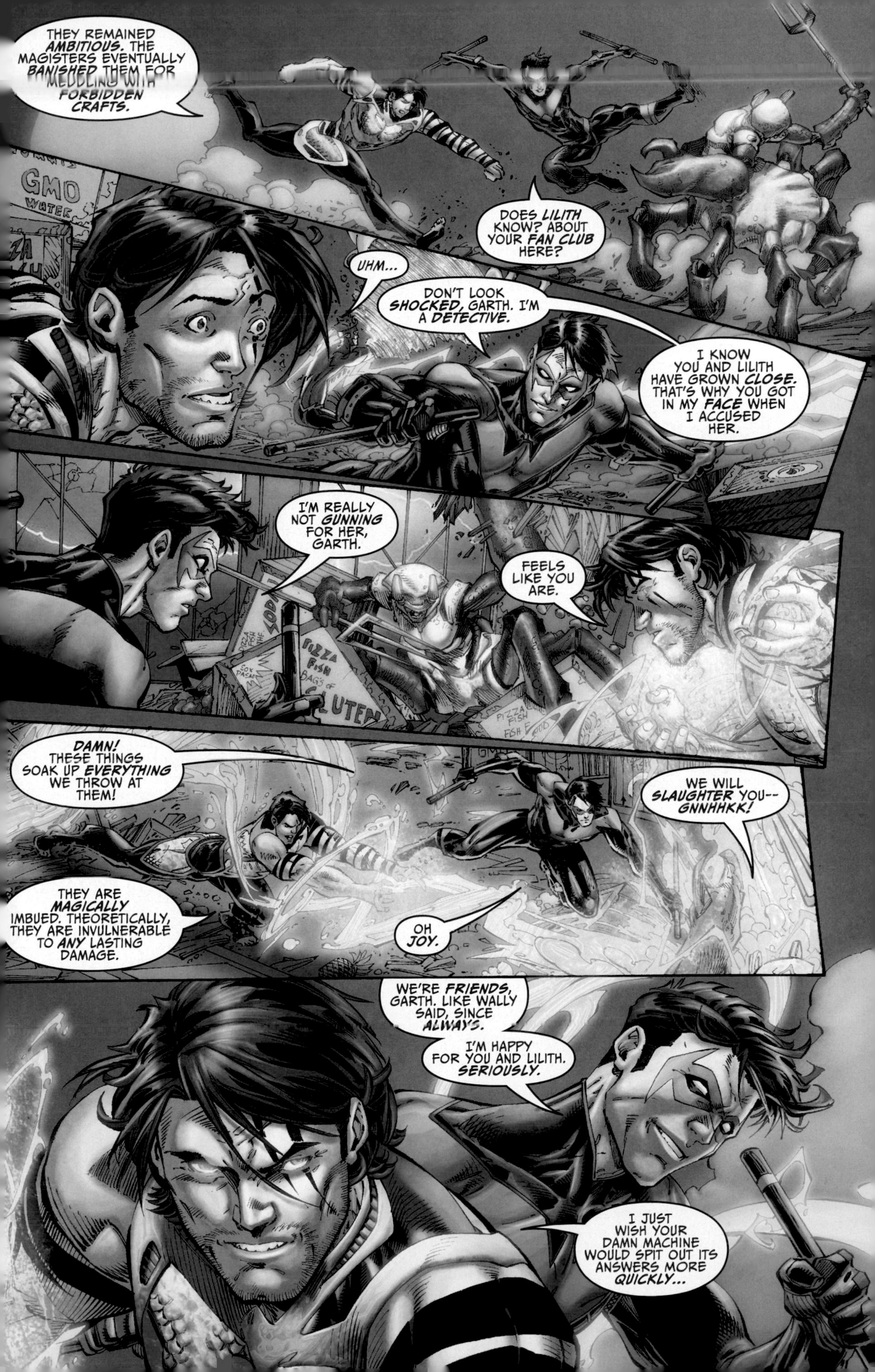
THEY REMAINED AMBITIOUS. THE MAGISTERS EVENTUALLY BANISHED THEM FOR MEDDLING WITH FORBIDDEN CRAFTS.
DOES LILITH KNOW? ABOUT YOUR FAN CLUB HERE?
UHM...
DON'T LOOK SHOCKED, GARTH. I'M A DETECTIVE.
I KNOW YOU AND LILITH HAVE GROWN CLOSE. THAT'S WHY YOU GOT IN MY FACE WHEN I ACCUSED HER.
GMO WATER
I'M REALLY NOT GUNNING FOR HER, GARTH.
FEELS LIKE YOU ARE.
PIZZA FISH
BAGS OF GLUTEN
DAMN! THESE THINGS SOAK UP EVERYTHING WE THROW AT THEM!
WE WILL SLAUGHTER YOU-- GNNHHKK!
THEY ARE MAGICALLY IMBUED. THEORETICALLY, THEY ARE INVULNERABLE TO ANY LASTING DAMAGE.
OH JOY.
WE'RE FRIENDS, GARTH. LIKE WALLY SAID, SINCE ALWAYS.
I'M HAPPY FOR YOU AND LILITH. SERIOUSLY.
I JUST WISH YOUR DAMN MACHINE WOULD SPIT OUT ITS ANSWERS MORE QUICKLY...

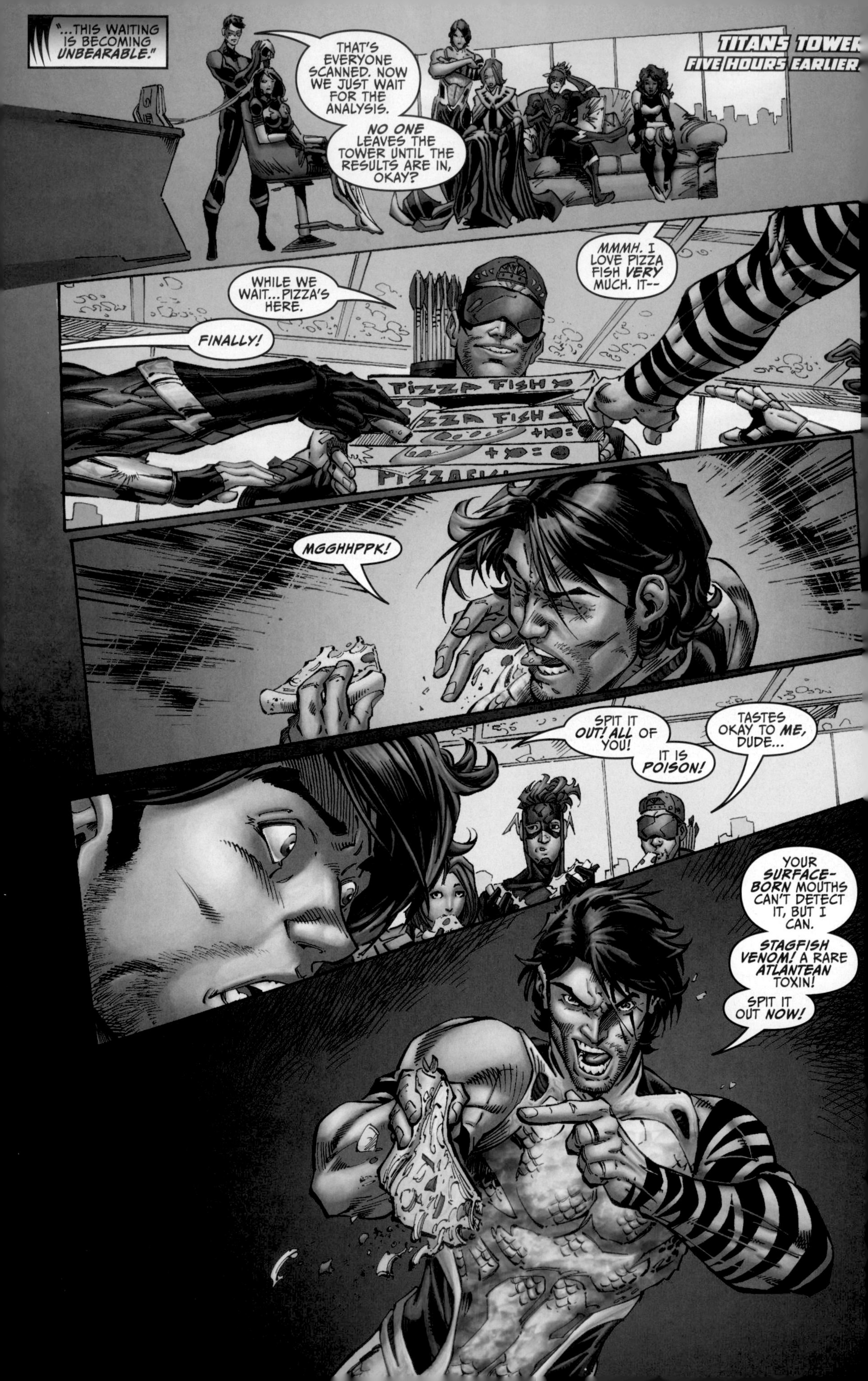
"...THIS WAITING IS BECOMING UNBEARABLE."
TITANS TOWER FIVE HOURS EARLIER.
THAT'S EVERYONE SCANNED. NOW WE JUST WAIT FOR THE ANALYSIS.
NO ONE LEAVES THE TOWER UNTIL THE RESULTS ARE IN, OKAY?
WHILE WE WAIT...PIZZA'S HERE.
MMMH. I LOVE PIZZA FISH VERY MUCH. IT--
FINALLY!
PIZZA FISH
MGGHHPPK!
SPIT IT OUT! ALL OF YOU!
IT IS POISON!
TASTES OKAY TO ME, DUDE...
YOUR SURFACE-BORN MOUTHS CAN'T DETECT IT, BUT I CAN.
STAGFISH VENOM! A RARE ATLANTEAN TOXIN!
SPIT IT OUT NOW!

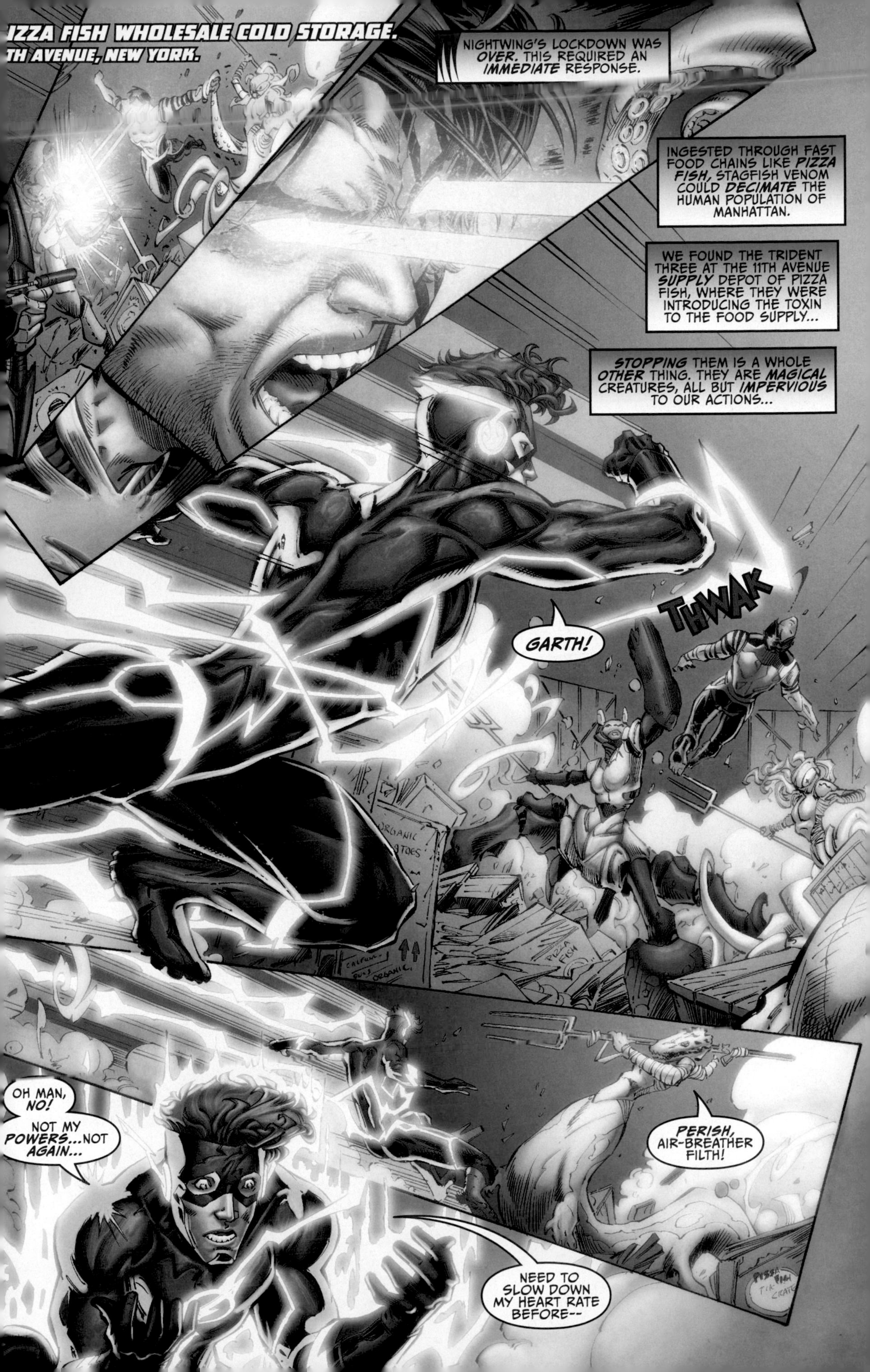
IZZA FISH WHOLESALE COLD STORAGE.
TH AVENUE, NEW YORK.
NIGHTWING'S LOCKDOWN WAS OVER. THIS REQUIRED AN IMMEDIATE RESPONSE.
INGESTED THROUGH FAST FOOD CHAINS LIKE PIZZA FISH, STAGFISH VENOM COULD DECIMATE THE HUMAN POPULATION OF MANHATTAN.
WE FOUND THE TRIDENT THREE AT THE 11TH AVENUE SUPPLY DEPOT OF PIZZA FISH, WHERE THEY WERE INTRODUCING THE TOXIN TO THE FOOD SUPPLY...
STOPPING THEM IS A WHOLE OTHER THING. THEY ARE MAGICAL CREATURES, ALL BUT IMPERVIOUS TO OUR ACTIONS...
THWAK
GARTH!
OH MAN, NO!
NOT MY POWERS...NOT AGAIN...
PERISH, AIR-BREATHER FILTH!
NEED TO SLOW DOWN MY HEART RATE BEFORE--

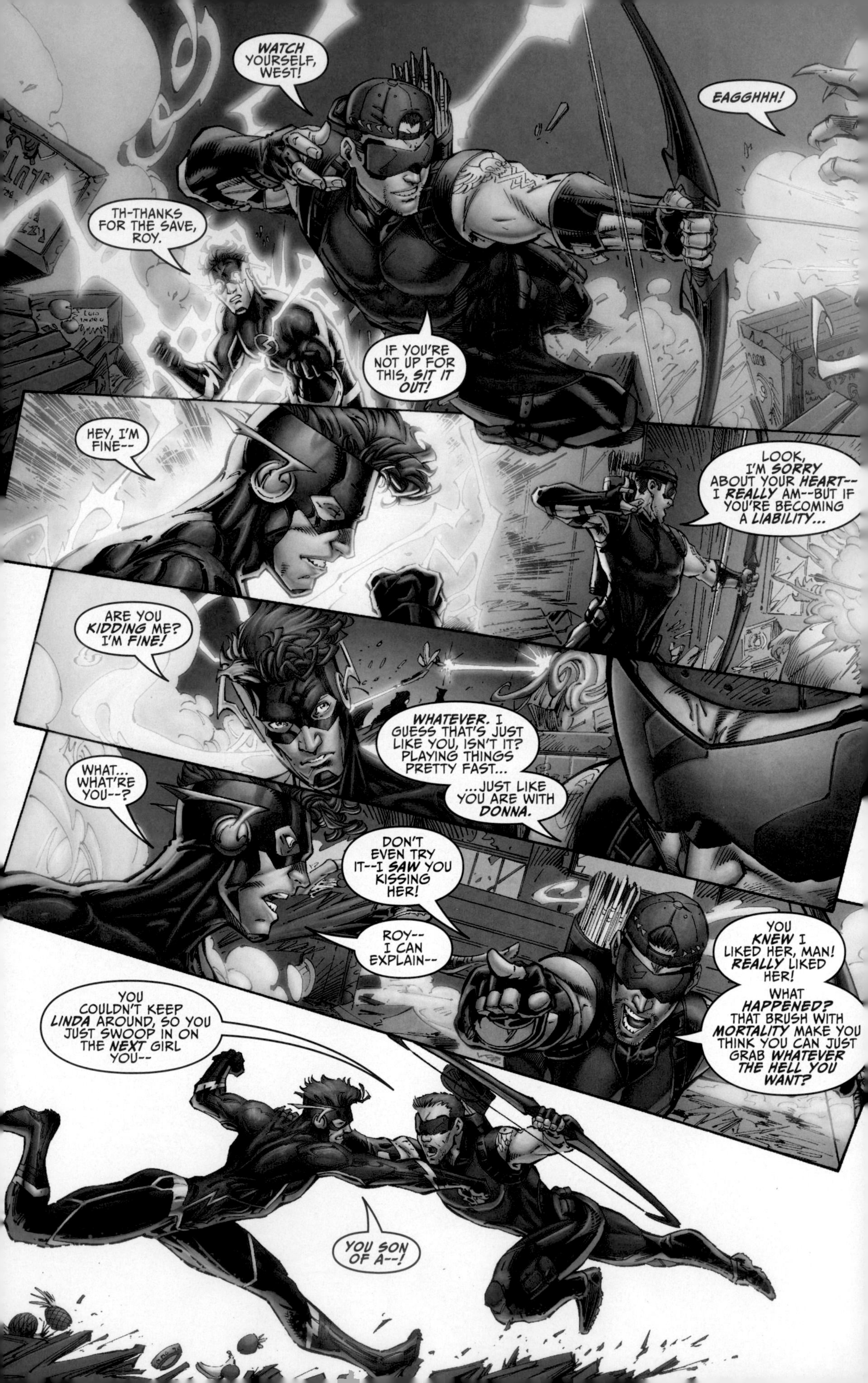
WATCH YOURSELF, WEST!
EAGGHHH!
TH-THANKS FOR THE SAVE, ROY.
IF YOU'RE NOT UP FOR THIS, SIT IT OUT!
HEY, I'M FINE--
LOOK, I'M SORRY ABOUT YOUR HEART-- I REALLY AM--BUT IF YOU'RE BECOMING A LIABILITY...
ARE YOU KIDDING ME? I'M FINE!
WHATEVER. I GUESS THAT'S JUST LIKE YOU, ISN'T IT? PLAYING THINGS PRETTY FAST...
...JUST LIKE YOU ARE WITH DONNA.
WHAT... WHAT'RE YOU--?
DON'T EVEN TRY IT--I SAW YOU KISSING HER!
ROY-- I CAN EXPLAIN--
YOU KNEW I LIKED HER, MAN! REALLY LIKED HER!
WHAT HAPPENED? THAT BRUSH WITH MORTALITY MAKE YOU THINK YOU CAN JUST GRAB WHATEVER THE HELL YOU WANT?
YOU COULDN'T KEEP LINDA AROUND, SO YOU JUST SWOOP IN ON THE NEXT GIRL YOU--
YOU SON OF A--!

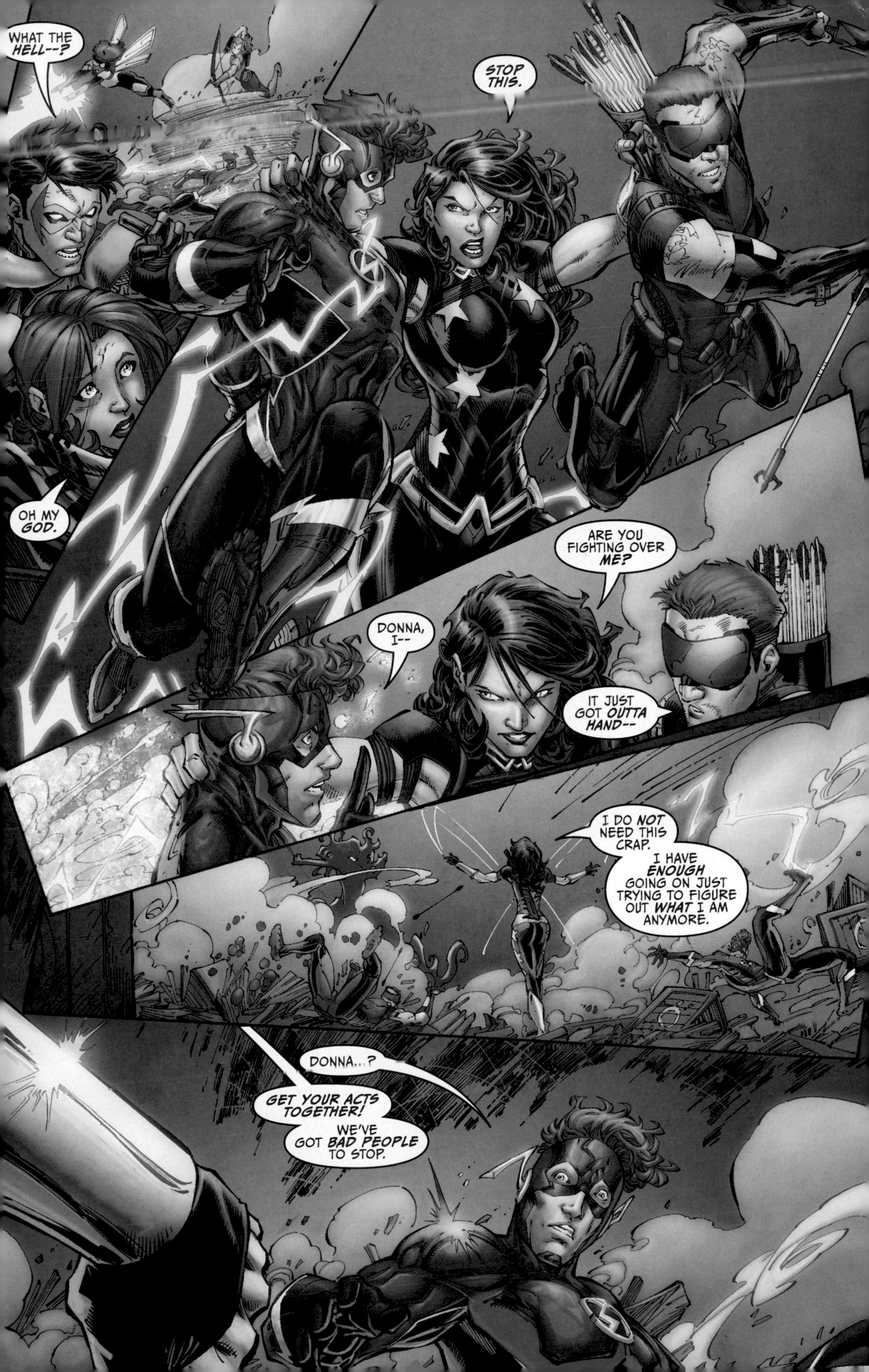

WHAT THE HELL--?
STOP THIS.
OH MY GOD.
ARE YOU FIGHTING OVER ME?
DONNA, I--
IT JUST GOT OUTTA HAND--
I DO NOT NEED THIS CRAP.
I HAVE ENOUGH GOING ON JUST TRYING TO FIGURE OUT WHAT I AM ANYMORE.
DONNA...?
GET YOUR ACTS TOGETHER!
WE'VE GOT BAD PEOPLE TO STOP.

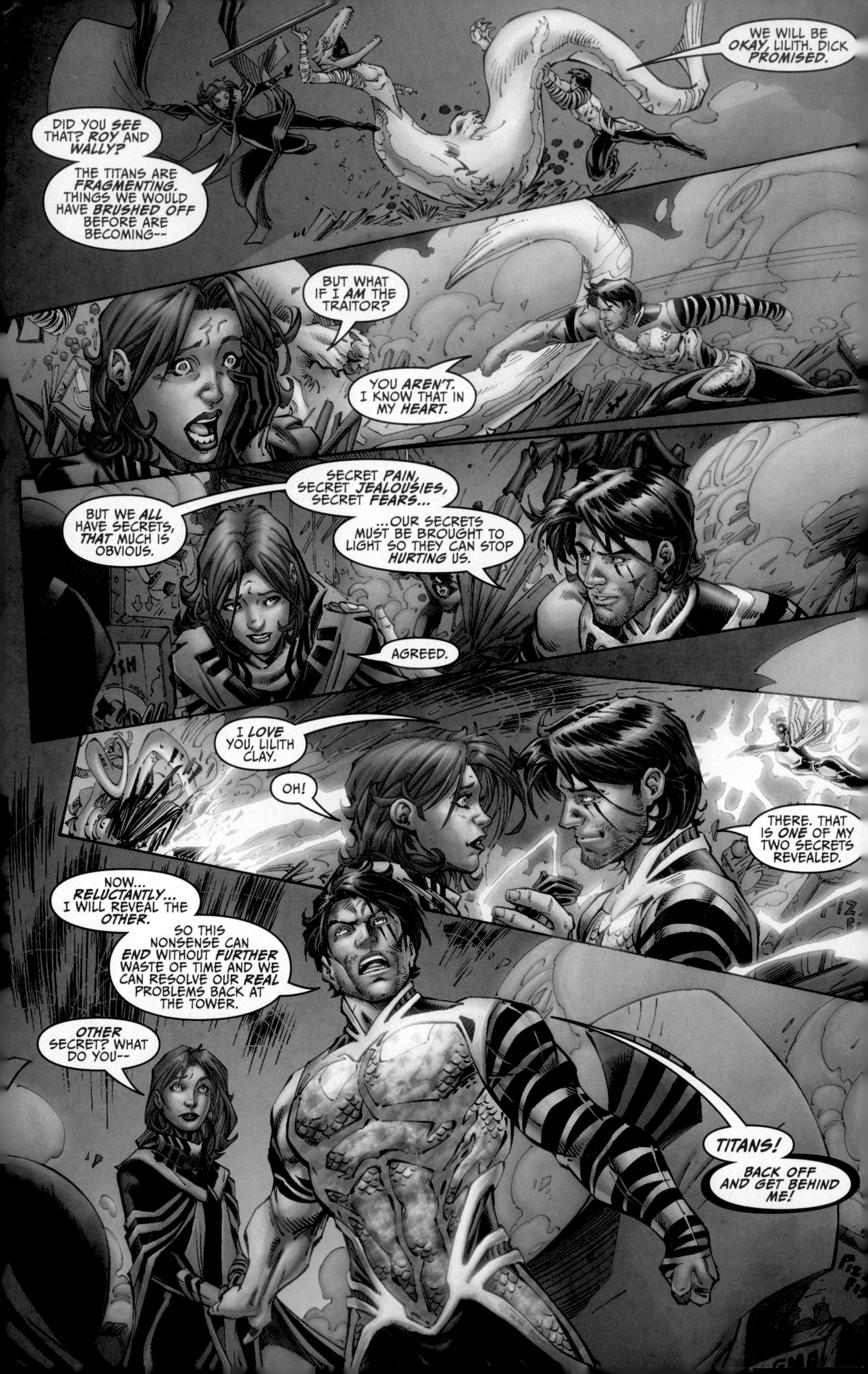

WE WILL BE OKAY, LILITH. DICK PROMISED.
DID YOU SEE THAT? ROY AND WALLY?
THE TITANS ARE FRAGMENTING. THINGS WE WOULD HAVE BRUSHED OFF BEFORE ARE BECOMING--
BUT WHAT IF I AM THE TRAITOR?
YOU AREN'T. I KNOW THAT IN MY HEART.
BUT WE ALL HAVE SECRETS, THAT MUCH IS OBVIOUS.
SECRET PAIN, SECRET JEALOUSIES, SECRET FEARS...
...OUR SECRETS MUST BE BROUGHT TO LIGHT SO THEY CAN STOP HURTING US.
AGREED.
I LOVE YOU, LILITH CLAY.
OH!
THERE. THAT IS ONE OF MY TWO SECRETS REVEALED.
NOW... RELUCTANTLY... I WILL REVEAL THE OTHER.
SO THIS NONSENSE CAN END WITHOUT FURTHER WASTE OF TIME AND WE CAN RESOLVE OUR REAL PROBLEMS BACK AT THE TOWER.
OTHER SECRET? WHAT DO YOU--
TITANS!
BACK OFF AND GET BEHIND ME!

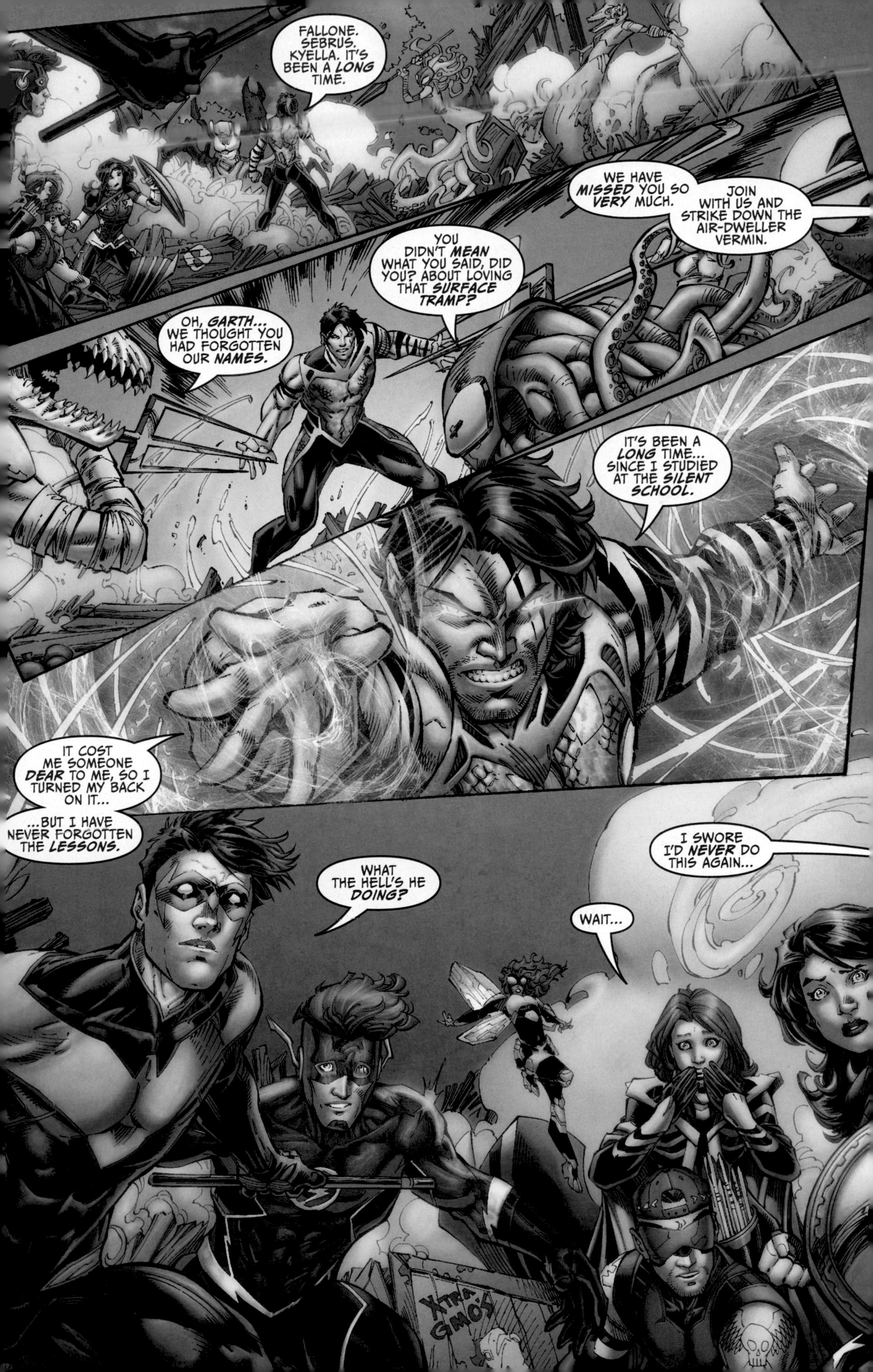
FALLONE. SEBRUS. KYELLA. IT'S BEEN A LONG TIME.
WE HAVE MISSED YOU SO VERY MUCH.
JOIN WITH US AND STRIKE DOWN THE AIR-DWELLER VERMIN.
YOU DIDN'T MEAN WHAT YOU SAID, DID YOU? ABOUT LOVING THAT SURFACE TRAMP?
OH, GARTH... WE THOUGHT YOU HAD FORGOTTEN OUR NAMES.
IT'S BEEN A LONG TIME... SINCE I STUDIED AT THE SILENT SCHOOL.
IT COST ME SOMEONE DEAR TO ME, SO I TURNED MY BACK ON IT...
...BUT I HAVE NEVER FORGOTTEN THE LESSONS.
I SWORE I'D NEVER DO THIS AGAIN...
WHAT THE HELL'S HE DOING?
WAIT...
XTRA GMO'S

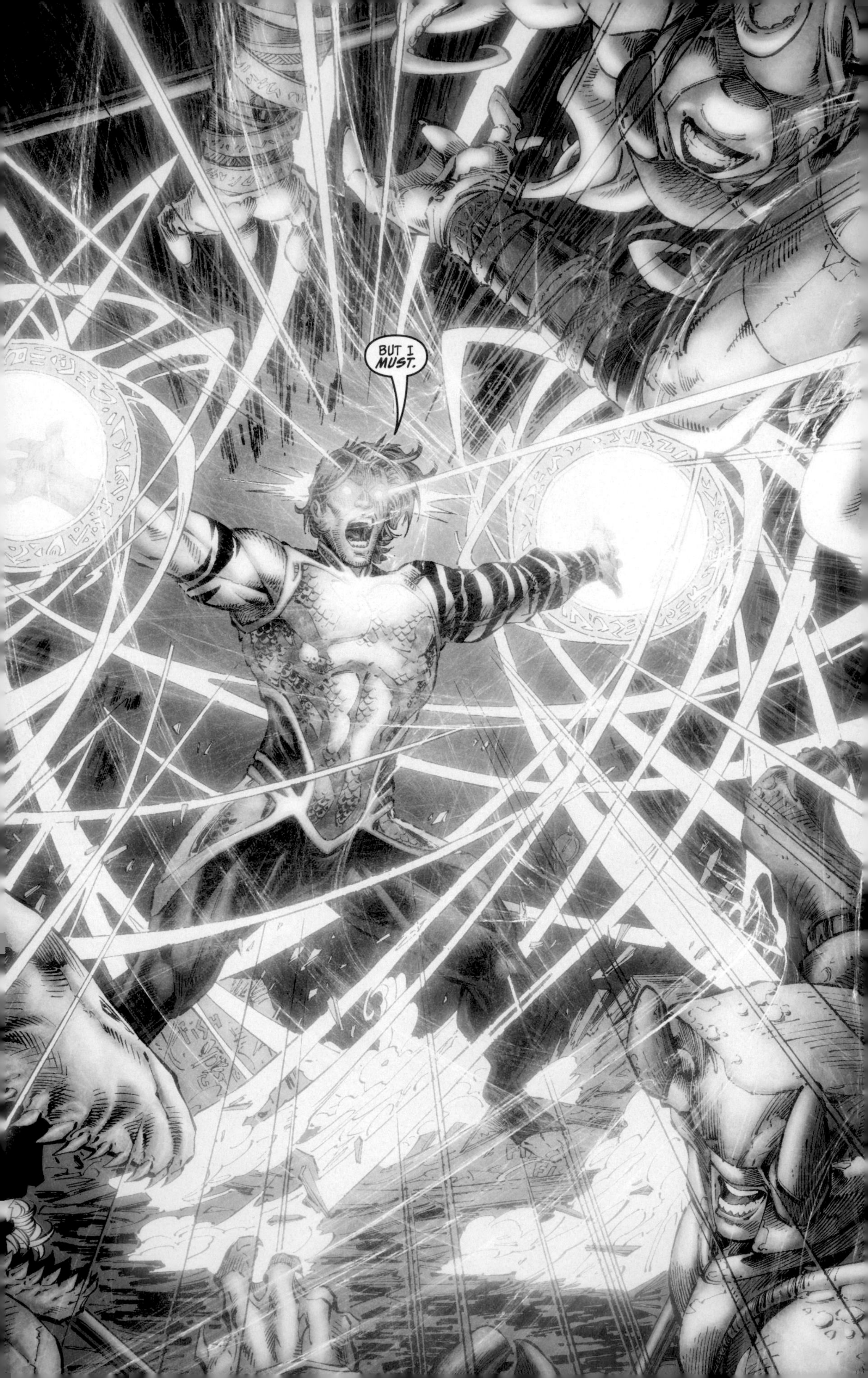
BUT I MUST.

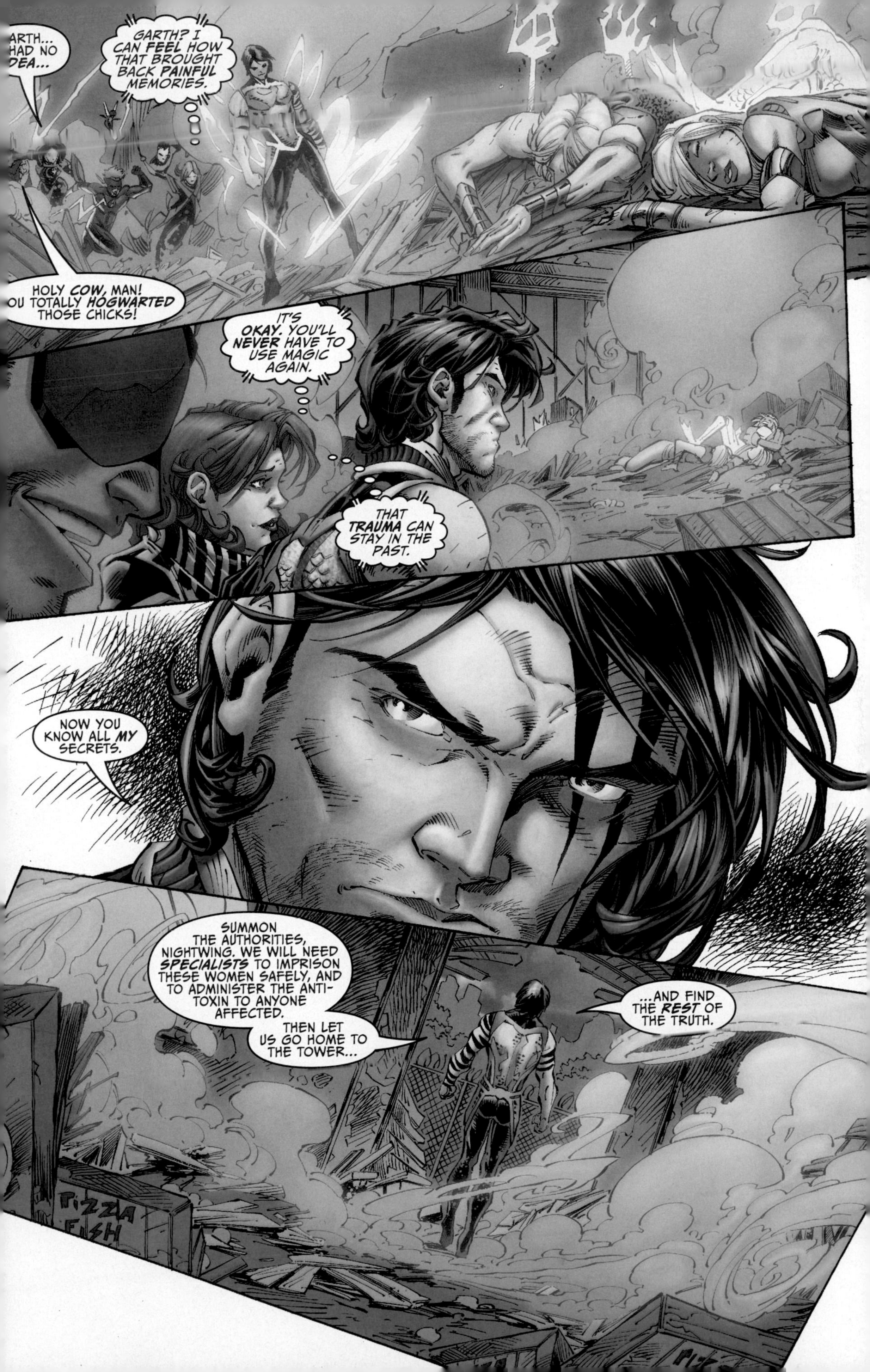
ARTH... HAD NO DEA...
GARTH? I CAN FEEL HOW THAT BROUGHT BACK PAINFUL MEMORIES.
HOLY COW, MAN! OU TOTALLY HOGWARTED THOSE CHICKS!
IT'S OKAY. YOU'LL NEVER HAVE TO USE MAGIC AGAIN.
THAT TRAUMA CAN STAY IN THE PAST.
NOW YOU KNOW ALL MY SECRETS.
SUMMON THE AUTHORITIES, NIGHTWING. WE WILL NEED SPECIALISTS TO IMPRISON THESE WOMEN SAFELY, AND TO ADMINISTER THE ANTI-TOXIN TO ANYONE AFFECTED.
THEN LET US GO HOME TO THE TOWER...
...AND FIND THE REST OF THE TRUTH.
PIZZA FISH

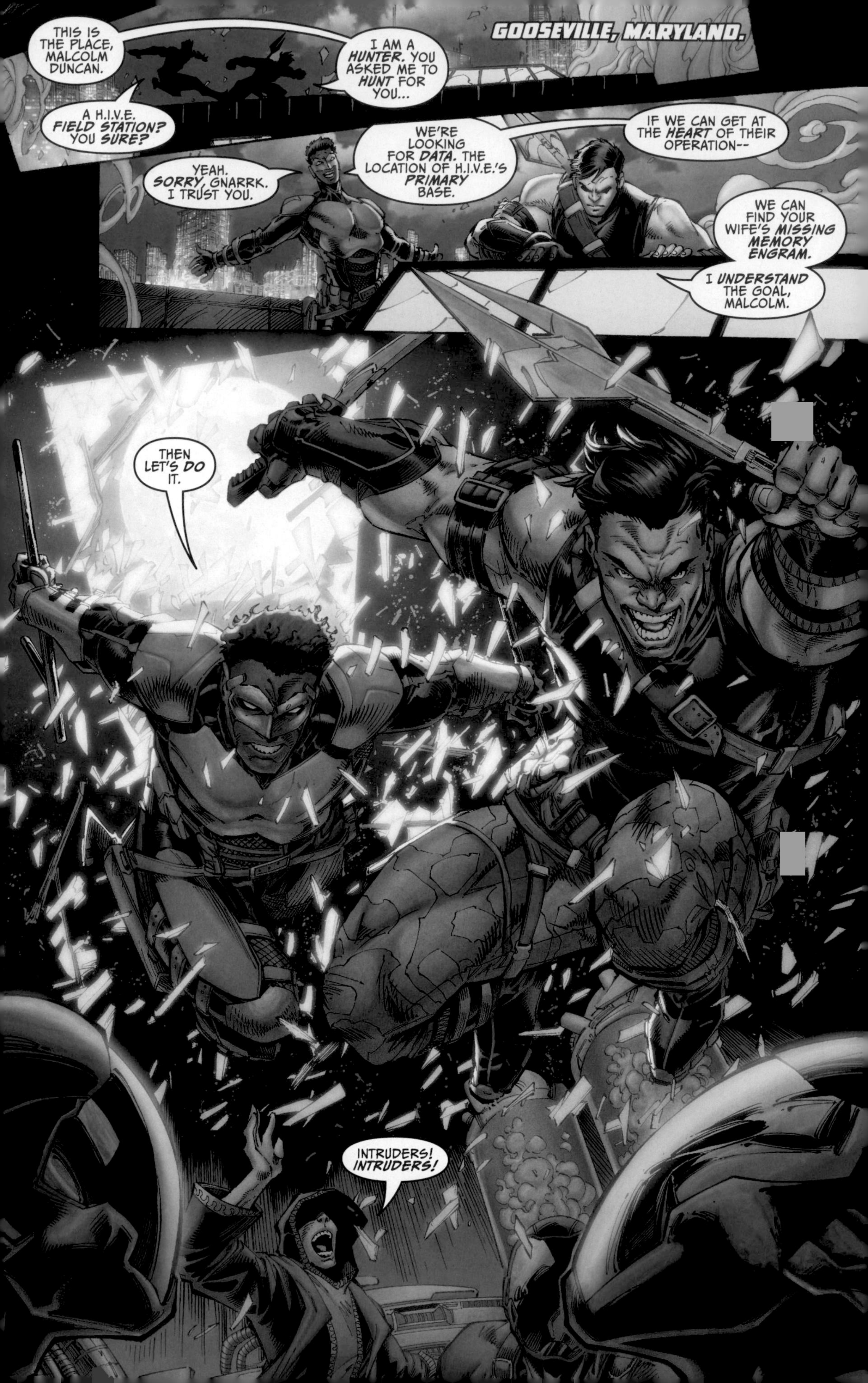
GOOSEVILLE, MARYLAND.
THIS IS THE PLACE, MALCOLM DUNCAN.
I AM A HUNTER. YOU ASKED ME TO HUNT FOR YOU...
A H.I.V.E. FIELD STATION? YOU SURE?
YEAH. SORRY, GNARRK. I TRUST YOU.
WE'RE LOOKING FOR DATA. THE LOCATION OF H.I.V.E.'S PRIMARY BASE.
IF WE CAN GET AT THE HEART OF THEIR OPERATION--
WE CAN FIND YOUR WIFE'S MISSING MEMORY ENGRAM.
I UNDERSTAND THE GOAL, MALCOLM.
THEN LET'S DO IT.
INTRUDERS! INTRUDERS!

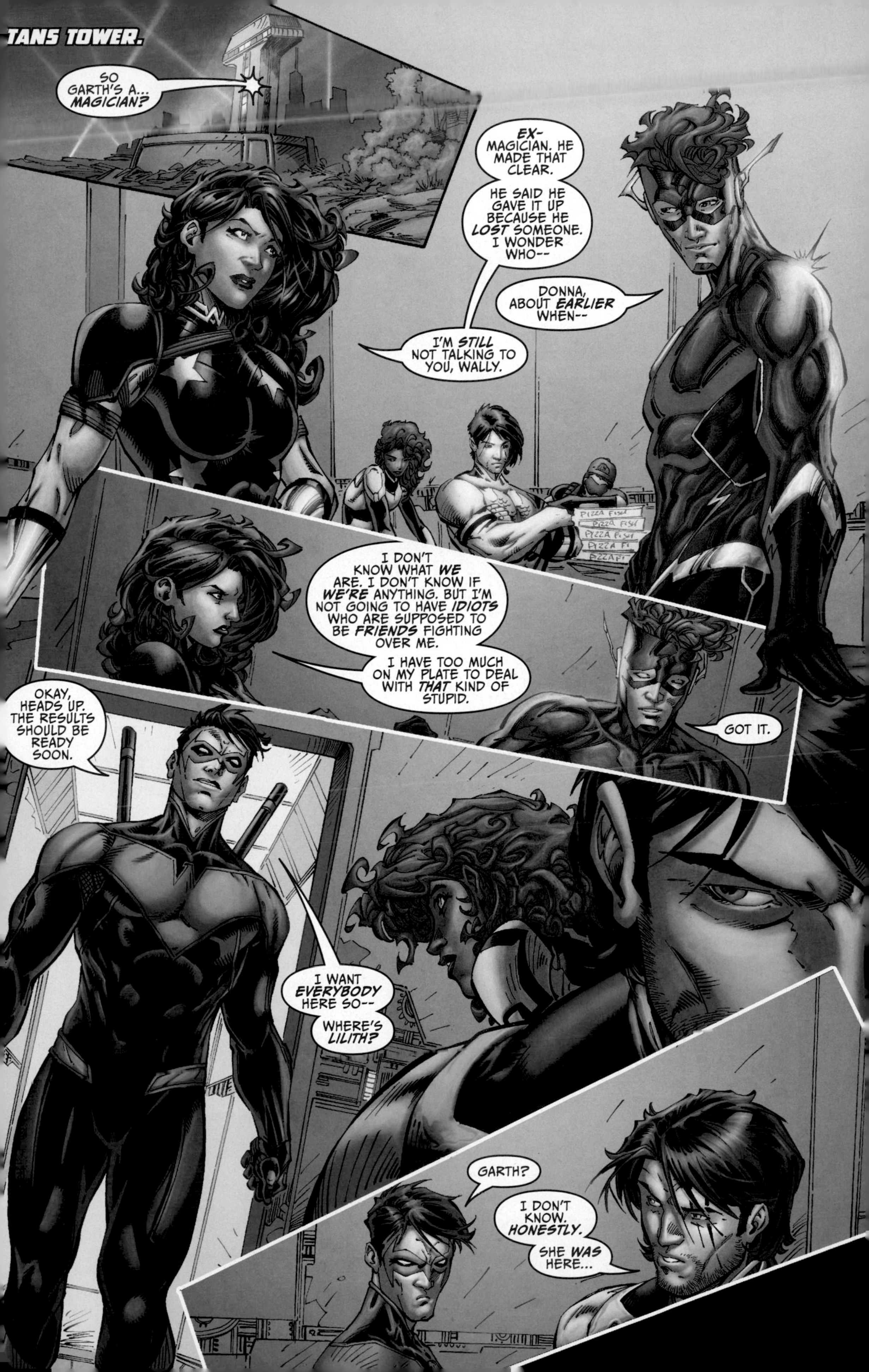
TANS TOWER.
SO GARTH'S A... MAGICIAN?
EX-MAGICIAN. HE MADE THAT CLEAR.
HE SAID HE GAVE IT UP BECAUSE HE LOST SOMEONE. I WONDER WHO--
DONNA, ABOUT EARLIER WHEN--
I'M STILL NOT TALKING TO YOU, WALLY.
PIZZA FISH
I DON'T KNOW WHAT WE ARE. I DON'T KNOW IF WE'RE ANYTHING. BUT I'M NOT GOING TO HAVE IDIOTS WHO ARE SUPPOSED TO BE FRIENDS FIGHTING OVER ME.
I HAVE TOO MUCH ON MY PLATE TO DEAL WITH THAT KIND OF STUPID.
GOT IT.
OKAY, HEADS UP. THE RESULTS SHOULD BE READY SOON.
I WANT EVERYBODY HERE SO--
WHERE'S LILITH?
GARTH?
I DON'T KNOW. HONESTLY.
SHE WAS HERE...

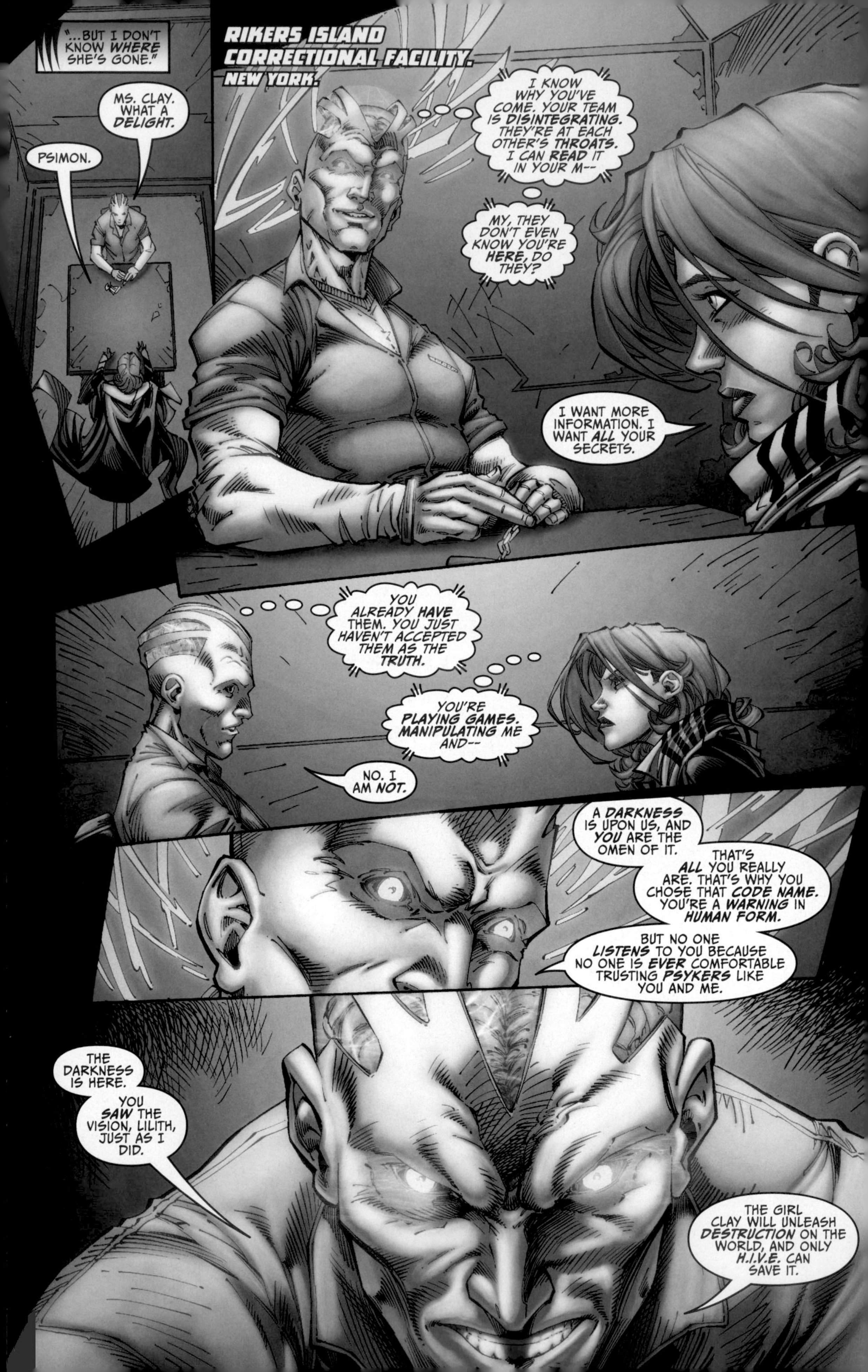

"...BUT I DON'T KNOW WHERE SHE'S GONE."
RIKERS ISLAND CORRECTIONAL FACILITY. NEW YORK.
PSIMON.
MS. CLAY. WHAT A DELIGHT.
I KNOW WHY YOU'VE COME. YOUR TEAM IS DISINTEGRATING. THEY'RE AT EACH OTHER'S THROATS. I CAN READ IT IN YOUR M--
MY, THEY DON'T EVEN KNOW YOU'RE HERE, DO THEY?
I WANT MORE INFORMATION. I WANT ALL YOUR SECRETS.
YOU ALREADY HAVE THEM. YOU JUST HAVEN'T ACCEPTED THEM AS THE TRUTH.
YOU'RE PLAYING GAMES. MANIPULATING ME AND--
NO. I AM NOT.
A DARKNESS IS UPON US, AND YOU ARE THE OMEN OF IT.
THAT'S ALL YOU REALLY ARE. THAT'S WHY YOU CHOSE THAT CODE NAME. YOU'RE A WARNING IN HUMAN FORM.
BUT NO ONE LISTENS TO YOU BECAUSE NO ONE IS EVER COMFORTABLE TRUSTING PSYKERS LIKE YOU AND ME.
THE DARKNESS IS HERE.
YOU SAW THE VISION, LILITH, JUST AS I DID.
THE GIRL CLAY WILL UNLEASH DESTRUCTION ON THE WORLD, AND ONLY H.I.V.E. CAN SAVE IT.

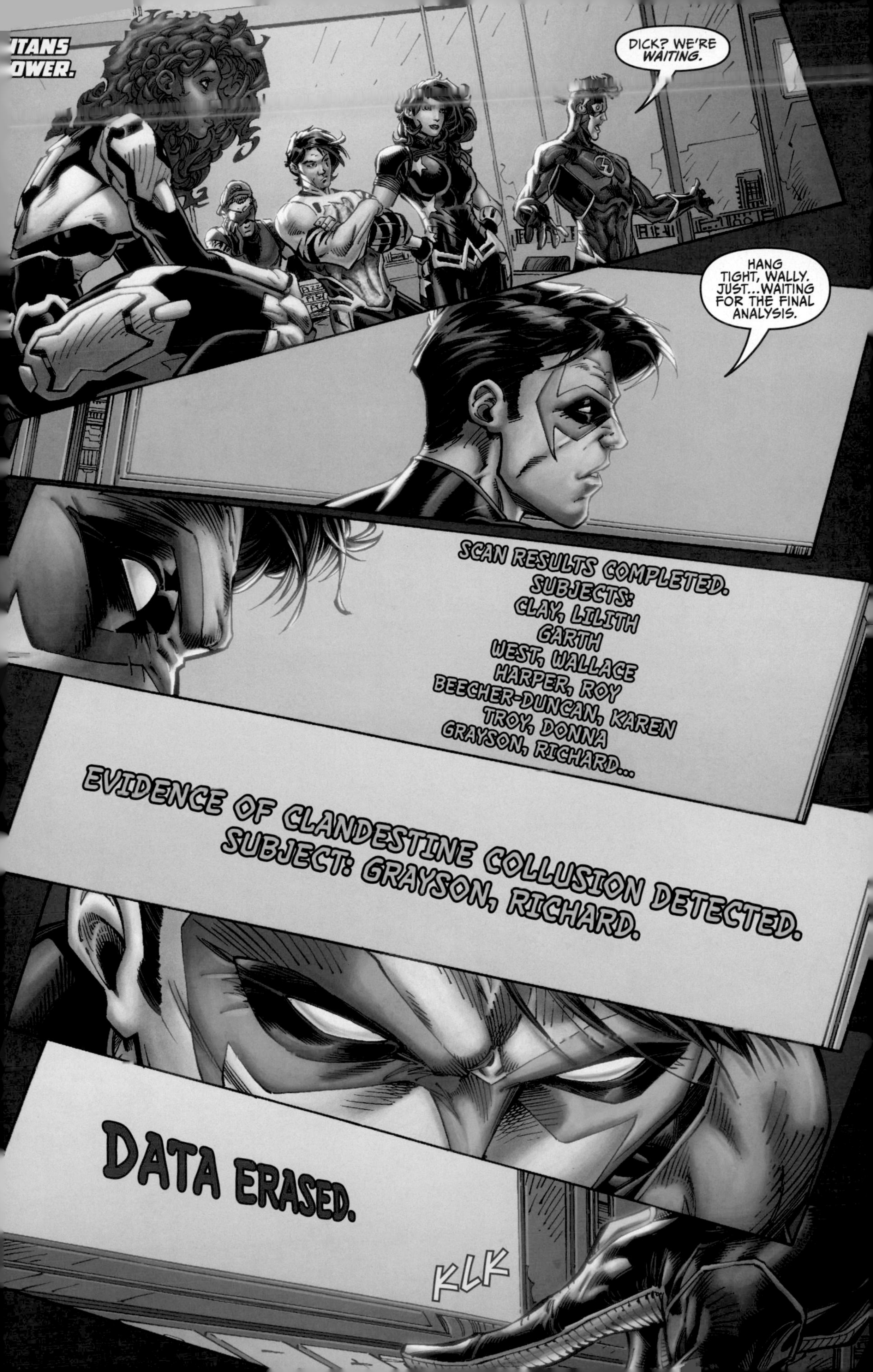

TITANS TOWER.
DICK? WE'RE WAITING.
HANG TIGHT, WALLY. JUST...WAITING FOR THE FINAL ANALYSIS.
SCAN RESULTS COMPLETED. SUBJECTS: CLAY, LILITH GARTH WEST, WALLACE HARPER, ROY BEECHER-DUNCAN, KAREN TROY, DONNA GRAYSON, RICHARD...
EVIDENCE OF CLANDESTINE COLLUSION DETECTED. SUBJECT: GRAYSON, RICHARD.
DATA ERASED.
KLK

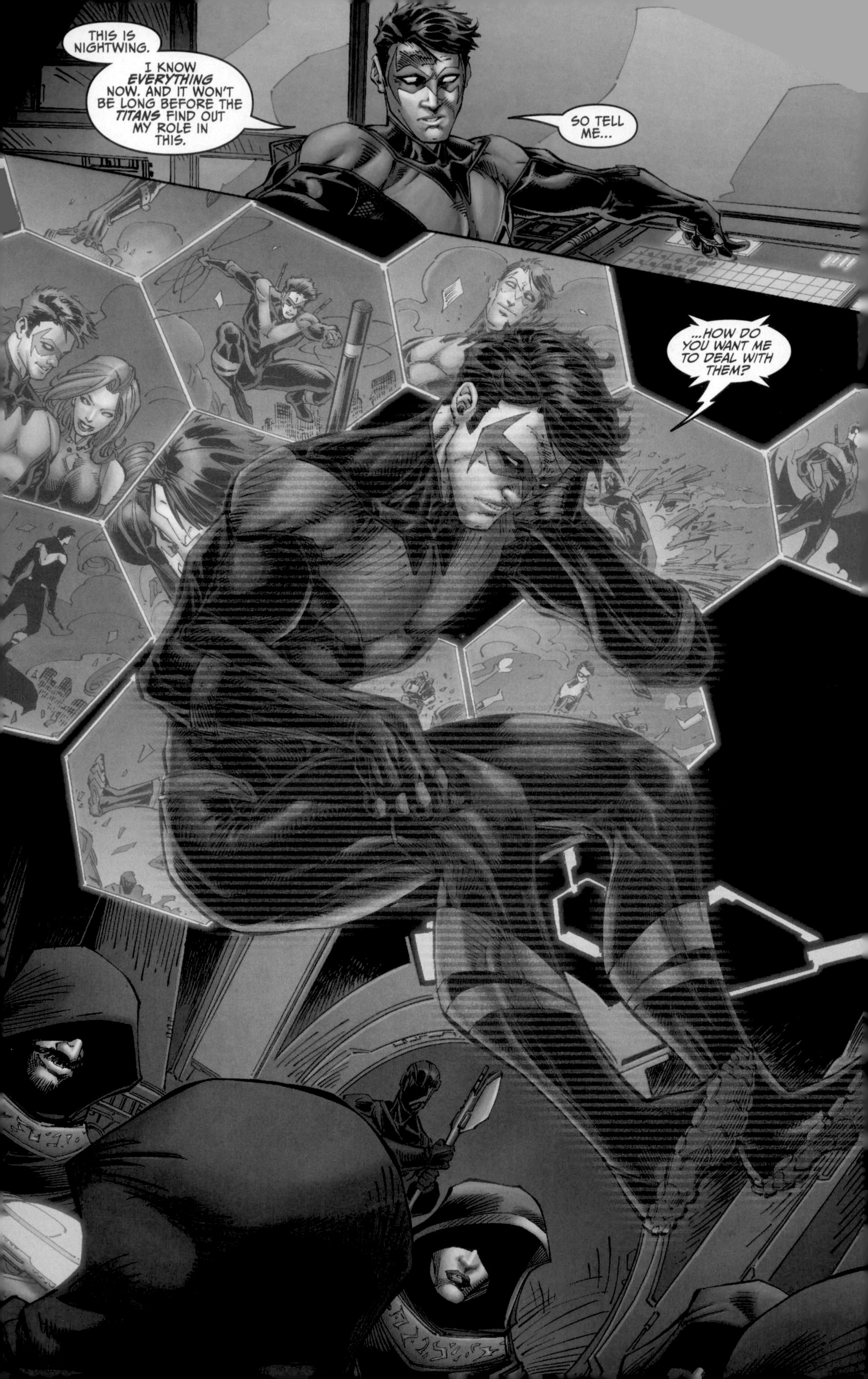
THIS IS NIGHTWING.
I KNOW EVERYTHING NOW. AND IT WON'T BE LONG BEFORE THE TITANS FIND OUT MY ROLE IN THIS.
SO TELL ME...
...HOW DO YOU WANT ME TO DEAL WITH THEM?

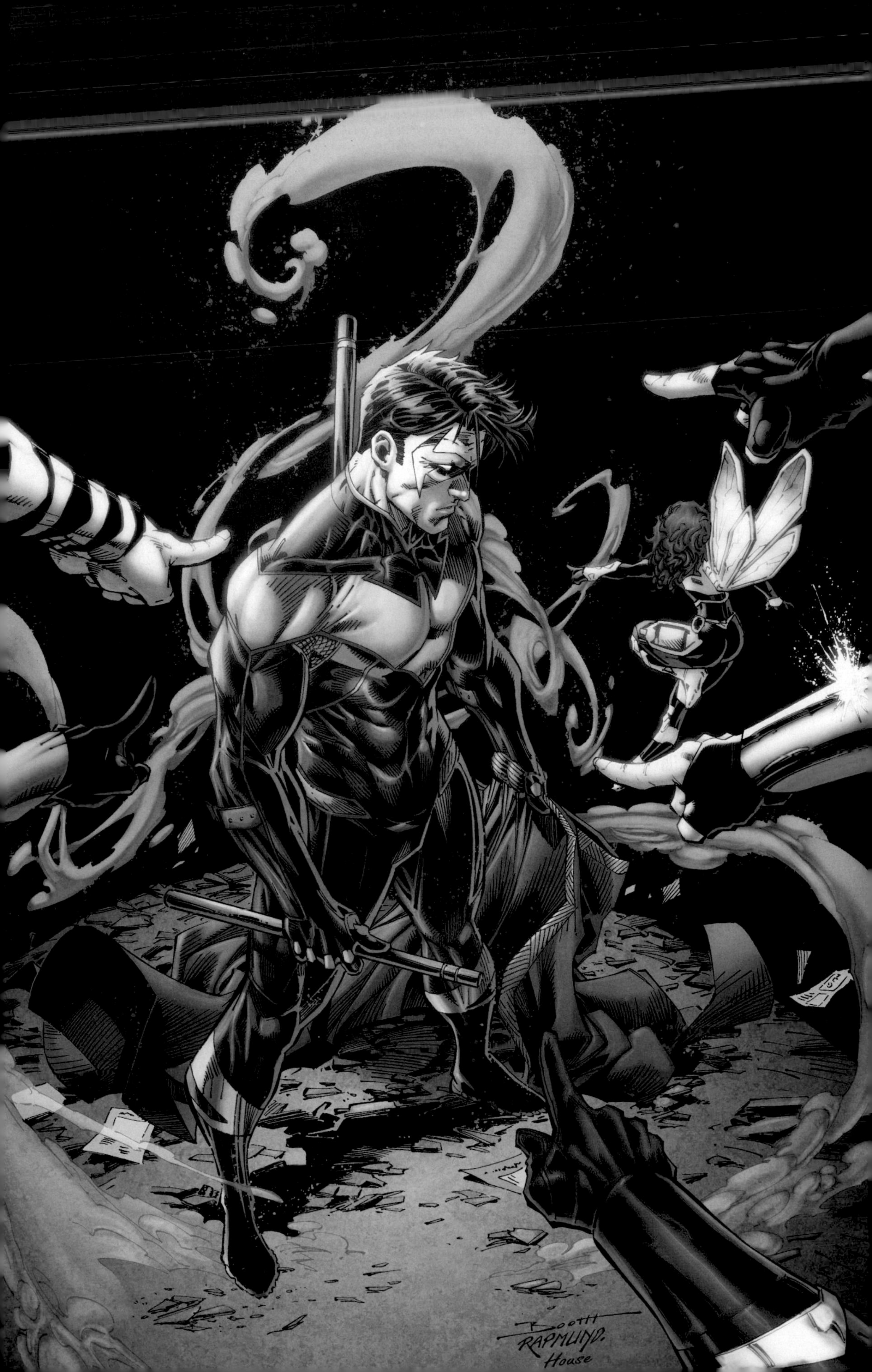
BOOTH
RAPMUND
House

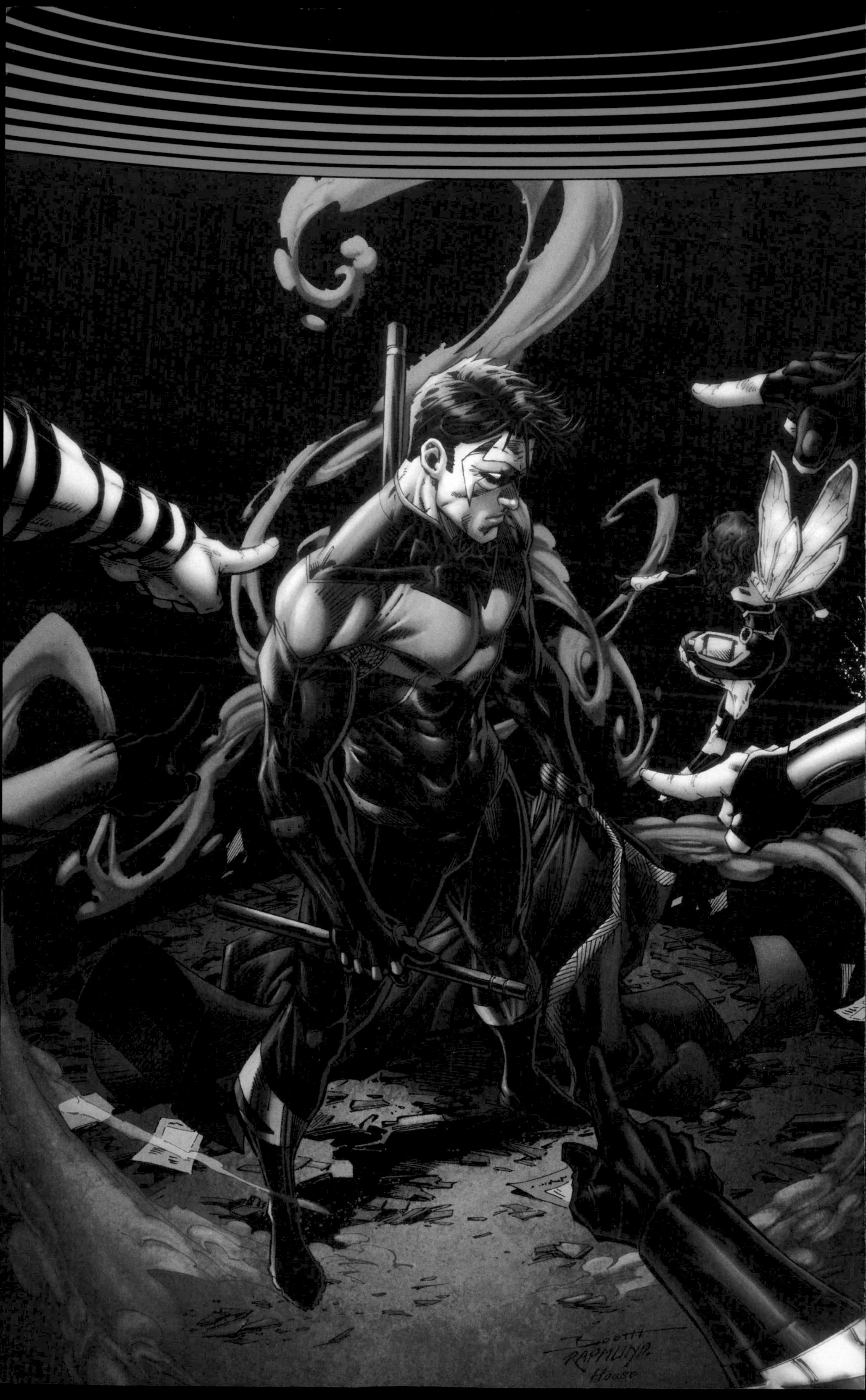
BOOTH
RAPMUND.
House

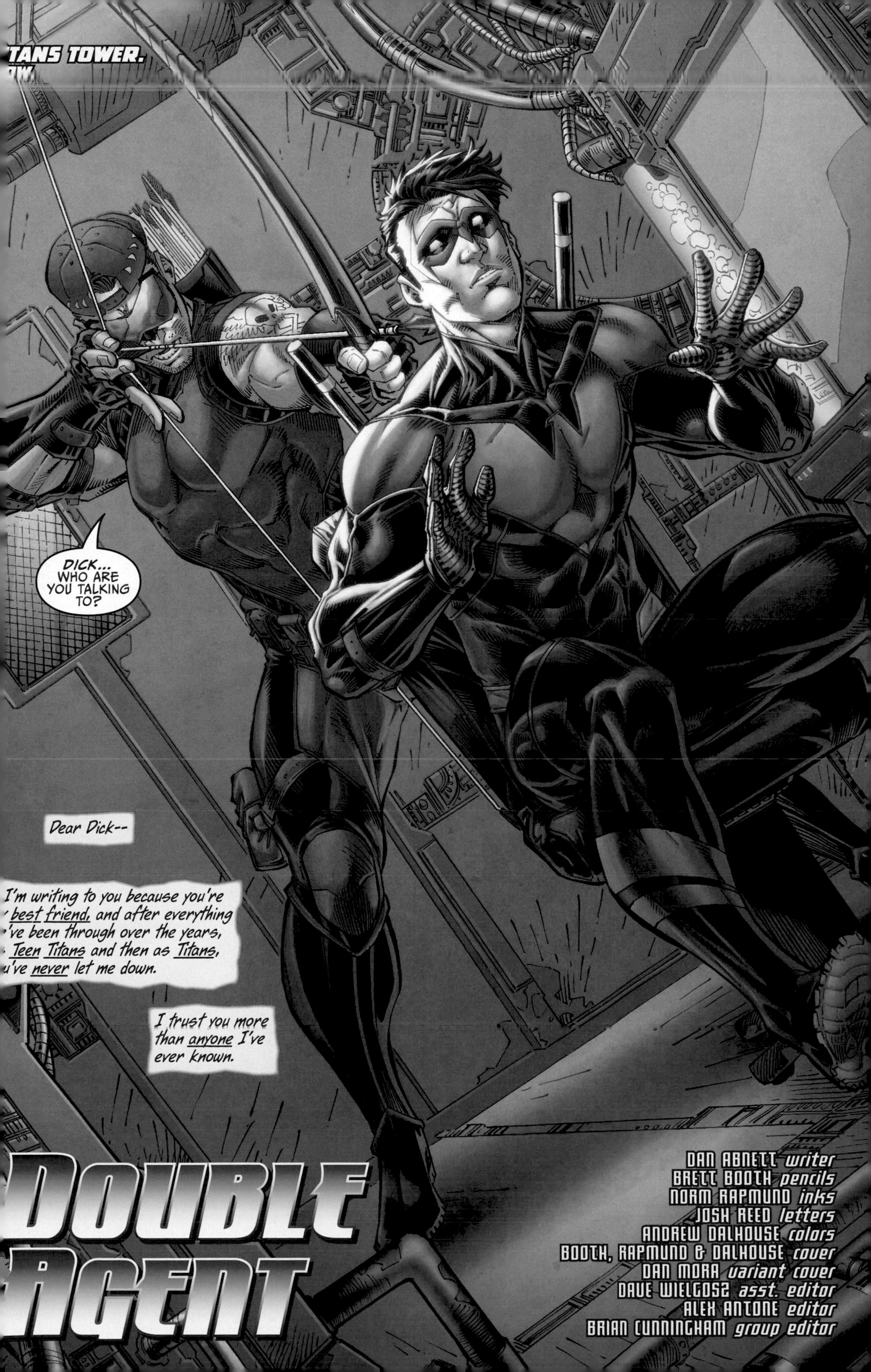
TANS TOWER.
DICK... WHO ARE YOU TALKING TO?
Dear Dick--
I'm writing to you because you're
best friend, and after everything
've been through over the years,
Teen Titans and then as Titans,
u've never let me down.
I trust you more than anyone I've ever known.
DOUBLE
AGENT
DAN ABNETT writer
BRETT BOOTH pencils
NORM RAPMUND inks
JOSH REED letters
ANDREW DALHOUSE colors
BOOTH, RAPMUND & DALHOUSE cover
DAN MORA variant cover
DAVE WIELGOSZ asst. editor
ALEX ANTONE editor
BRIAN CUNNINGHAM group editor

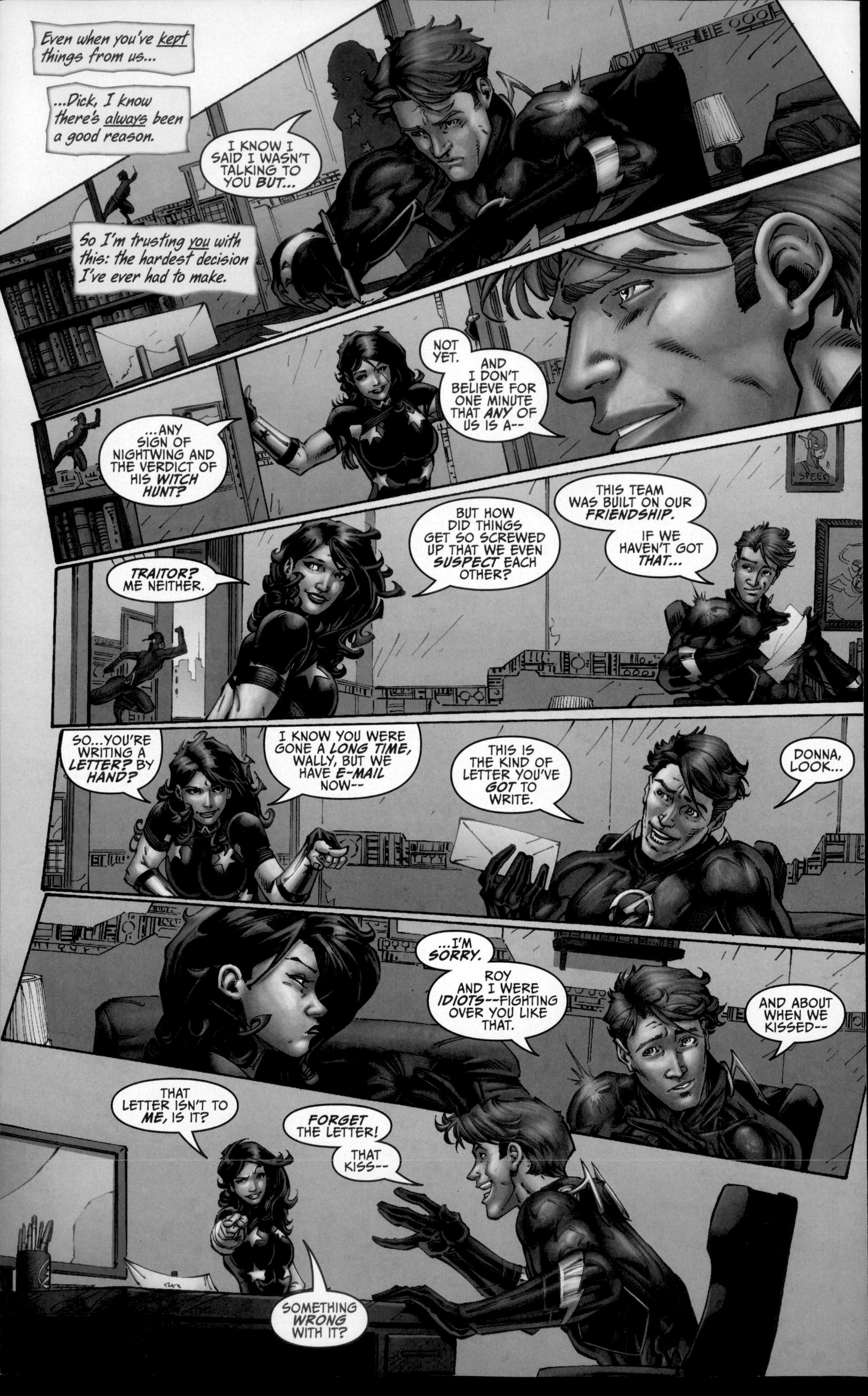
Even when you've kept things from us...
...Dick, I know there's always been a good reason.
I KNOW I SAID I WASN'T TALKING TO YOU BUT...
So I'm trusting you with this: the hardest decision I've ever had to make.
NOT YET.
AND I DON'T BELIEVE FOR ONE MINUTE THAT ANY OF US IS A--
...ANY SIGN OF NIGHTWING AND THE VERDICT OF HIS WITCH HUNT?
SPEED
TRAITOR? ME NEITHER.
BUT HOW DID THINGS GET SO SCREWED UP THAT WE EVEN SUSPECT EACH OTHER?
THIS TEAM WAS BUILT ON OUR FRIENDSHIP.
IF WE HAVEN'T GOT THAT...
SO...YOU'RE WRITING A LETTER? BY HAND?
I KNOW YOU WERE GONE A LONG TIME, WALLY, BUT WE HAVE E-MAIL NOW--
THIS IS THE KIND OF LETTER YOU'VE GOT TO WRITE.
DONNA, LOOK...
...I'M SORRY.
ROY AND I WERE IDIOTS--FIGHTING OVER YOU LIKE THAT.
AND ABOUT WHEN WE KISSED--
THAT LETTER ISN'T TO ME, IS IT?
FORGET THE LETTER!
THAT KISS--
SOMETHING WRONG WITH IT?

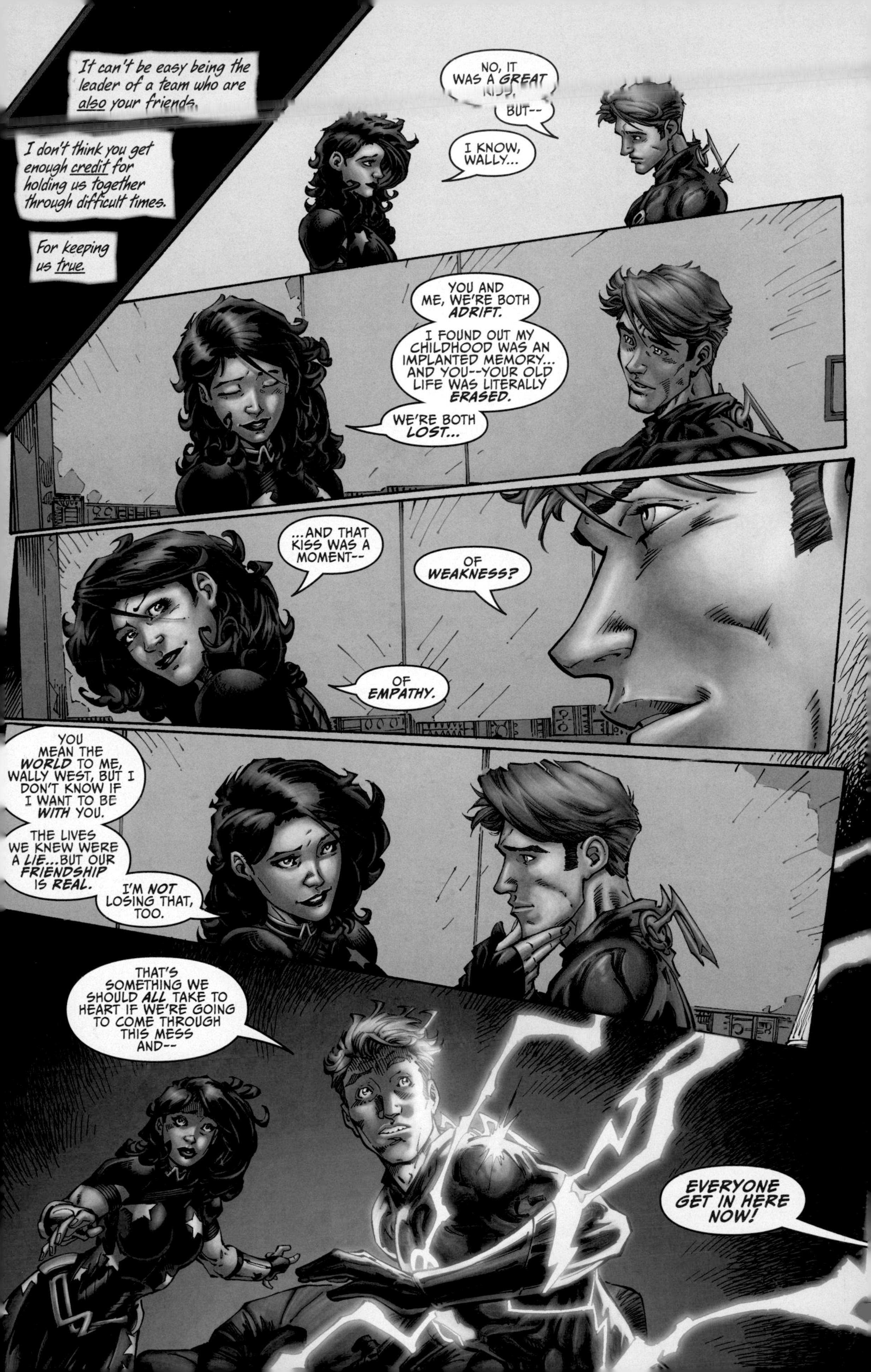

It can't be easy being the leader of a team who are also your friends.
NO, IT WAS A GREAT KISS, BUT--
I KNOW, WALLY...
I don't think you get enough credit for holding us together through difficult times.
For keeping us true.
YOU AND ME, WE'RE BOTH ADRIFT.
I FOUND OUT MY CHILDHOOD WAS AN IMPLANTED MEMORY... AND YOU--YOUR OLD LIFE WAS LITERALLY ERASED.
WE'RE BOTH LOST...
...AND THAT KISS WAS A MOMENT--
OF WEAKNESS?
OF EMPATHY.
YOU MEAN THE WORLD TO ME, WALLY WEST, BUT I DON'T KNOW IF I WANT TO BE WITH YOU.
THE LIVES WE KNEW WERE A LIE...BUT OUR FRIENDSHIP IS REAL.
I'M NOT LOSING THAT, TOO.
THAT'S SOMETHING WE SHOULD ALL TAKE TO HEART IF WE'RE GOING TO COME THROUGH THIS MESS AND--
EVERYONE GET IN HERE NOW!

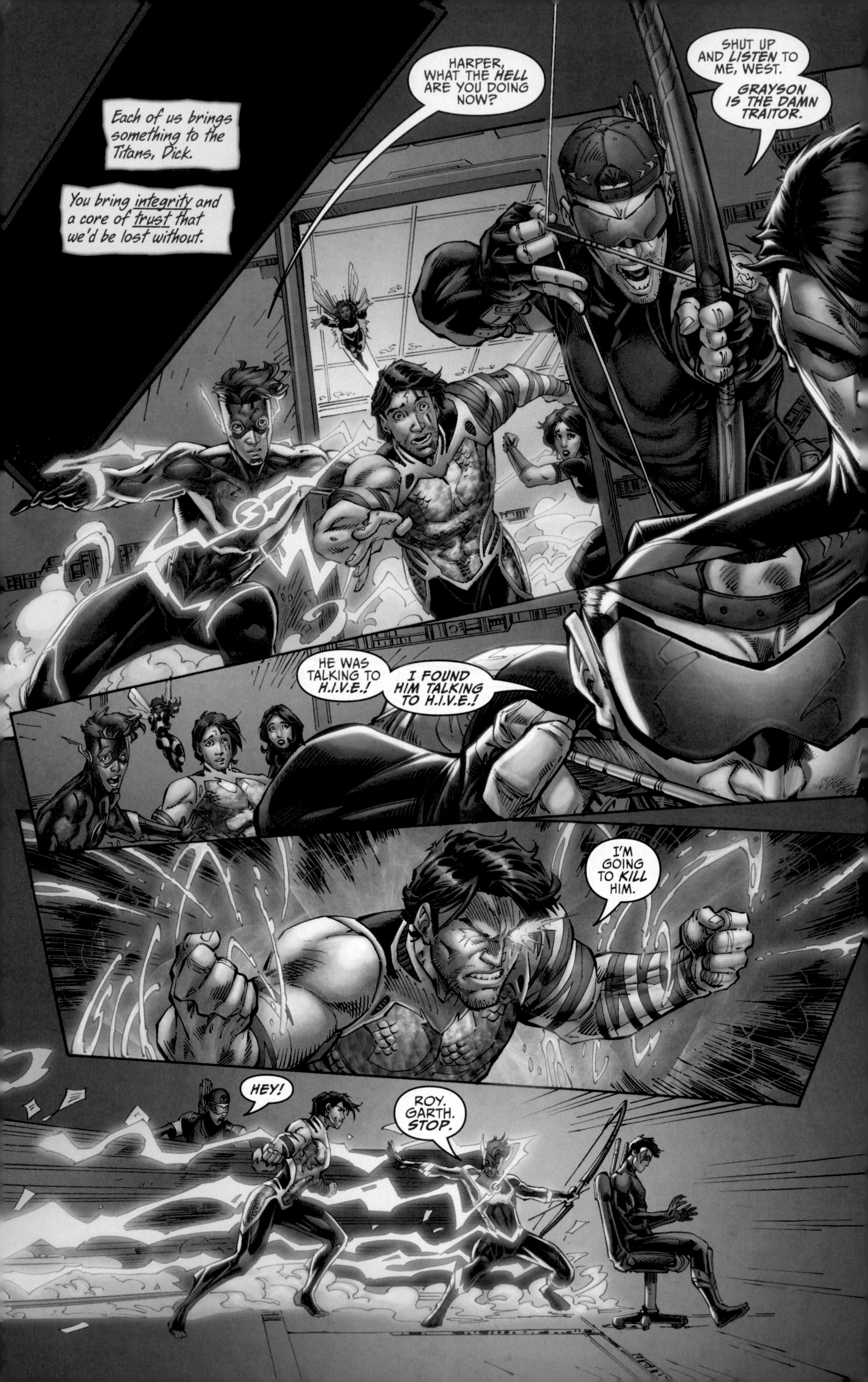
Each of us brings something to the Titans, Dick.
You bring integrity and a core of trust that we'd be lost without.
HARPER, WHAT THE HELL ARE YOU DOING NOW?
SHUT UP AND LISTEN TO ME, WEST.
GRAYSON IS THE DAMN TRAITOR.
HE WAS TALKING TO H.I.V.E.!
I FOUND HIM TALKING TO H.I.V.E.!
I'M GOING TO KILL HIM.
HEY!
ROY. GARTH. STOP.

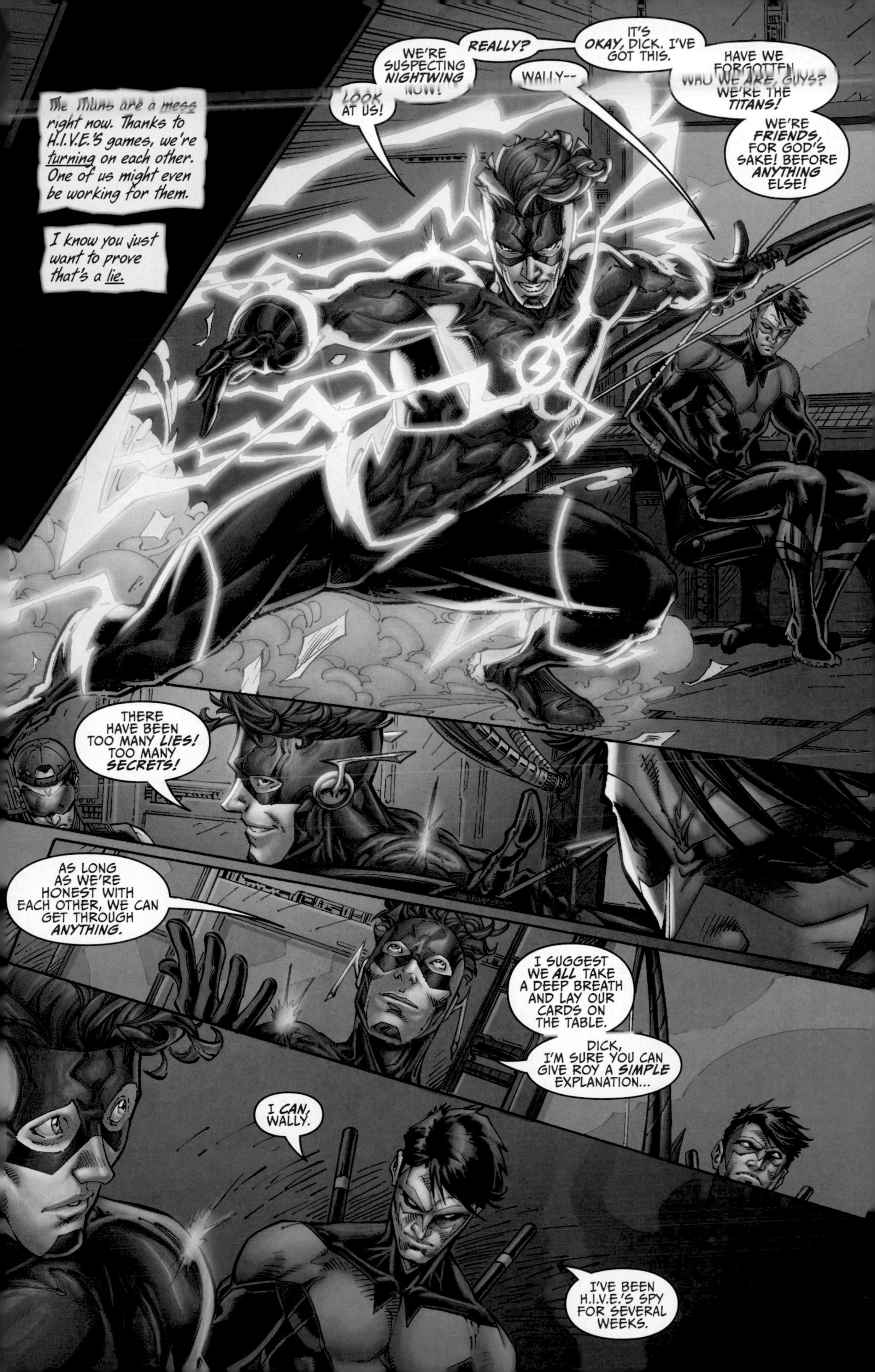

are a mess right now. Thanks to H.I.V.E.'S games, we're turning on each other. One of us might even be working for them.
I know you just want to prove that's a lie.
WE'RE SUSPECTING NIGHTWING NOW!
LOOK AT US!
REALLY?
WALLY--
IT'S OKAY, DICK. I'VE GOT THIS.
HAVE WE FORGOTTEN WHO WE ARE, GUYS? WE'RE THE TITANS!
WE'RE FRIENDS, FOR GOD'S SAKE! BEFORE ANYTHING ELSE!
THERE HAVE BEEN TOO MANY LIES! TOO MANY SECRETS!
AS LONG AS WE'RE HONEST WITH EACH OTHER, WE CAN GET THROUGH ANYTHING.
I SUGGEST WE ALL TAKE A DEEP BREATH AND LAY OUR CARDS ON THE TABLE.
DICK, I'M SURE YOU CAN GIVE ROY A SIMPLE EXPLANATION...
I CAN, WALLY.
I'VE BEEN H.I.V.E.'S SPY FOR SEVERAL WEEKS.

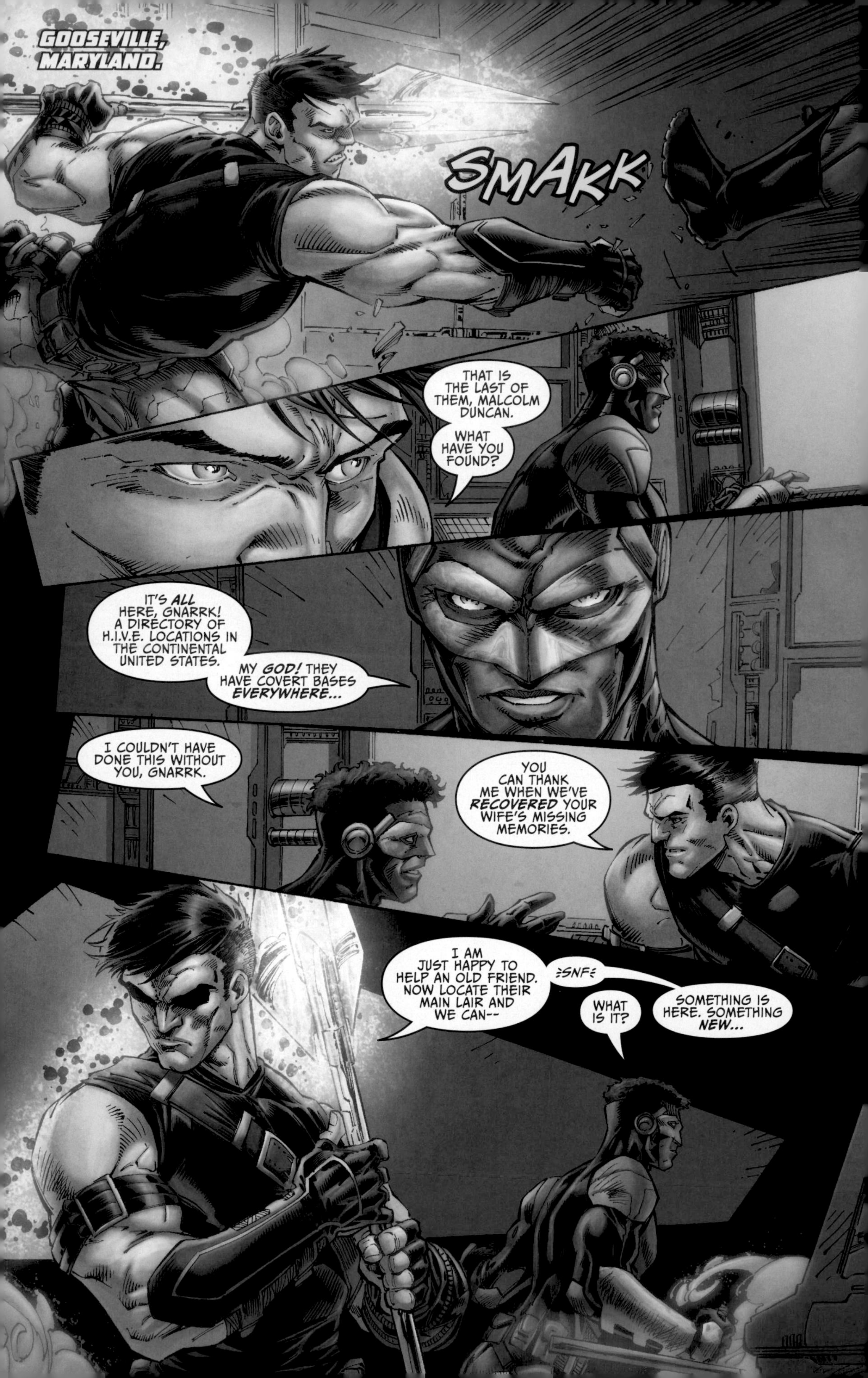
GOOSEVILLE, MARYLAND.
SMAKK
THAT IS THE LAST OF THEM, MALCOLM DUNCAN.
WHAT HAVE YOU FOUND?
IT'S ALL HERE, GNARRK! A DIRECTORY OF H.I.V.E. LOCATIONS IN THE CONTINENTAL UNITED STATES.
MY GOD! THEY HAVE COVERT BASES EVERYWHERE...
I COULDN'T HAVE DONE THIS WITHOUT YOU, GNARRK.
YOU CAN THANK ME WHEN WE'VE RECOVERED YOUR WIFE'S MISSING MEMORIES.
I AM JUST HAPPY TO HELP AN OLD FRIEND. NOW LOCATE THEIR MAIN LAIR AND WE CAN--
SNF
SOMETHING IS HERE. SOMETHING NEW...
WHAT IS IT?

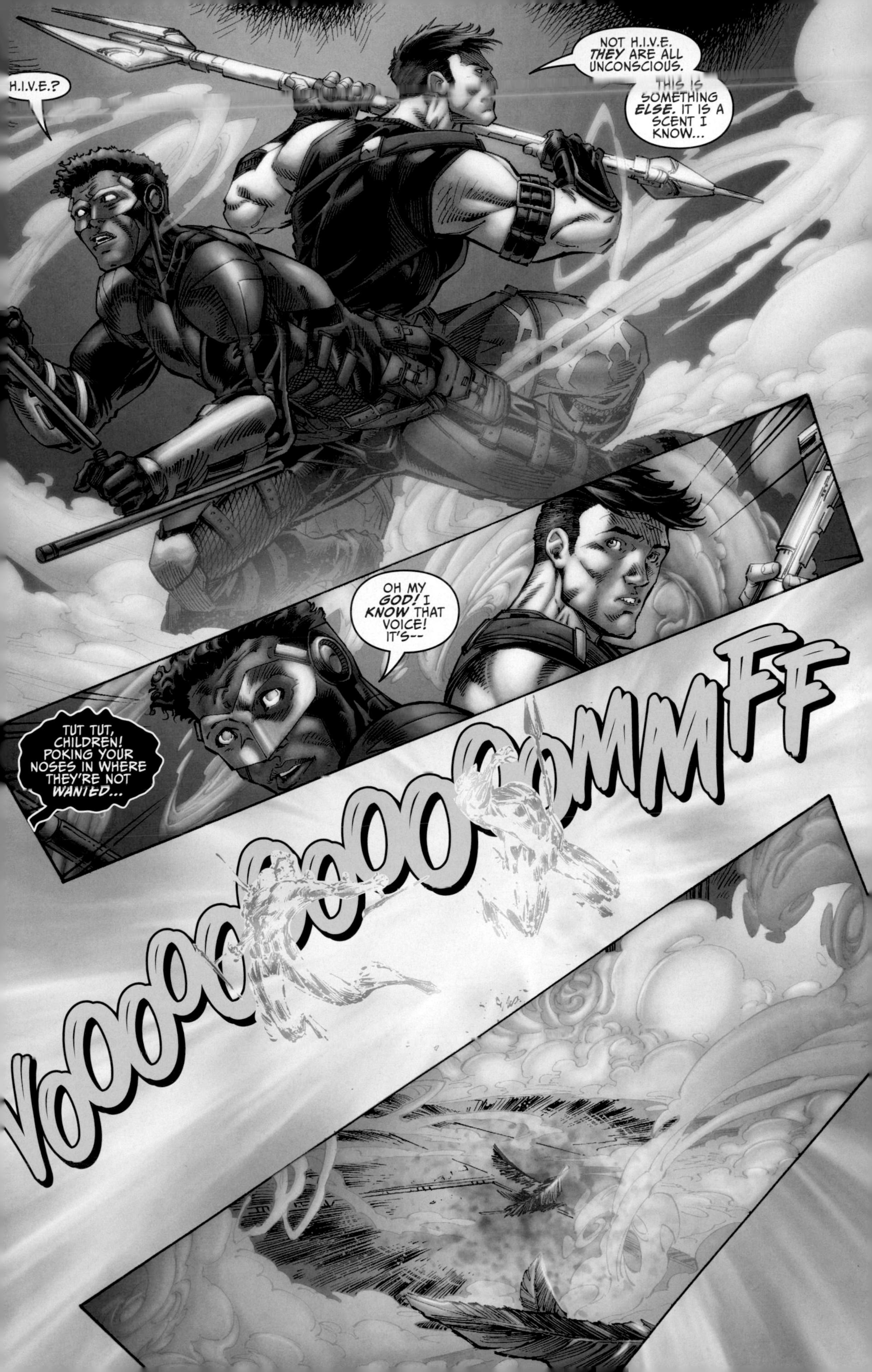
H.I.V.E.?
NOT H.I.V.E. THEY ARE ALL UNCONSCIOUS.
THIS IS SOMETHING ELSE. IT IS A SCENT I KNOW...
OH MY GOD! I KNOW THAT VOICE! IT'S--
TUT TUT, CHILDREN! POKING YOUR NOSES IN WHERE THEY'RE NOT WANTED...
VOOOOOOOOOMMFF

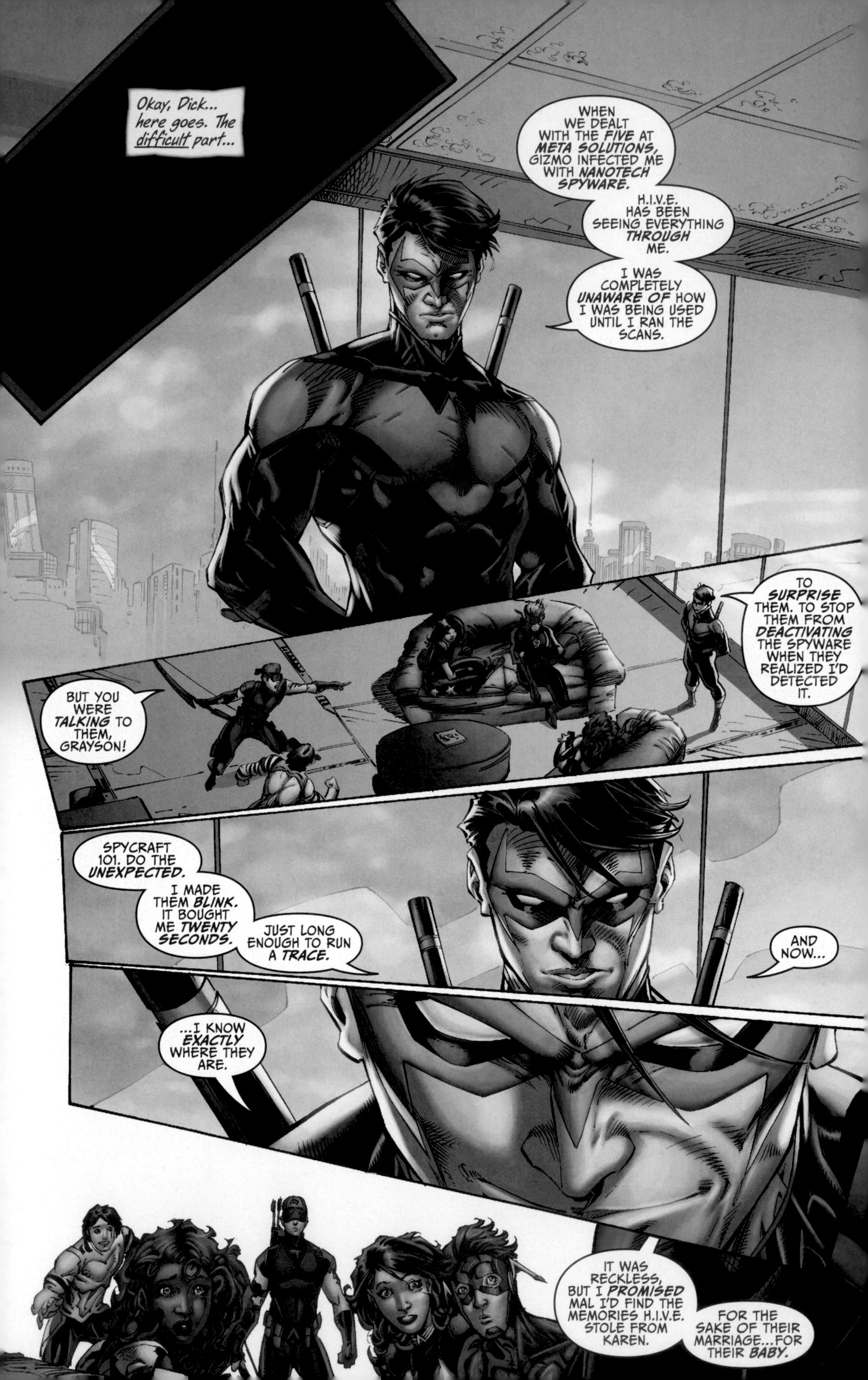
Okay, Dick... here goes. The difficult part...
WHEN WE DEALT WITH THE FIVE AT META SOLUTIONS, GIZMO INFECTED ME WITH NANOTECH SPYWARE.
H.I.V.E. HAS BEEN SEEING EVERYTHING THROUGH ME.
I WAS COMPLETELY UNAWARE OF HOW I WAS BEING USED UNTIL I RAN THE SCANS.
BUT YOU WERE TALKING TO THEM, GRAYSON!
TO SURPRISE THEM. TO STOP THEM FROM DEACTIVATING THE SPYWARE WHEN THEY REALIZED I'D DETECTED IT.
SPYCRAFT 101. DO THE UNEXPECTED.
I MADE THEM BLINK. IT BOUGHT ME TWENTY SECONDS.
JUST LONG ENOUGH TO RUN A TRACE.
AND NOW...
...I KNOW EXACTLY WHERE THEY ARE.
IT WAS RECKLESS, BUT I PROMISED MAL I'D FIND THE MEMORIES H.I.V.E. STOLE FROM KAREN.
FOR THE SAKE OF THEIR MARRIAGE...FOR THEIR BABY.

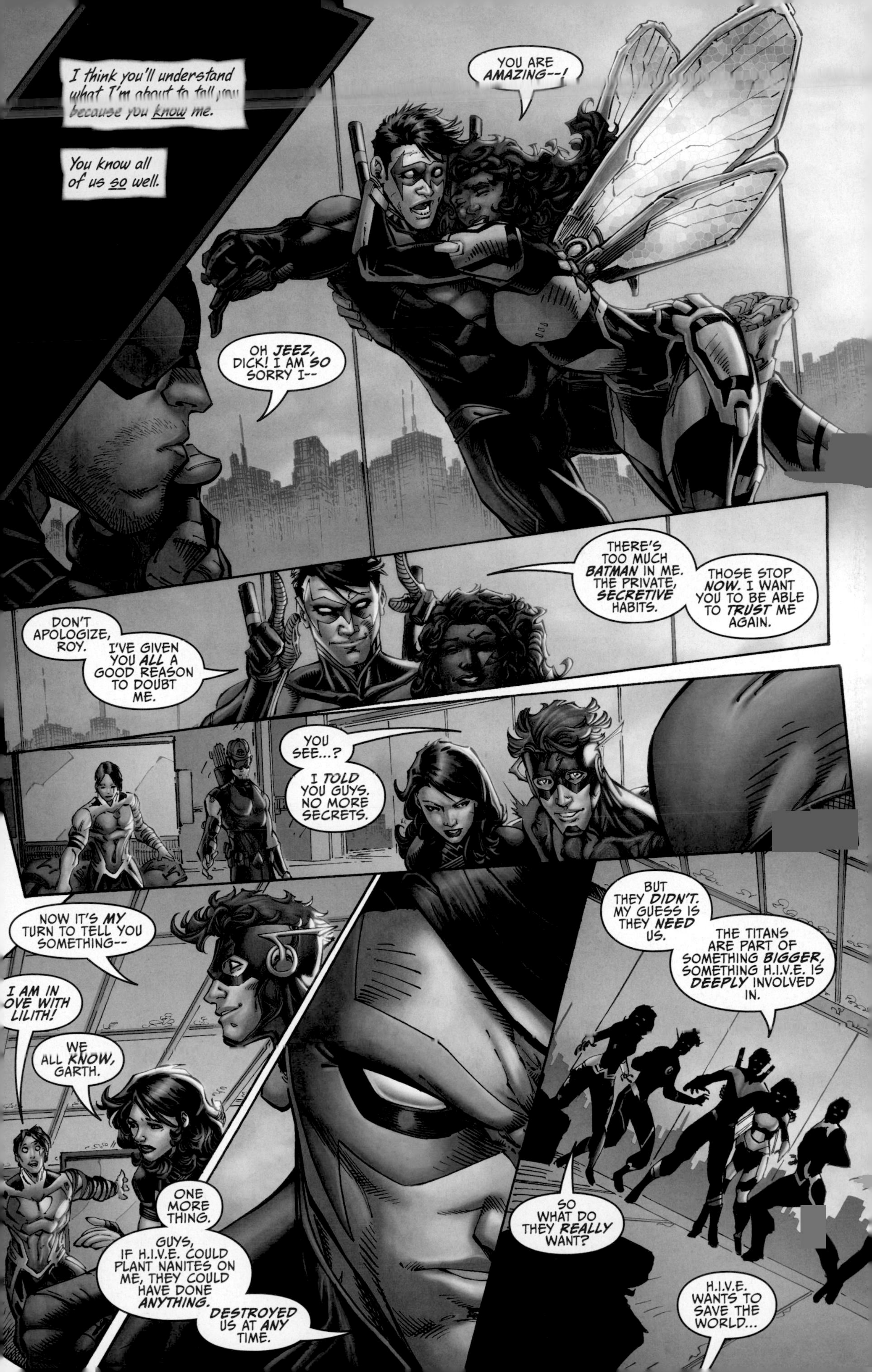
I think you'll understand what I'm about to tell you because you know me.
You know all of us so well.
YOU ARE AMAZING--!
OH JEEZ, DICK! I AM SO SORRY I--
DON'T APOLOGIZE, ROY.
I'VE GIVEN YOU ALL A GOOD REASON TO DOUBT ME.
THERE'S TOO MUCH BATMAN IN ME. THE PRIVATE, SECRETIVE HABITS.
THOSE STOP NOW. I WANT YOU TO BE ABLE TO TRUST ME AGAIN.
YOU SEE...?
I TOLD YOU GUYS. NO MORE SECRETS.
NOW IT'S MY TURN TO TELL YOU SOMETHING--
I AM IN OVE WITH LILITH!
WE ALL KNOW, GARTH.
ONE MORE THING.
GUYS, IF H.I.V.E. COULD PLANT NANITES ON ME, THEY COULD HAVE DONE ANYTHING.
DESTROYED US AT ANY TIME.
BUT THEY DIDN'T. MY GUESS IS THEY NEED US.
THE TITANS ARE PART OF SOMETHING BIGGER, SOMETHING H.I.V.E. IS DEEPLY INVOLVED IN.
SO WHAT DO THEY REALLY WANT?
H.I.V.E. WANTS TO SAVE THE WORLD...

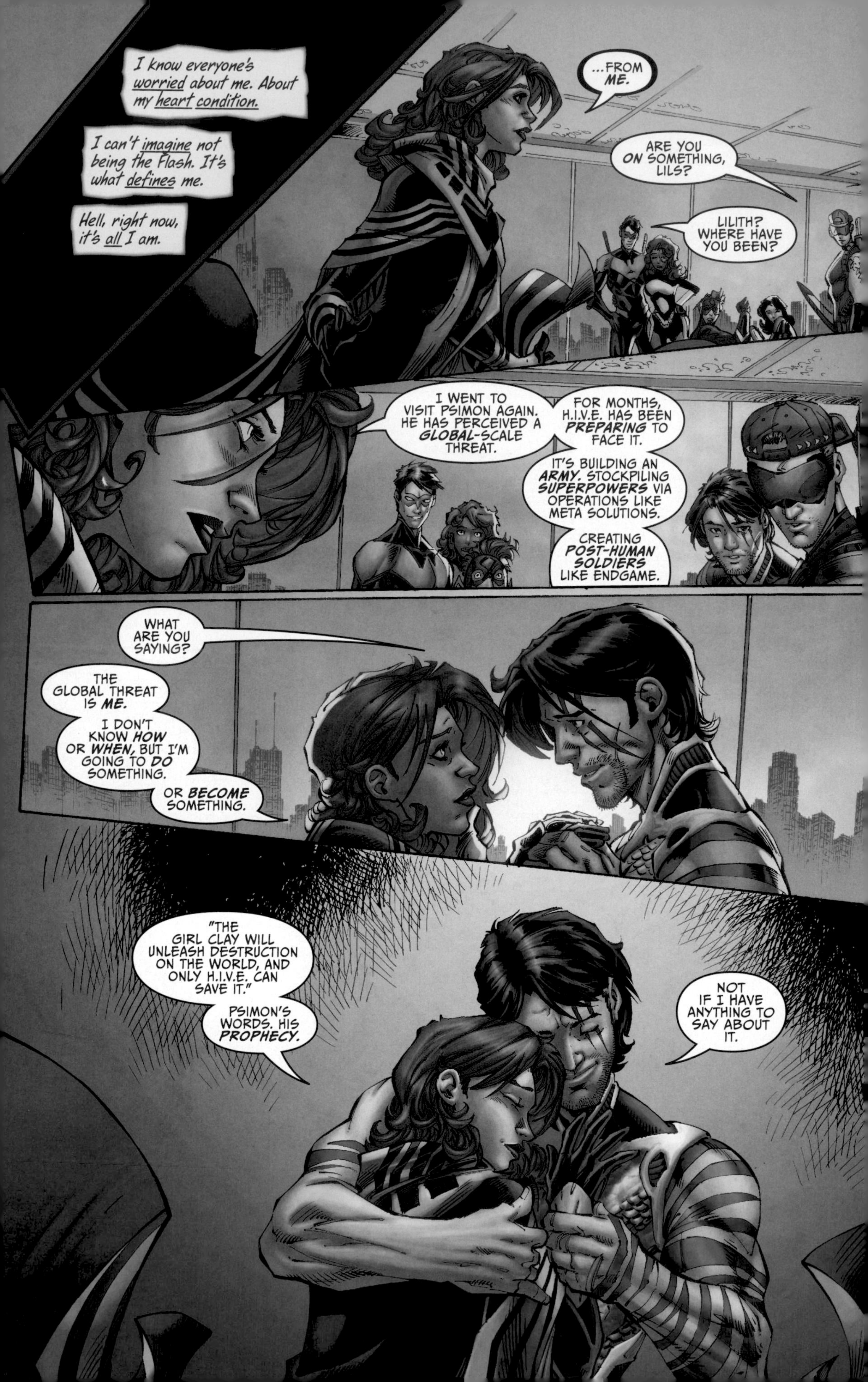

I know everyone's worried about me. About my heart condition.
I can't imagine not being the Flash. It's what defines me.
Hell, right now, it's all I am.
...FROM ME.
ARE YOU ON SOMETHING, LILS?
LILITH? WHERE HAVE YOU BEEN?
I WENT TO VISIT PSIMON AGAIN. HE HAS PERCEIVED A GLOBAL-SCALE THREAT.
FOR MONTHS, H.I.V.E. HAS BEEN PREPARING TO FACE IT.
IT'S BUILDING AN ARMY. STOCKPILING SUPERPOWERS VIA OPERATIONS LIKE META SOLUTIONS.
CREATING POST-HUMAN SOLDIERS LIKE ENDGAME.
WHAT ARE YOU SAYING?
THE GLOBAL THREAT IS ME.
I DON'T KNOW HOW OR WHEN, BUT I'M GOING TO DO SOMETHING.
OR BECOME SOMETHING.
"THE GIRL CLAY WILL UNLEASH DESTRUCTION ON THE WORLD, AND ONLY H.I.V.E. CAN SAVE IT."
PSIMON'S WORDS. HIS PROPHECY.
NOT IF I HAVE ANYTHING TO SAY ABOUT IT.

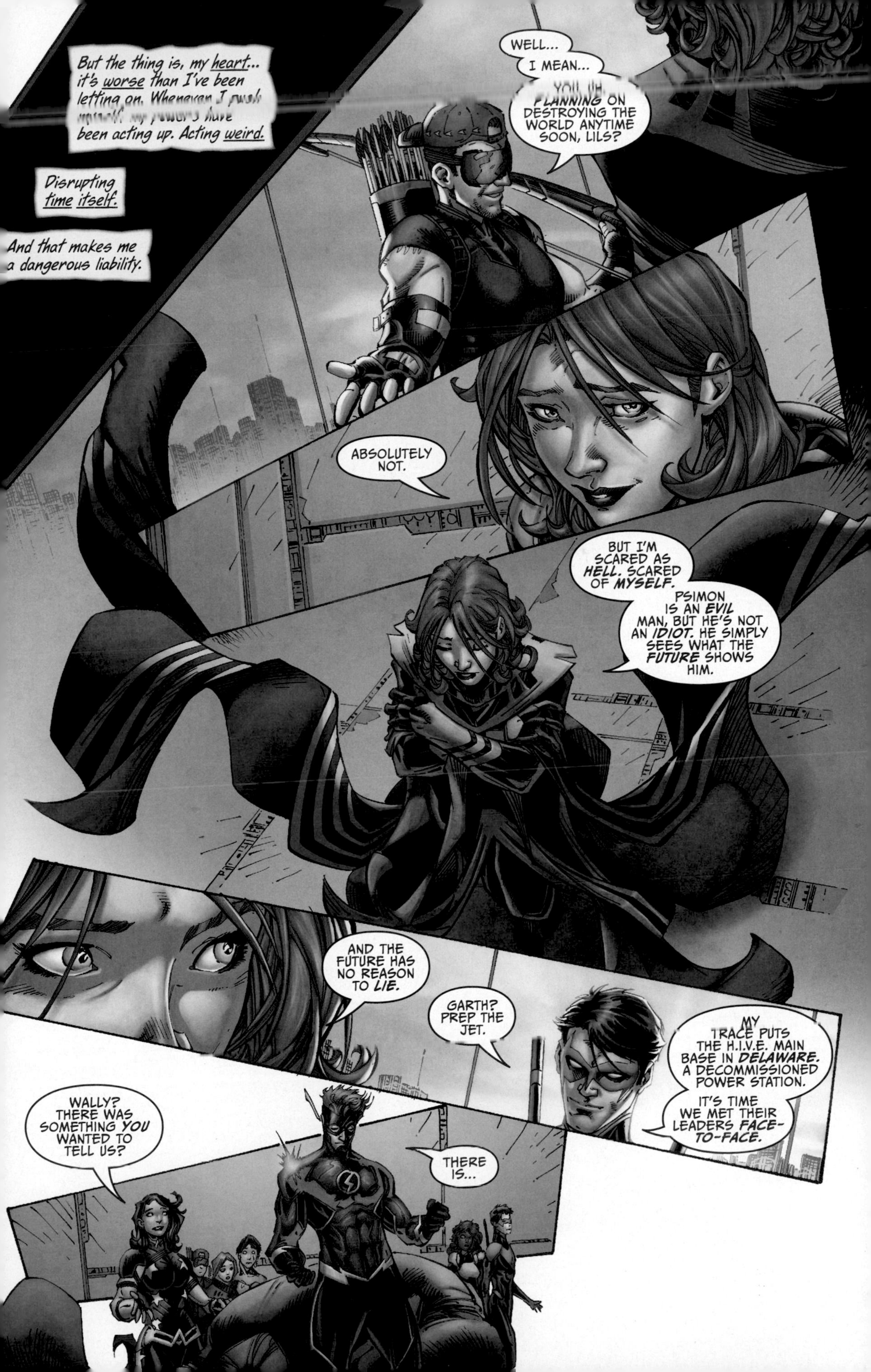

But the thing is, my heart... it's worse than I've been letting on.
been acting up. Acting weird.
Disrupting time itself.
And that makes me a dangerous liability.
WELL...
I MEAN...
PLANNING ON DESTROYING THE WORLD ANYTIME SOON, LILS?
ABSOLUTELY NOT.
BUT I'M SCARED AS HELL. SCARED OF MYSELF.
PSIMON IS AN EVIL MAN, BUT HE'S NOT AN IDIOT. HE SIMPLY SEES WHAT THE FUTURE SHOWS HIM.
AND THE FUTURE HAS NO REASON TO LIE.
GARTH? PREP THE JET.
MY TRACE PUTS THE H.I.V.E. MAIN BASE IN DELAWARE. A DECOMMISSIONED POWER STATION.
IT'S TIME WE MET THEIR LEADERS FACE-TO-FACE.
WALLY? THERE WAS SOMETHING YOU WANTED TO TELL US?
THERE IS...

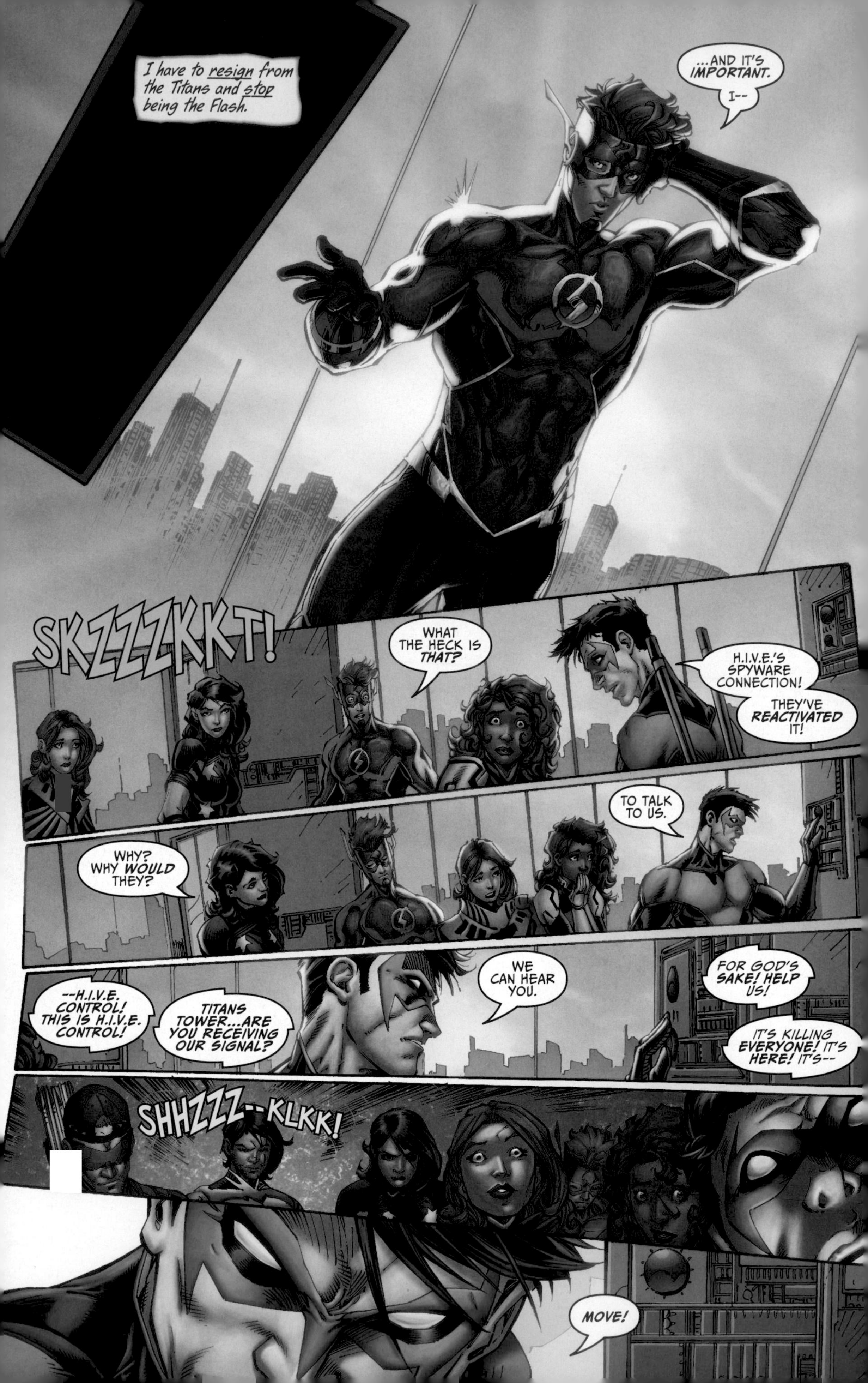
I have to resign from the Titans and stop being the Flash.
...AND IT'S IMPORTANT.
I--
SKZZZKKT!
WHAT THE HECK IS THAT?
H.I.V.E.'S SPYWARE CONNECTION!
THEY'VE REACTIVATED IT!
TO TALK TO US.
WHY? WHY WOULD THEY?
--H.I.V.E. CONTROL! THIS IS H.I.V.E. CONTROL!
TITANS TOWER...ARE YOU RECEIVING OUR SIGNAL?
WE CAN HEAR YOU.
FOR GOD'S SAKE! HELP US!
IT'S KILLING EVERYONE! IT'S HERE! IT'S--
SHHZZZ--KLKK!
MOVE!

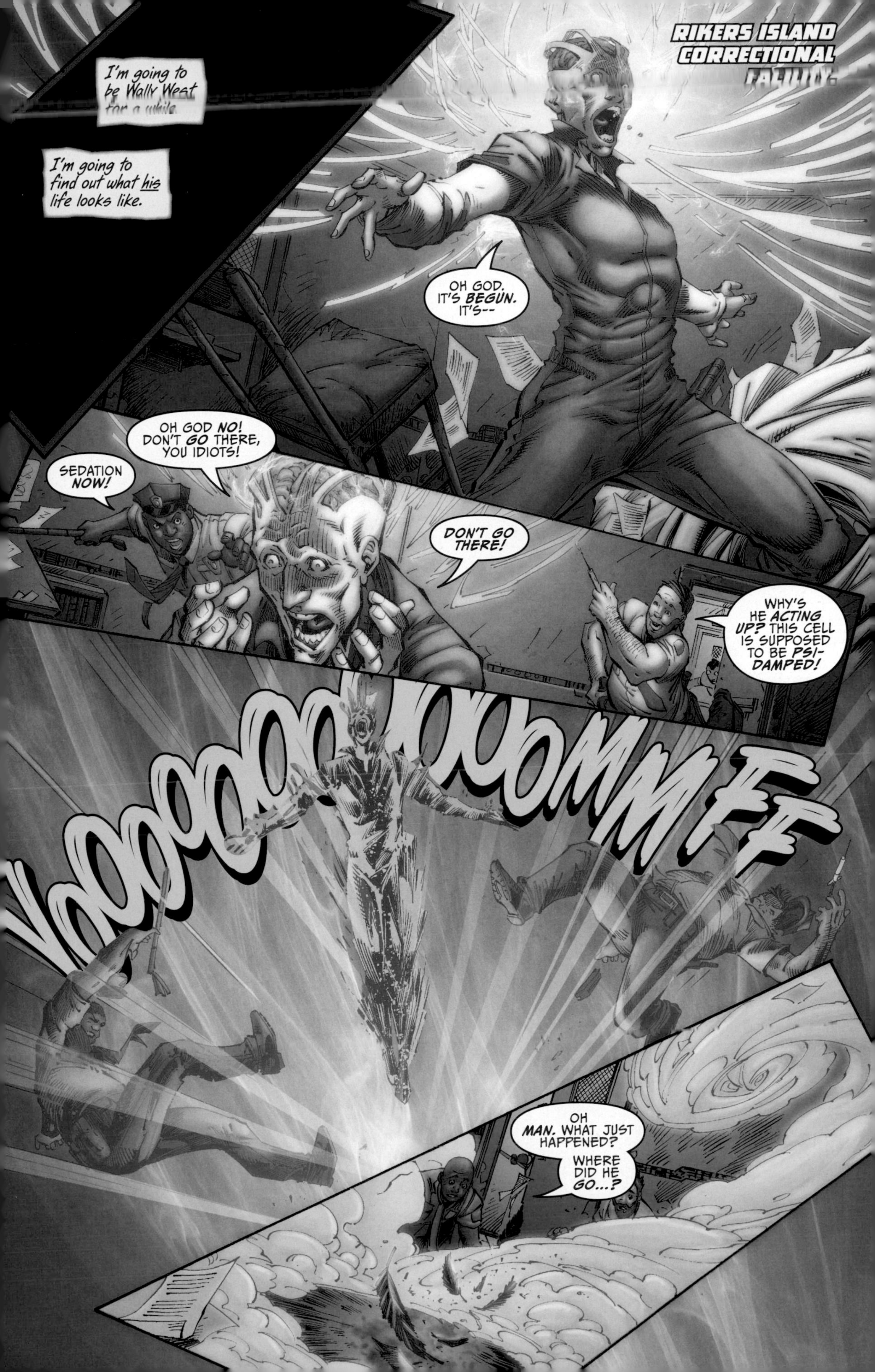

I'm going to be Wally West for a while.
I'm going to find out what his life looks like.
RIKERS ISLAND CORRECTIONAL
OH GOD. IT'S BEGUN. IT'S--
SEDATION NOW!
OH GOD NO! DON'T GO THERE, YOU IDIOTS!
DON'T GO THERE!
WHY'S HE ACTING UP? THIS CELL IS SUPPOSED TO BE PSI-DAMPED!
VOOOOOOOOOOOMMFF
OH MAN. WHAT JUST HAPPENED?
WHERE DID HE GO...?

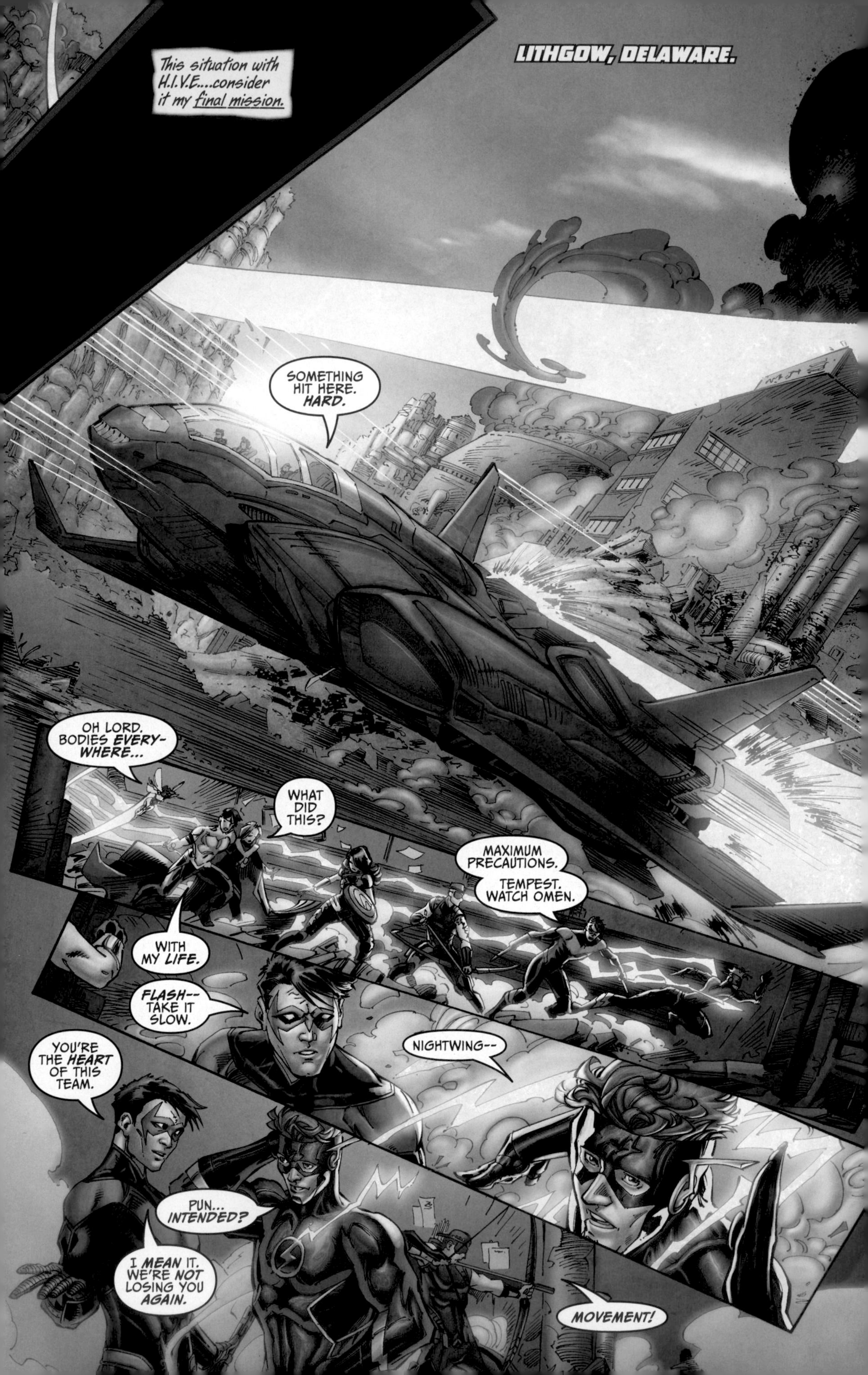
This situation with H.I.V.E....consider it my final mission.
LITHGOW, DELAWARE.
SOMETHING HIT HERE. HARD.
OH LORD. BODIES EVERY-WHERE...
WHAT DID THIS?
MAXIMUM PRECAUTIONS.
TEMPEST. WATCH OMEN.
WITH MY LIFE.
FLASH-- TAKE IT SLOW.
NIGHTWING--
YOU'RE THE HEART OF THIS TEAM.
PUN... INTENDED?
I MEAN IT. WE'RE NOT LOSING YOU AGAIN.
MOVEMENT!

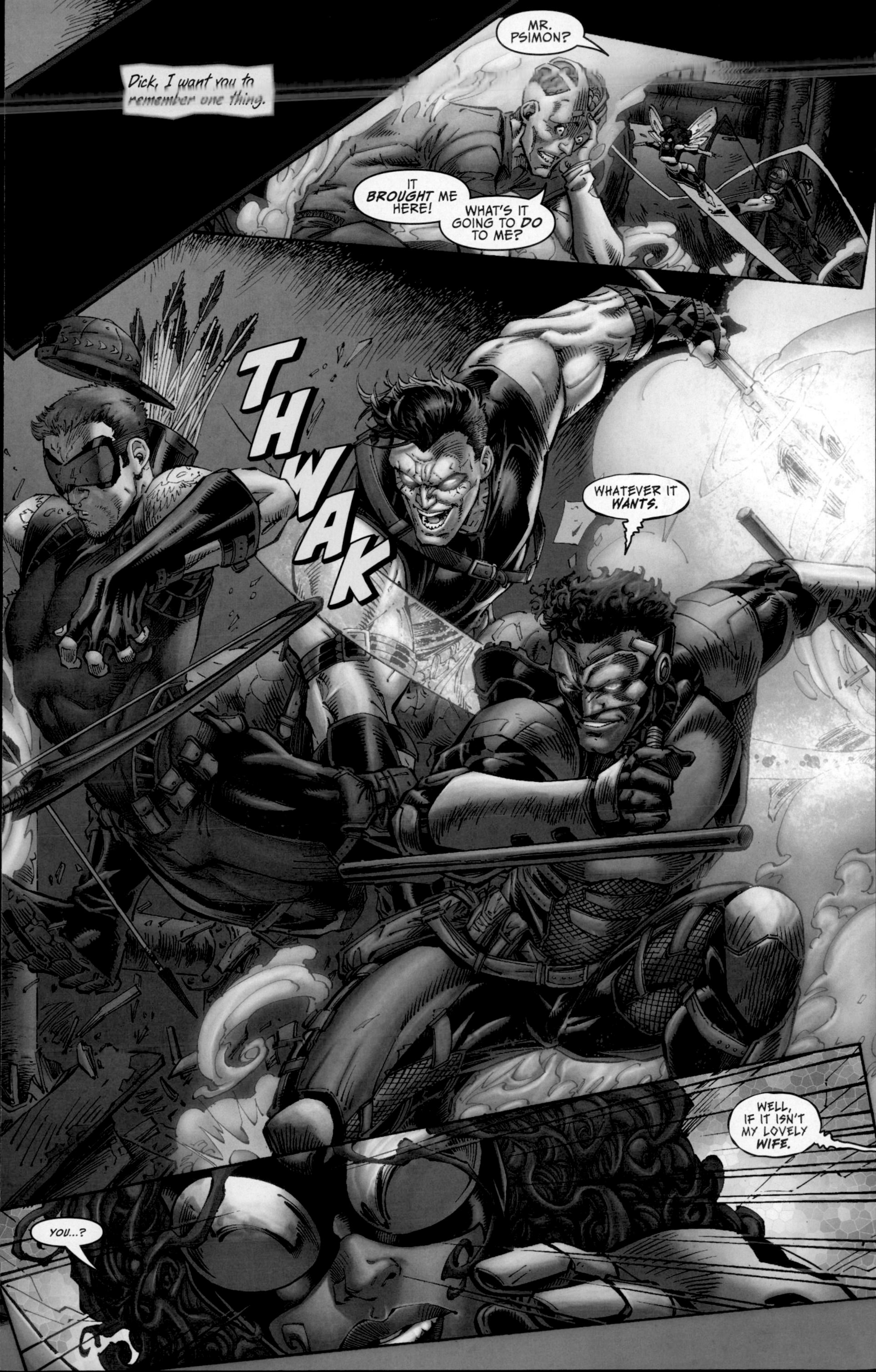

Dick, I want you to remember one thing.
MR. PSIMON?
IT BROUGHT ME HERE!
WHAT'S IT GOING TO DO TO ME?
THWAK
WHATEVER IT WANTS.
WELL, IF IT ISN'T MY LOVELY WIFE.
YOU...?

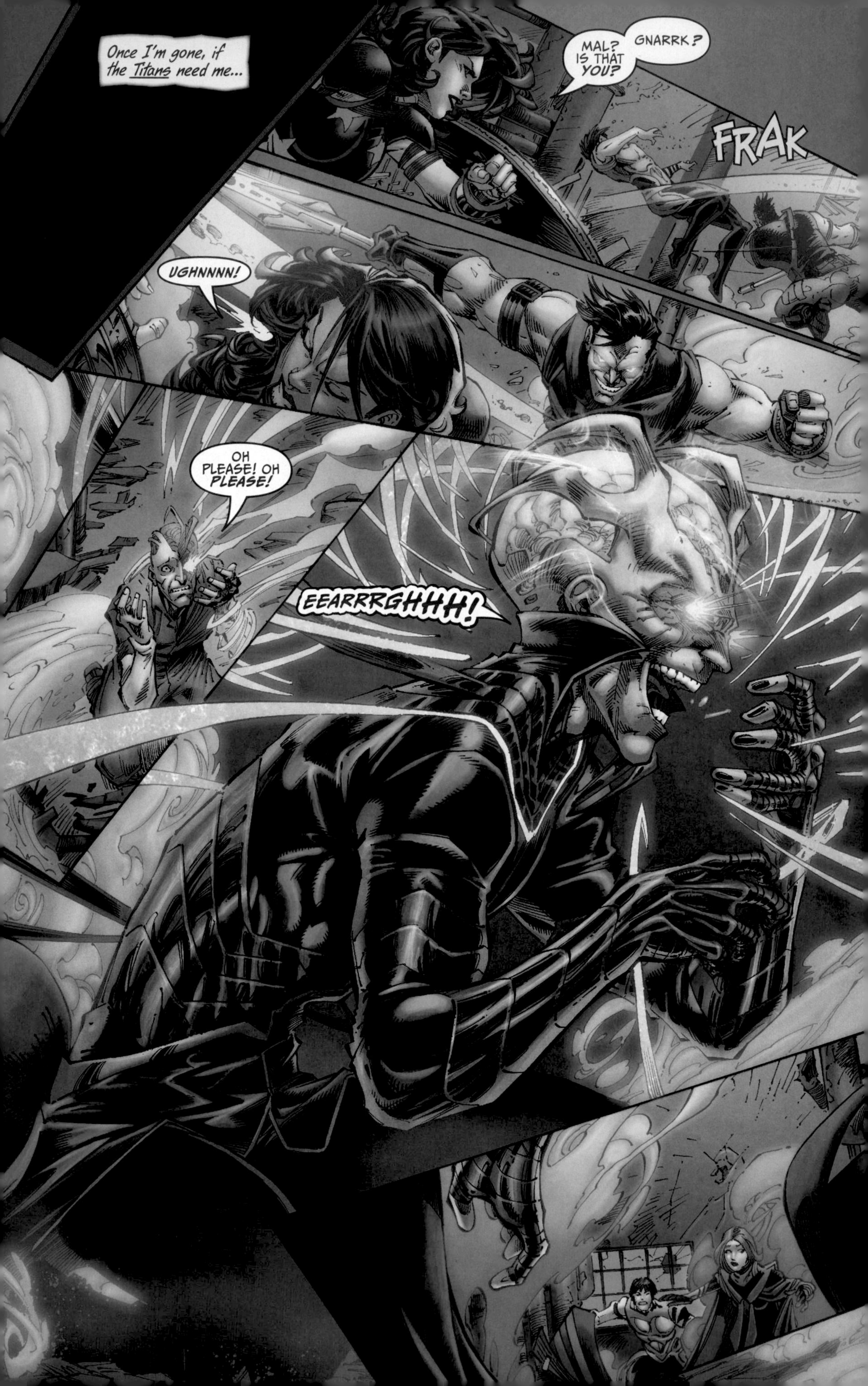
Once I'm gone, if the Titans need me...
MAL? IS THAT YOU?
GNARRK?
FRAK
UGHNNNN!
OH PLEASE! OH PLEASE!
EEARRRGHHH!

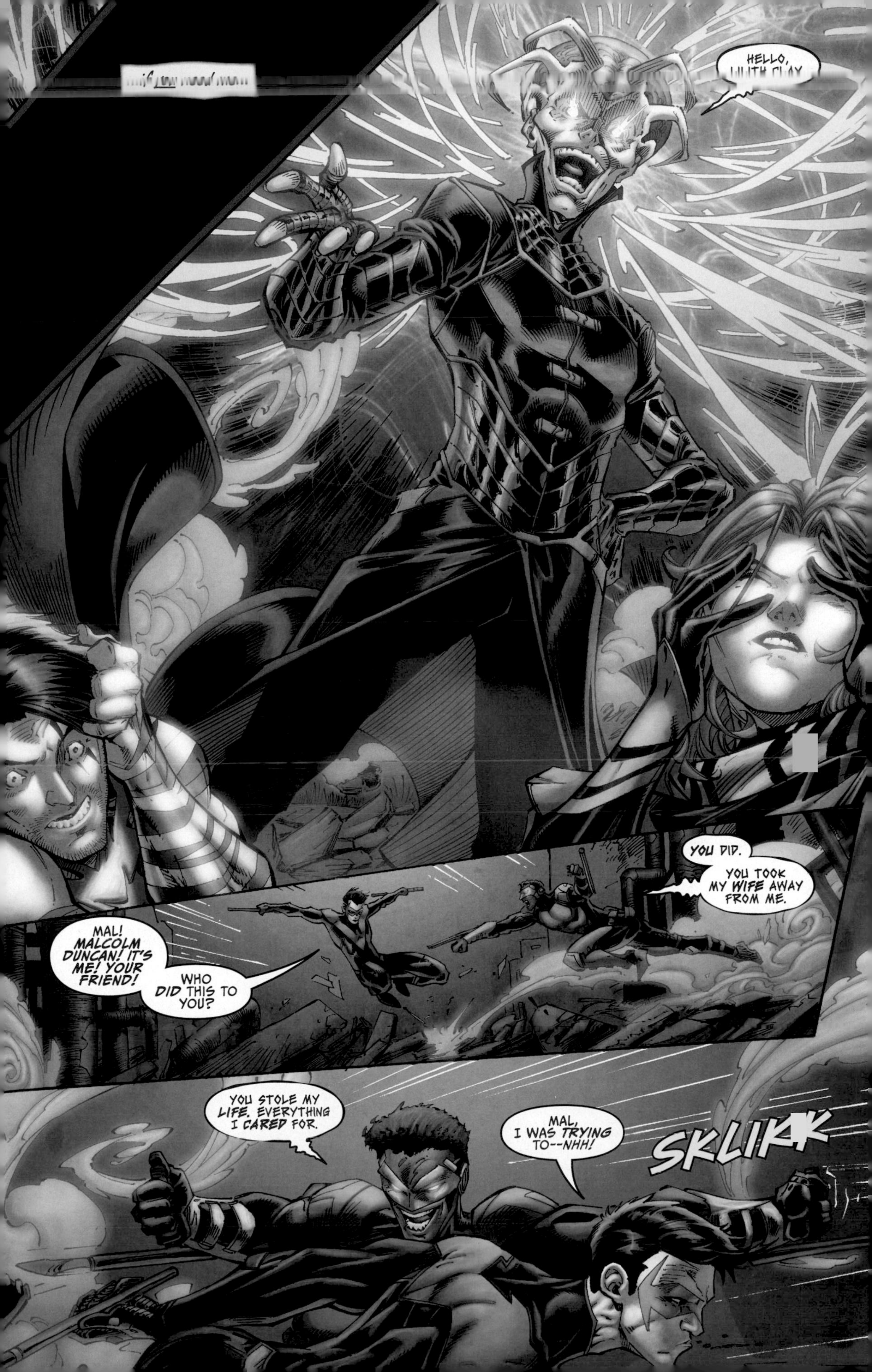
HELLO,
YOU DID.
YOU TOOK MY WIFE AWAY FROM ME.
MAL! MALCOLM DUNCAN! IT'S ME! YOUR FRIEND!
WHO DID THIS TO YOU?
YOU STOLE MY LIFE. EVERYTHING I CARED FOR.
MAL, I WAS TRYING TO--NHH!
SKLIKK

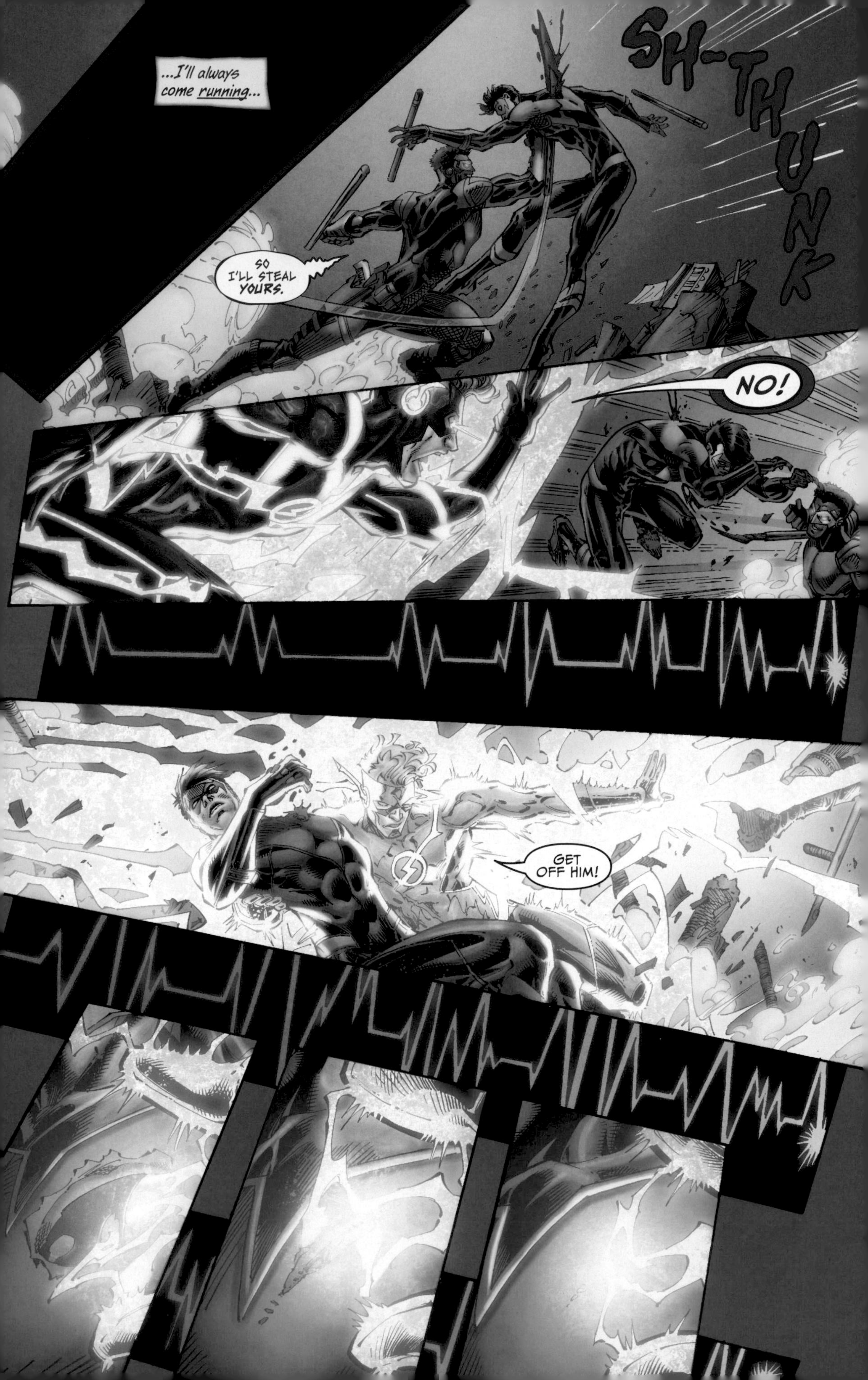

...I'll always come running...
SH-THUNK
SO I'LL STEAL YOURS.
NO!
GET OFF HIM!

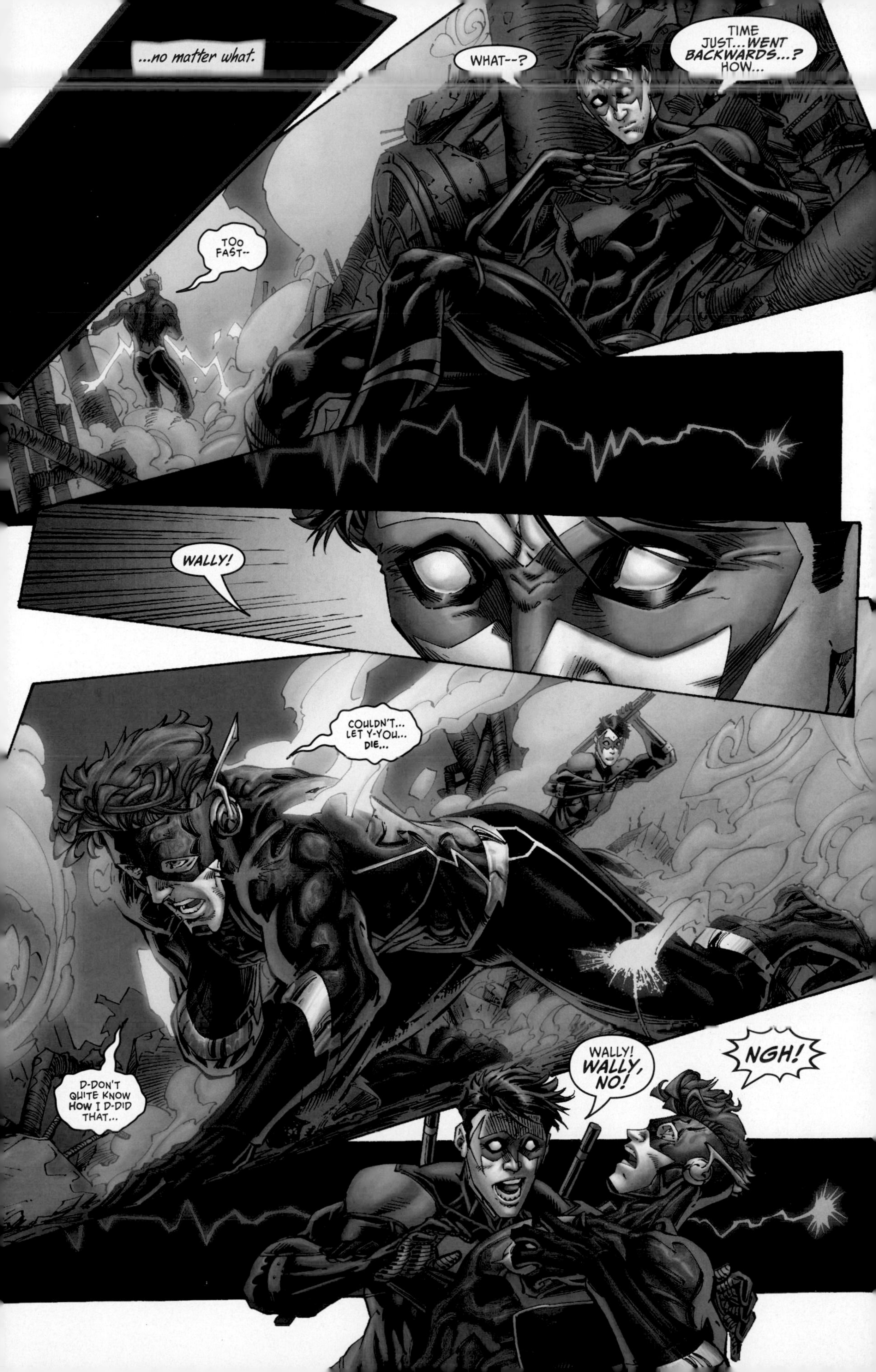
...no matter what.
WHAT--?
TIME JUST...WENT BACKWARDS...? HOW...
TOO FAST--
WALLY!
COULDN'T... LET Y-YOU... DIE...
D-DON'T QUITE KNOW HOW I D-DID THAT...
WALLY! WALLY, NO!
NGH!

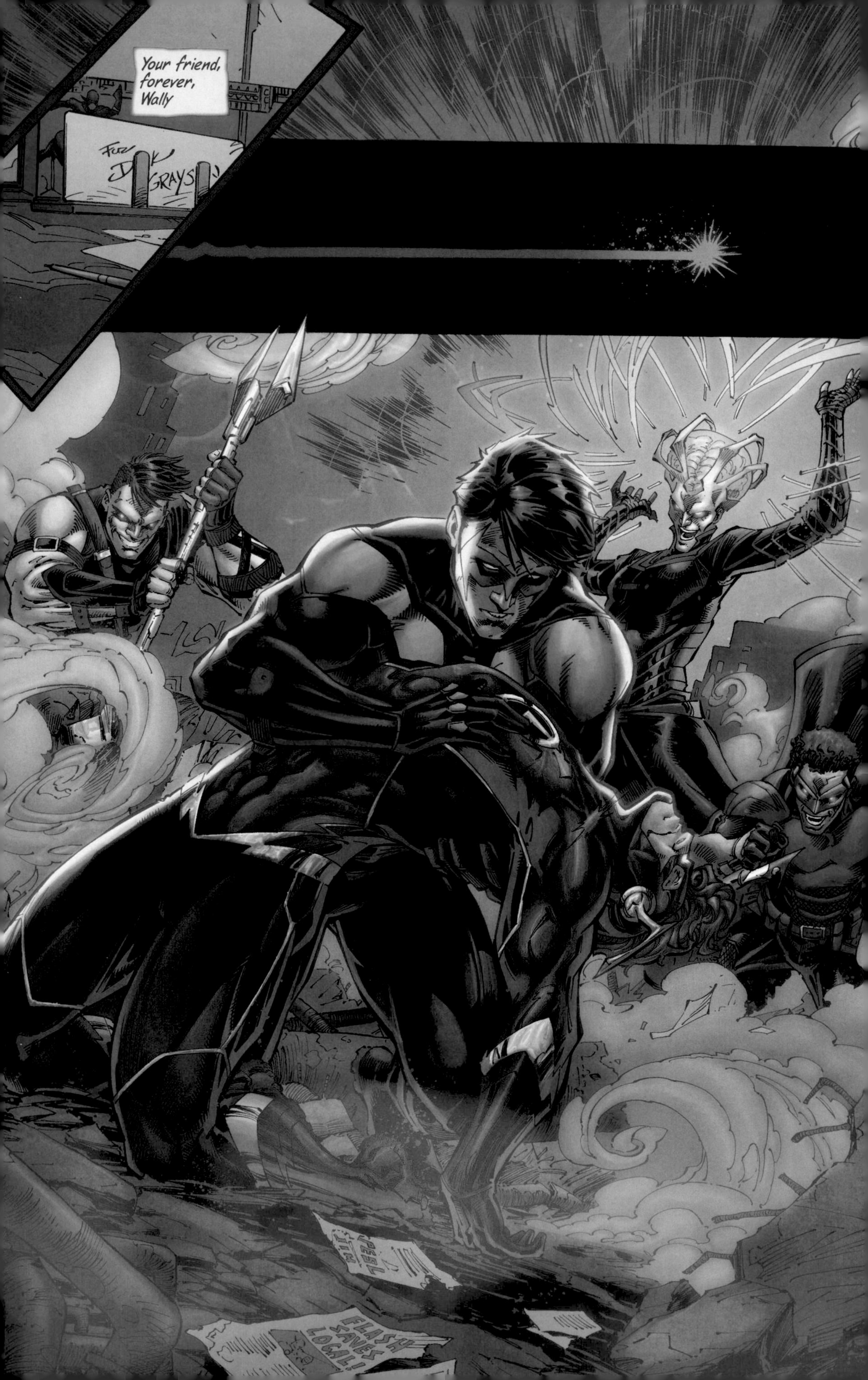
Your friend, forever, Wally
FLASH SAVES LOCAL!

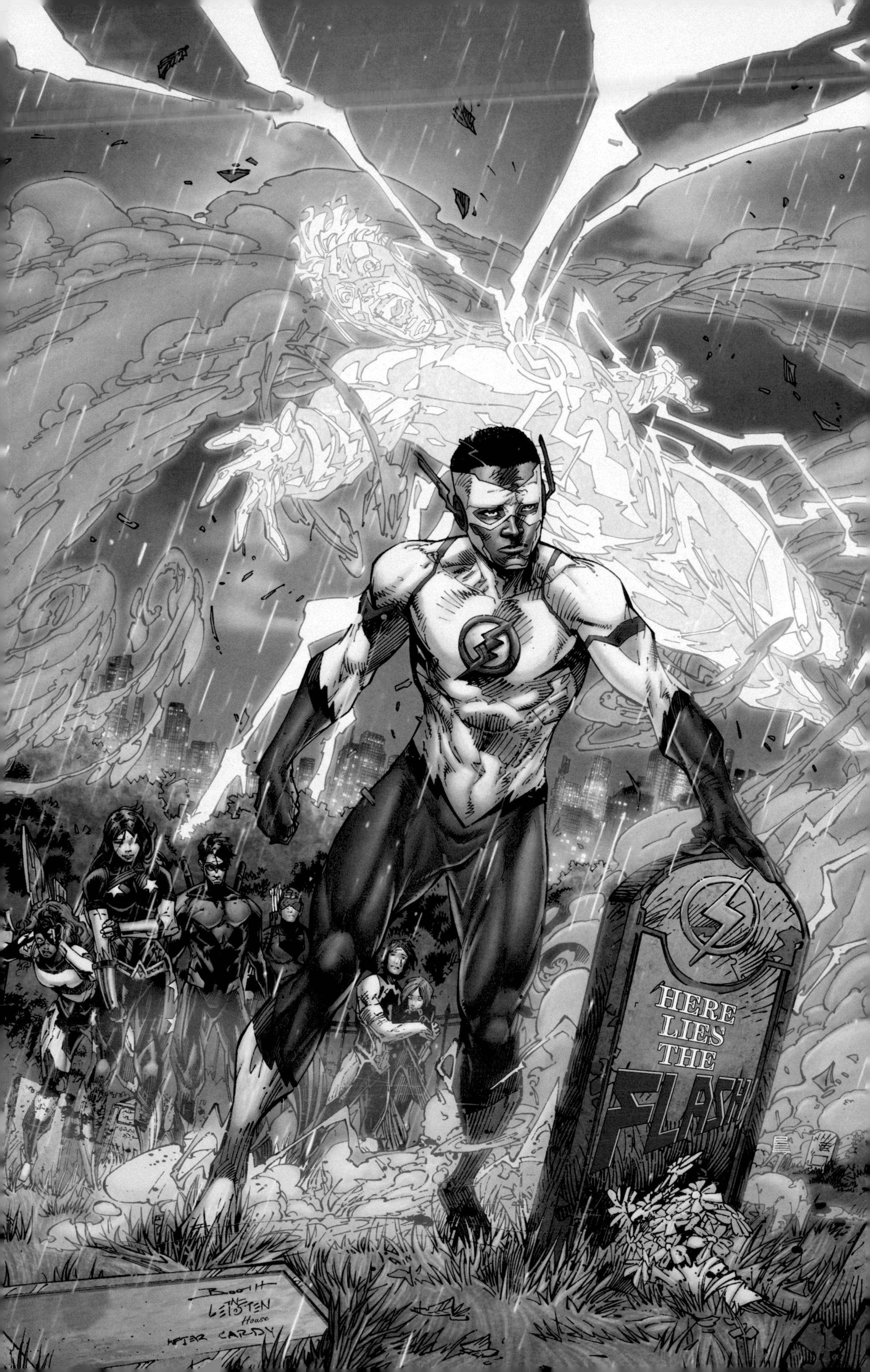
HERE
LIES
THE
FLASH
BOOTH
LEISTEN
House
PETER CARDY

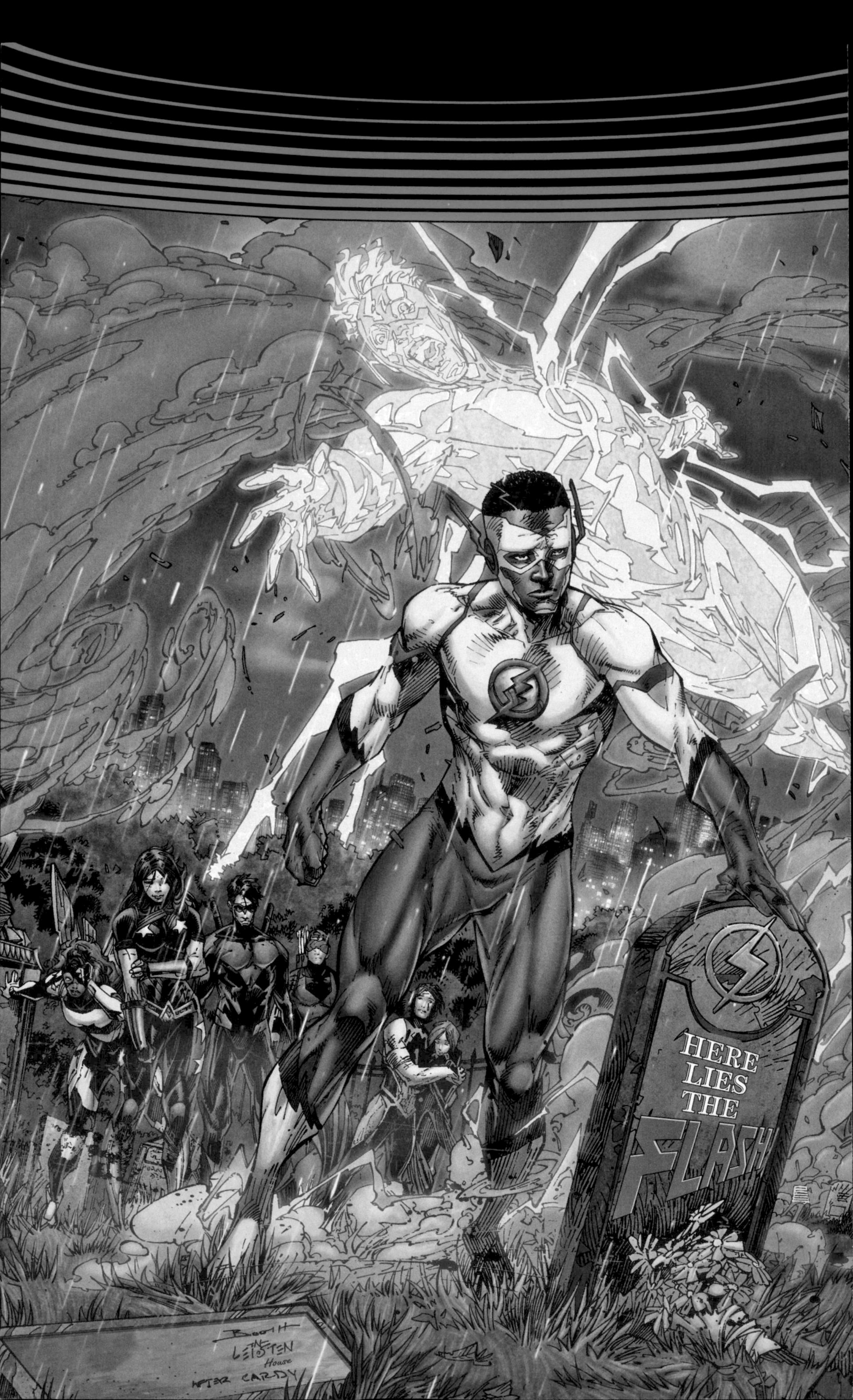
HERE
LIES
THE
FLASH

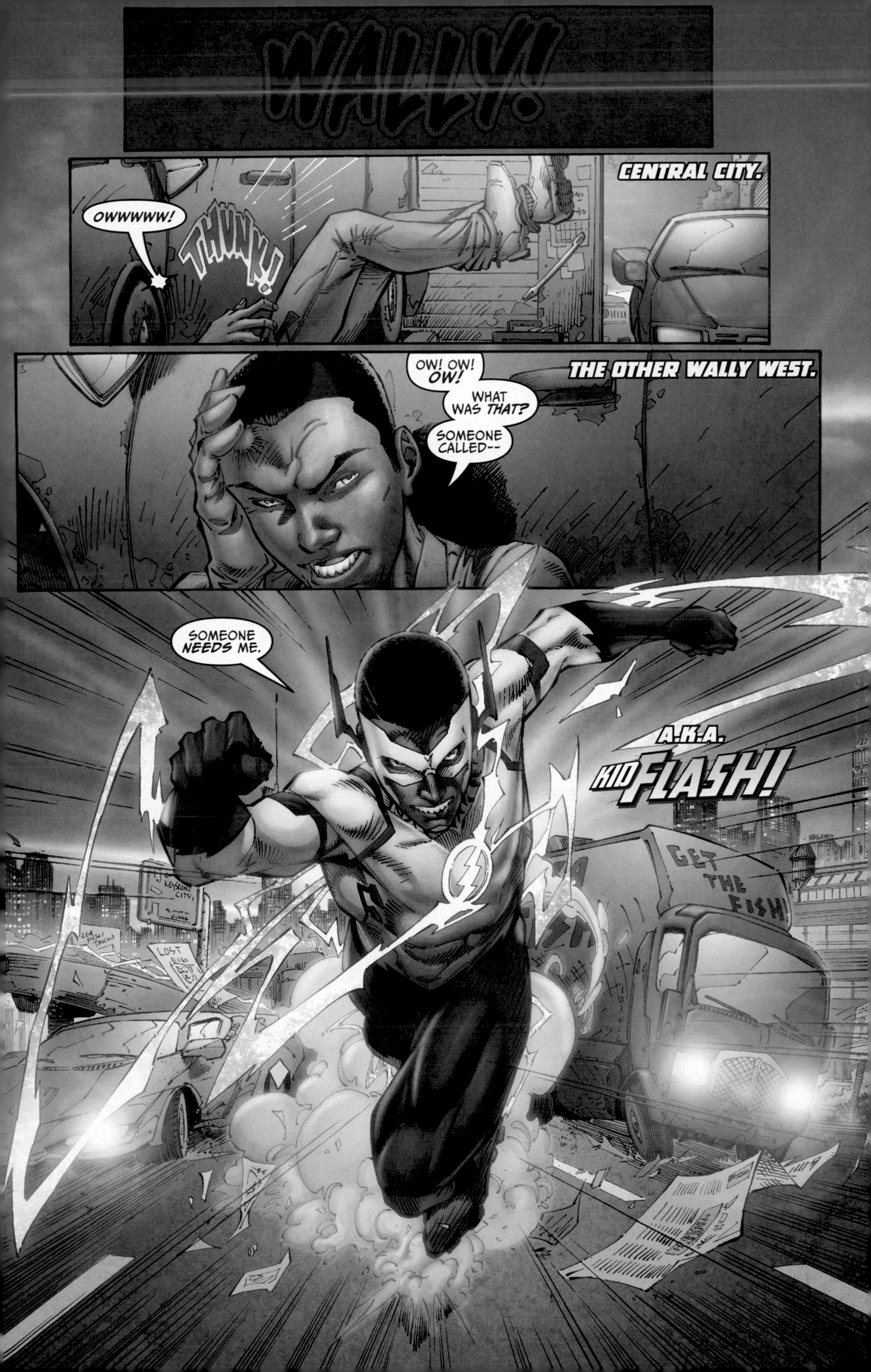
WALLY!
CENTRAL CITY.
OWWWWW!
THUNK!
THE OTHER WALLY WEST.
OW! OW! OW!
WHAT WAS THAT?
SOMEONE CALLED--
SOMEONE NEEDS ME.
A.K.A. KID FLASH!
GET THE FISH!
LOST DOG

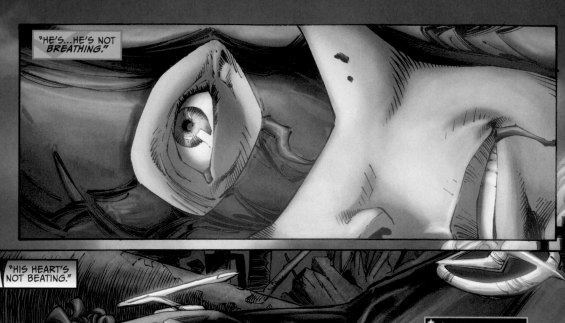

"HE'S...HE'S NOT *BREATHING.*"

"HIS HEART'S NOT *BEATING.*"

"WALLY? WALLY... *PLEASE...*"

"WHAT DID HE *DO?* WHAT *CRAZY STUNT* WAS WEST TRYING TO PULL--?"

"HE WAS *SAVING* ME. HE *WOUND TIME BACKWARDS* TO SAVE ME..."

"BUT HIS *HEART--*"

"I KNOW."

"THIS ISN'T *HAPPENING.* THIS ISN'T *REAL...*"

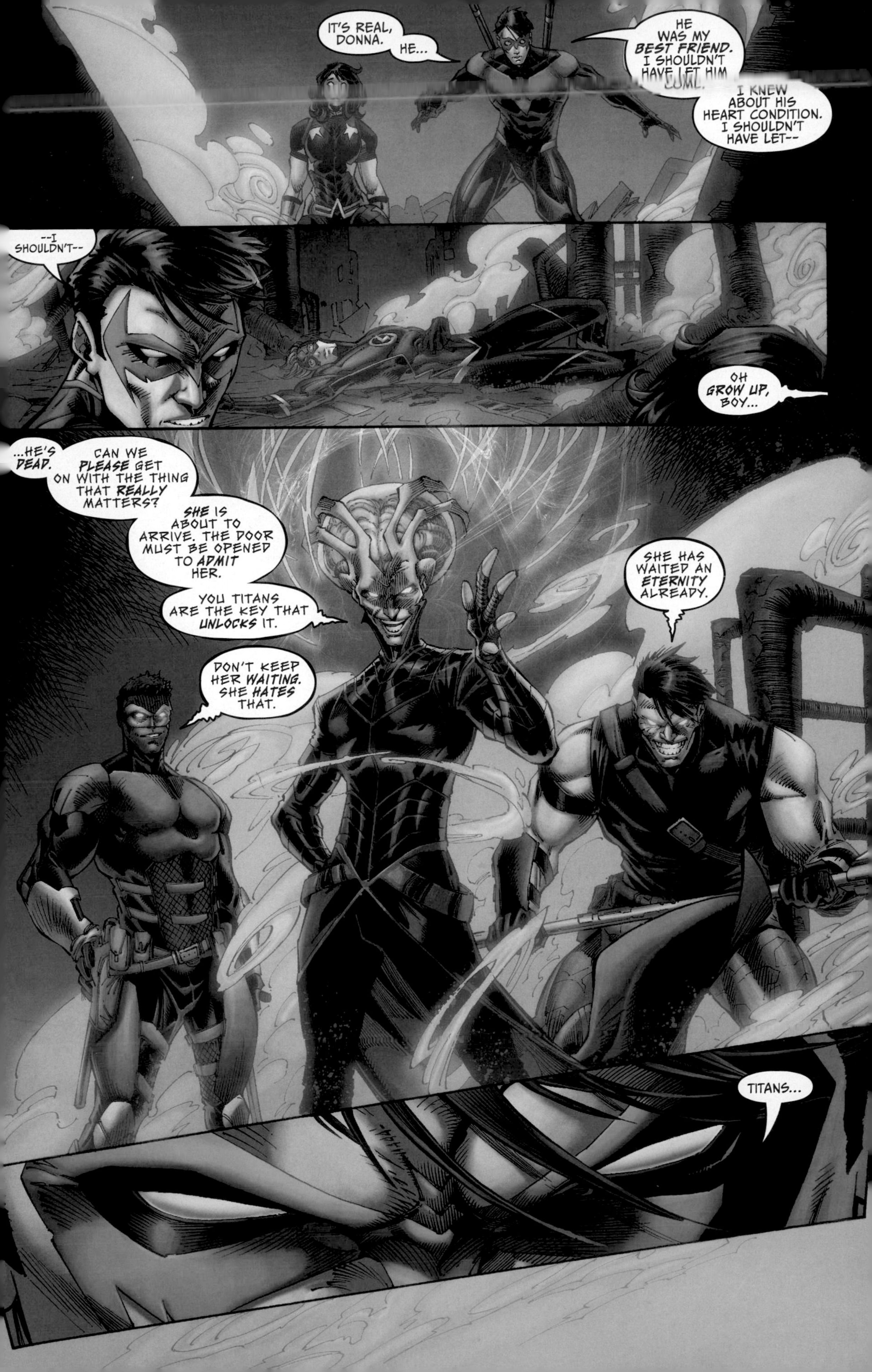
IT'S REAL, DONNA. HE...
HE WAS MY BEST FRIEND. I SHOULDN'T HAVE LET HIM COME.
I KNEW ABOUT HIS HEART CONDITION. I SHOULDN'T HAVE LET--
--I SHOULDN'T--
OH GROW UP, BOY...
...HE'S DEAD.
CAN WE PLEASE GET ON WITH THE THING THAT REALLY MATTERS?
SHE IS ABOUT TO ARRIVE. THE DOOR MUST BE OPENED TO ADMIT HER.
YOU TITANS ARE THE KEY THAT UNLOCKS IT.
SHE HAS WAITED AN ETERNITY ALREADY.
DON'T KEEP HER WAITING. SHE HATES THAT.
TITANS...

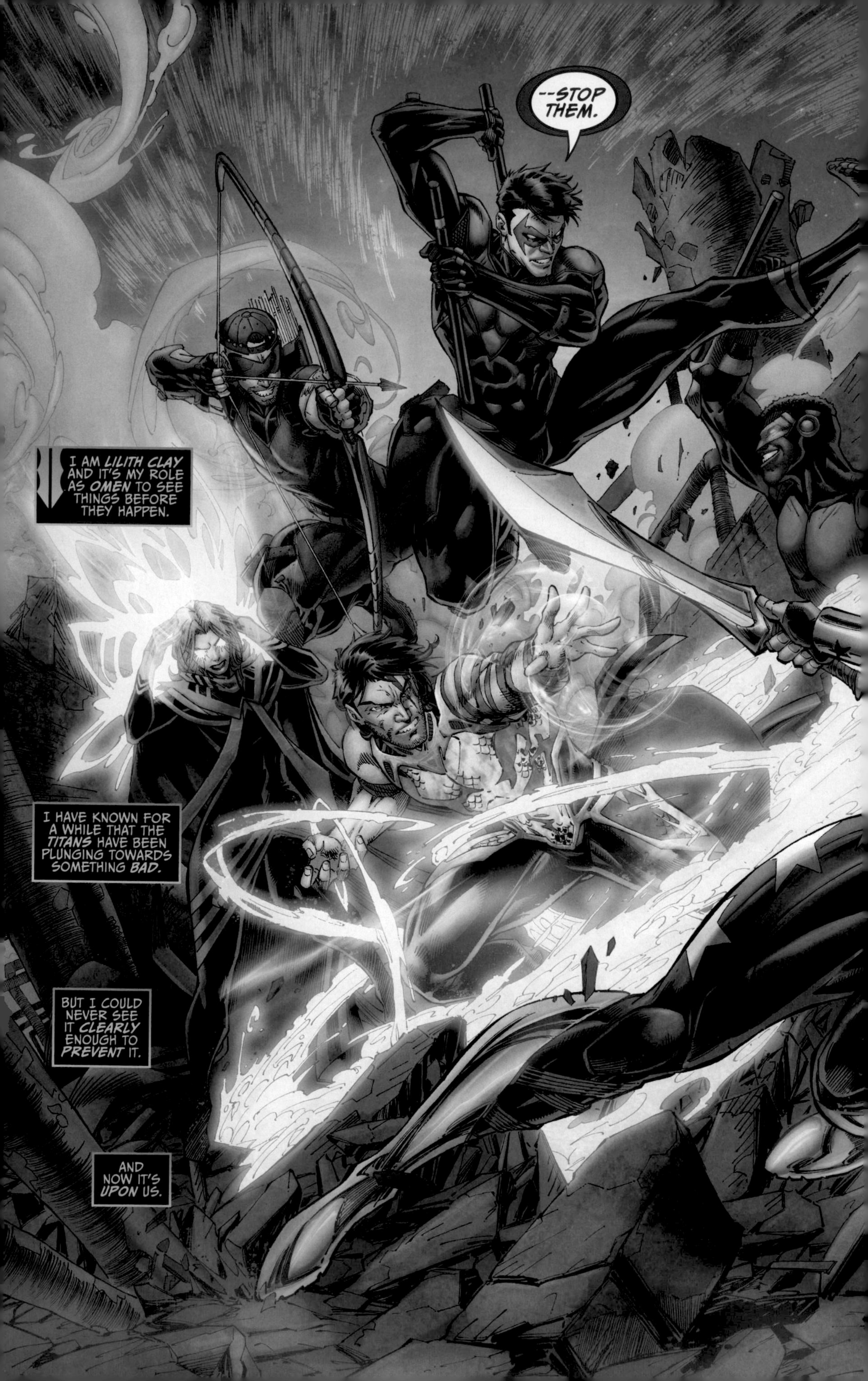
--STOP THEM.
I AM LILITH CLAY AND IT'S MY ROLE AS OMEN TO SEE THINGS BEFORE THEY HAPPEN.
I HAVE KNOWN FOR A WHILE THAT THE TITANS HAVE BEEN PLUNGING TOWARDS SOMETHING BAD.
BUT I COULD NEVER SEE IT CLEARLY ENOUGH TO PREVENT IT.
AND NOW IT'S UPON US.

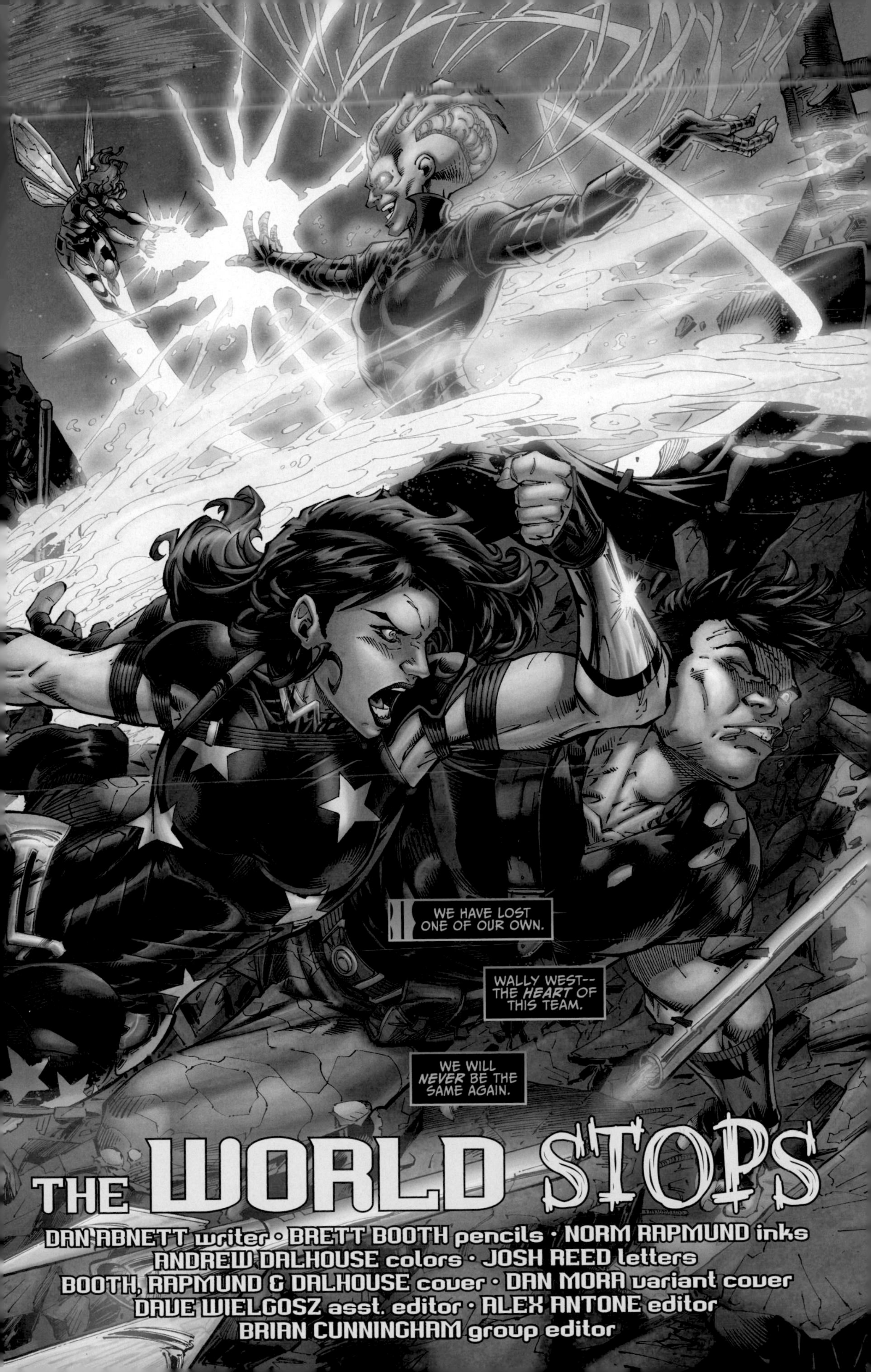

WE HAVE LOST ONE OF OUR OWN.
WALLY WEST-- THE *HEART* OF THIS TEAM.
WE WILL *NEVER* BE THE SAME AGAIN.
THE WORLD STOPS
DAN ABNETT writer · BRETT BOOTH pencils · NORM RAPMUND inks
ANDREW DALHOUSE colors · JOSH REED letters
BOOTH, RAPMUND & DALHOUSE cover · DAN MORA variant cover
DAVE WIELGOSZ asst. editor · ALEX ANTONE editor
BRIAN CUNNINGHAM group editor

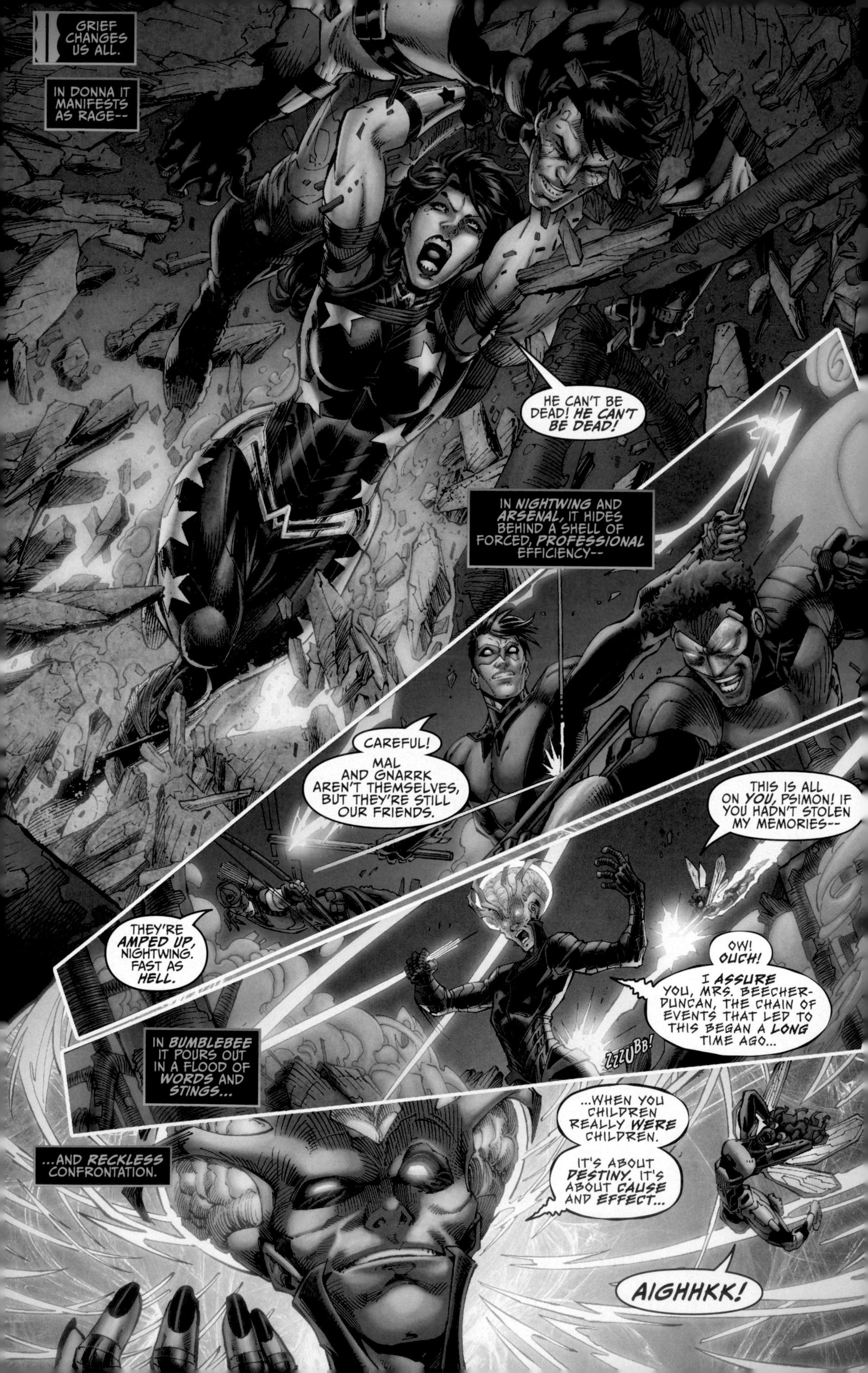
GRIEF CHANGES US ALL.
IN DONNA IT MANIFESTS AS RAGE--
HE CAN'T BE DEAD! HE CAN'T BE DEAD!
IN NIGHTWING AND ARSENAL, IT HIDES BEHIND A SHELL OF FORCED, PROFESSIONAL EFFICIENCY--
CAREFUL! MAL AND GNARRK AREN'T THEMSELVES, BUT THEY'RE STILL OUR FRIENDS.
THEY'RE AMPED UP, NIGHTWING. FAST AS HELL.
IN BUMBLEBEE IT POURS OUT IN A FLOOD OF WORDS AND STINGS...
THIS IS ALL ON YOU, PSIMON! IF YOU HADN'T STOLEN MY MEMORIES--
OW! OUCH!
I ASSURE YOU, MRS. BEECHER-DUNCAN, THE CHAIN OF EVENTS THAT LED TO THIS BEGAN A LONG TIME AGO...
ZZZUBB!
...AND RECKLESS CONFRONTATION.
...WHEN YOU CHILDREN REALLY WERE CHILDREN.
IT'S ABOUT DESTINY. IT'S ABOUT CAUSE AND EFFECT...
AIGHHKK!

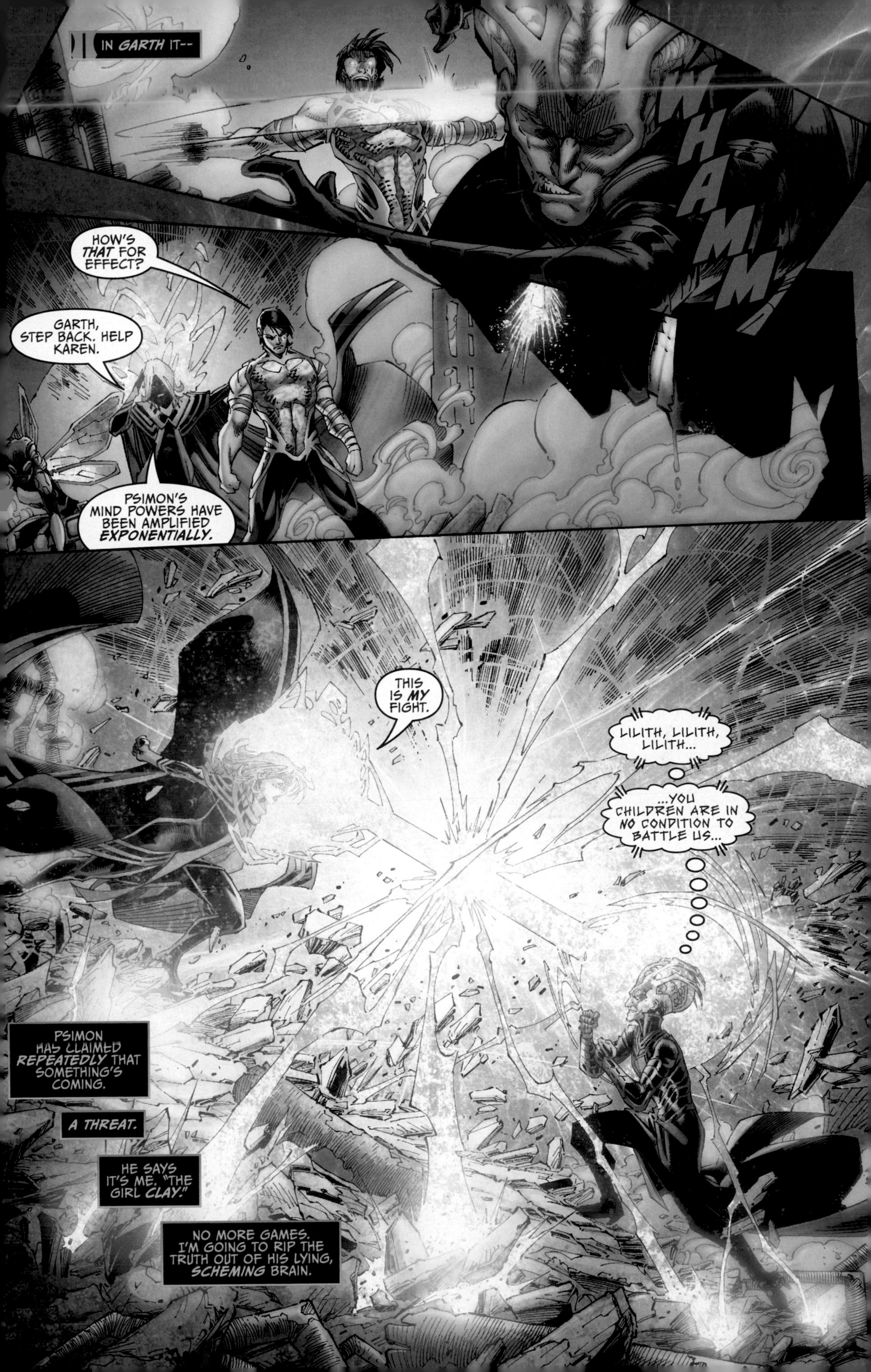
IN GARTH IT--
WHAMM!
HOW'S THAT FOR EFFECT?
GARTH, STEP BACK. HELP KAREN.
PSIMON'S MIND POWERS HAVE BEEN AMPLIFIED EXPONENTIALLY.
THIS IS MY FIGHT.
LILITH, LILITH, LILITH...
...YOU CHILDREN ARE IN NO CONDITION TO BATTLE US...
PSIMON HAS CLAIMED REPEATEDLY THAT SOMETHING'S COMING.
A THREAT.
HE SAYS IT'S ME. "THE GIRL CLAY."
NO MORE GAMES. I'M GOING TO RIP THE TRUTH OUT OF HIS LYING, SCHEMING BRAIN.

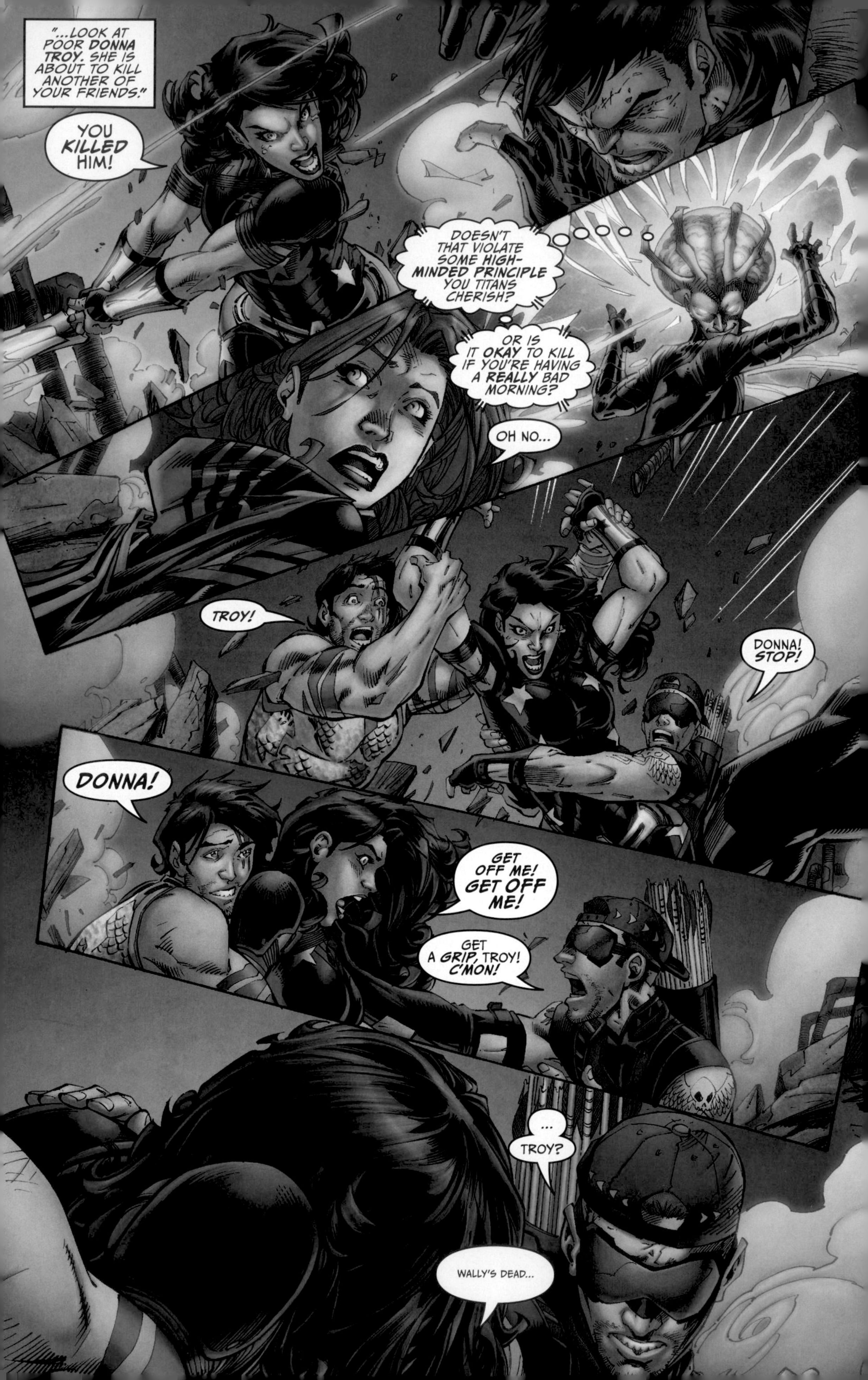
"...LOOK AT POOR DONNA TROY. SHE IS ABOUT TO KILL ANOTHER OF YOUR FRIENDS."
YOU KILLED HIM!
DOESN'T THAT VIOLATE SOME HIGH-MINDED PRINCIPLE YOU TITANS CHERISH?
OR IS IT OKAY TO KILL IF YOU'RE HAVING A REALLY BAD MORNING?
OH NO...
TROY!
DONNA! STOP!
DONNA!
GET OFF ME! GET OFF ME!
GET A GRIP, TROY! C'MON!
... TROY?
WALLY'S DEAD...

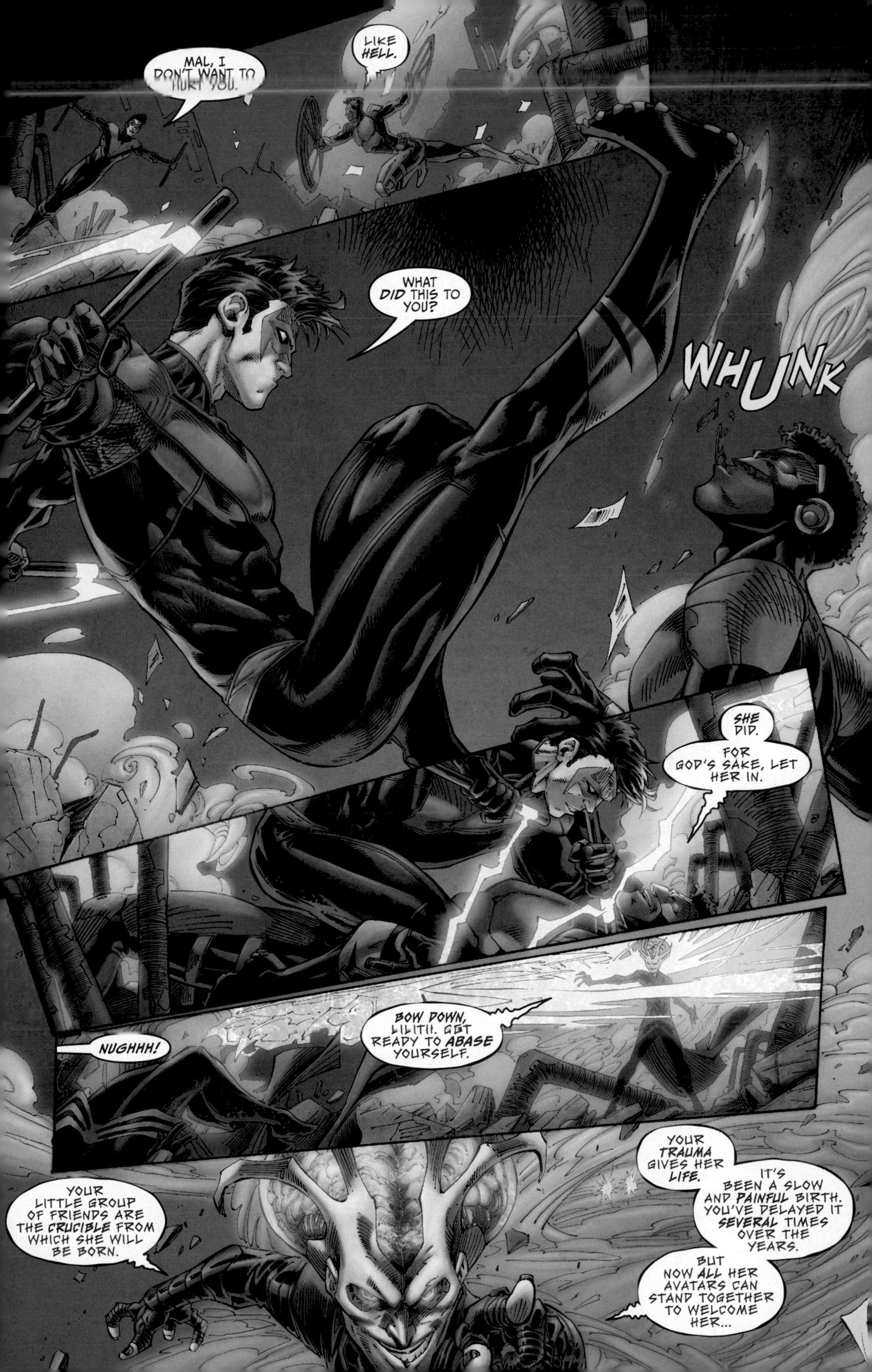

MAL, I DON'T WANT TO HURT YOU.
LIKE HELL.
WHAT DID THIS TO YOU?
WHUNK
SHE DID.
FOR GOD'S SAKE, LET HER IN.
NUGHHH!
BOW DOWN, LILITH. GET READY TO ABASE YOURSELF.
YOUR LITTLE GROUP OF FRIENDS ARE THE CRUCIBLE FROM WHICH SHE WILL BE BORN.
YOUR TRAUMA GIVES HER LIFE.
IT'S BEEN A SLOW AND PAINFUL BIRTH. YOU'VE DELAYED IT SEVERAL TIMES OVER THE YEARS.
BUT NOW ALL HER AVATARS CAN STAND TOGETHER TO WELCOME HER...

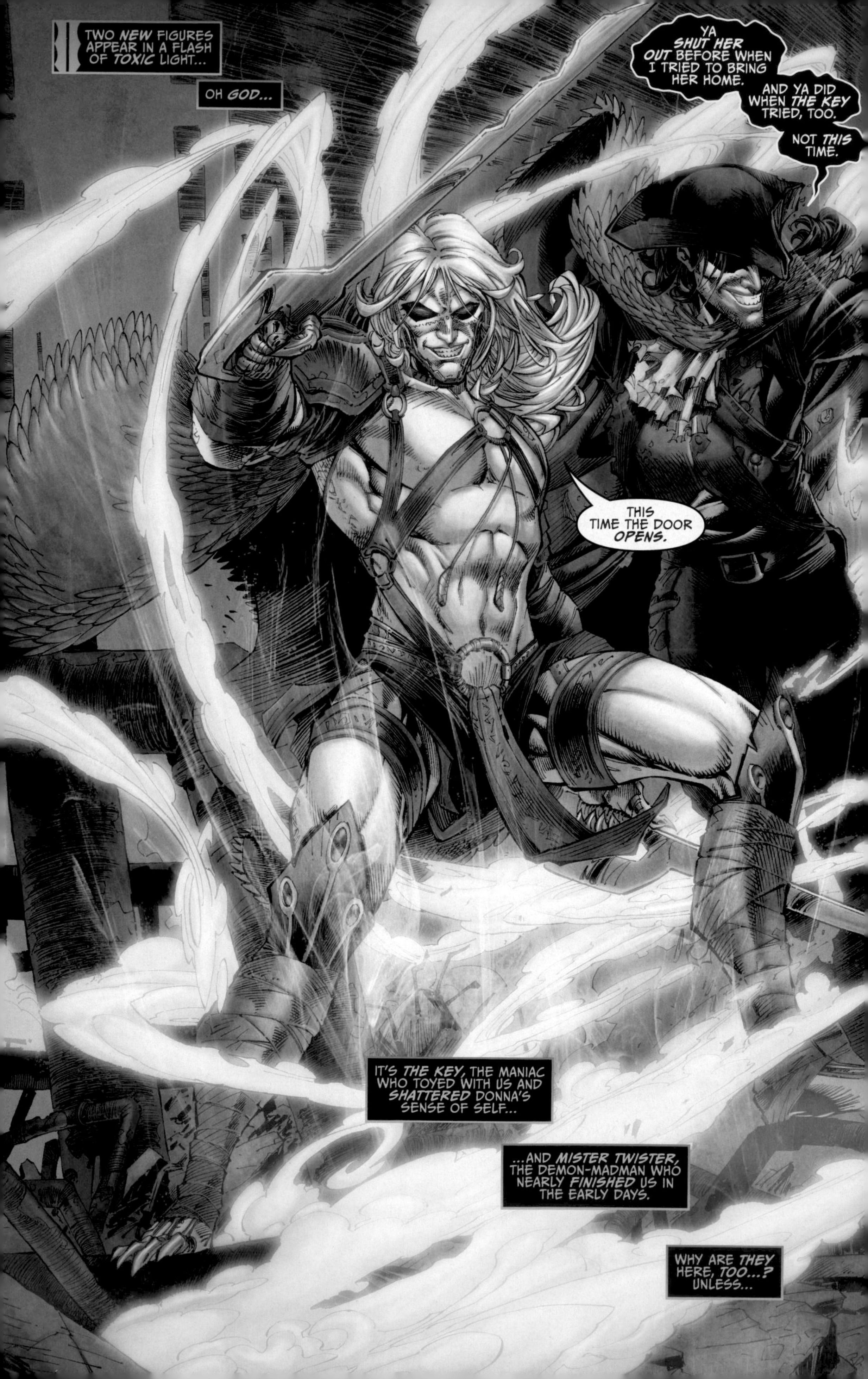
TWO NEW FIGURES APPEAR IN A FLASH OF TOXIC LIGHT...
OH GOD...
YA SHUT HER OUT BEFORE WHEN I TRIED TO BRING HER HOME.
AND YA DID WHEN THE KEY TRIED, TOO.
NOT THIS TIME.
THIS TIME THE DOOR OPENS.
IT'S THE KEY, THE MANIAC WHO TOYED WITH US AND SHATTERED DONNA'S SENSE OF SELF...
...AND MISTER TWISTER, THE DEMON-MADMAN WHO NEARLY FINISHED US IN THE EARLY DAYS.
WHY ARE THEY HERE, TOO...? UNLESS...

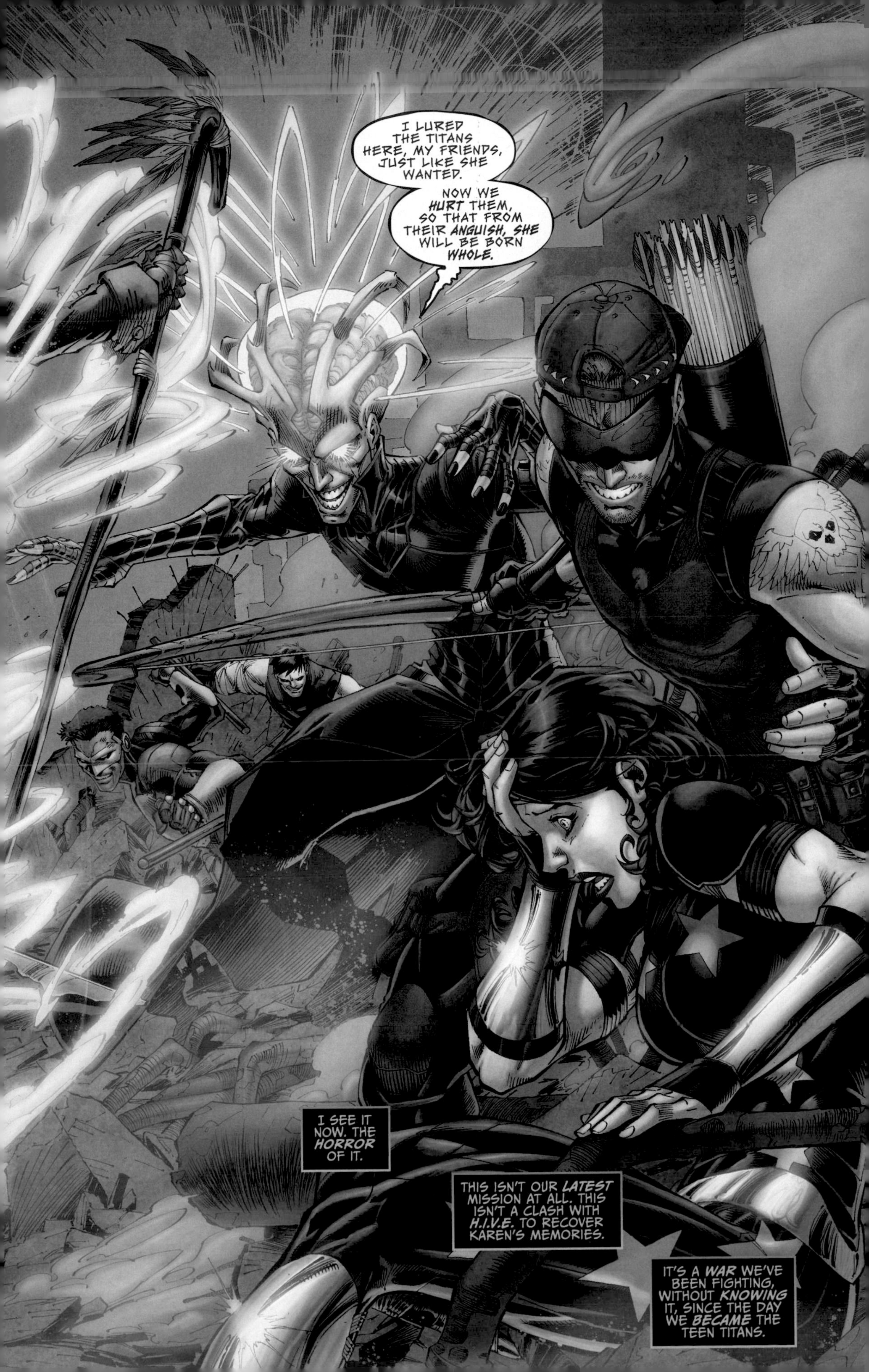
I LURED THE TITANS HERE, MY FRIENDS, JUST LIKE SHE WANTED.
NOW WE HURT THEM, SO THAT FROM THEIR ANGUISH, SHE WILL BE BORN WHOLE.
I SEE IT NOW. THE HORROR OF IT.
THIS ISN'T OUR LATEST MISSION AT ALL. THIS ISN'T A CLASH WITH H.I.V.E. TO RECOVER KAREN'S MEMORIES.
IT'S A WAR WE'VE BEEN FIGHTING, WITHOUT KNOWING IT, SINCE THE DAY WE BECAME THE TEEN TITANS.

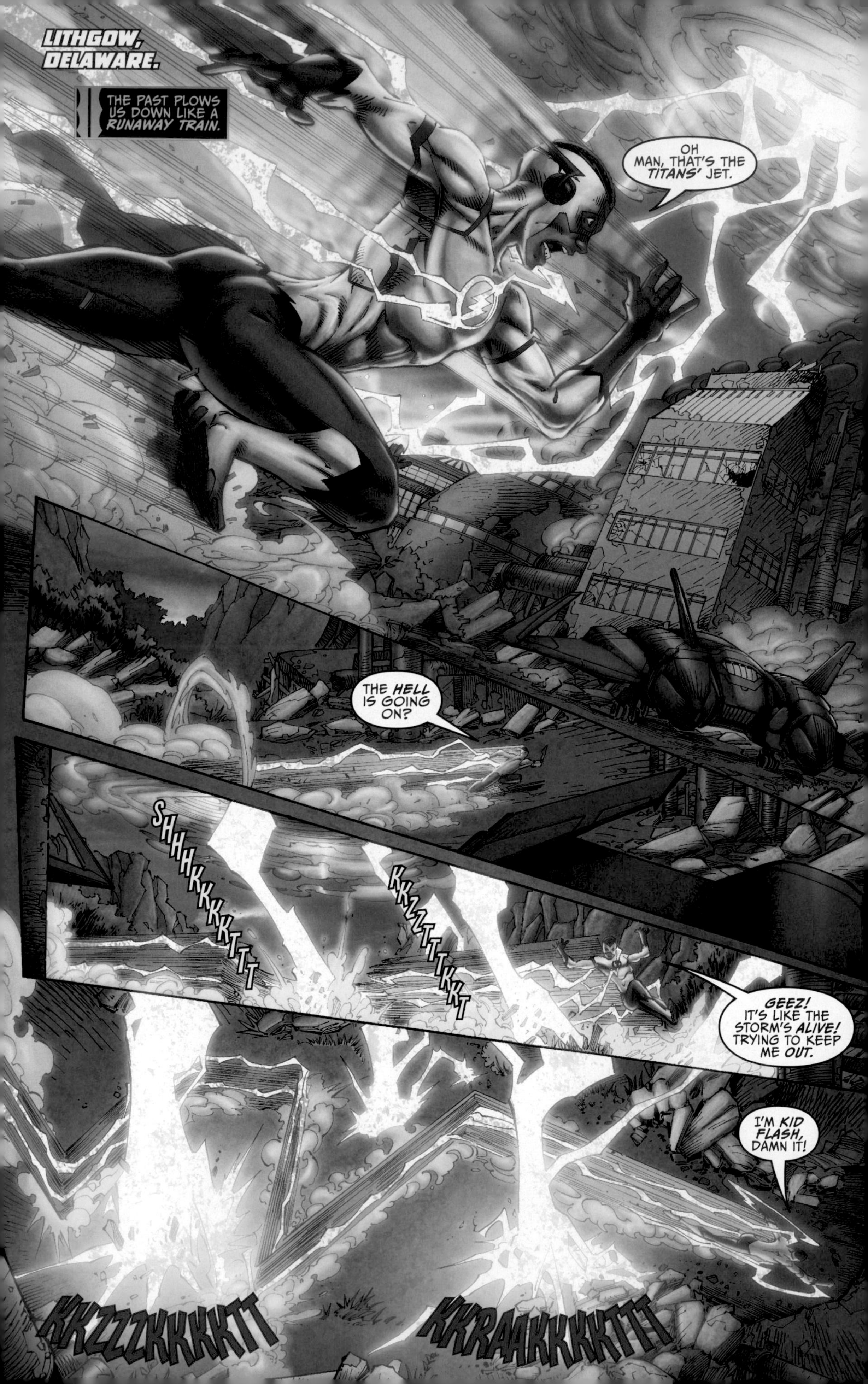
LITHGOW, DELAWARE.
THE PAST PLOWS US DOWN LIKE A RUNAWAY TRAIN.
OH MAN, THAT'S THE TITANS' JET.
THE HELL IS GOING ON?
SHHHKKKKKTTTT
KKZZTTTKKT
GEEZ! IT'S LIKE THE STORM'S ALIVE! TRYING TO KEEP ME OUT.
I'M KID FLASH, DAMN IT!
KKZZZKKKKTT
KKRAAKKKKTTT

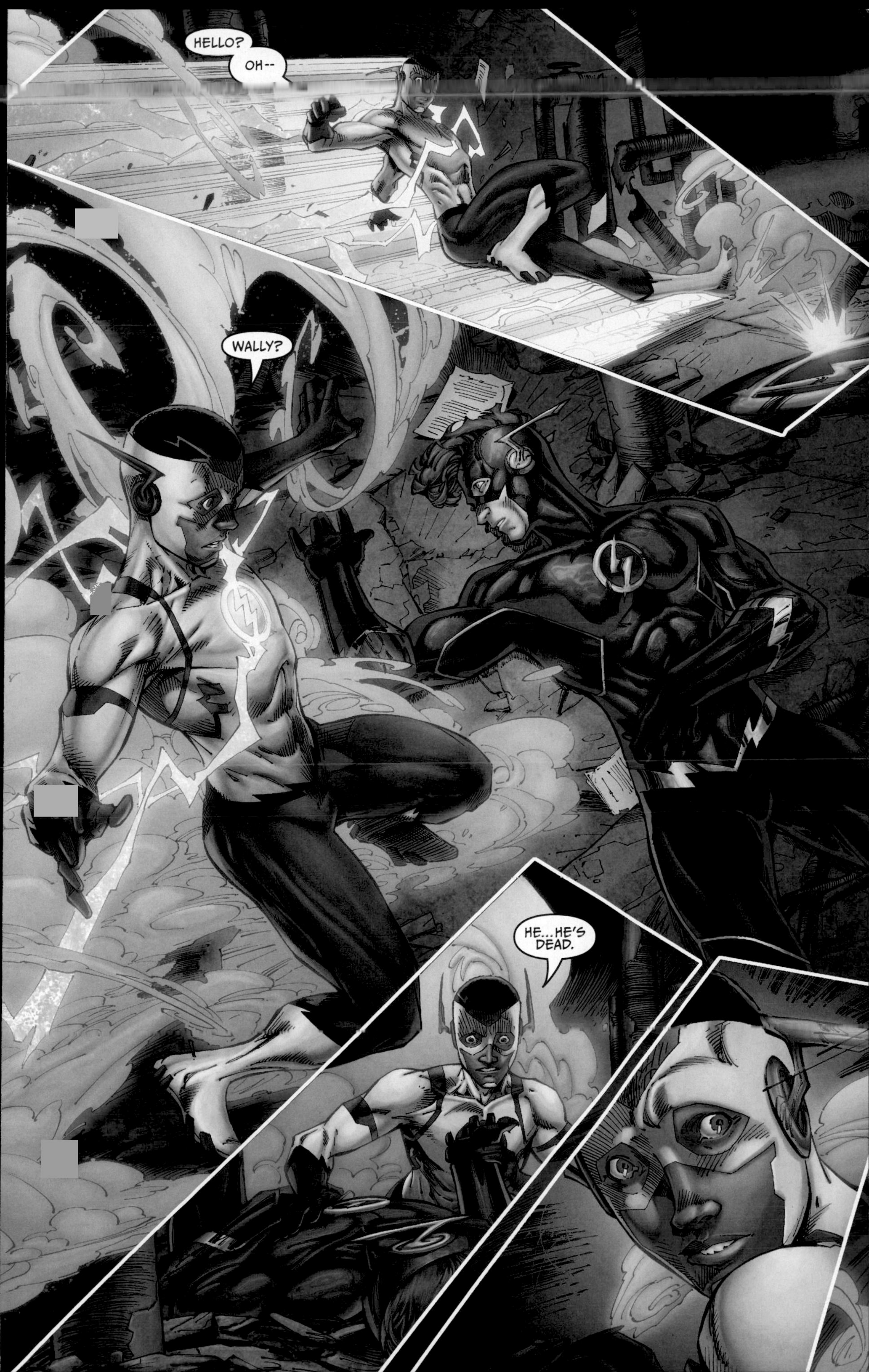
HELLO?
OH--
WALLY?
HE...HE'S DEAD.

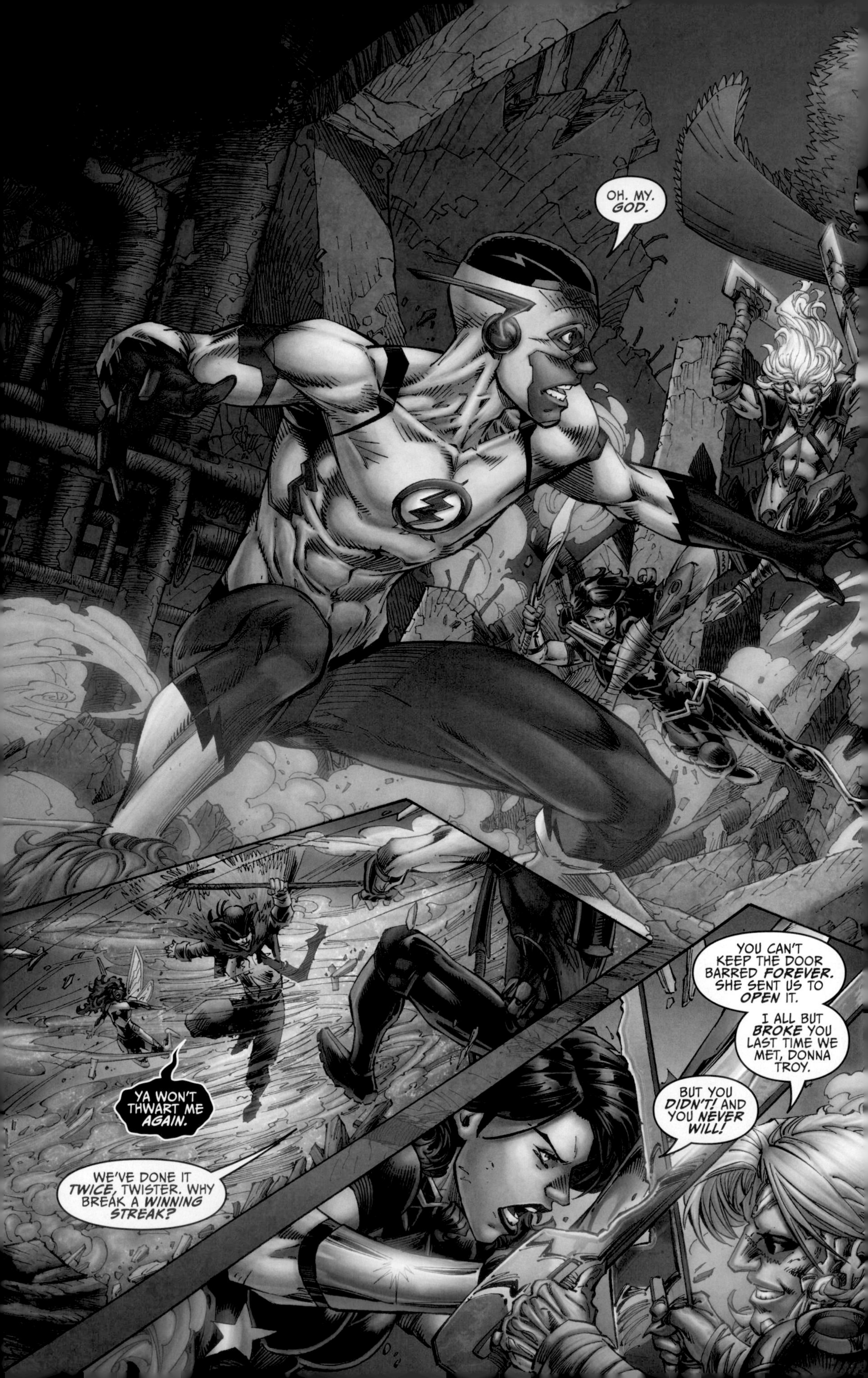
OH. MY. GOD.
YOU CAN'T KEEP THE DOOR BARRED FOREVER. SHE SENT US TO OPEN IT.
I ALL BUT BROKE YOU LAST TIME WE MET, DONNA TROY.
BUT YOU DIDN'T! AND YOU NEVER WILL!
YA WON'T THWART ME AGAIN.
WE'VE DONE IT TWICE, TWISTER. WHY BREAK A WINNING STREAK?

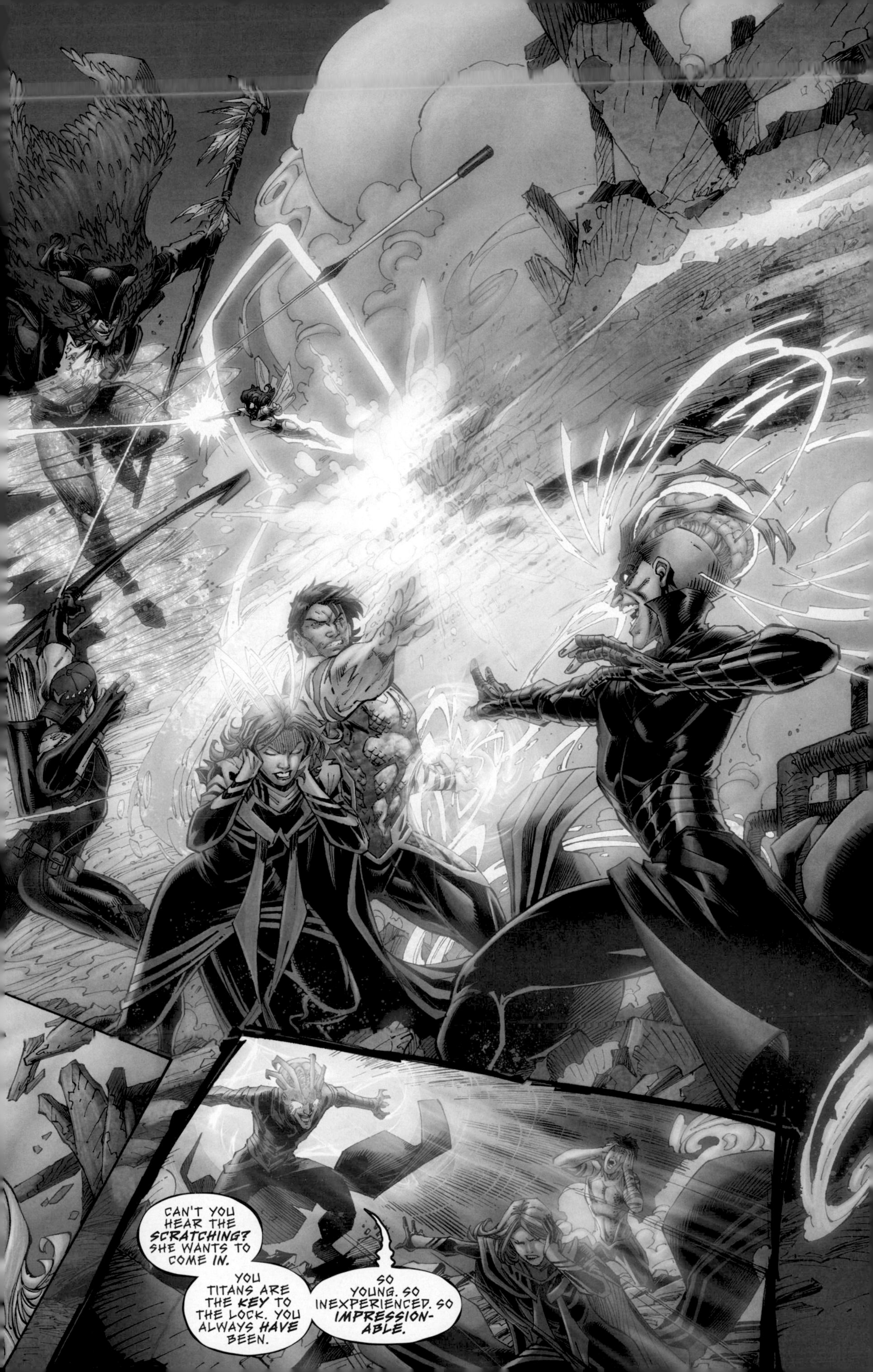

CAN'T YOU HEAR THE SCRATCHING? SHE WANTS TO COME IN.
YOU TITANS ARE THE KEY TO THE LOCK. YOU ALWAYS HAVE BEEN.
SO YOUNG. SO INEXPERIENCED. SO IMPRESSION-ABLE.

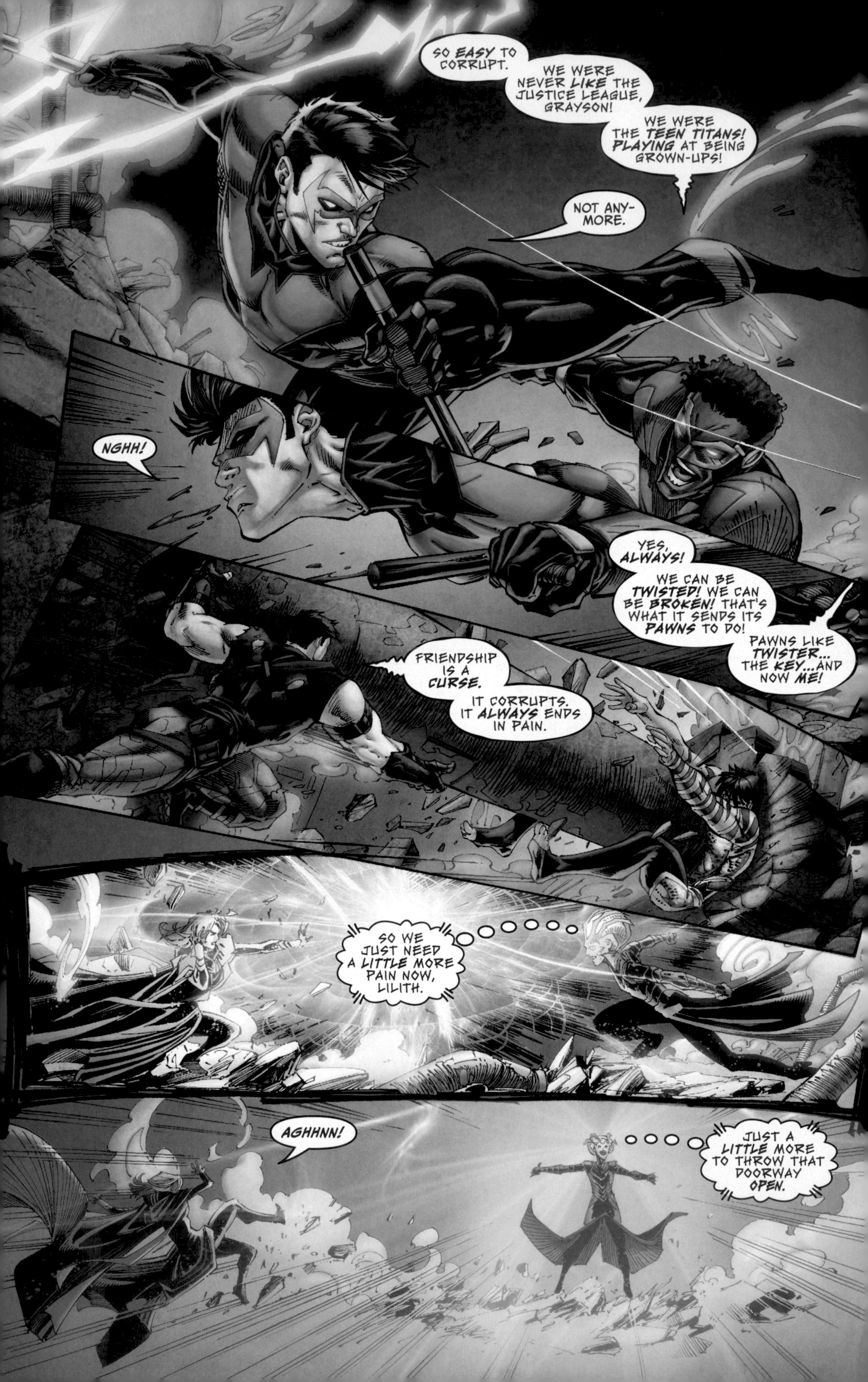
SO EASY TO CORRUPT.
WE WERE NEVER LIKE THE JUSTICE LEAGUE, GRAYSON!
WE WERE THE TEEN TITANS! PLAYING AT BEING GROWN-UPS!
NOT ANY-MORE.
NGHH!
YES, ALWAYS!
WE CAN BE TWISTED! WE CAN BE BROKEN! THAT'S WHAT IT SENDS ITS PAWNS TO DO!
PAWNS LIKE TWISTER... THE KEY...AND NOW ME!
FRIENDSHIP IS A CURSE.
IT CORRUPTS. IT ALWAYS ENDS IN PAIN.
SO WE JUST NEED A LITTLE MORE PAIN NOW, LILITH.
AGHHNN!
JUST A LITTLE MORE TO THROW THAT DOORWAY OPEN.

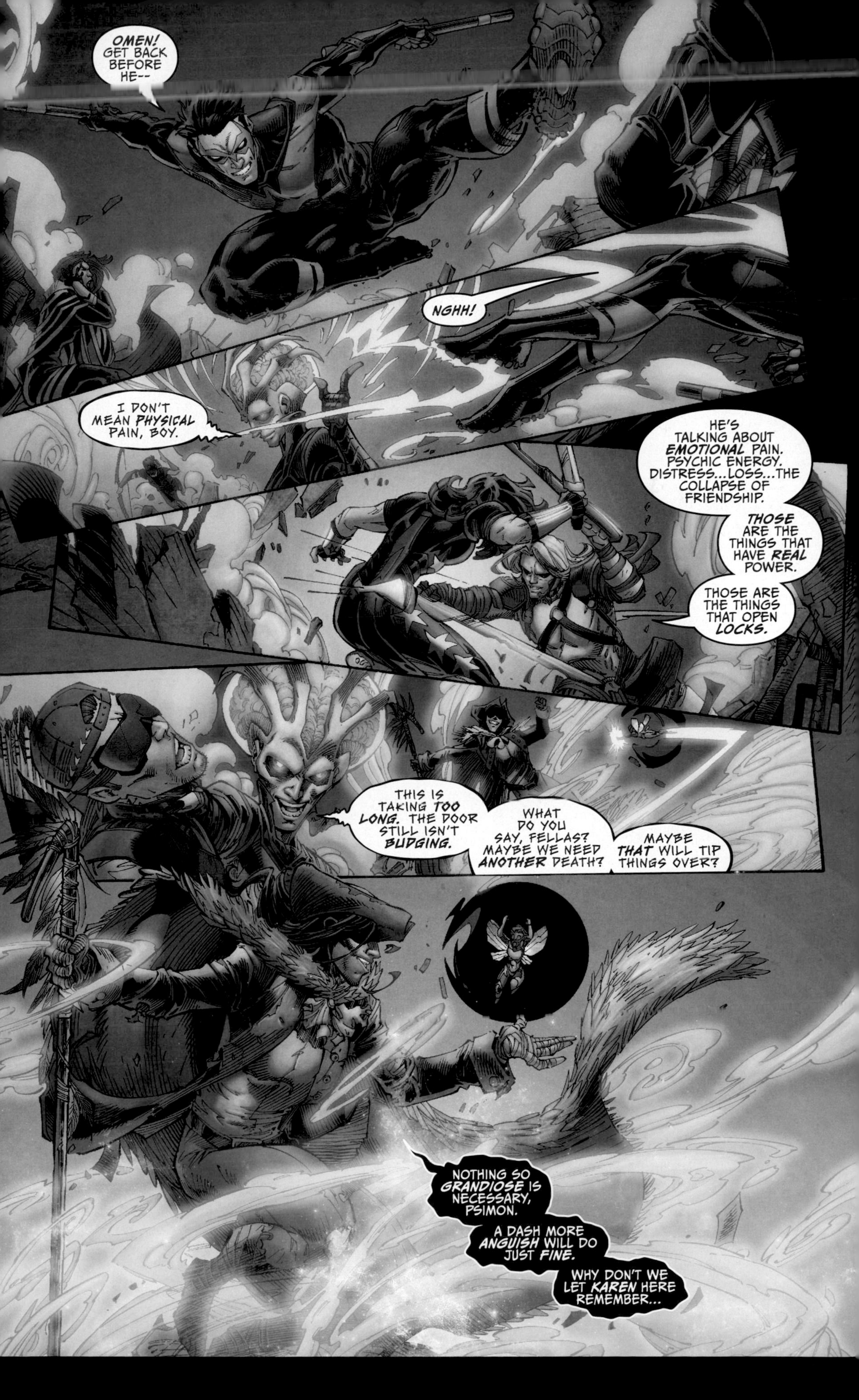

OMEN! GET BACK BEFORE HE--
NGHH!
I DON'T MEAN PHYSICAL PAIN, BOY.
HE'S TALKING ABOUT EMOTIONAL PAIN. PSYCHIC ENERGY. DISTRESS...LOSS...THE COLLAPSE OF FRIENDSHIP.
THOSE ARE THE THINGS THAT HAVE REAL POWER.
THOSE ARE THE THINGS THAT OPEN LOCKS.
THIS IS TAKING TOO LONG. THE DOOR STILL ISN'T BUDGING.
WHAT DO YOU SAY, FELLAS? MAYBE WE NEED ANOTHER DEATH?
MAYBE THAT WILL TIP THINGS OVER?
NOTHING SO GRANDIOSE IS NECESSARY, PSIMON.
A DASH MORE ANGUISH WILL DO JUST FINE.
WHY DON'T WE LET KAREN HERE REMEMBER...

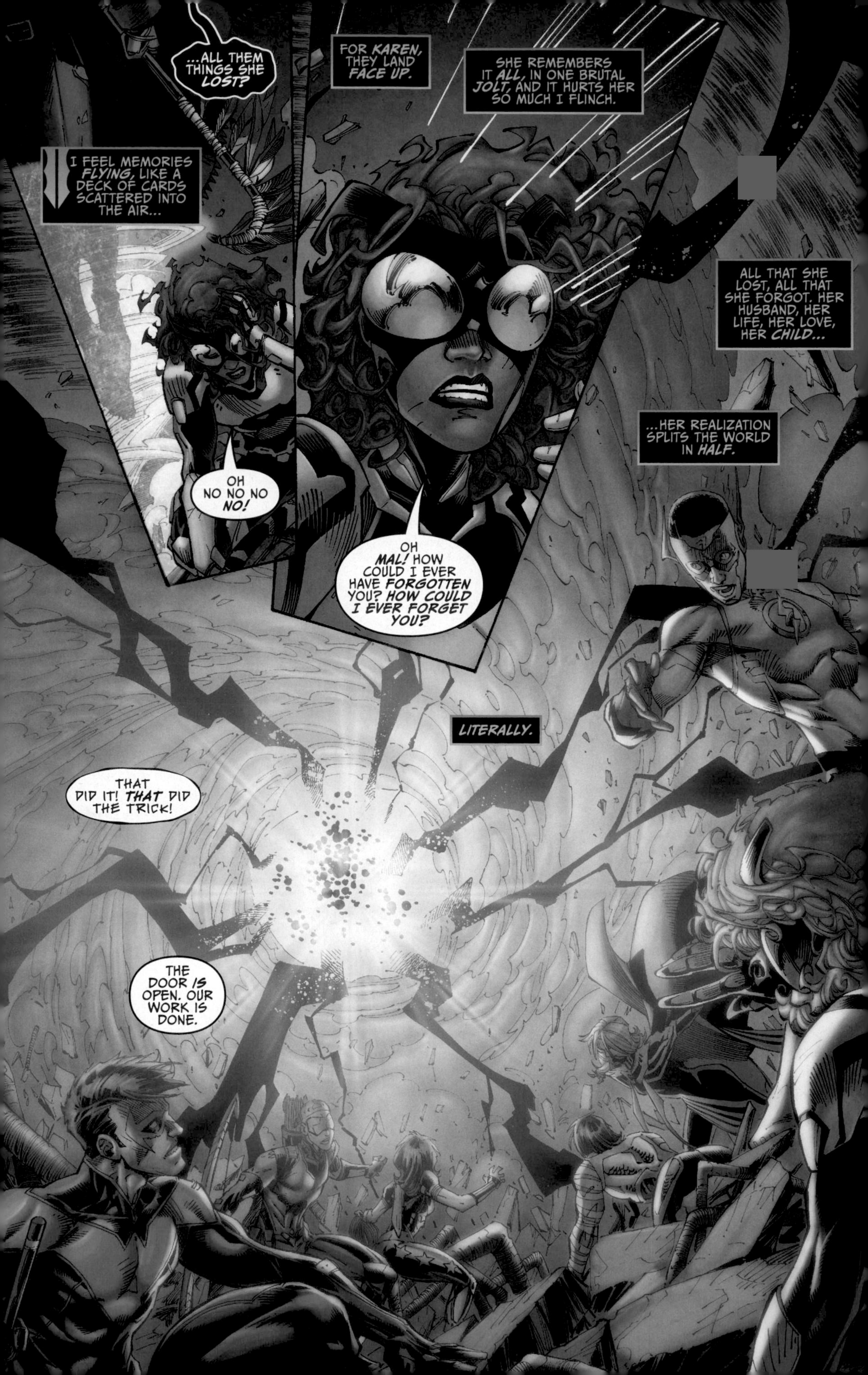

I FEEL MEMORIES FLYING, LIKE A DECK OF CARDS SCATTERED INTO THE AIR...
...ALL THEM THINGS SHE LOST?
OH NO NO NO NO!
FOR KAREN, THEY LAND FACE UP.
SHE REMEMBERS IT ALL, IN ONE BRUTAL JOLT, AND IT HURTS HER SO MUCH I FLINCH.
OH MAL! HOW COULD I EVER HAVE FORGOTTEN YOU? HOW COULD I EVER FORGET YOU?
ALL THAT SHE LOST, ALL THAT SHE FORGOT. HER HUSBAND, HER LIFE, HER LOVE, HER CHILD...
...HER REALIZATION SPLITS THE WORLD IN HALF.
LITERALLY.
THAT DID IT! THAT DID THE TRICK!
THE DOOR IS OPEN. OUR WORK IS DONE.

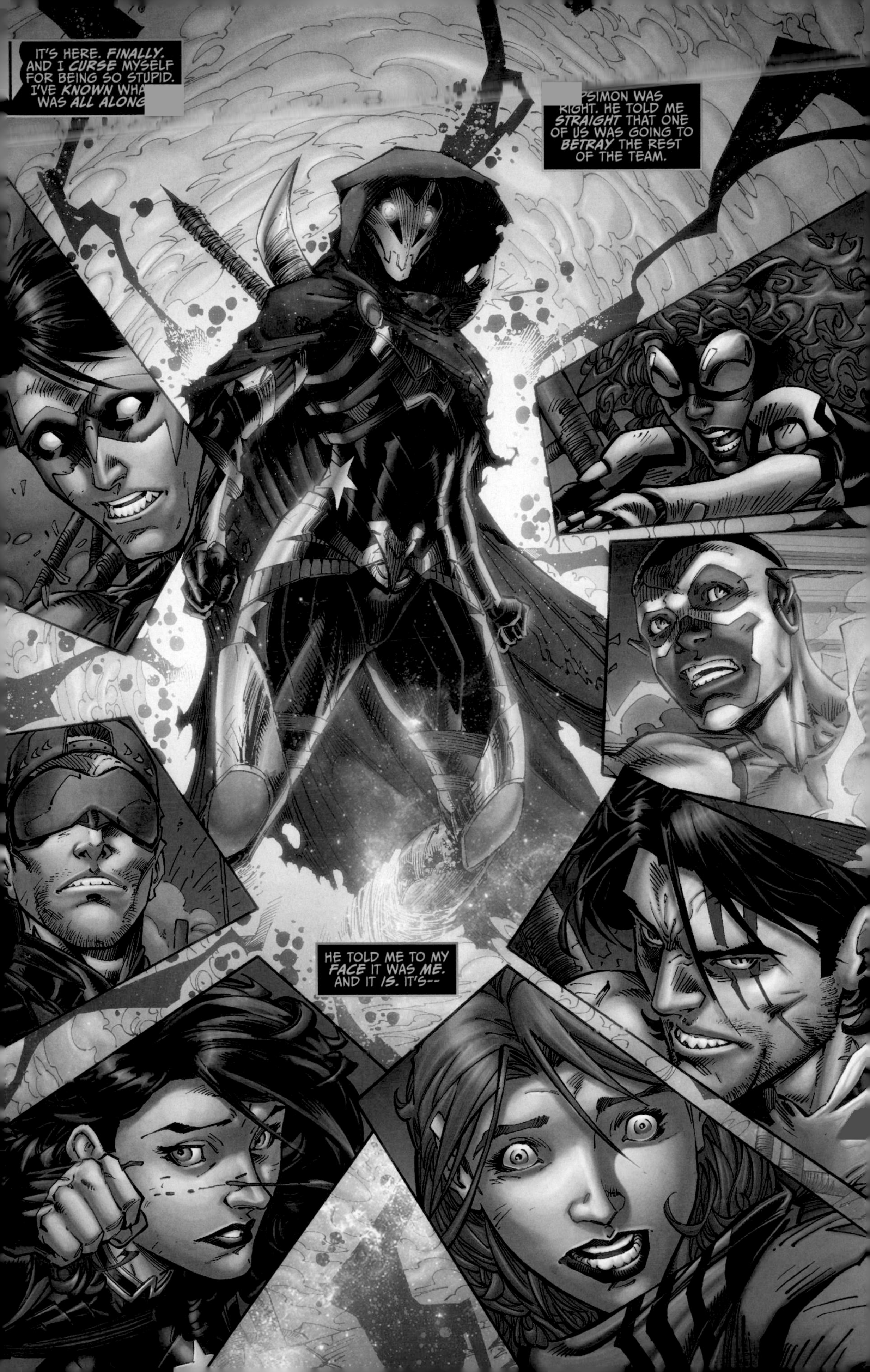
IT'S HERE. FINALLY. AND I CURSE MYSELF FOR BEING SO STUPID. I'VE KNOWN WHA WAS ALL ALONG
PSIMON WAS RIGHT. HE TOLD ME STRAIGHT THAT ONE OF US WAS GOING TO BETRAY THE REST OF THE TEAM.
HE TOLD ME TO MY FACE IT WAS ME. AND IT IS. IT'S--

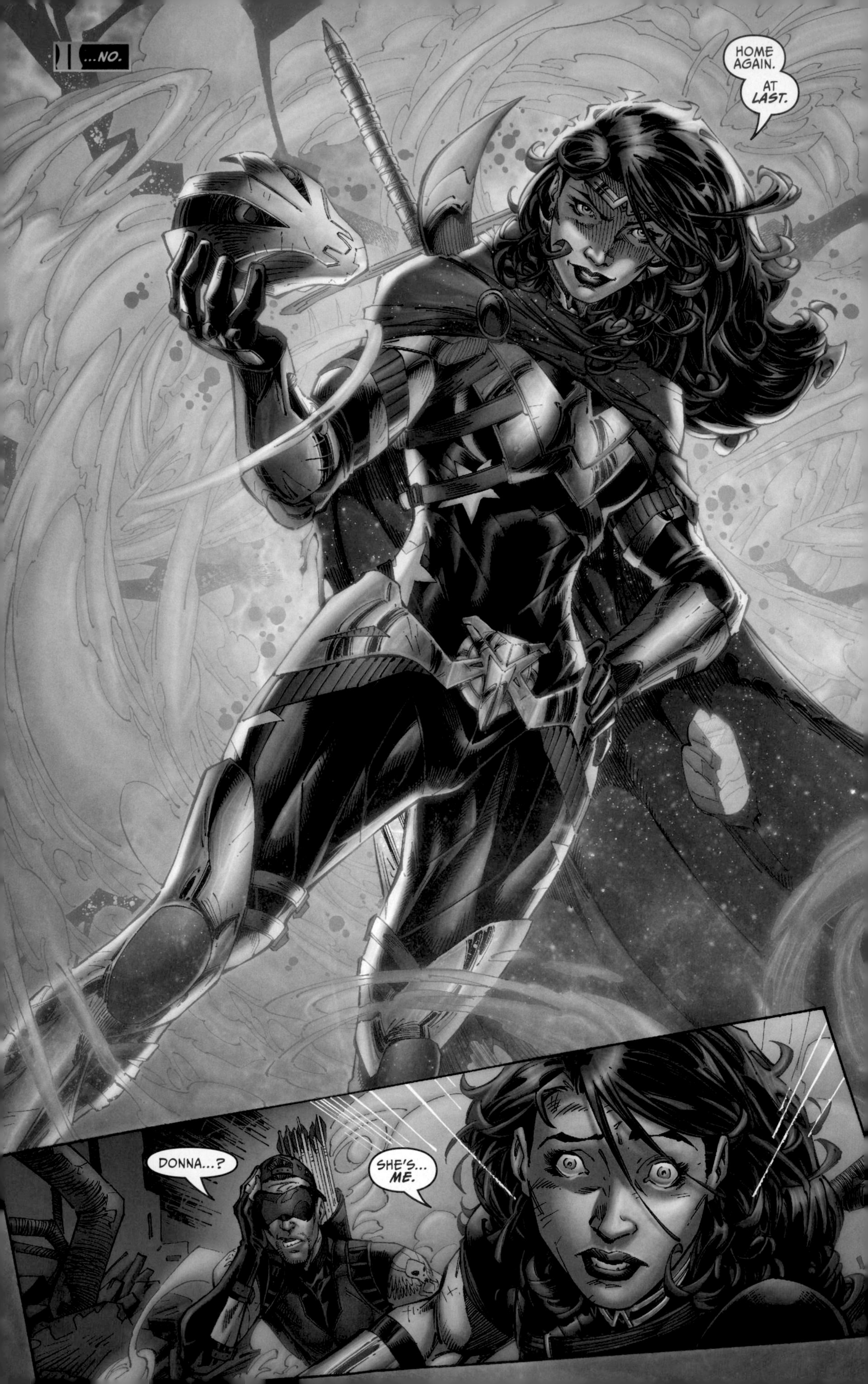

...NO.
HOME AGAIN. AT LAST.
DONNA...?
SHE'S... ME.

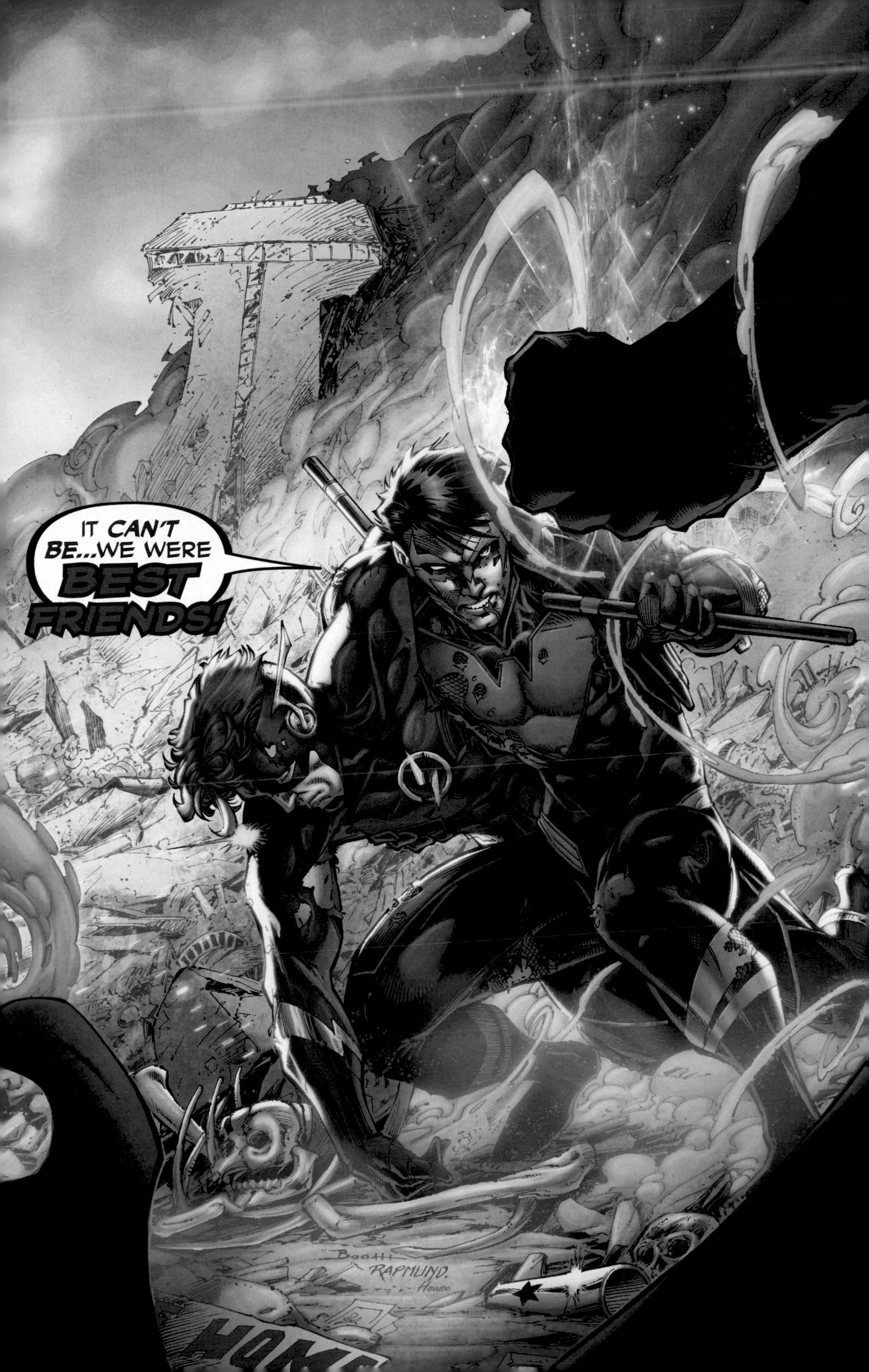
IT CAN'T BE...WE WERE BEST FRIENDS!
Booth
RAPMUND.
House

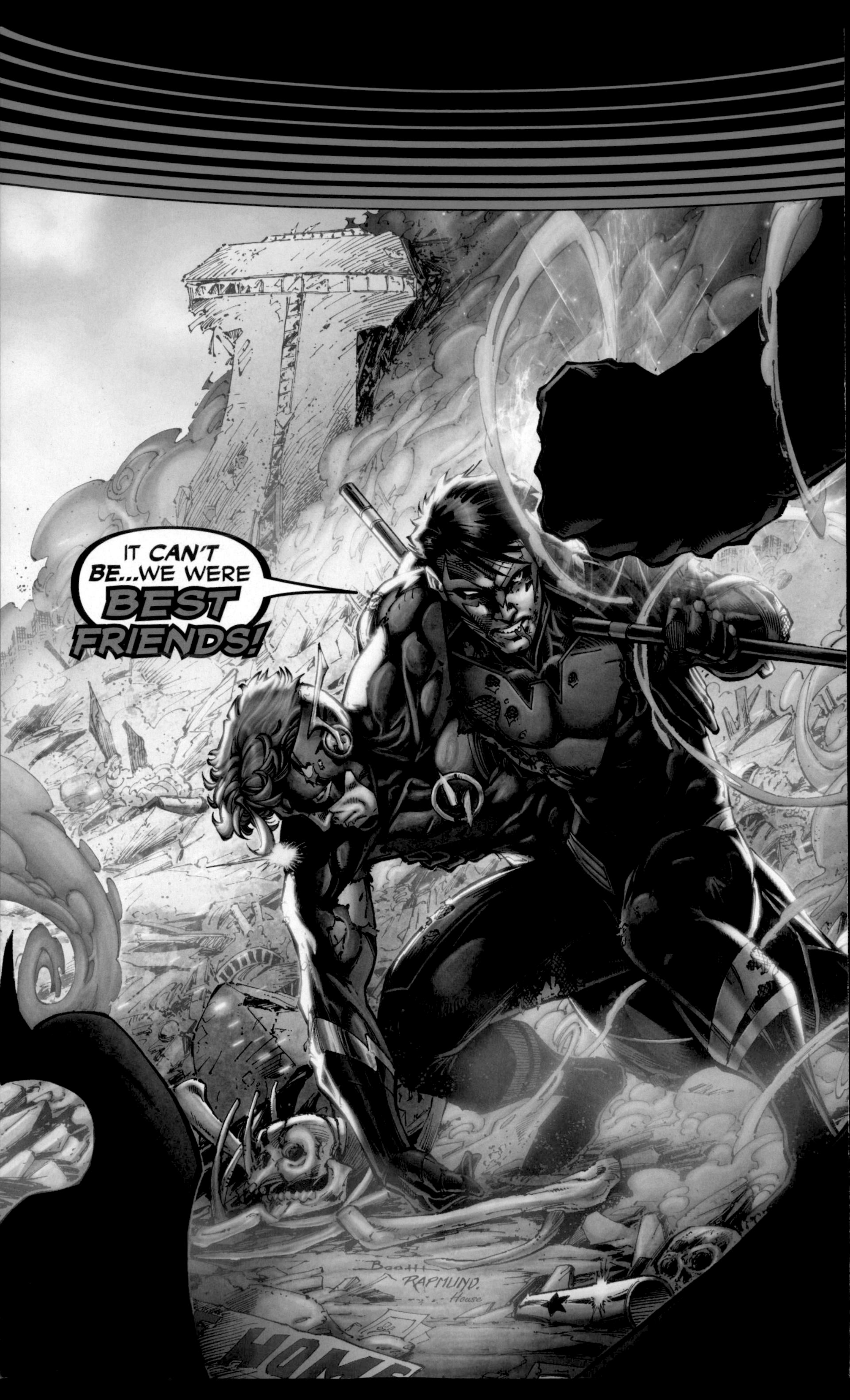
IT CAN'T BE...WE WERE BEST FRIENDS!

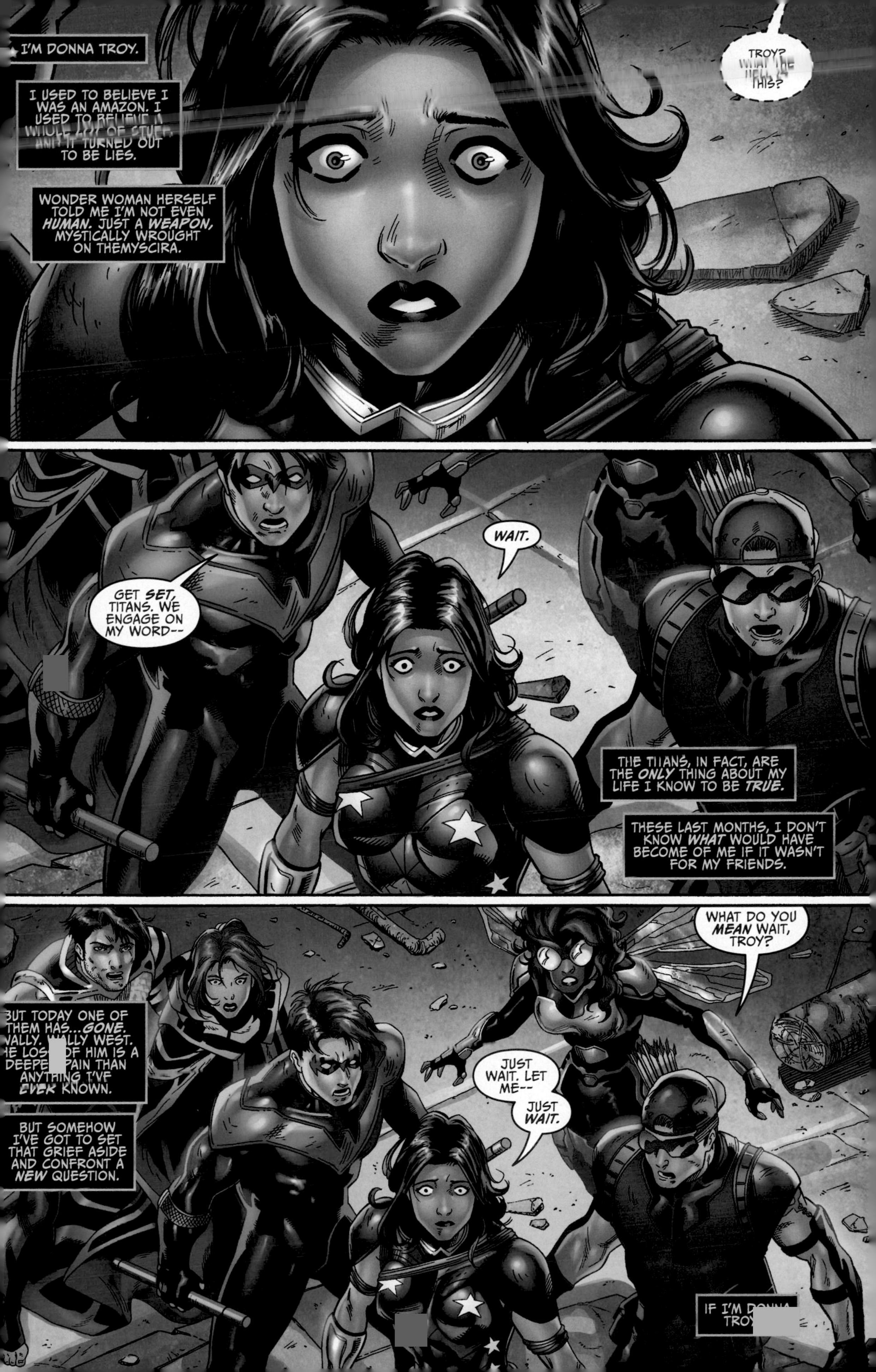
I'M DONNA TROY.
I USED TO BELIEVE I WAS AN AMAZON. I USED TO BELIEVE A WHOLE LOT OF STUFF. AND IT TURNED OUT TO BE LIES.
WONDER WOMAN HERSELF TOLD ME I'M NOT EVEN *HUMAN.* JUST A *WEAPON,* MYSTICALLY WROUGHT ON THEMYSCIRA.
TROY? WHAT THE HELL IS THIS?
GET *SET,* TITANS. WE ENGAGE ON MY WORD--
WAIT.
THE TITANS, IN FACT, ARE THE *ONLY* THING ABOUT MY LIFE I KNOW TO BE *TRUE.*
THESE LAST MONTHS, I DON'T KNOW *WHAT* WOULD HAVE BECOME OF ME IF IT WASN'T FOR MY FRIENDS.
BUT TODAY ONE OF THEM HAS...*GONE.* WALLY. WALLY WEST. THE LOSS OF HIM IS A DEEPER PAIN THAN ANYTHING I'VE *EVER* KNOWN.
BUT SOMEHOW I'VE GOT TO SET THAT GRIEF ASIDE AND CONFRONT A *NEW* QUESTION.
WHAT DO YOU *MEAN* WAIT, TROY?
JUST WAIT. LET ME--
JUST *WAIT.*
IF I'M DONNA TROY

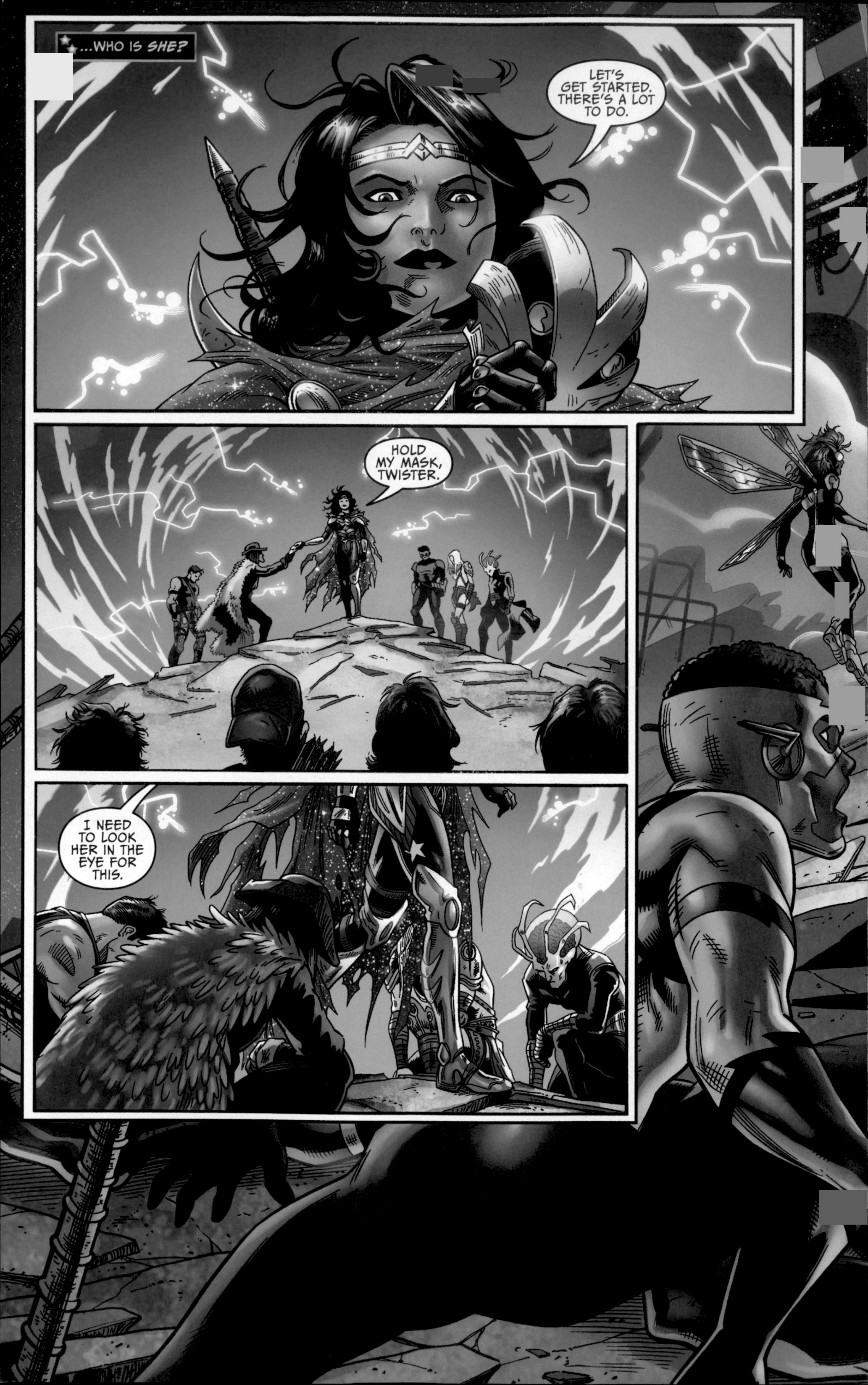
...WHO IS SHE?
LET'S GET STARTED. THERE'S A LOT TO DO.
HOLD MY MASK, TWISTER.
I NEED TO LOOK HER IN THE EYE FOR THIS.

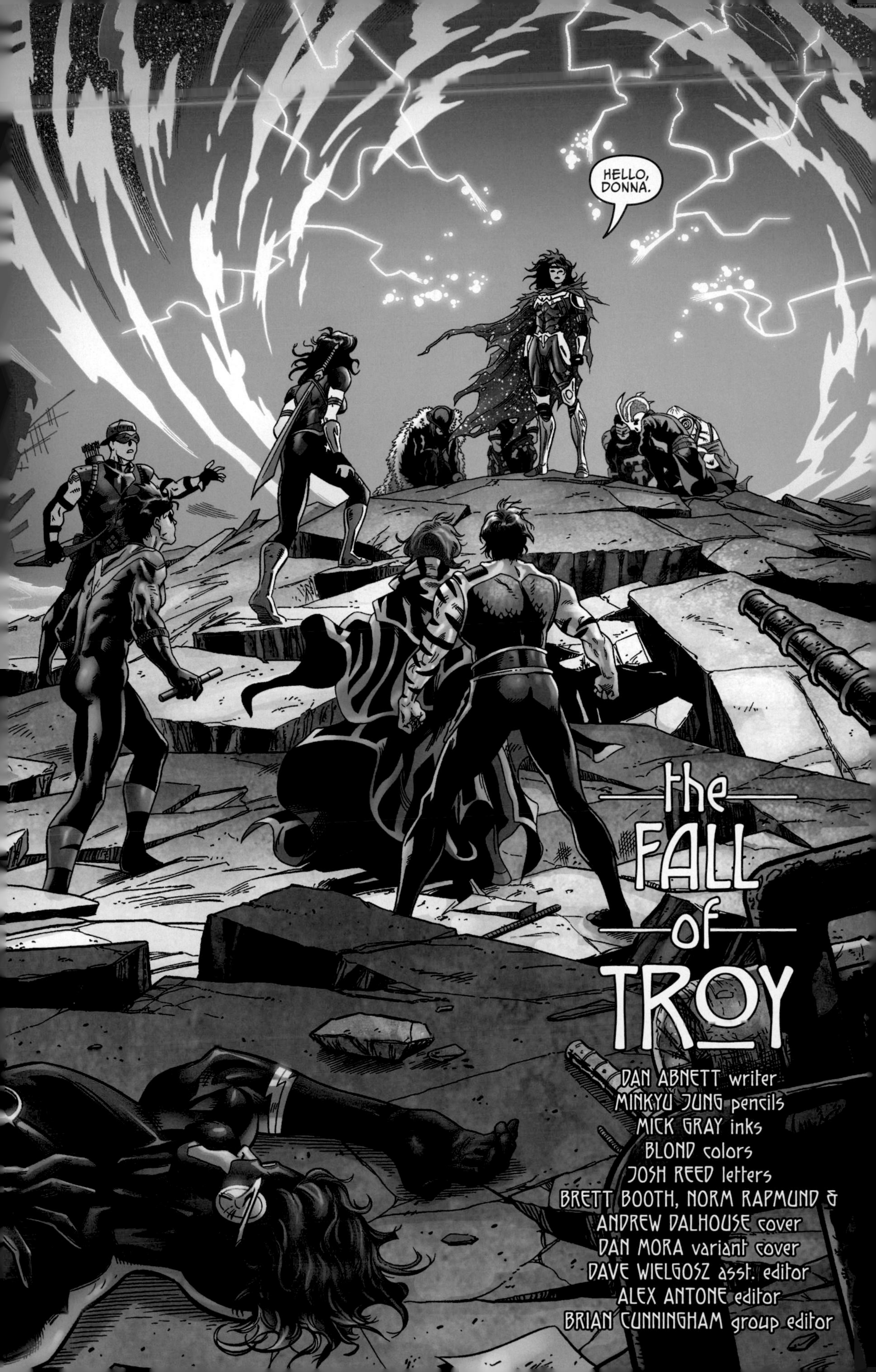
HELLO, DONNA.
the FALL of TROY
DAN ABNETT writer
MINKYU JUNG pencils
MICK GRAY inks
BLOND colors
JOSH REED letters
BRETT BOOTH, NORM RAPMUND &
ANDREW DALHOUSE cover
DAN MORA variant cover
DAVE WIELGOSZ asst. editor
ALEX ANTONE editor
BRIAN CUNNINGHAM group editor

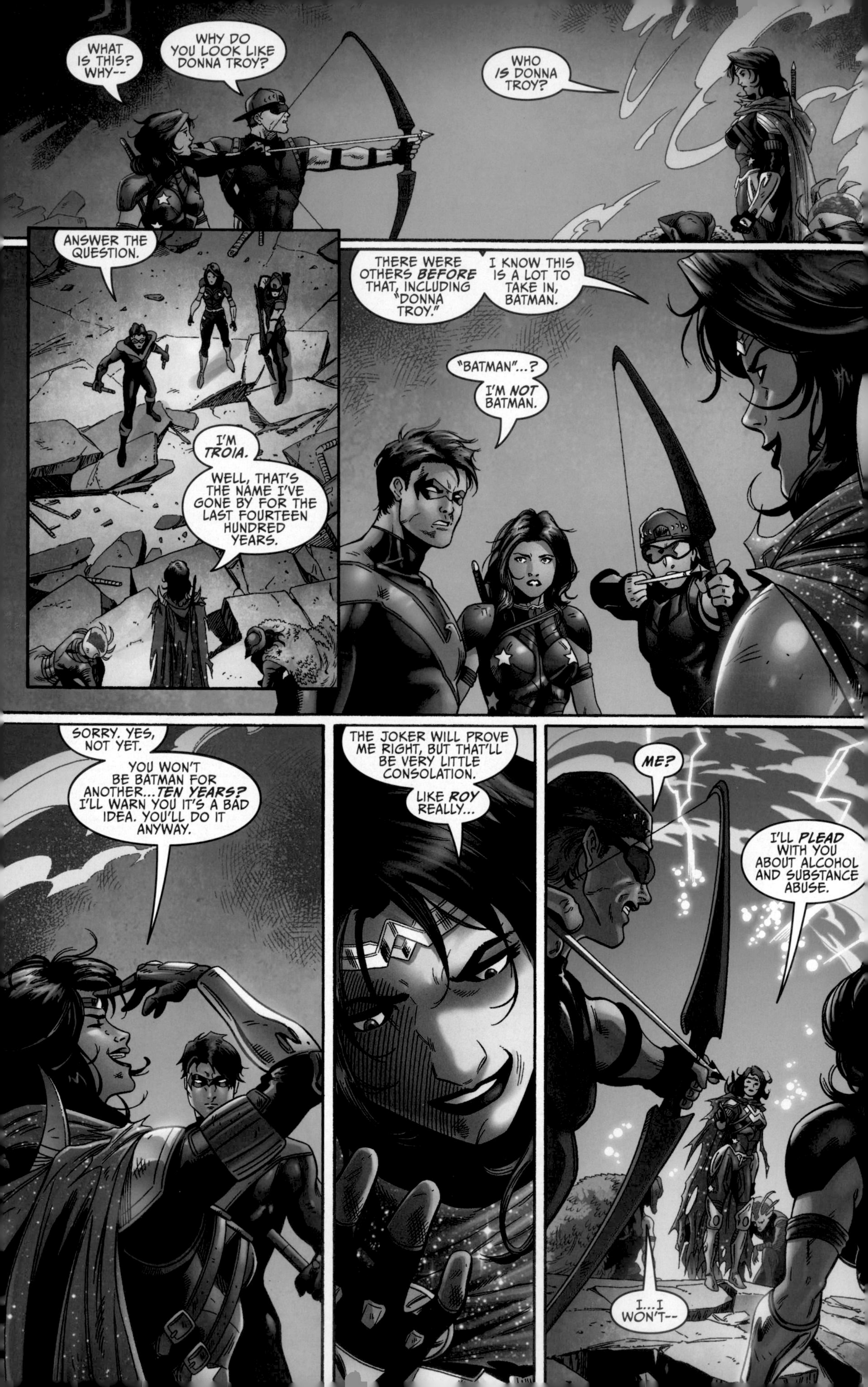
WHAT IS THIS? WHY--
WHY DO YOU LOOK LIKE DONNA TROY?
WHO *IS* DONNA TROY?
ANSWER THE QUESTION.
I'M *TROIA.*
WELL, THAT'S THE NAME I'VE GONE BY FOR THE LAST FOURTEEN HUNDRED YEARS.
THERE WERE OTHERS *BEFORE* THAT, INCLUDING "DONNA TROY."
I KNOW THIS IS A LOT TO TAKE IN, BATMAN.
"BATMAN"...?
I'M *NOT* BATMAN.
SORRY. YES, NOT YET.
YOU WON'T BE BATMAN FOR ANOTHER...*TEN YEARS?* I'LL WARN YOU IT'S A BAD IDEA. YOU'LL DO IT ANYWAY.
THE JOKER WILL PROVE ME RIGHT, BUT THAT'LL BE VERY LITTLE CONSOLATION.
LIKE *ROY* REALLY...
ME?
I'LL *PLEAD* WITH YOU ABOUT ALCOHOL AND SUBSTANCE ABUSE.
I...I WON'T--

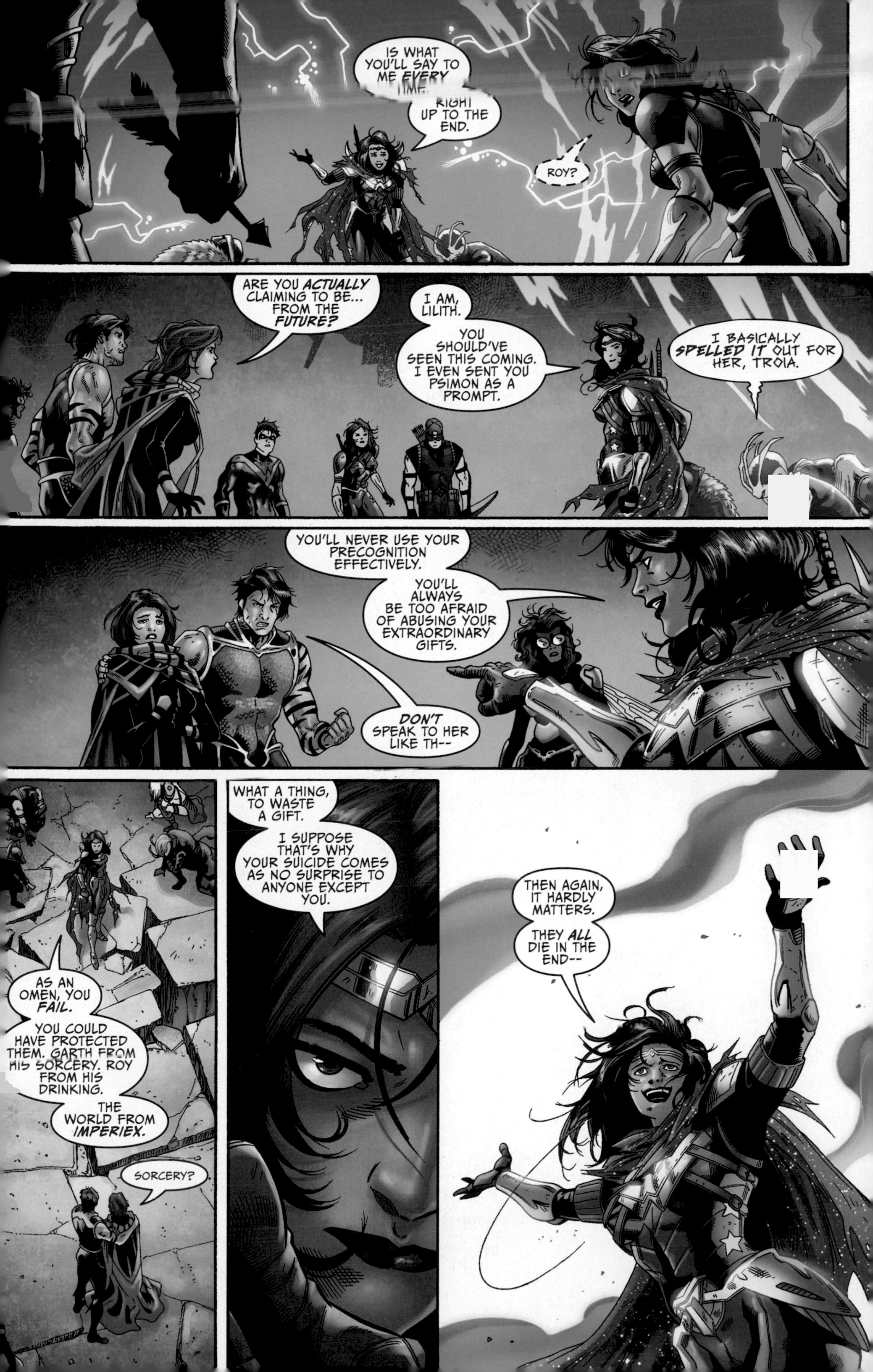
IS WHAT YOU'LL SAY TO ME EVERY
RIGHT UP TO THE END.
ROY?
ARE YOU ACTUALLY CLAIMING TO BE... FROM THE FUTURE?
I AM, LILITH.
YOU SHOULD'VE SEEN THIS COMING. I EVEN SENT YOU PSIMON AS A PROMPT.
I BASICALLY SPELLED IT OUT FOR HER, TROIA.
YOU'LL NEVER USE YOUR PRECOGNITION EFFECTIVELY.
YOU'LL ALWAYS BE TOO AFRAID OF ABUSING YOUR EXTRAORDINARY GIFTS.
DON'T SPEAK TO HER LIKE TH--
AS AN OMEN, YOU FAIL.
YOU COULD HAVE PROTECTED THEM. GARTH FROM HIS SORCERY. ROY FROM HIS DRINKING.
THE WORLD FROM IMPERIEX.
SORCERY?
WHAT A THING, TO WASTE A GIFT.
I SUPPOSE THAT'S WHY YOUR SUICIDE COMES AS NO SURPRISE TO ANYONE EXCEPT YOU.
THEN AGAIN, IT HARDLY MATTERS.
THEY ALL DIE IN THE END--

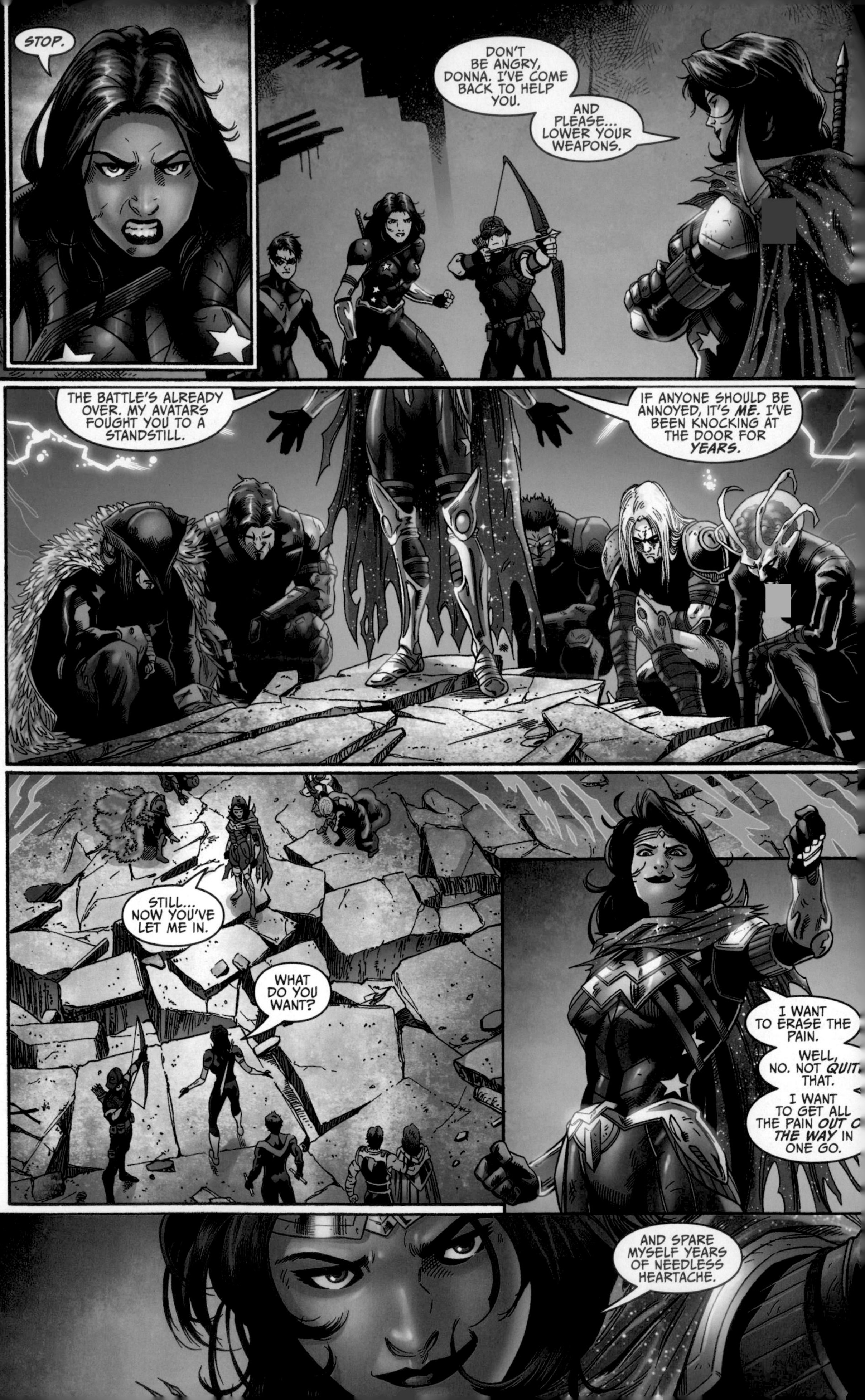
STOP.
DON'T BE ANGRY, DONNA. I'VE COME BACK TO HELP YOU.
AND PLEASE... LOWER YOUR WEAPONS.
THE BATTLE'S ALREADY OVER. MY AVATARS FOUGHT YOU TO A STANDSTILL.
IF ANYONE SHOULD BE ANNOYED, IT'S ME. I'VE BEEN KNOCKING AT THE DOOR FOR YEARS.
STILL... NOW YOU'VE LET ME IN.
WHAT DO YOU WANT?
I WANT TO ERASE THE PAIN.
WELL, NO. NOT QUIT THAT.
I WANT TO GET ALL THE PAIN OUT O THE WAY IN ONE GO.
AND SPARE MYSELF YEARS OF NEEDLESS HEARTACHE.

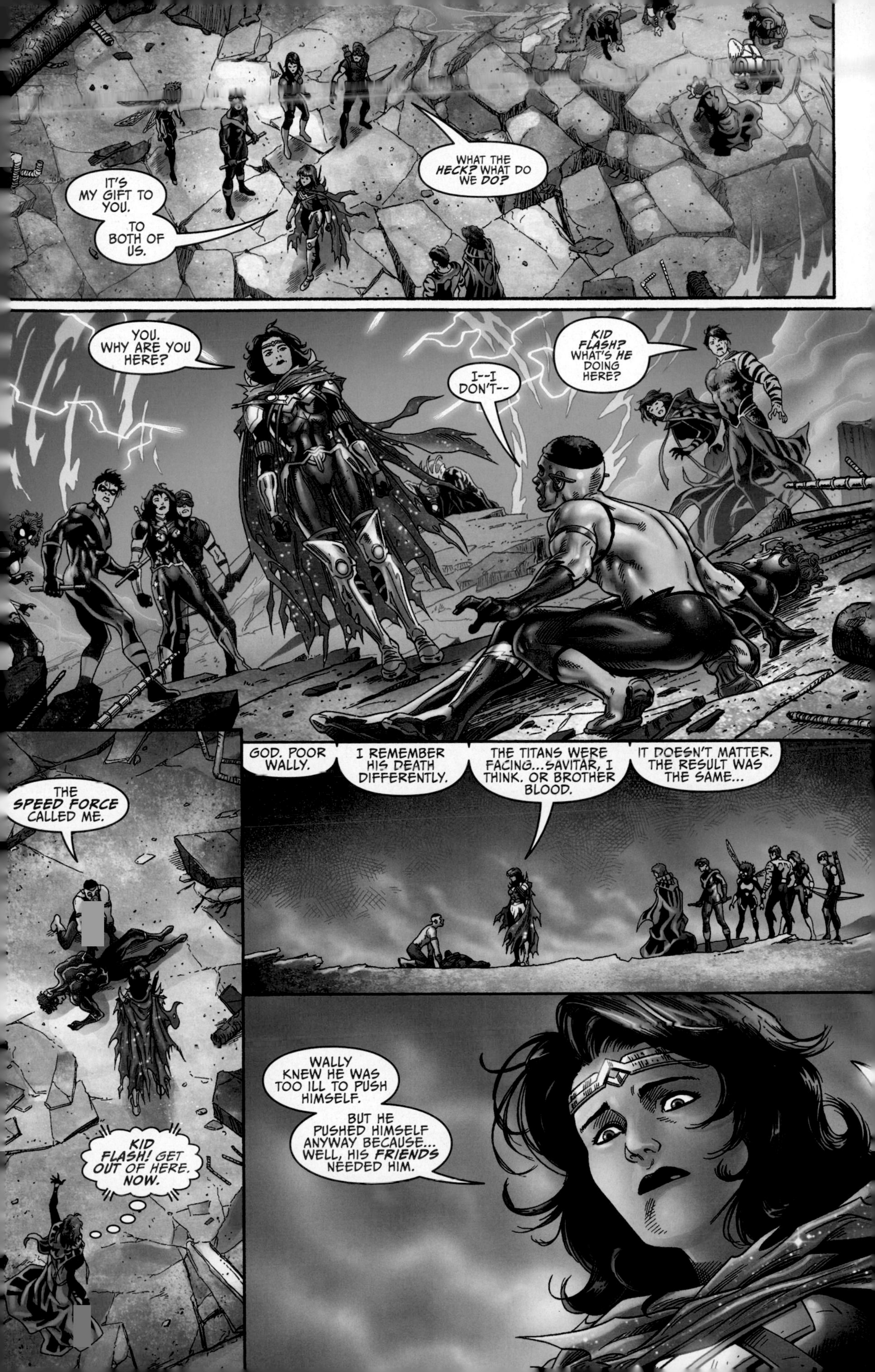
IT'S MY GIFT TO YOU.
TO BOTH OF US.
WHAT THE HECK? WHAT DO WE DO?
YOU. WHY ARE YOU HERE?
I--I DON'T--
KID FLASH? WHAT'S HE DOING HERE?
THE SPEED FORCE CALLED ME.
KID FLASH! GET OUT OF HERE. NOW.
GOD. POOR WALLY.
I REMEMBER HIS DEATH DIFFERENTLY.
THE TITANS WERE FACING...SAVITAR, I THINK. OR BROTHER BLOOD.
IT DOESN'T MATTER. THE RESULT WAS THE SAME...
WALLY KNEW HE WAS TOO ILL TO PUSH HIMSELF.
BUT HE PUSHED HIMSELF ANYWAY BECAUSE... WELL, HIS FRIENDS NEEDED HIM.

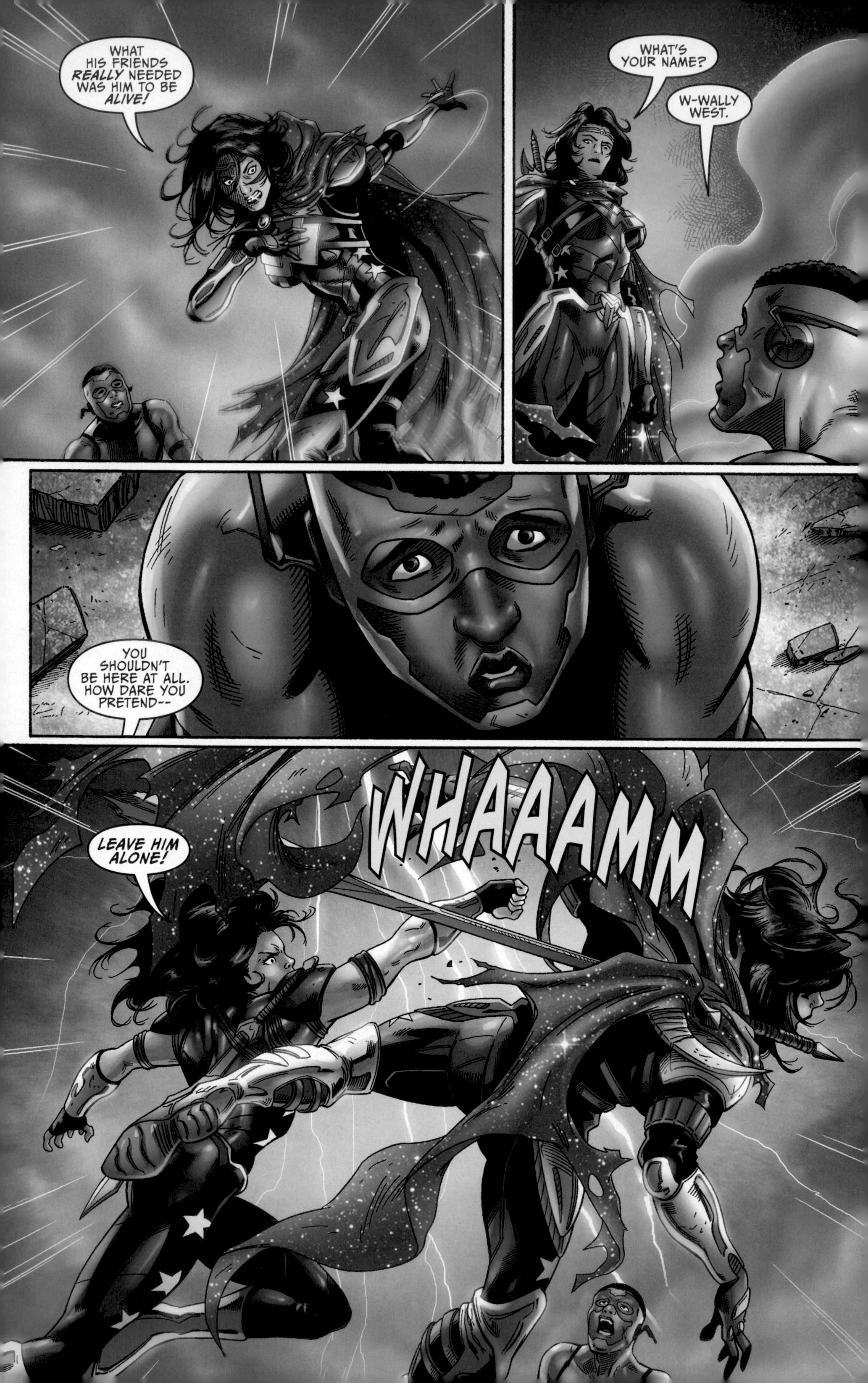
WHAT HIS FRIENDS *REALLY* NEEDED WAS HIM TO BE *ALIVE!*
WHAT'S YOUR NAME?
W-WALLY WEST.
YOU SHOULDN'T BE HERE AT ALL. HOW DARE YOU PRETEND--
LEAVE HIM ALONE!
WHAAAMM

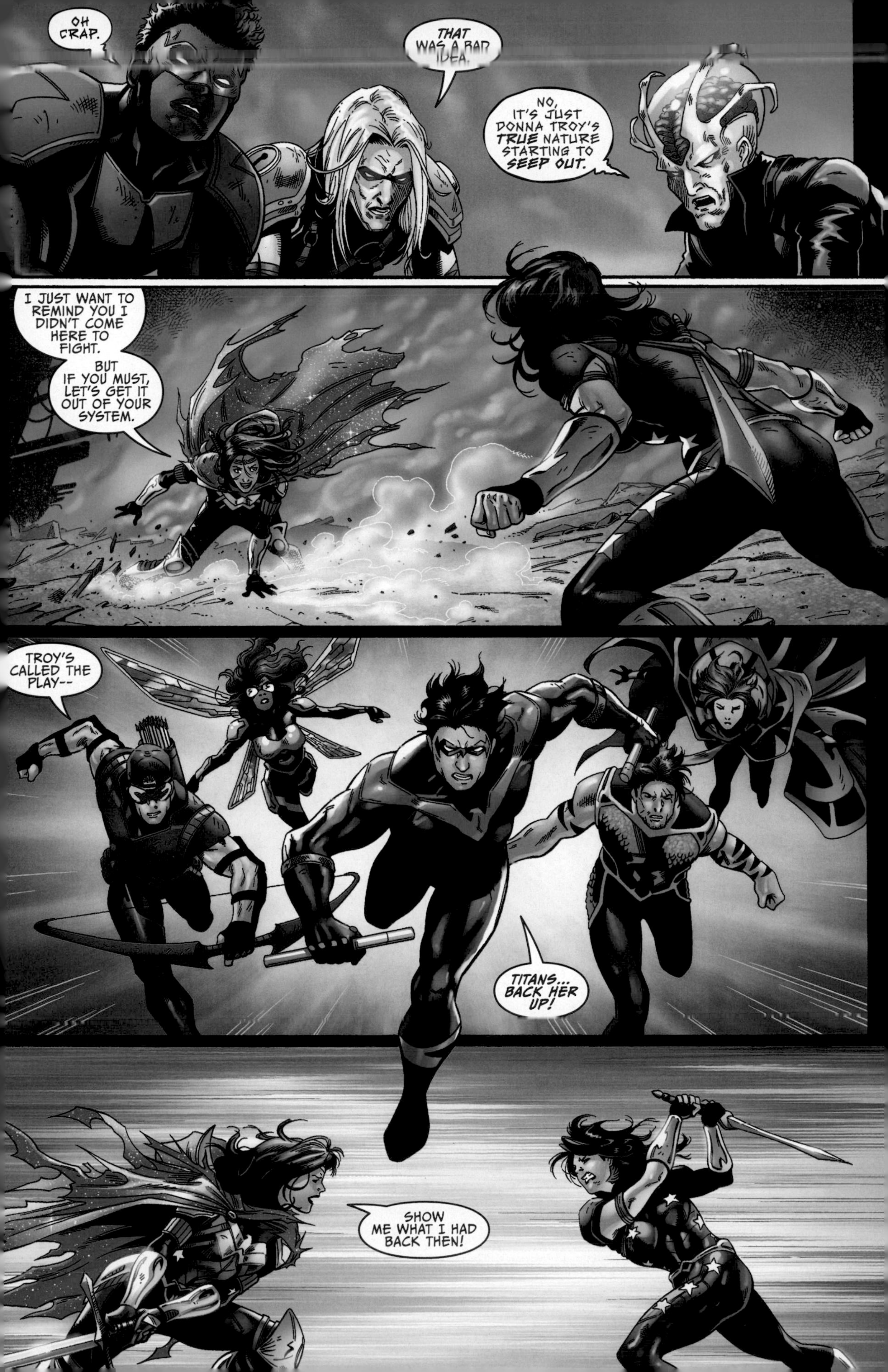

OH CRAP.
THAT WAS A BAD IDEA.
NO, IT'S JUST DONNA TROY'S TRUE NATURE STARTING TO SEEP OUT.
I JUST WANT TO REMIND YOU I DIDN'T COME HERE TO FIGHT.
BUT IF YOU MUST, LET'S GET IT OUT OF YOUR SYSTEM.
TROY'S CALLED THE PLAY--
TITANS... BACK HER UP!
SHOW ME WHAT I HAD BACK THEN!

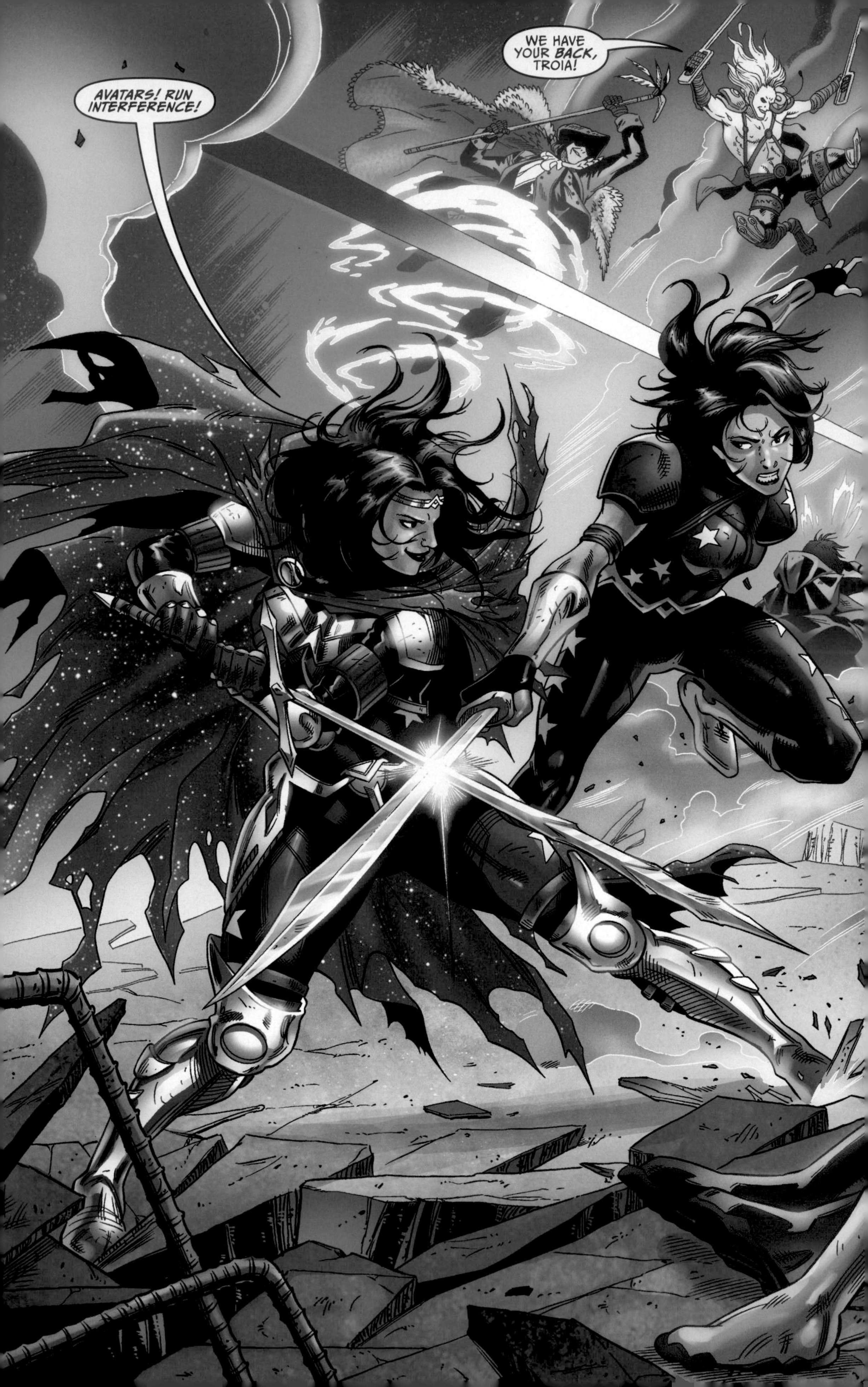
AVATARS! RUN INTERFERENCE!
WE HAVE YOUR BACK, TROIA!

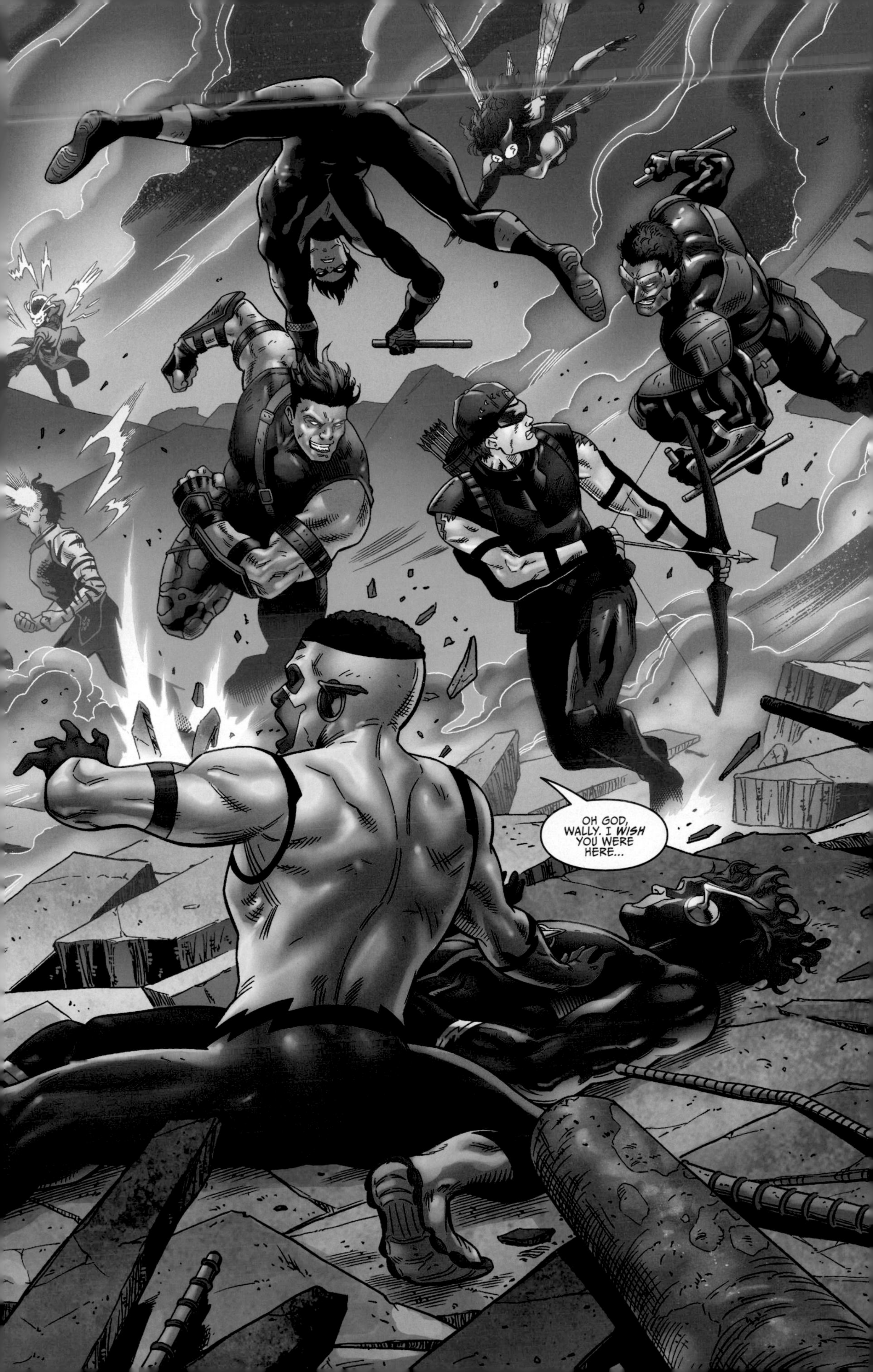
OH GOD, WALLY. I WISH YOU WERE HERE...

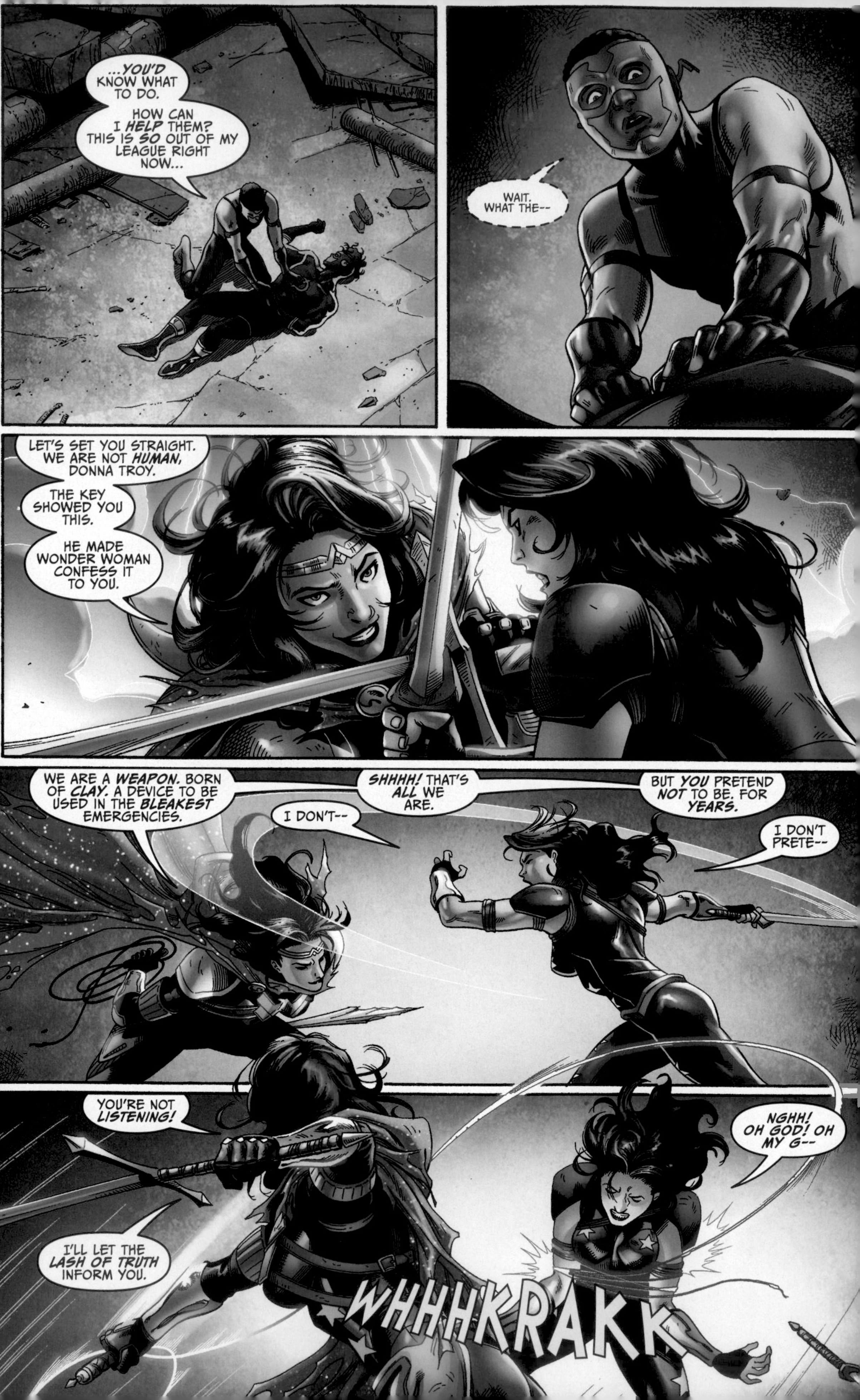
...YOU'D KNOW WHAT TO DO.
HOW CAN I HELP THEM? THIS IS SO OUT OF MY LEAGUE RIGHT NOW...
WAIT. WHAT THE--
LET'S SET YOU STRAIGHT. WE ARE NOT HUMAN, DONNA TROY.
THE KEY SHOWED YOU THIS.
HE MADE WONDER WOMAN CONFESS IT TO YOU.
WE ARE A WEAPON. BORN OF CLAY. A DEVICE TO BE USED IN THE BLEAKEST EMERGENCIES.
I DON'T--
SHHHH! THAT'S ALL WE ARE.
BUT YOU PRETEND NOT TO BE. FOR YEARS.
I DON'T PRETE--
YOU'RE NOT LISTENING!
I'LL LET THE LASH OF TRUTH INFORM YOU.
NGHH! OH GOD! OH MY G--
WHHHKRAKK

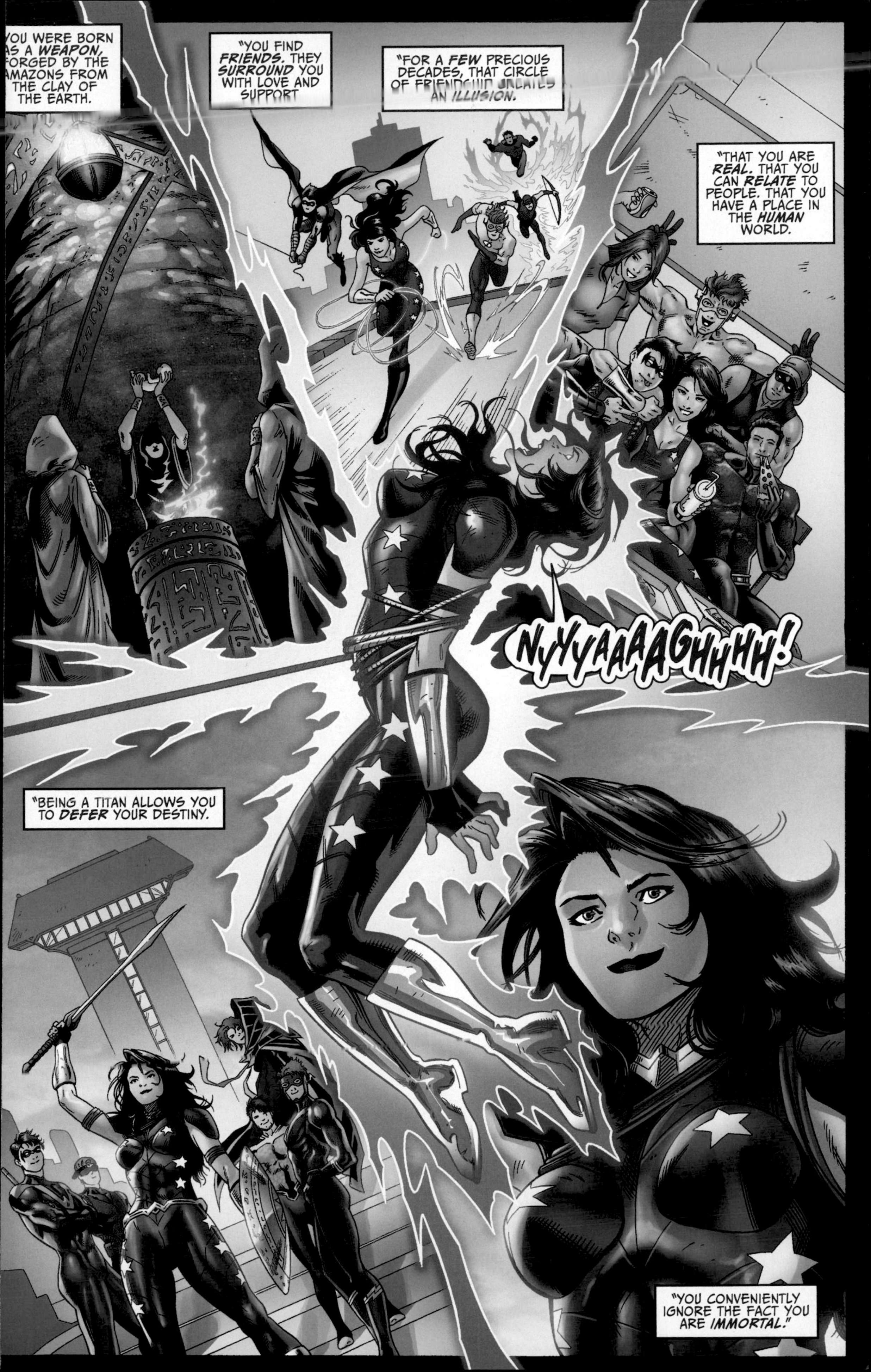
"YOU WERE BORN AS A *WEAPON*, FORGED BY THE AMAZONS FROM THE CLAY OF THE EARTH.
"YOU FIND *FRIENDS*. THEY *SURROUND* YOU WITH LOVE AND SUPPORT
"FOR A *FEW* PRECIOUS DECADES, THAT CIRCLE OF FRIENDSHIP CREATES AN *ILLUSION*.
"THAT YOU ARE *REAL*. THAT YOU CAN *RELATE* TO PEOPLE. THAT YOU HAVE A PLACE IN THE *HUMAN* WORLD.
NYYYAAAAGHHHH!
"BEING A TITAN ALLOWS YOU TO *DEFER* YOUR DESTINY.
"YOU CONVENIENTLY IGNORE THE FACT YOU ARE *IMMORTAL*."

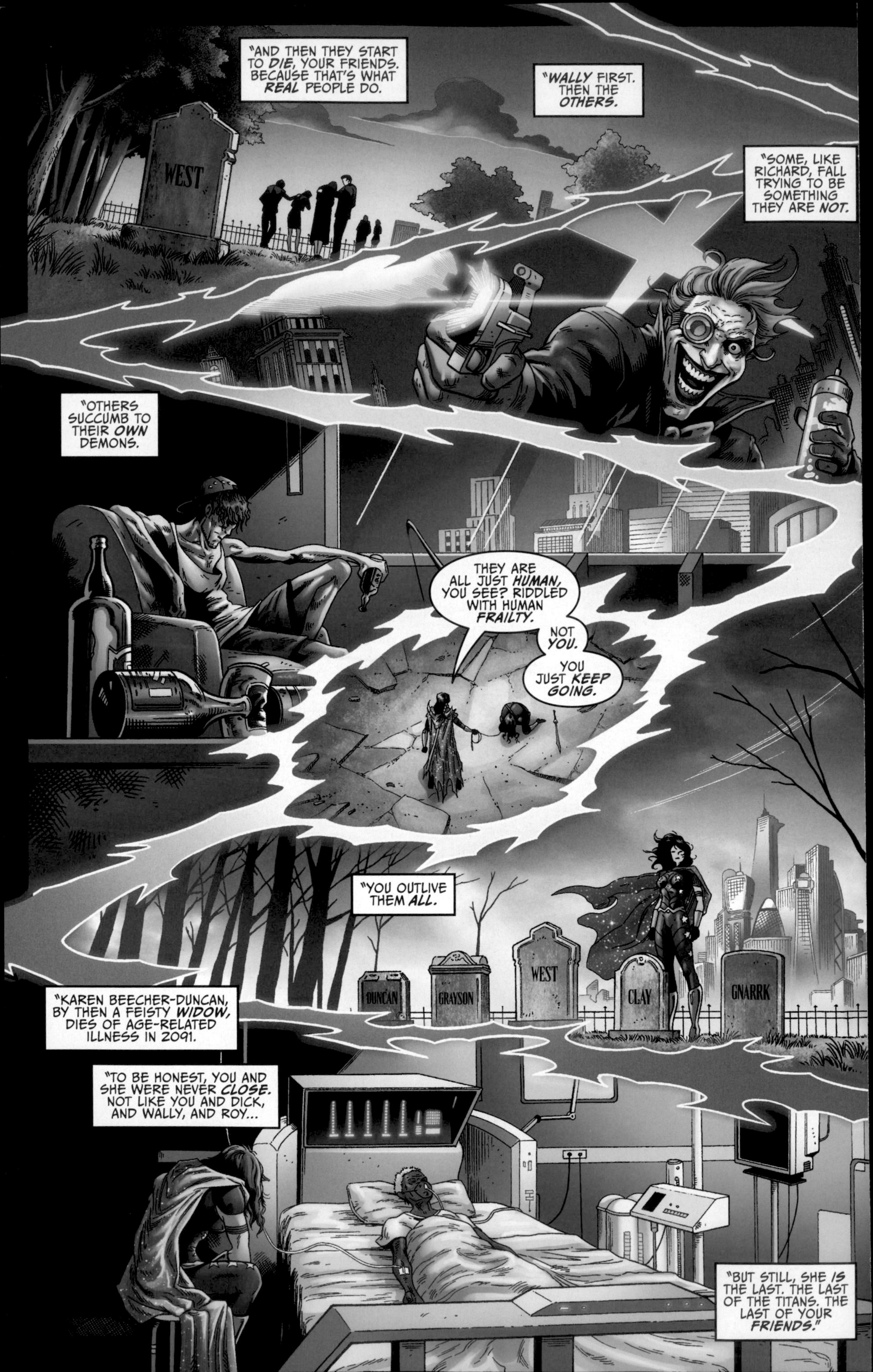
"AND THEN THEY START TO DIE, YOUR FRIENDS. BECAUSE THAT'S WHAT REAL PEOPLE DO.
WEST
"WALLY FIRST. THEN THE OTHERS.
"SOME, LIKE RICHARD, FALL TRYING TO BE SOMETHING THEY ARE NOT.
"OTHERS SUCCUMB TO THEIR OWN DEMONS.
THEY ARE ALL JUST HUMAN, YOU SEE? RIDDLED WITH HUMAN FRAILTY.
NOT YOU.
YOU JUST KEEP GOING.
"YOU OUTLIVE THEM ALL.
DUNCAN
GRAYSON
WEST
CLAY
GNARRK
"KAREN BEECHER-DUNCAN, BY THEN A FEISTY WIDOW, DIES OF AGE-RELATED ILLNESS IN 2091.
"TO BE HONEST, YOU AND SHE WERE NEVER CLOSE. NOT LIKE YOU AND DICK, AND WALLY, AND ROY...
"BUT STILL, SHE IS THE LAST. THE LAST OF THE TITANS. THE LAST OF YOUR FRIENDS."

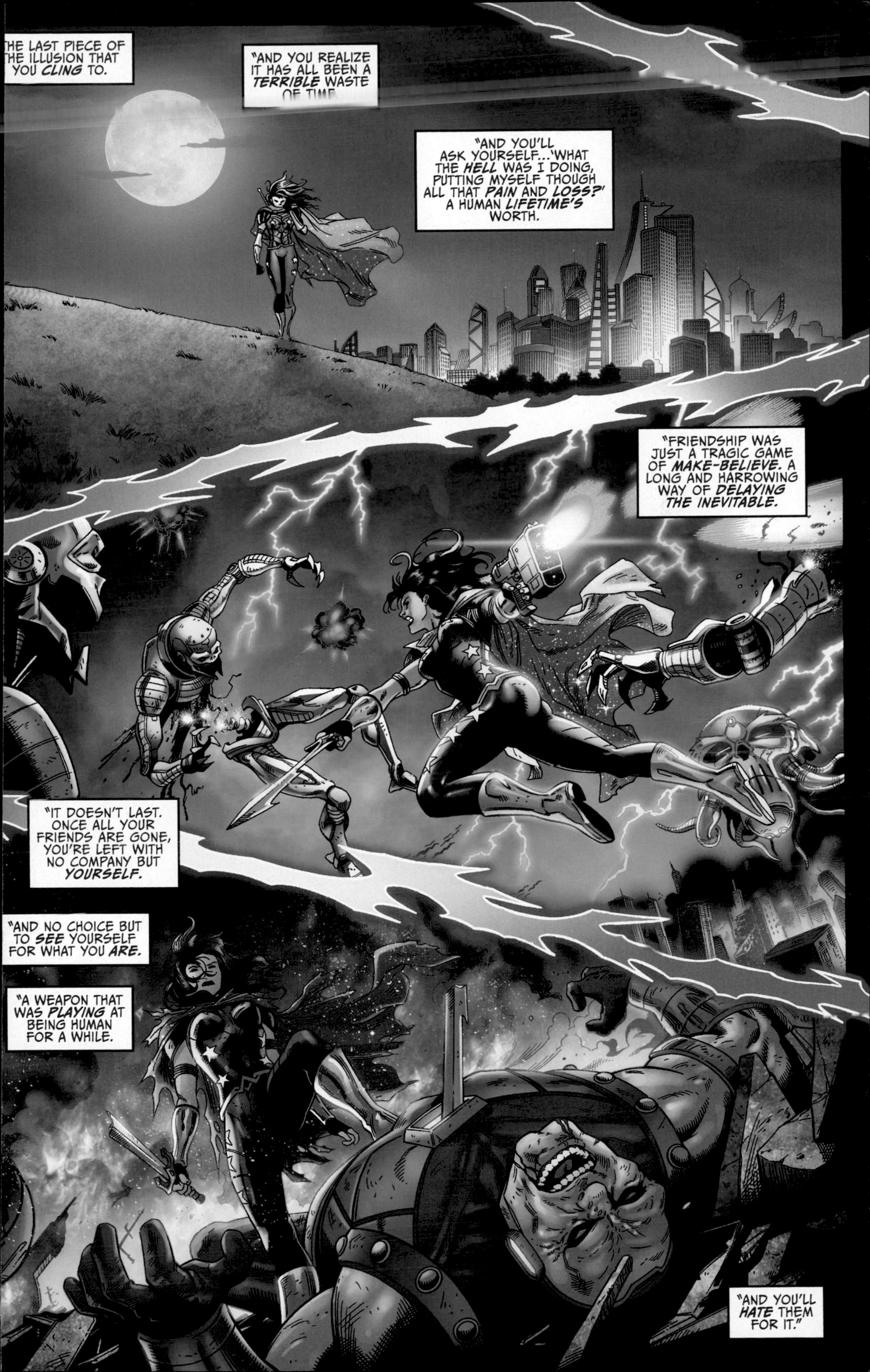

THE LAST PIECE OF THE ILLUSION THAT YOU CLING TO.
"AND YOU REALIZE IT HAS ALL BEEN A TERRIBLE WASTE OF TIME.
"AND YOU'LL ASK YOURSELF...'WHAT THE HELL WAS I DOING, PUTTING MYSELF THOUGH ALL THAT PAIN AND LOSS?' A HUMAN LIFETIME'S WORTH.
"FRIENDSHIP WAS JUST A TRAGIC GAME OF MAKE-BELIEVE. A LONG AND HARROWING WAY OF DELAYING THE INEVITABLE.
"IT DOESN'T LAST. ONCE ALL YOUR FRIENDS ARE GONE, YOU'RE LEFT WITH NO COMPANY BUT YOURSELF.
"AND NO CHOICE BUT TO SEE YOURSELF FOR WHAT YOU ARE.
"A WEAPON THAT WAS PLAYING AT BEING HUMAN FOR A WHILE.
"AND YOU'LL HATE THEM FOR IT."

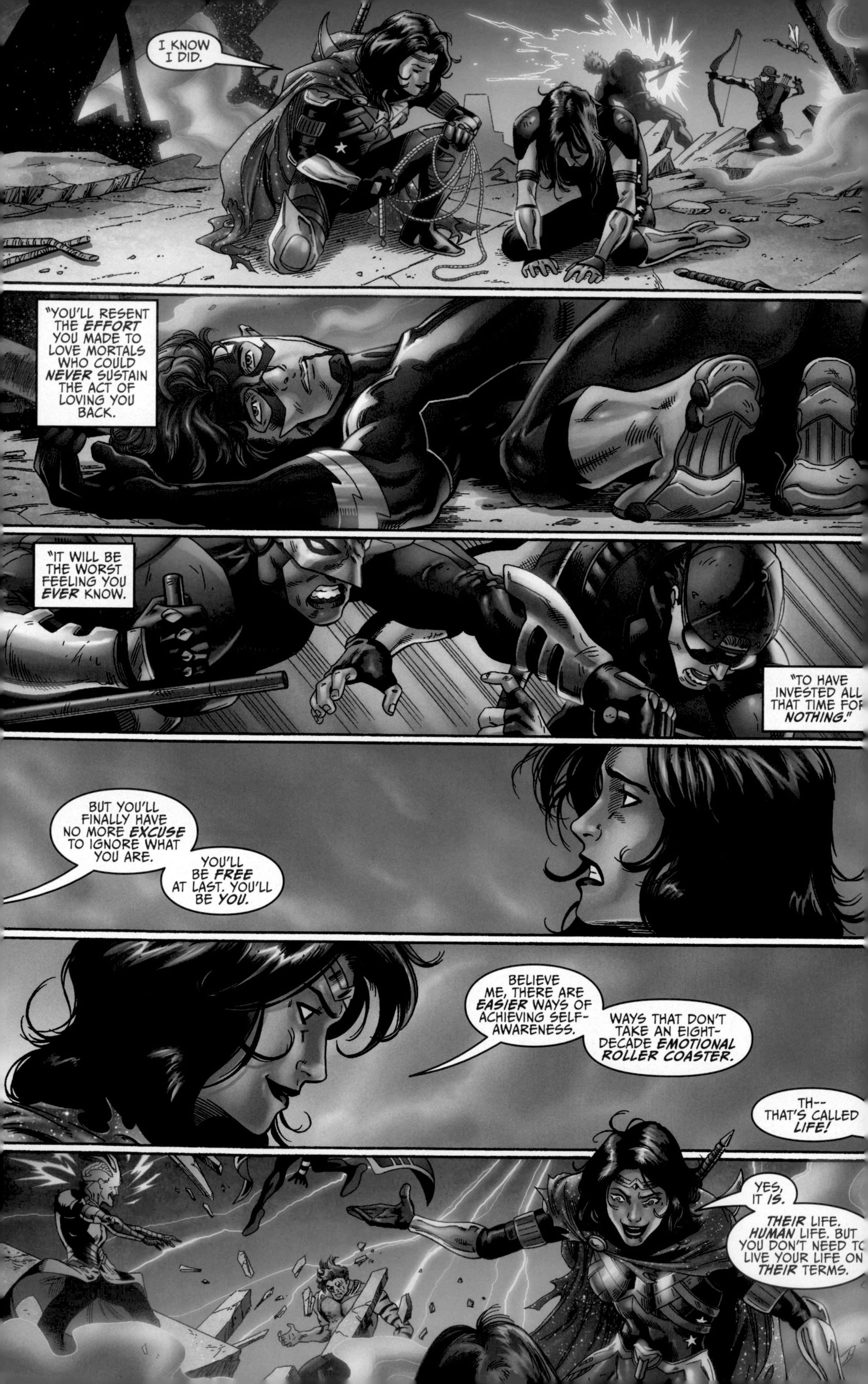

I KNOW I DID.
"YOU'LL RESENT THE EFFORT YOU MADE TO LOVE MORTALS WHO COULD NEVER SUSTAIN THE ACT OF LOVING YOU BACK.
"IT WILL BE THE WORST FEELING YOU EVER KNOW.
"TO HAVE INVESTED ALL THAT TIME FOR NOTHING."
BUT YOU'LL FINALLY HAVE NO MORE EXCUSE TO IGNORE WHAT YOU ARE.
YOU'LL BE FREE AT LAST. YOU'LL BE YOU.
BELIEVE ME, THERE ARE EASIER WAYS OF ACHIEVING SELF-AWARENESS.
WAYS THAT DON'T TAKE AN EIGHT-DECADE EMOTIONAL ROLLER COASTER.
TH-- THAT'S CALLED LIFE!
YES, IT IS.
THEIR LIFE. HUMAN LIFE. BUT YOU DON'T NEED TO LIVE YOUR LIFE ON THEIR TERMS.

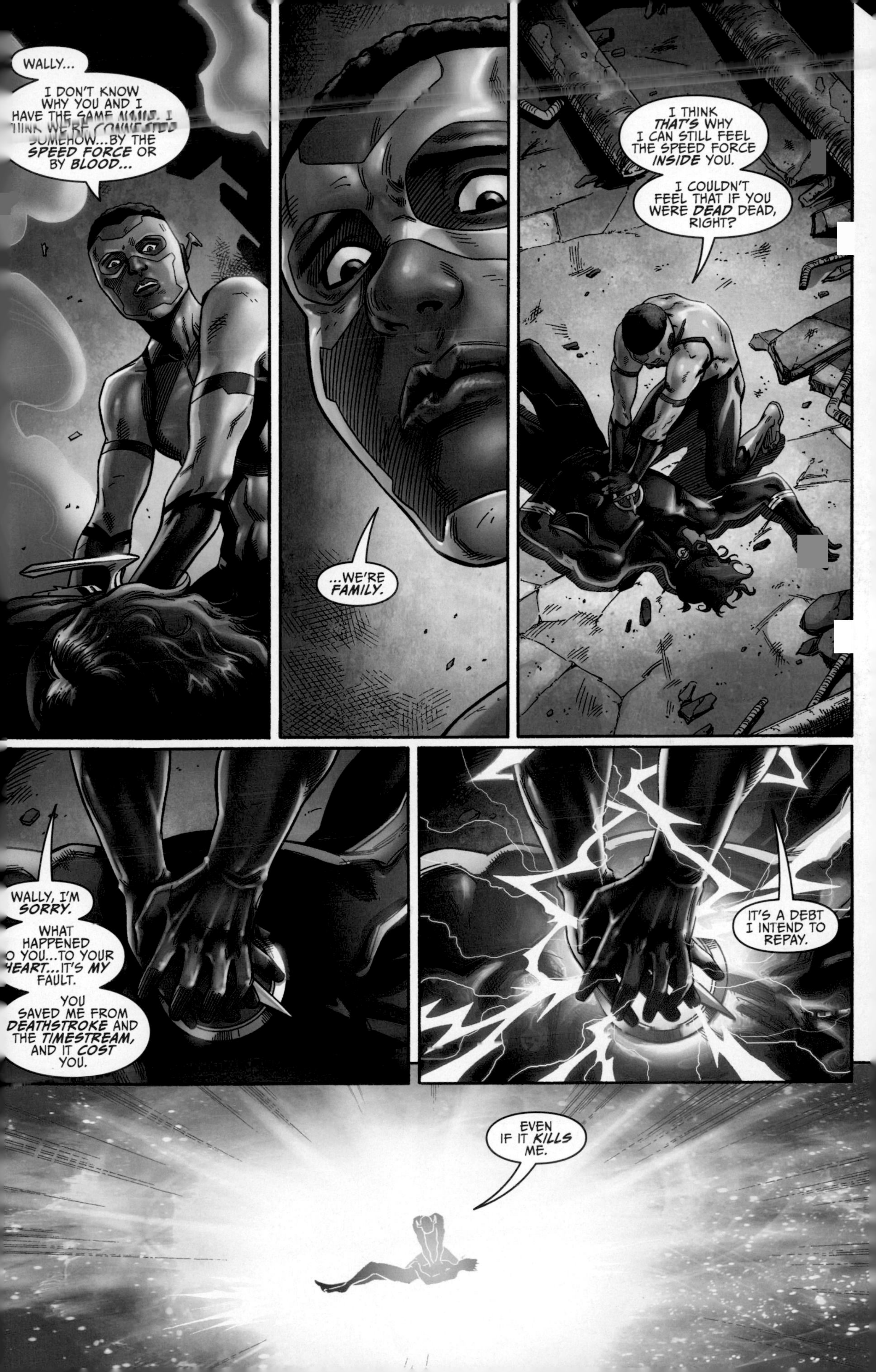
WALLY...
I DON'T KNOW WHY YOU AND I HAVE THE SAME
I THINK WE'RE CONNECTED SOMEHOW...BY THE SPEED FORCE OR BY BLOOD...
...WE'RE FAMILY.
I THINK THAT'S WHY I CAN STILL FEEL THE SPEED FORCE INSIDE YOU.
I COULDN'T FEEL THAT IF YOU WERE DEAD DEAD, RIGHT?
WALLY, I'M SORRY.
WHAT HAPPENED O YOU...TO YOUR EART...IT'S MY FAULT.
YOU SAVED ME FROM DEATHSTROKE AND THE TIMESTREAM, AND IT COST YOU.
IT'S A DEBT I INTEND TO REPAY.
EVEN IF IT KILLS ME.

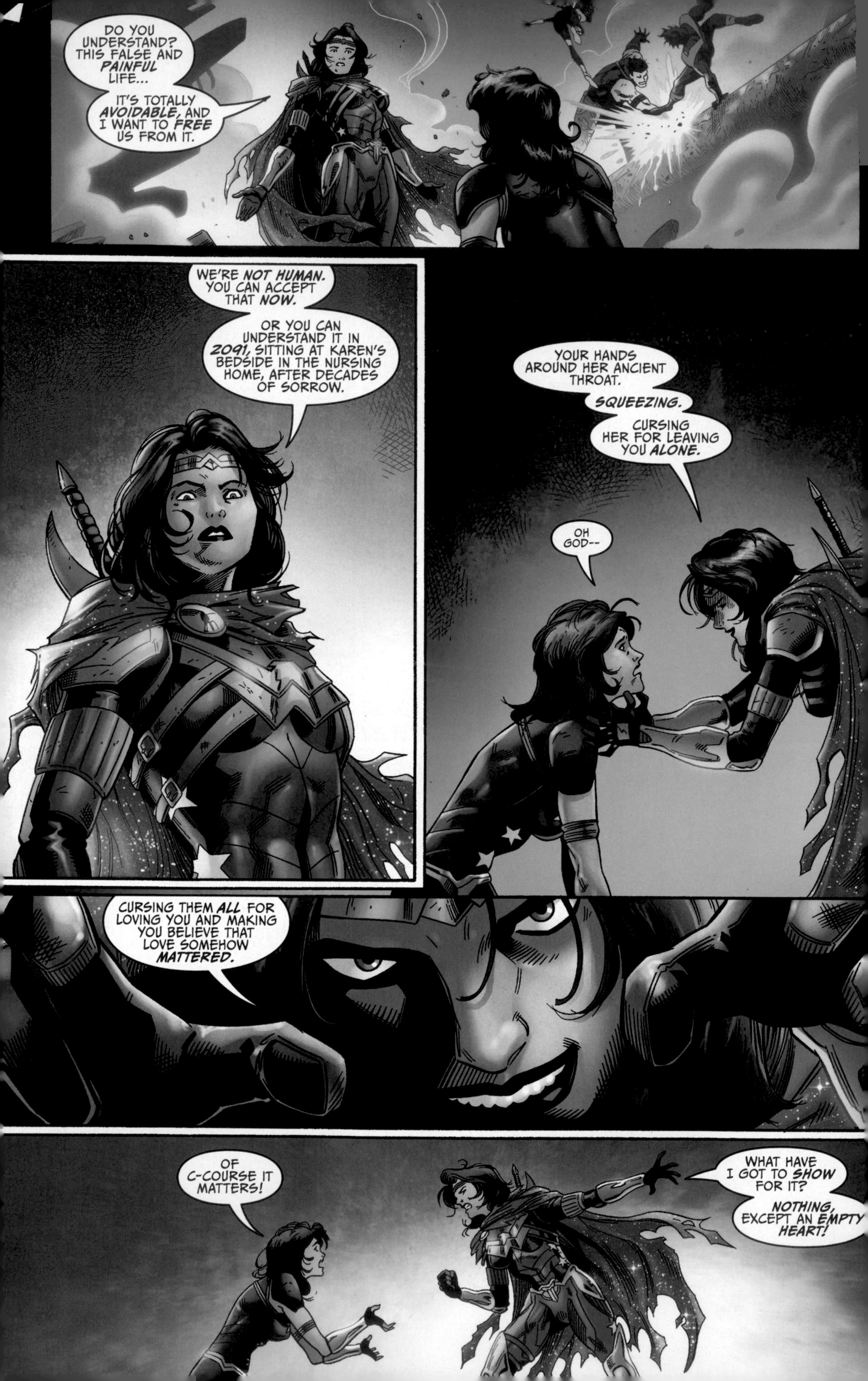
DO YOU UNDERSTAND? THIS FALSE AND PAINFUL LIFE...
IT'S TOTALLY AVOIDABLE, AND I WANT TO FREE US FROM IT.
WE'RE NOT HUMAN. YOU CAN ACCEPT THAT NOW.
OR YOU CAN UNDERSTAND IT IN 2091, SITTING AT KAREN'S BEDSIDE IN THE NURSING HOME, AFTER DECADES OF SORROW.
YOUR HANDS AROUND HER ANCIENT THROAT.
SQUEEZING.
CURSING HER FOR LEAVING YOU ALONE.
OH GOD--
CURSING THEM ALL FOR LOVING YOU AND MAKING YOU BELIEVE THAT LOVE SOMEHOW MATTERED.
OF C-COURSE IT MATTERS!
WHAT HAVE I GOT TO SHOW FOR IT?
NOTHING, EXCEPT AN EMPTY HEART!

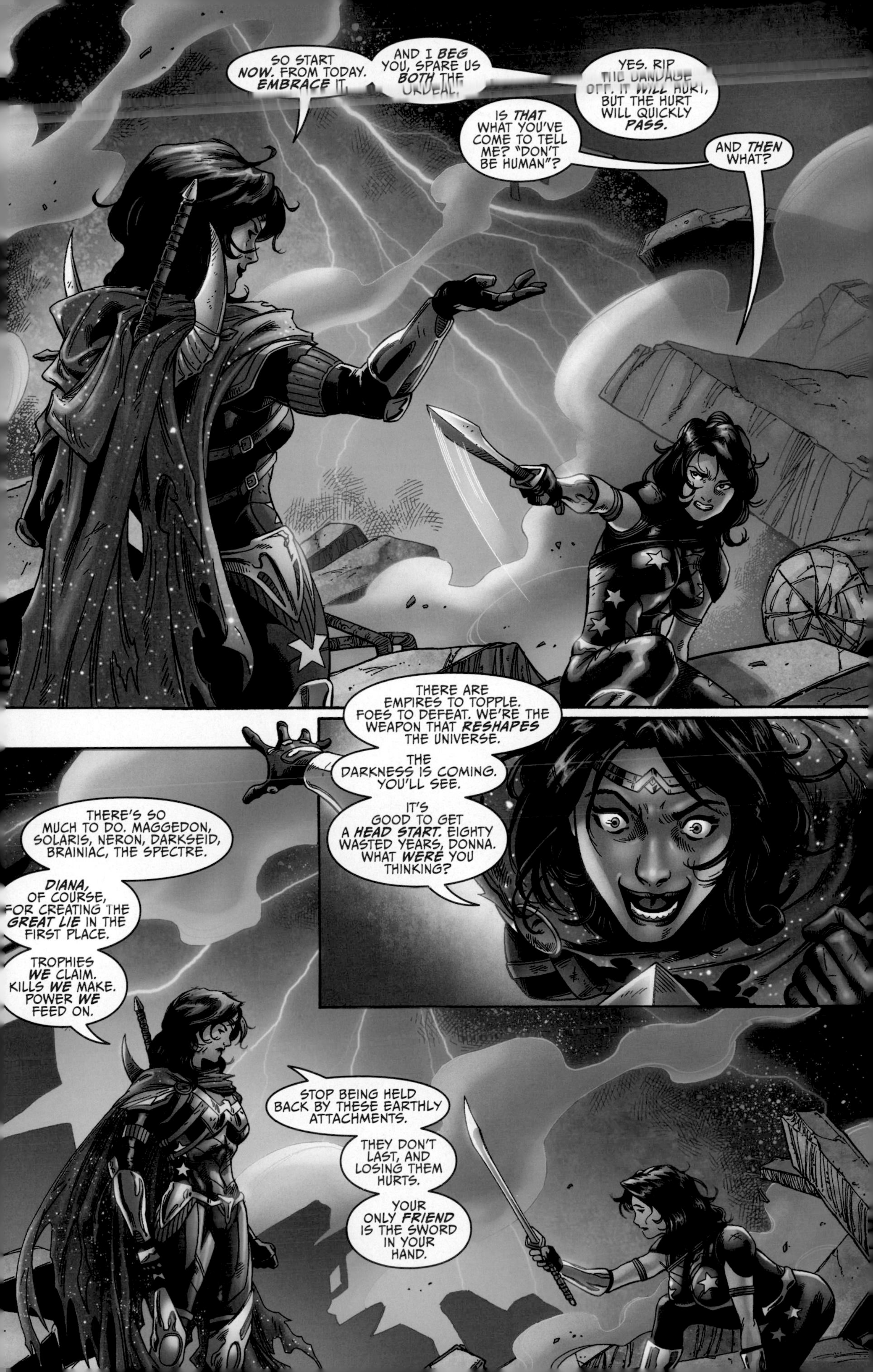
SO START NOW. FROM TODAY. EMBRACE IT.
AND I BEG YOU, SPARE US BOTH THE ORDEAL.
YES. RIP THE BANDAGE OFF. IT WILL HURT, BUT THE HURT WILL QUICKLY PASS.
IS THAT WHAT YOU'VE COME TO TELL ME? "DON'T BE HUMAN"?
AND THEN WHAT?
THERE ARE EMPIRES TO TOPPLE. FOES TO DEFEAT. WE'RE THE WEAPON THAT RESHAPES THE UNIVERSE.
THE DARKNESS IS COMING. YOU'LL SEE.
IT'S GOOD TO GET A HEAD START. EIGHTY WASTED YEARS, DONNA. WHAT WERE YOU THINKING?
THERE'S SO MUCH TO DO. MAGGEDON, SOLARIS, NERON, DARKSEID, BRAINIAC, THE SPECTRE.
DIANA, OF COURSE, FOR CREATING THE GREAT LIE IN THE FIRST PLACE.
TROPHIES WE CLAIM. KILLS WE MAKE. POWER WE FEED ON.
STOP BEING HELD BACK BY THESE EARTHLY ATTACHMENTS.
THEY DON'T LAST, AND LOSING THEM HURTS.
YOUR ONLY FRIEND IS THE SWORD IN YOUR HAND.

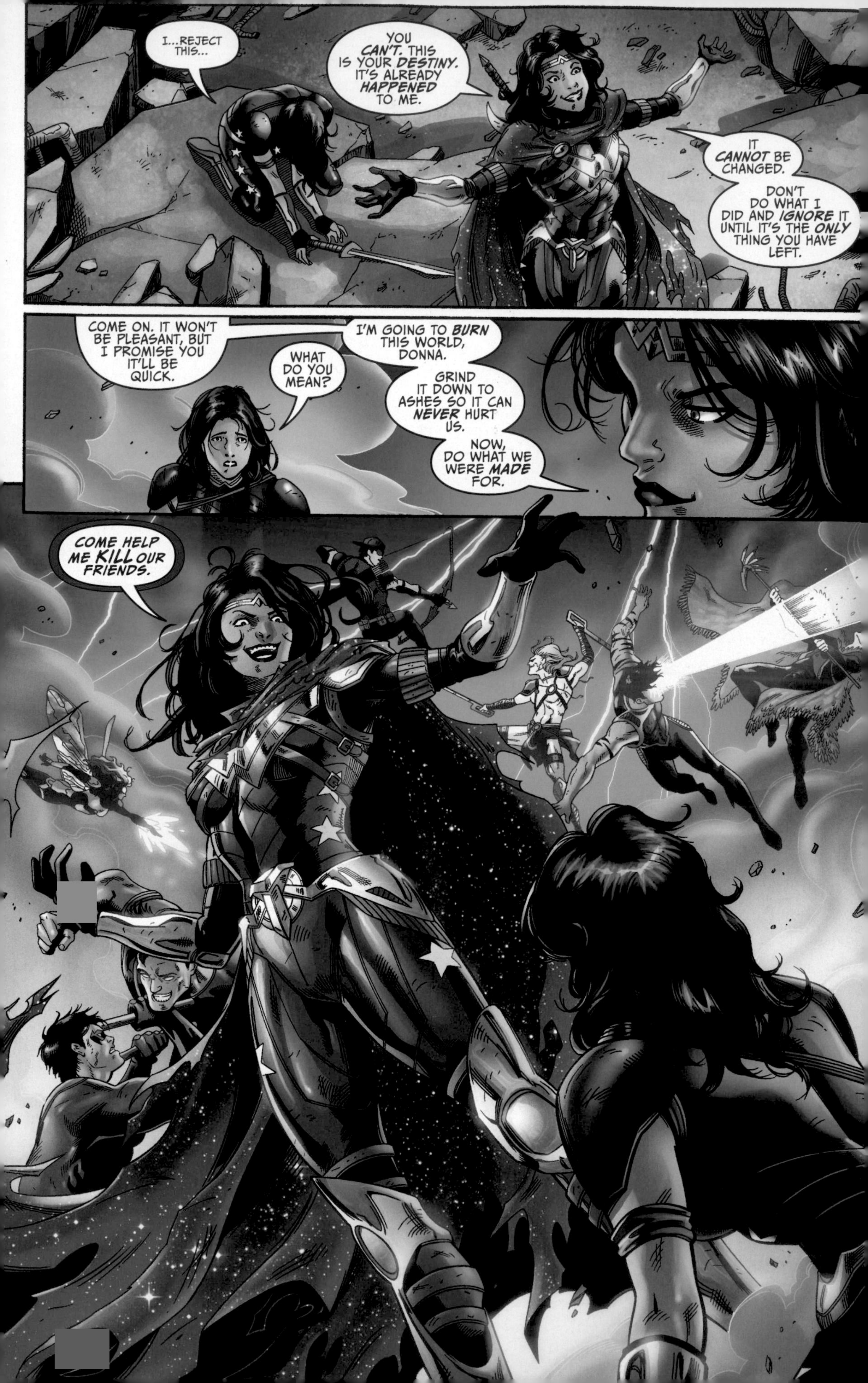
I...REJECT THIS...
YOU CAN'T. THIS IS YOUR DESTINY. IT'S ALREADY HAPPENED TO ME.
IT CANNOT BE CHANGED.
DON'T DO WHAT I DID AND IGNORE IT UNTIL IT'S THE ONLY THING YOU HAVE LEFT.
COME ON. IT WON'T BE PLEASANT, BUT I PROMISE YOU IT'LL BE QUICK.
WHAT DO YOU MEAN?
I'M GOING TO BURN THIS WORLD, DONNA.
GRIND IT DOWN TO ASHES SO IT CAN NEVER HURT US.
NOW, DO WHAT WE WERE MADE FOR.
COME HELP ME KILL OUR FRIENDS.

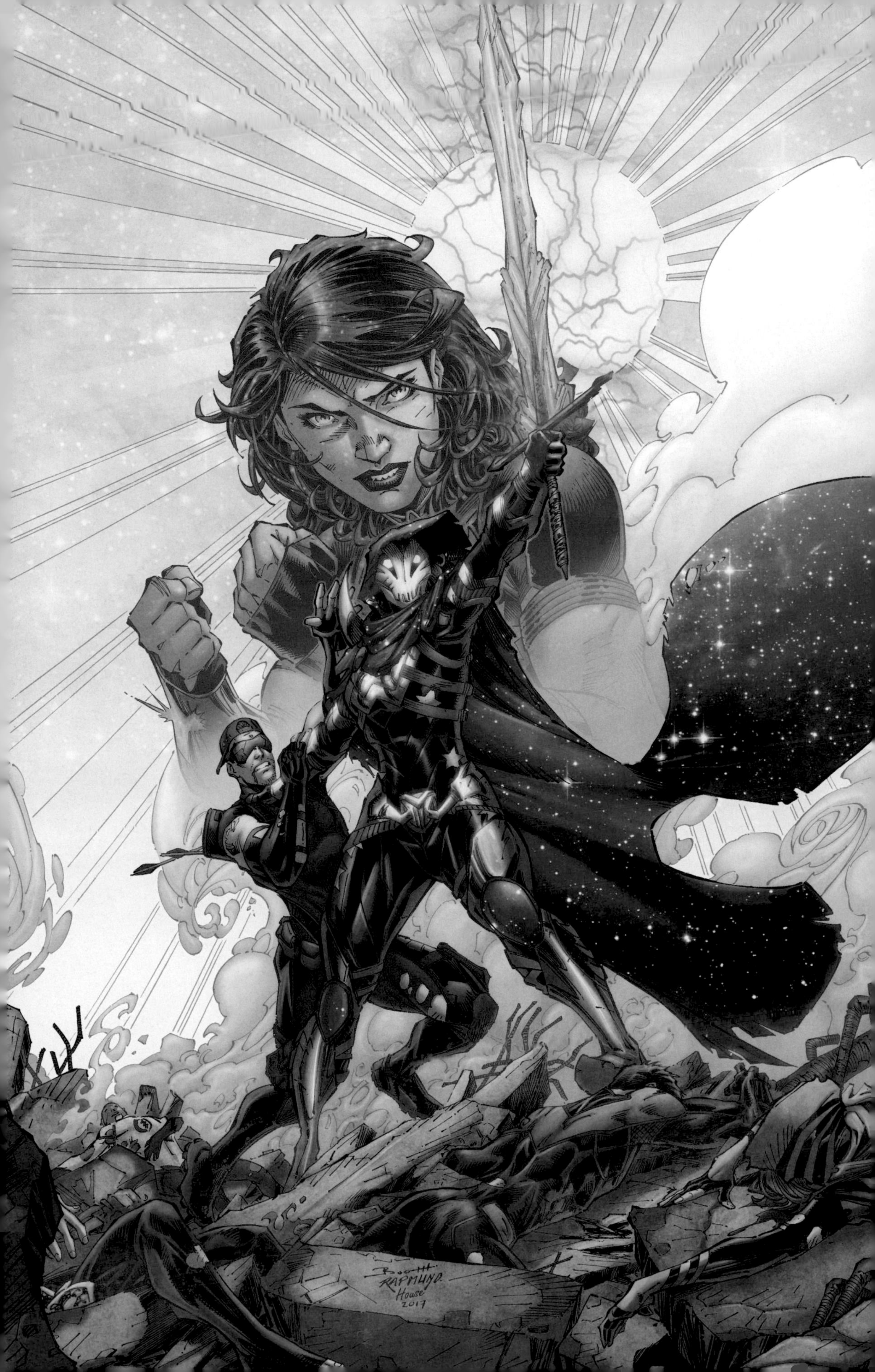

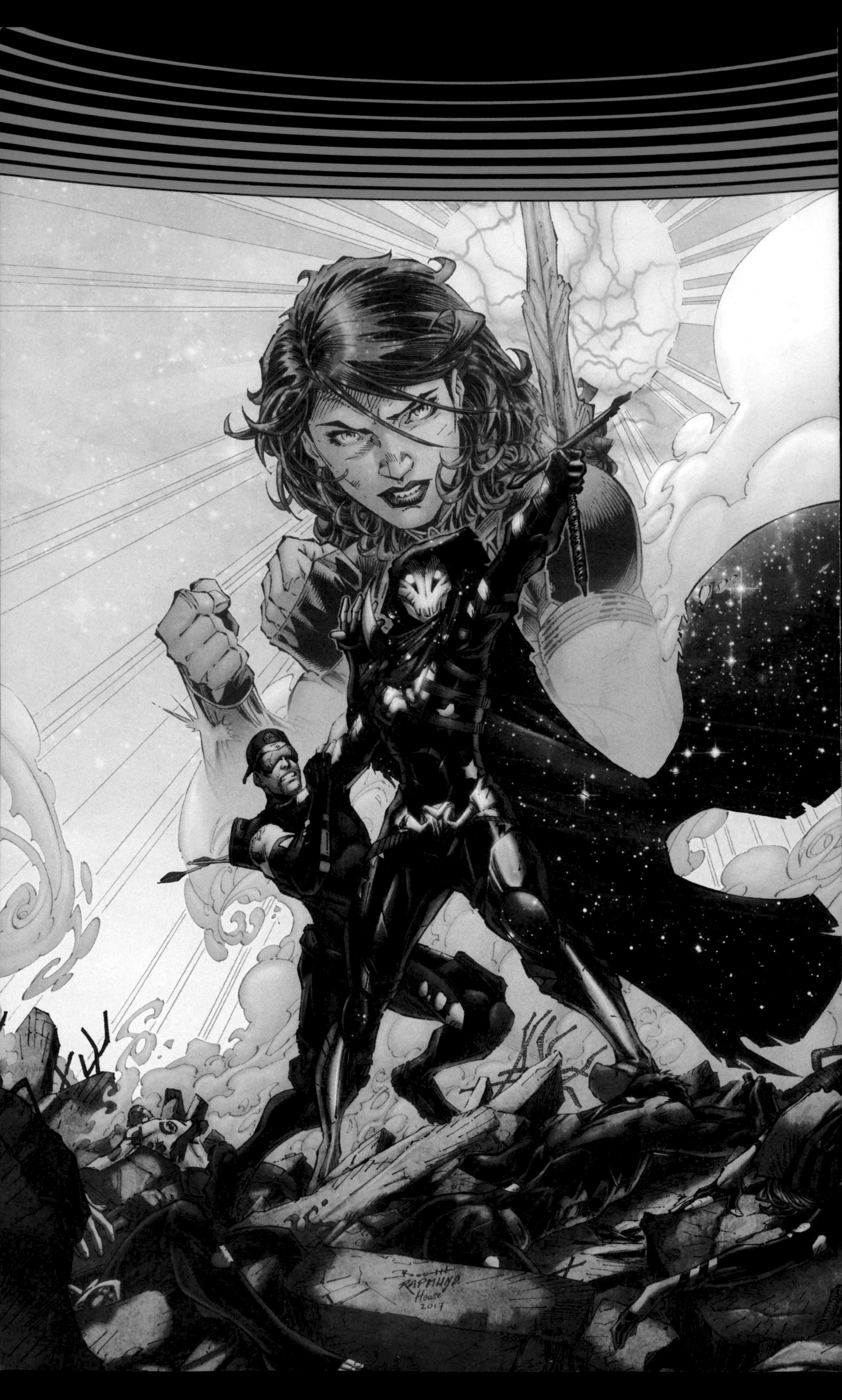

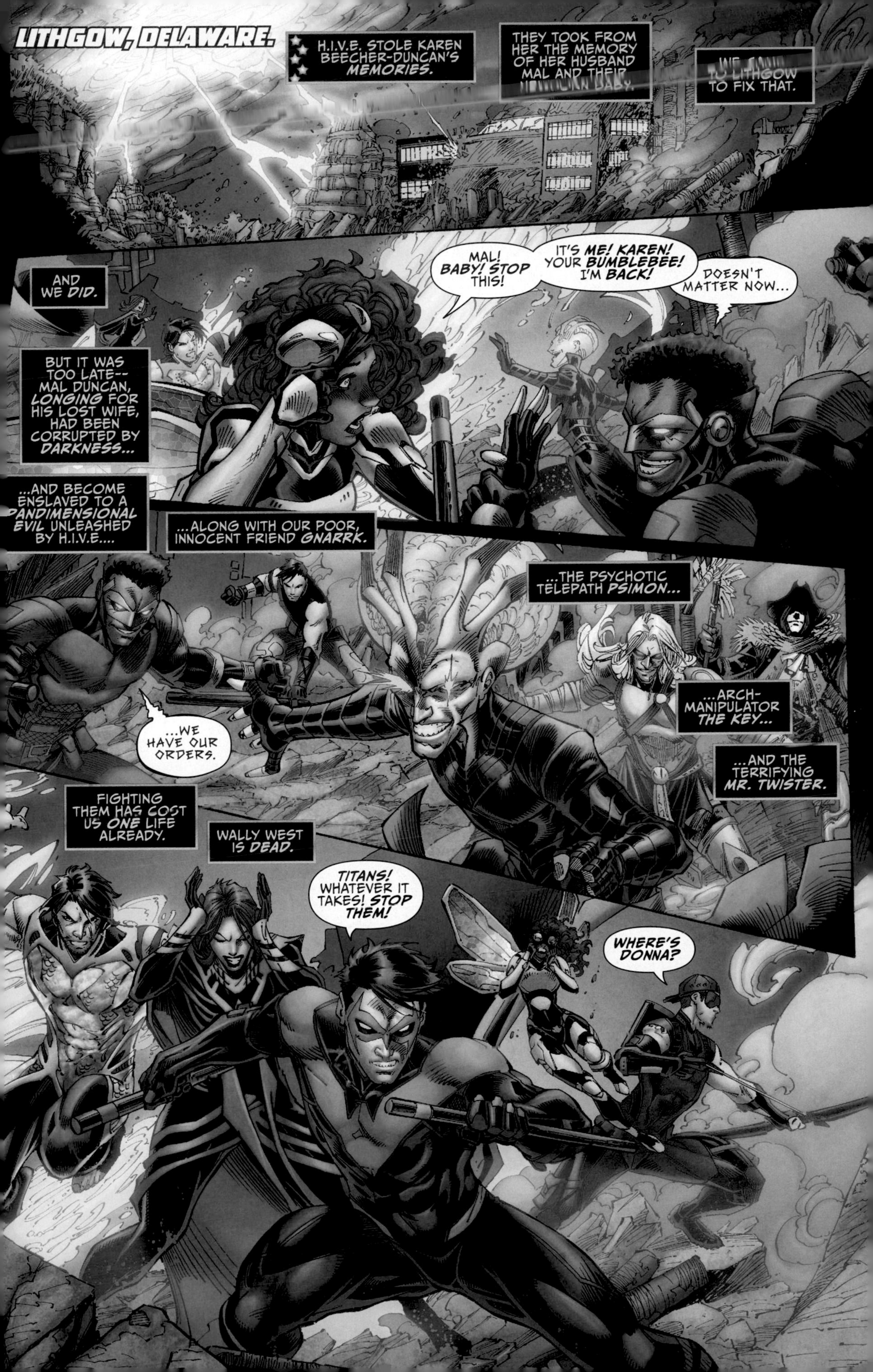
LITHGOW, DELAWARE.
H.I.V.E. STOLE KAREN BEECHER-DUNCAN'S MEMORIES.
THEY TOOK FROM HER THE MEMORY OF HER HUSBAND MAL AND THEIR
TO LITHGOW TO FIX THAT.
AND WE DID.
MAL! BABY! STOP THIS!
IT'S ME! KAREN! YOUR BUMBLEBEE! I'M BACK!
DOESN'T MATTER NOW...
BUT IT WAS TOO LATE--MAL DUNCAN, LONGING FOR HIS LOST WIFE, HAD BEEN CORRUPTED BY DARKNESS...
...AND BECOME ENSLAVED TO A PANDIMENSIONAL EVIL UNLEASHED BY H.I.V.E....
...ALONG WITH OUR POOR, INNOCENT FRIEND GNARRK.
...THE PSYCHOTIC TELEPATH PSIMON...
...WE HAVE OUR ORDERS.
...ARCH-MANIPULATOR THE KEY...
...AND THE TERRIFYING MR. TWISTER.
FIGHTING THEM HAS COST US ONE LIFE ALREADY.
WALLY WEST IS DEAD.
TITANS! WHATEVER IT TAKES! STOP THEM!
WHERE'S DONNA?

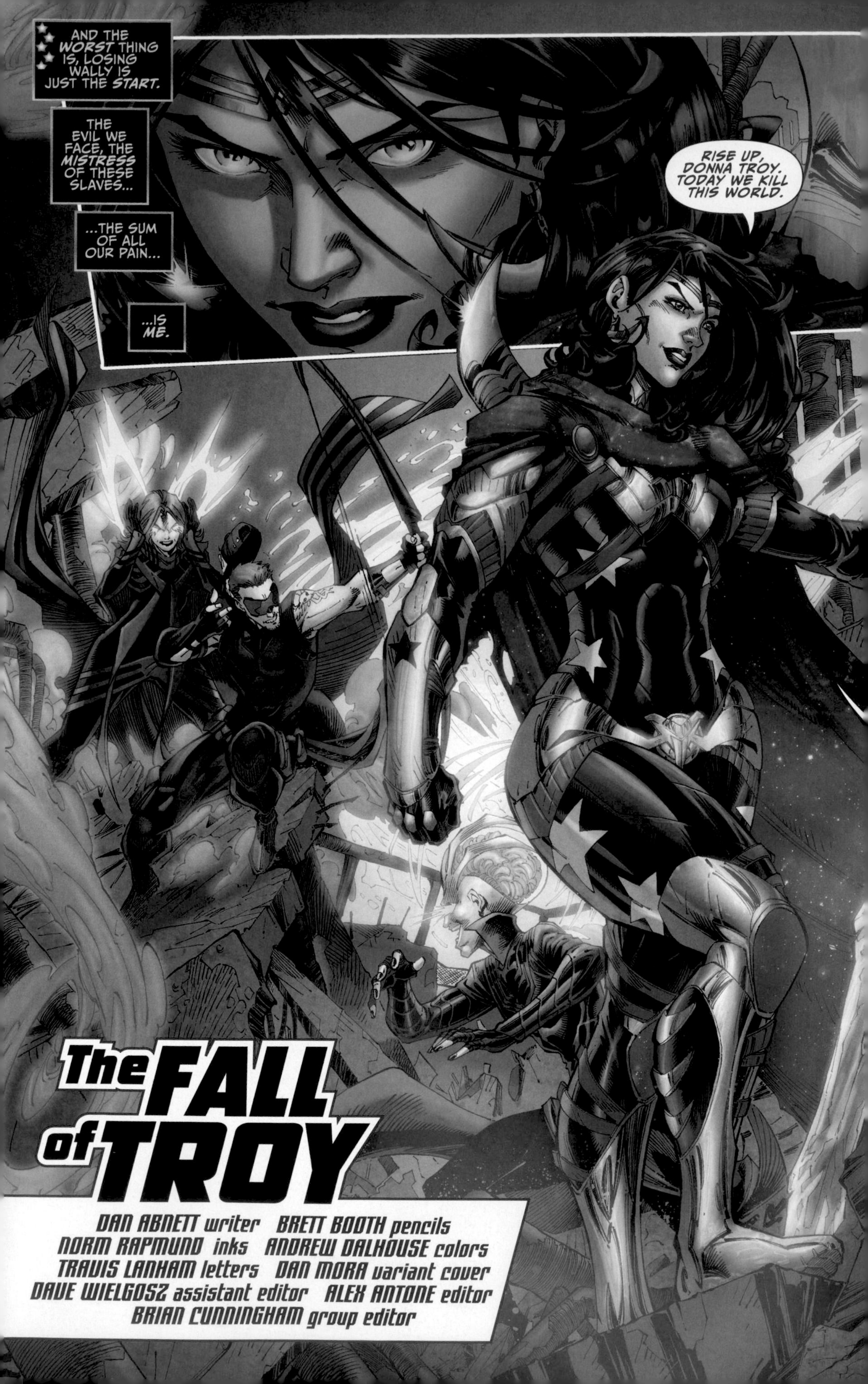
AND THE WORST THING IS, LOSING WALLY IS JUST THE START.
THE EVIL WE FACE, THE MISTRESS OF THESE SLAVES...
...THE SUM OF ALL OUR PAIN...
...IS ME.
RISE UP, DONNA TROY. TODAY WE KILL THIS WORLD.
The FALL of TROY
DAN ABNETT writer BRETT BOOTH pencils
NORM RAPMUND inks ANDREW DALHOUSE colors
TRAVIS LANHAM letters DAN MORA variant cover
DAVE WIELGOSZ assistant editor ALEX ANTONE editor
BRIAN CUNNINGHAM group editor

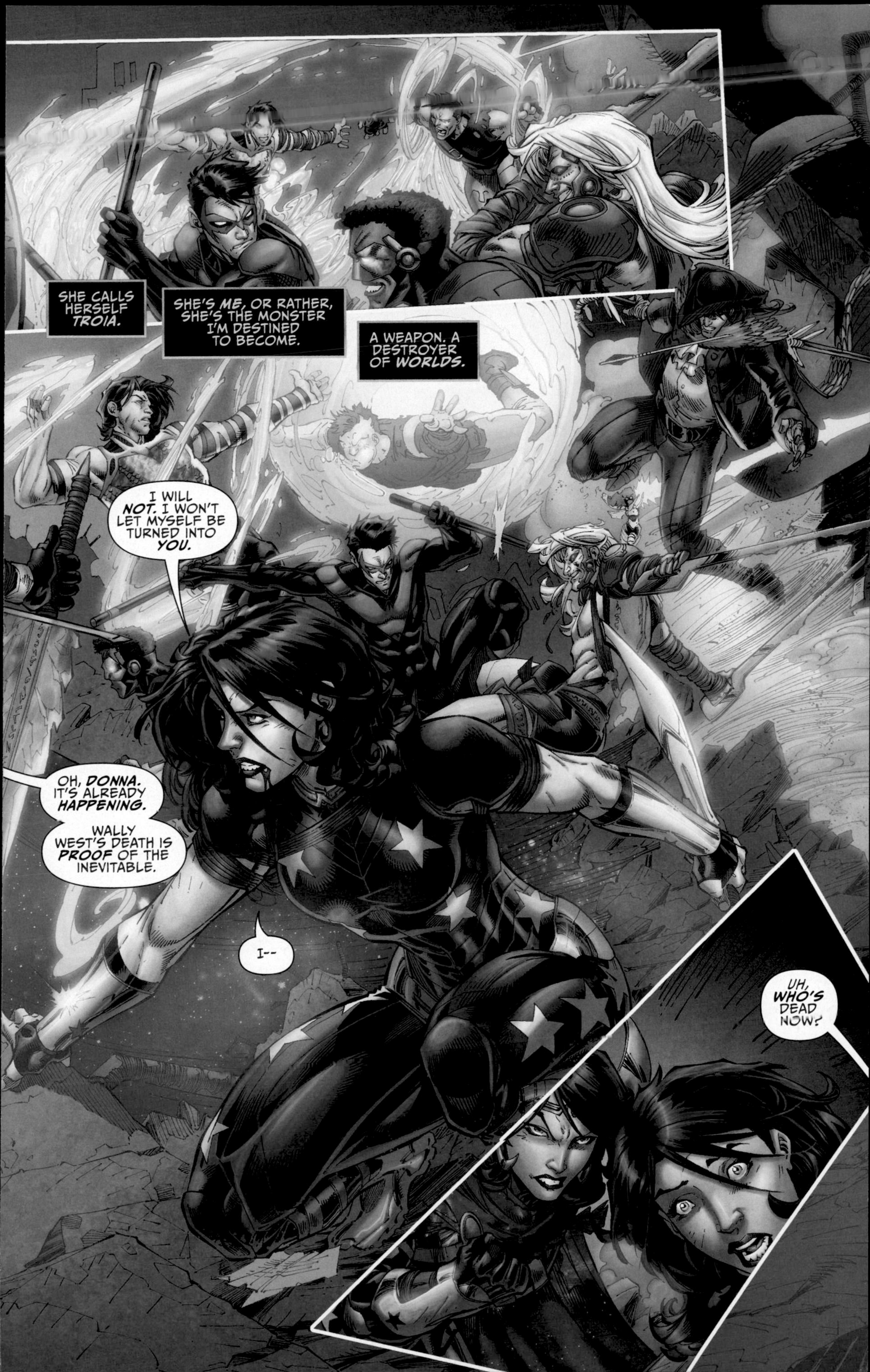
SHE CALLS HERSELF TROIA.
SHE'S ME, OR RATHER, SHE'S THE MONSTER I'M DESTINED TO BECOME.
A WEAPON. A DESTROYER OF WORLDS.
I WILL NOT. I WON'T LET MYSELF BE TURNED INTO YOU.
OH, DONNA. IT'S ALREADY HAPPENING.
WALLY WEST'S DEATH IS PROOF OF THE INEVITABLE.
I--
UH, WHO'S DEAD NOW?

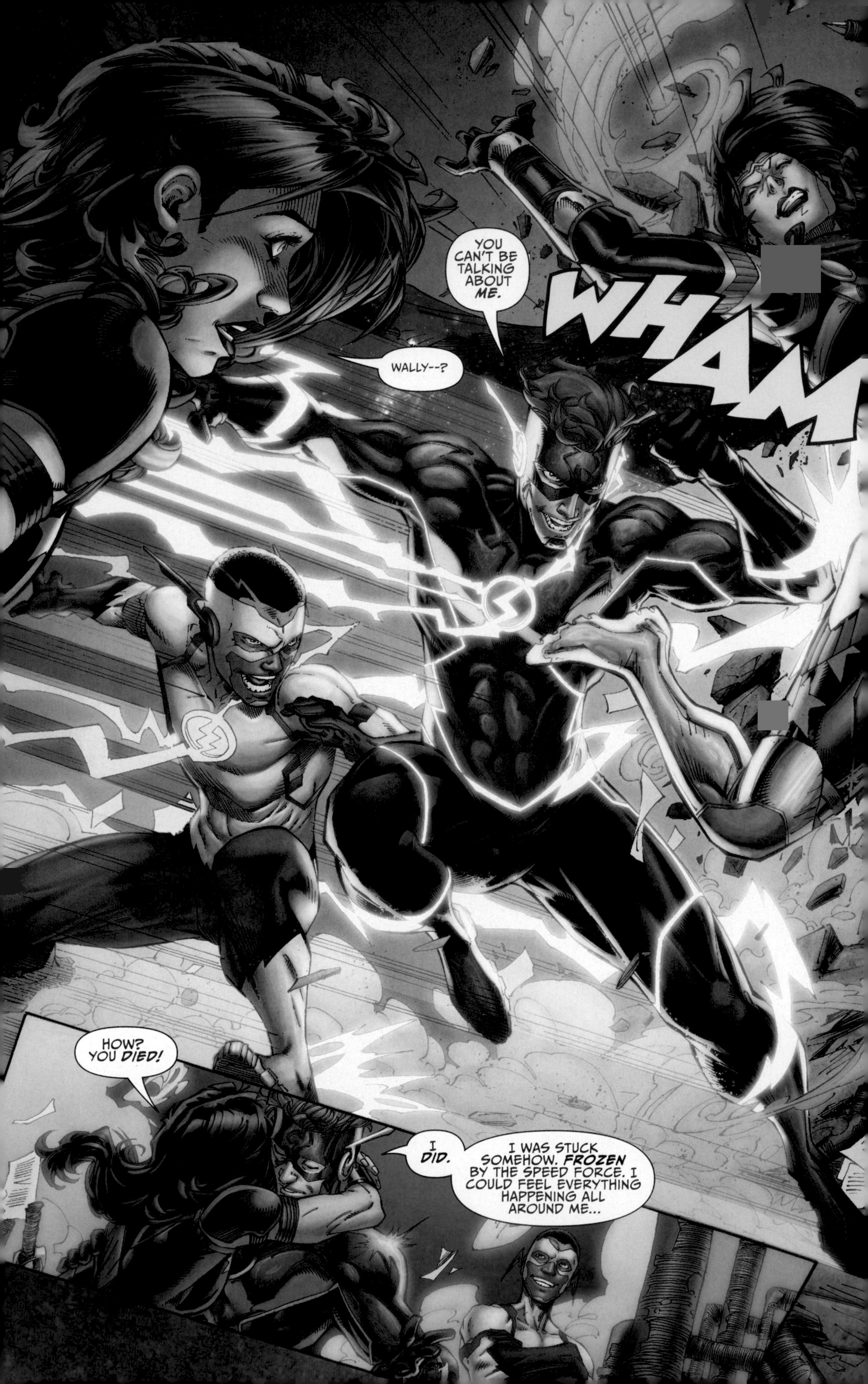
YOU CAN'T BE TALKING ABOUT ME.
WHAM
WALLY--?
HOW? YOU DIED!
I DID.
I WAS STUCK SOMEHOW. FROZEN BY THE SPEED FORCE. I COULD FEEL EVERYTHING HAPPENING ALL AROUND ME...

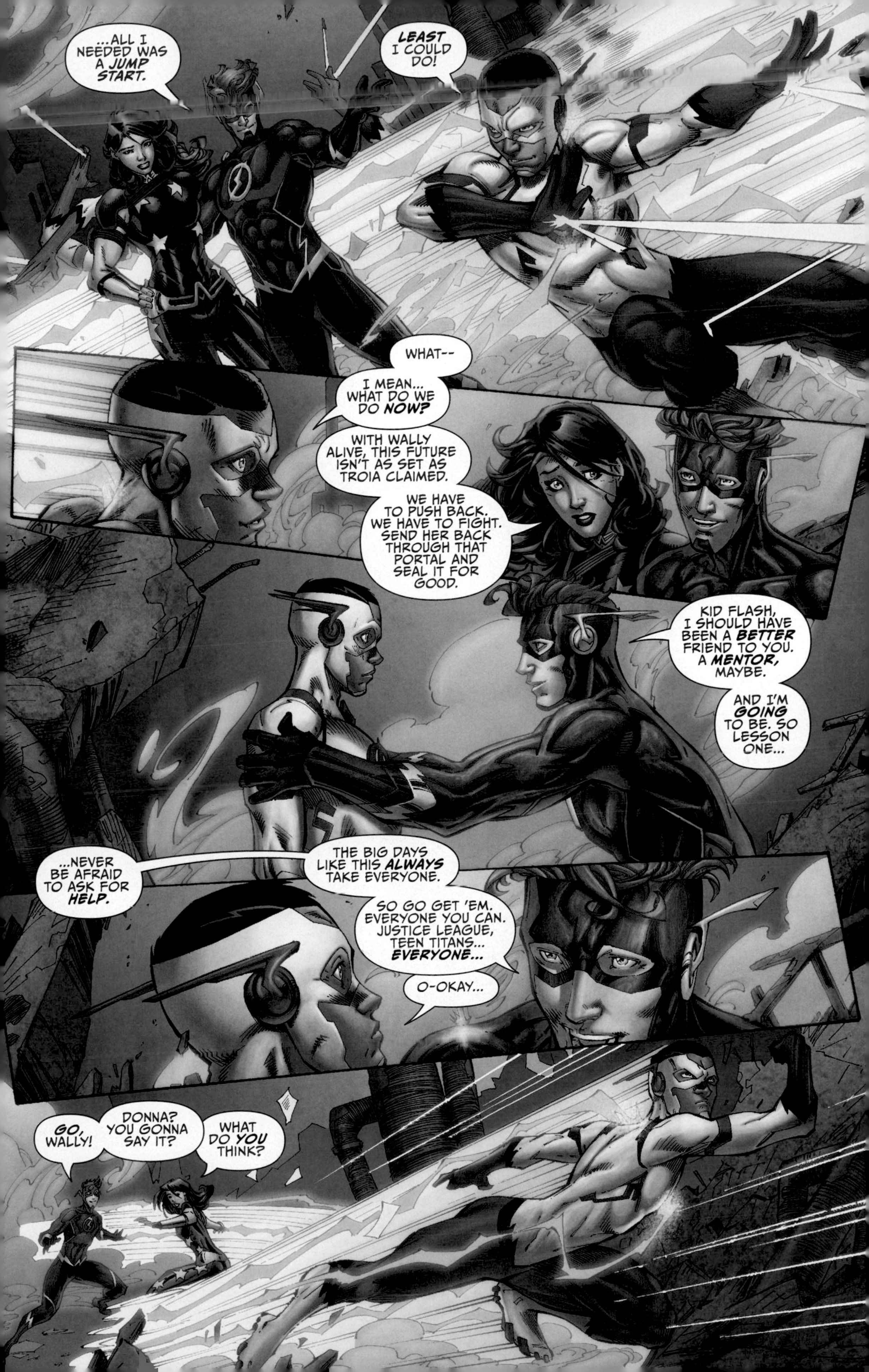
...ALL I NEEDED WAS A JUMP START.
LEAST I COULD DO!
WHAT--
I MEAN... WHAT DO WE DO NOW?
WITH WALLY ALIVE, THIS FUTURE ISN'T AS SET AS TROIA CLAIMED.
WE HAVE TO PUSH BACK. WE HAVE TO FIGHT. SEND HER BACK THROUGH THAT PORTAL AND SEAL IT FOR GOOD.
KID FLASH, I SHOULD HAVE BEEN A BETTER FRIEND TO YOU. A MENTOR, MAYBE.
AND I'M GOING TO BE. SO LESSON ONE...
...NEVER BE AFRAID TO ASK FOR HELP.
THE BIG DAYS LIKE THIS ALWAYS TAKE EVERYONE.
SO GO GET 'EM. EVERYONE YOU CAN. JUSTICE LEAGUE, TEEN TITANS... EVERYONE...
O-OKAY...
GO, WALLY!
DONNA? YOU GONNA SAY IT?
WHAT DO YOU THINK?

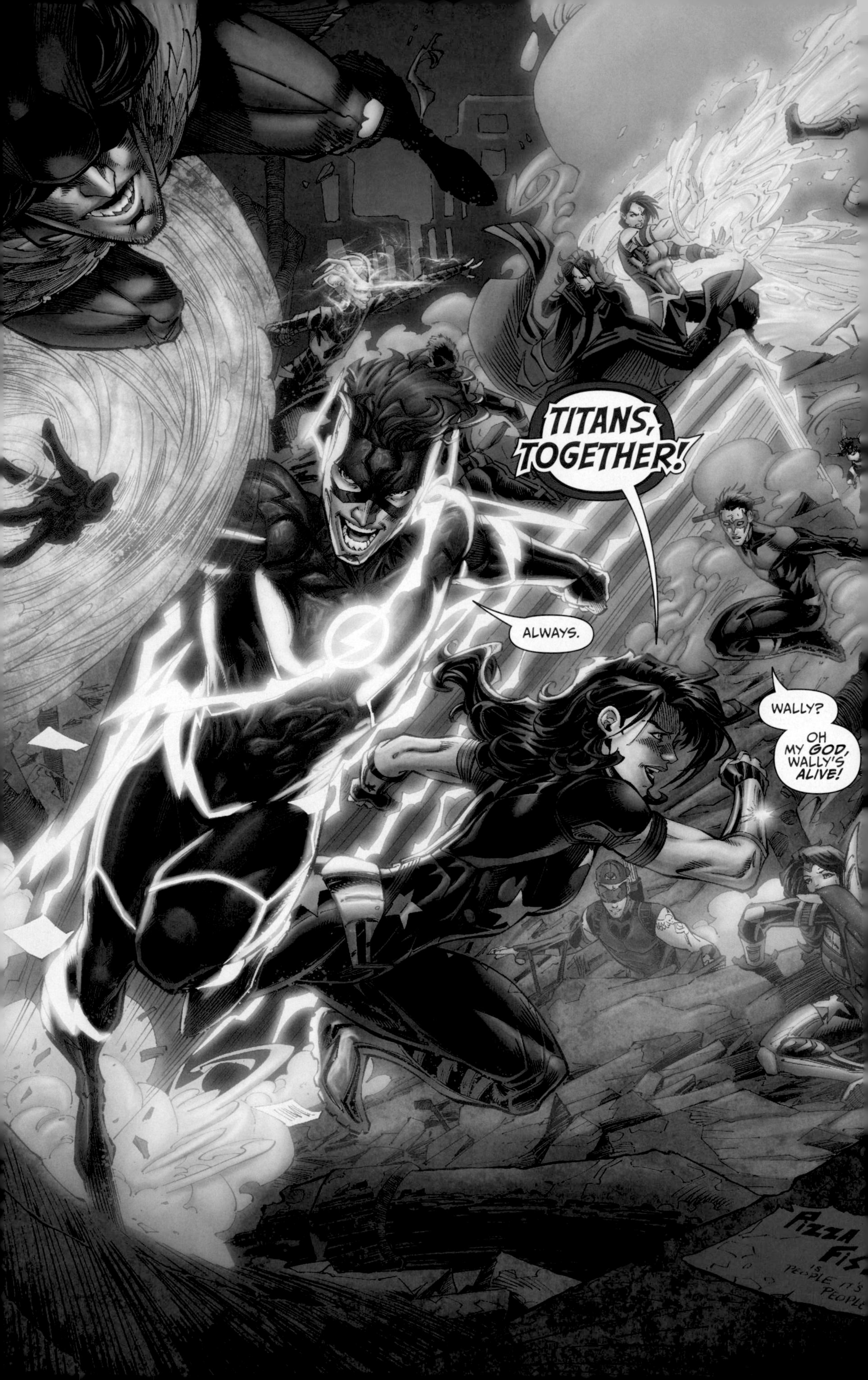
TITANS, TOGETHER!
ALWAYS.
WALLY?
OH MY GOD, WALLY'S ALIVE!

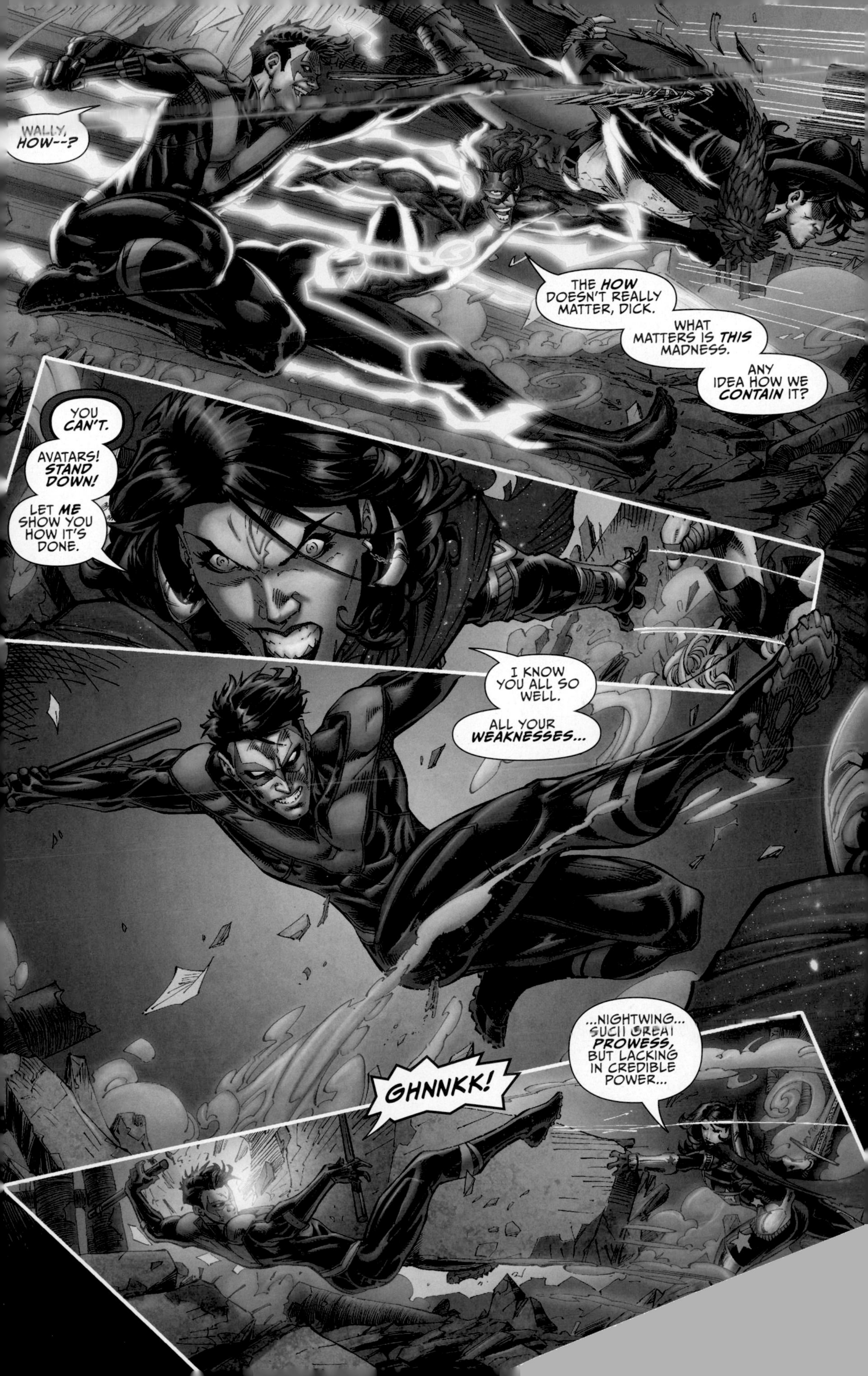
WALLY, HOW--?
THE HOW DOESN'T REALLY MATTER, DICK.
WHAT MATTERS IS THIS MADNESS.
ANY IDEA HOW WE CONTAIN IT?
YOU CAN'T.
AVATARS! STAND DOWN!
LET ME SHOW YOU HOW IT'S DONE.
I KNOW YOU ALL SO WELL.
ALL YOUR WEAKNESSES...
GHNNKK!
...NIGHTWING... SUCH GREAT PROWESS, BUT LACKING IN CREDIBLE POWER...

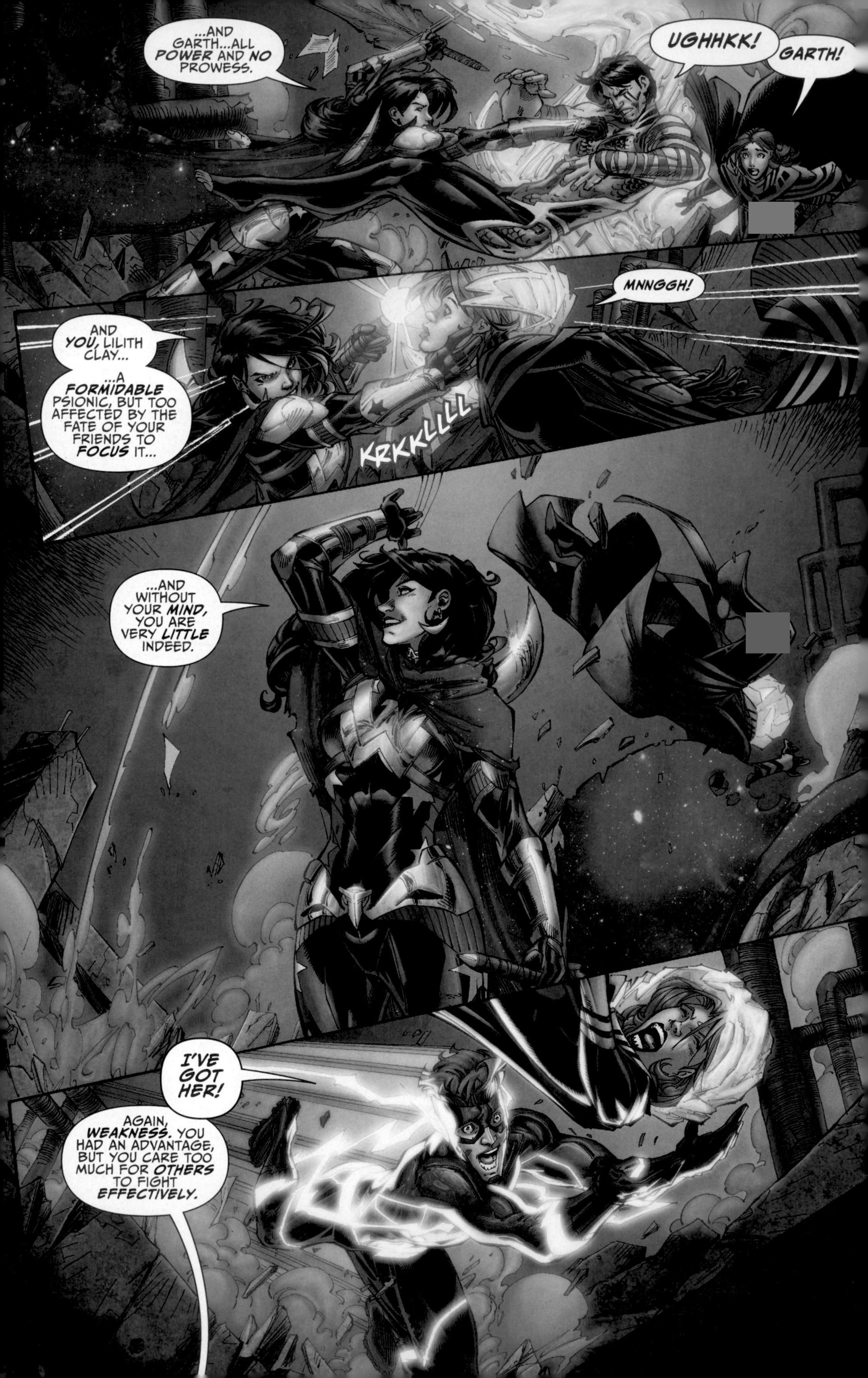
...AND GARTH...ALL POWER AND NO PROWESS.
UGHHKK!
GARTH!
MNNGGH!
AND YOU, LILITH CLAY...
...A FORMIDABLE PSIONIC, BUT TOO AFFECTED BY THE FATE OF YOUR FRIENDS TO FOCUS IT...
KRKKLLLL
...AND WITHOUT YOUR MIND, YOU ARE VERY LITTLE INDEED.
I'VE GOT HER!
AGAIN, WEAKNESS. YOU HAD AN ADVANTAGE, BUT YOU CARE TOO MUCH FOR OTHERS TO FIGHT EFFECTIVELY.

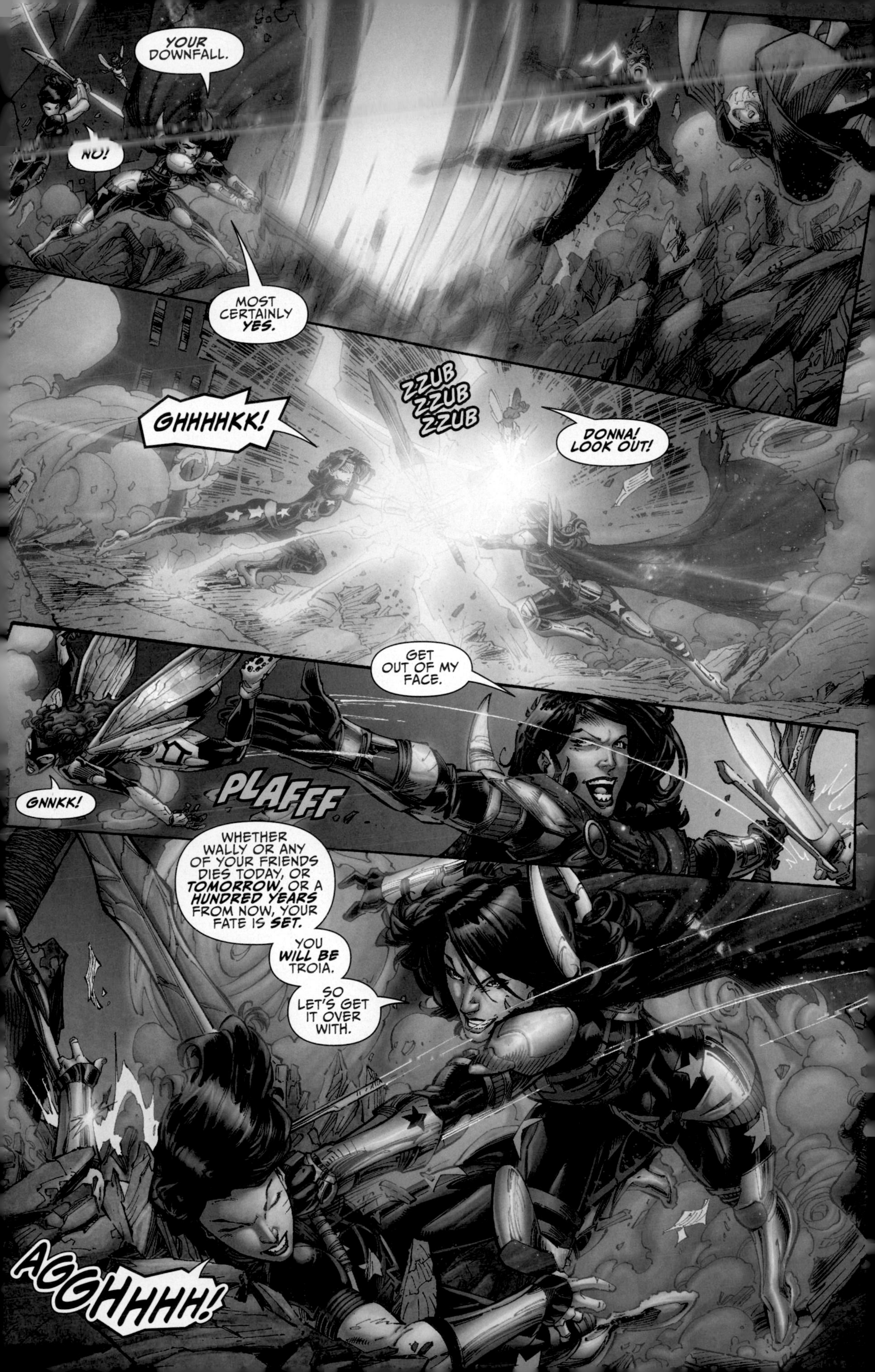
YOUR DOWNFALL.
NO!
MOST CERTAINLY YES.
GHHHHKK!
ZZUB ZZUB ZZUB
DONNA! LOOK OUT!
GET OUT OF MY FACE.
GNNKK!
PLAFFF
WHETHER WALLY OR ANY OF YOUR FRIENDS DIES TODAY, OR TOMORROW, OR A HUNDRED YEARS FROM NOW, YOUR FATE IS SET.
YOU WILL BE TROIA.
SO LET'S GET IT OVER WITH.
AGGHHHHH!

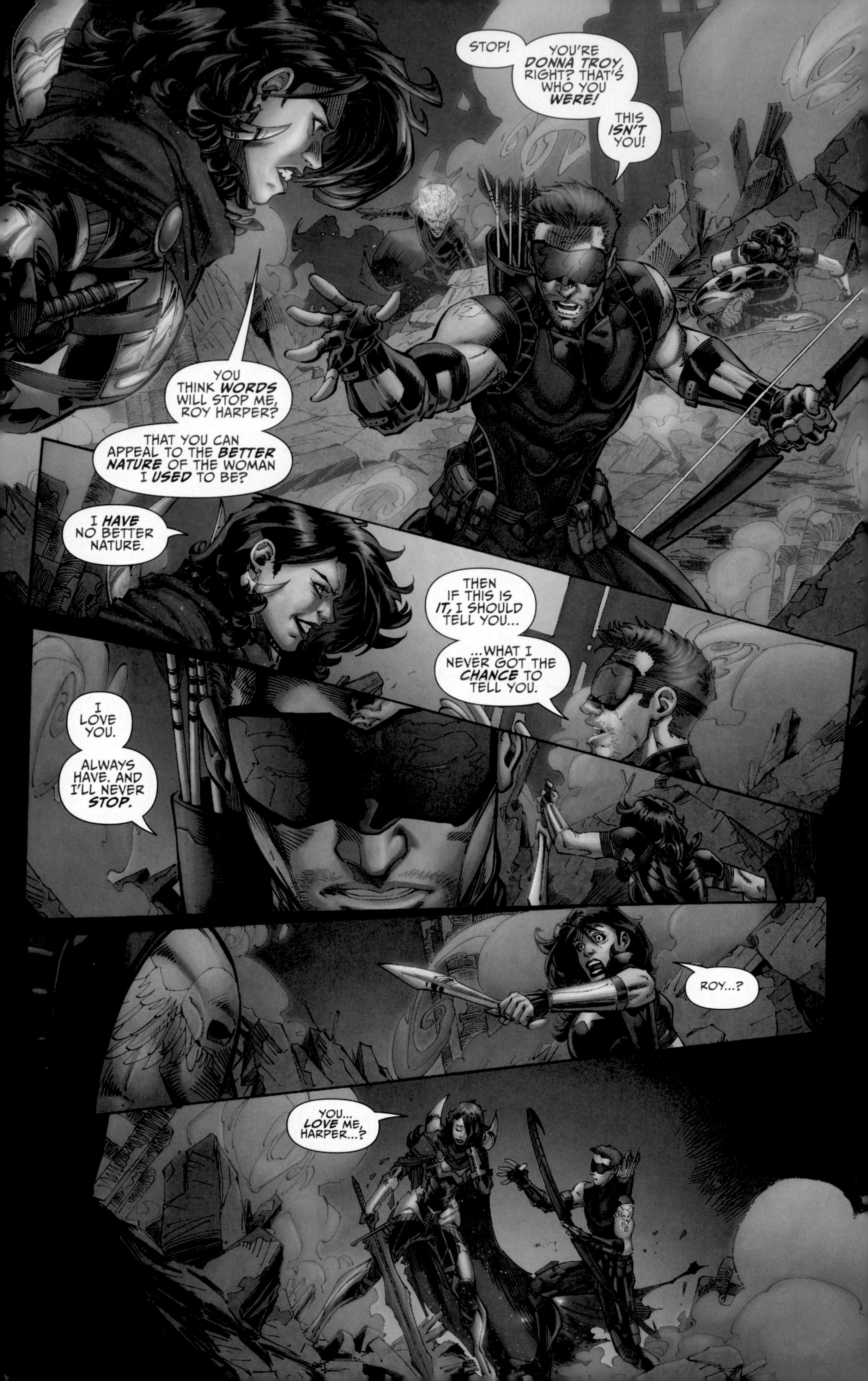
STOP!
YOU'RE DONNA TROY, RIGHT? THAT'S WHO YOU WERE!
THIS ISN'T YOU!
YOU THINK WORDS WILL STOP ME, ROY HARPER?
THAT YOU CAN APPEAL TO THE BETTER NATURE OF THE WOMAN I USED TO BE?
I HAVE NO BETTER NATURE.
THEN IF THIS IS IT, I SHOULD TELL YOU...
...WHAT I NEVER GOT THE CHANCE TO TELL YOU.
I LOVE YOU.
ALWAYS HAVE. AND I'LL NEVER STOP.
ROY...?
YOU... LOVE ME, HARPER...?

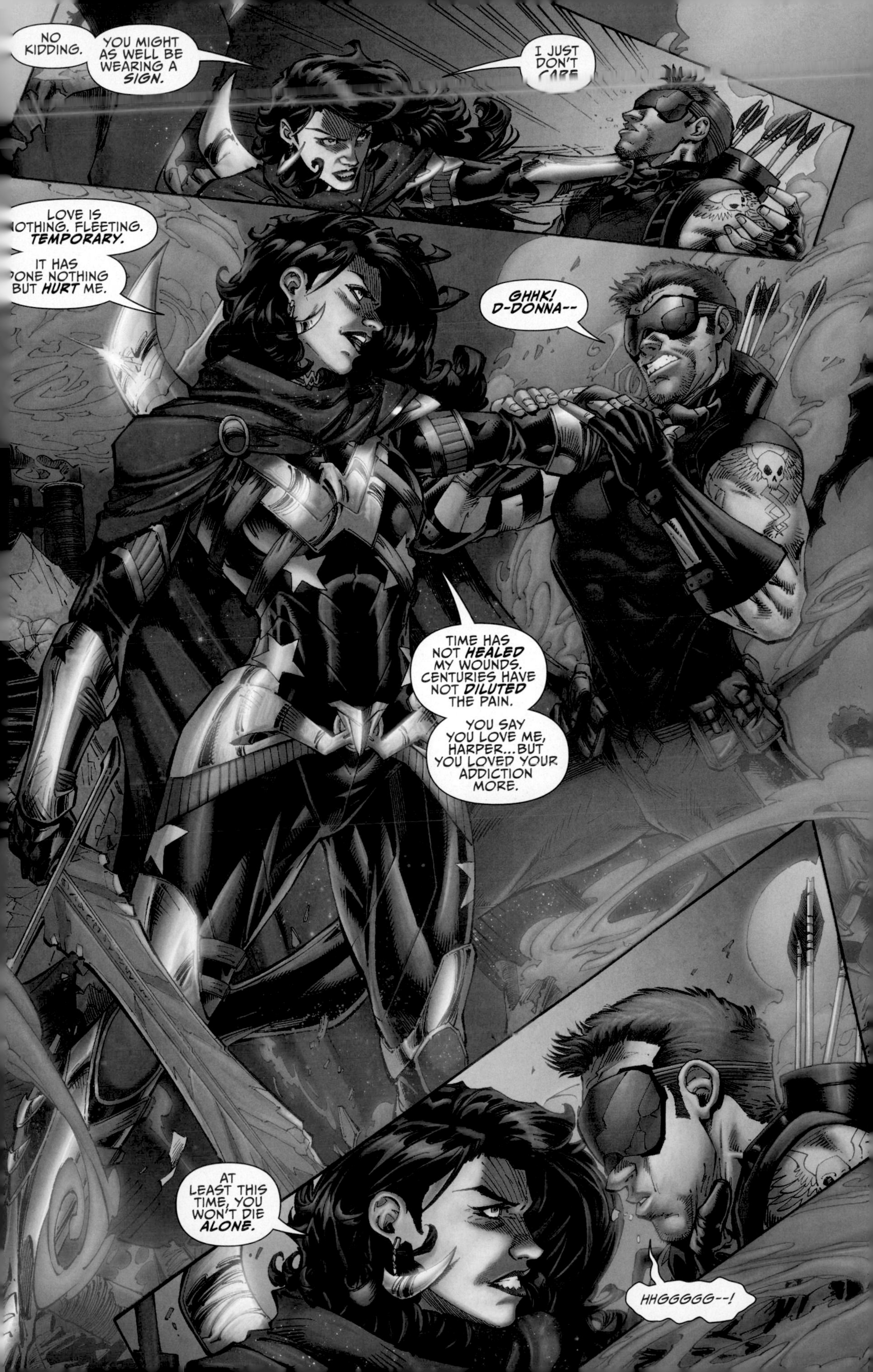
NO KIDDING.
YOU MIGHT AS WELL BE WEARING A SIGN.
I JUST DON'T CARE
LOVE IS NOTHING. FLEETING. TEMPORARY.
IT HAS DONE NOTHING BUT HURT ME.
GHHK! D-DONNA--
TIME HAS NOT HEALED MY WOUNDS. CENTURIES HAVE NOT DILUTED THE PAIN.
YOU SAY YOU LOVE ME, HARPER...BUT YOU LOVED YOUR ADDICTION MORE.
AT LEAST THIS TIME, YOU WON'T DIE ALONE.
HHGGGGG--!

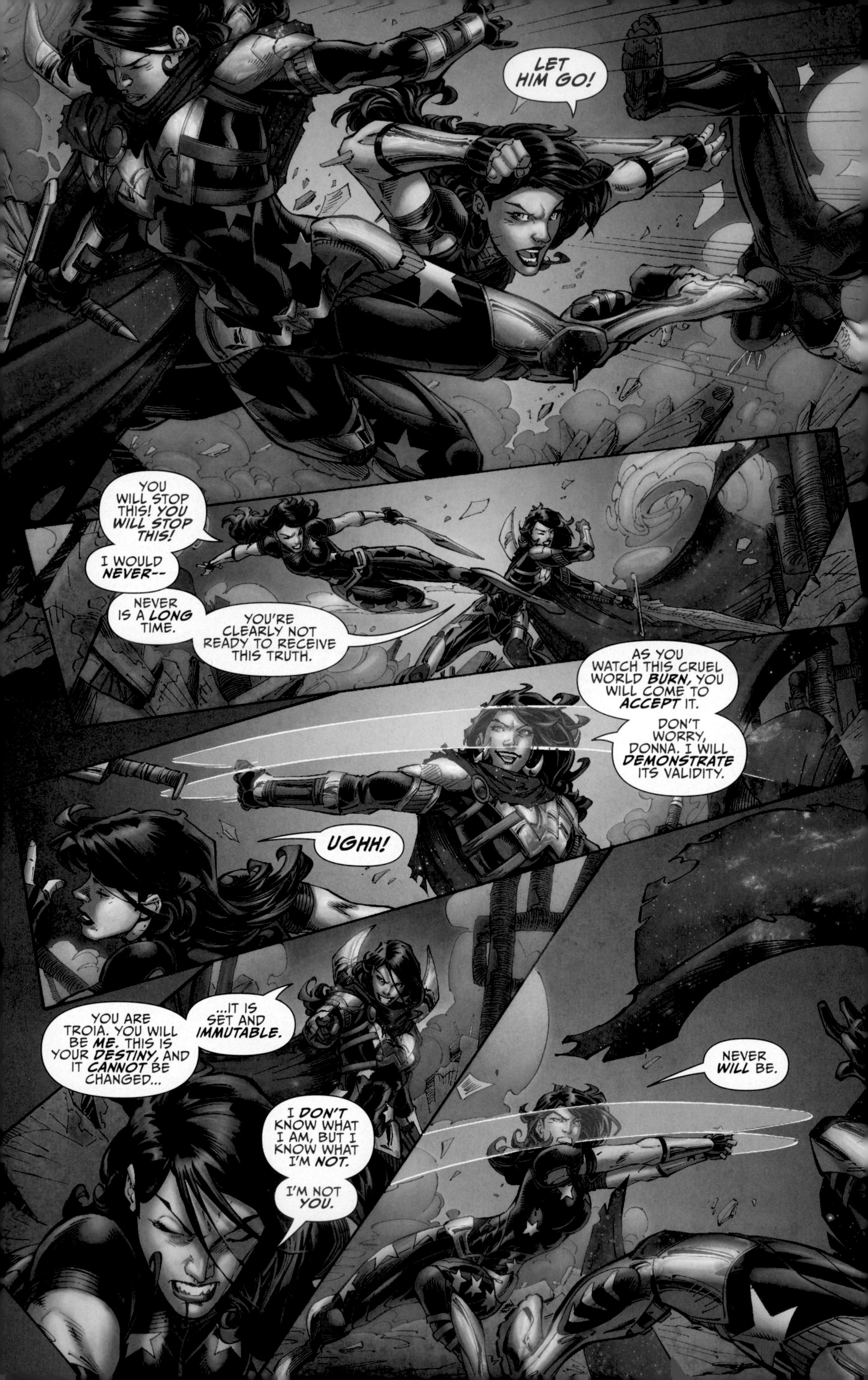
LET HIM GO!
YOU WILL STOP THIS! YOU WILL STOP THIS!
I WOULD NEVER--
NEVER IS A LONG TIME.
YOU'RE CLEARLY NOT READY TO RECEIVE THIS TRUTH.
AS YOU WATCH THIS CRUEL WORLD BURN, YOU WILL COME TO ACCEPT IT.
DON'T WORRY, DONNA. I WILL DEMONSTRATE ITS VALIDITY.
UGHH!
YOU ARE TROIA. YOU WILL BE ME. THIS IS YOUR DESTINY, AND IT CANNOT BE CHANGED...
...IT IS SET AND IMMUTABLE.
I DON'T KNOW WHAT I AM, BUT I KNOW WHAT I'M NOT.
I'M NOT YOU.
NEVER WILL BE.

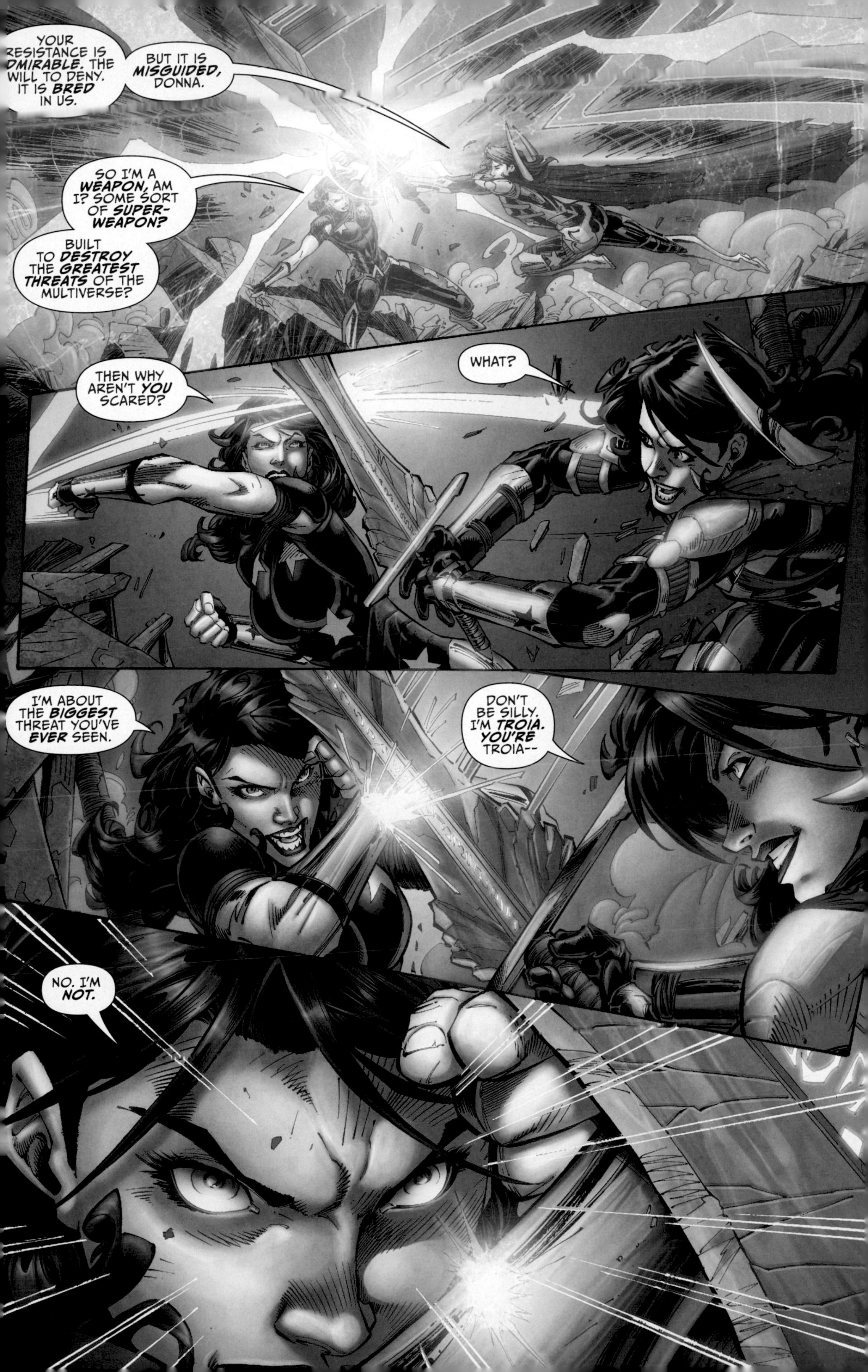
YOUR RESISTANCE IS ADMIRABLE. THE WILL TO DENY. IT IS BRED IN US.
BUT IT IS MISGUIDED, DONNA.
SO I'M A WEAPON, AM I? SOME SORT OF SUPER-WEAPON?
BUILT TO DESTROY THE GREATEST THREATS OF THE MULTIVERSE?
THEN WHY AREN'T YOU SCARED?
WHAT?
I'M ABOUT THE BIGGEST THREAT YOU'VE EVER SEEN.
DON'T BE SILLY. I'M TROIA. YOU'RE TROIA--
NO. I'M NOT.

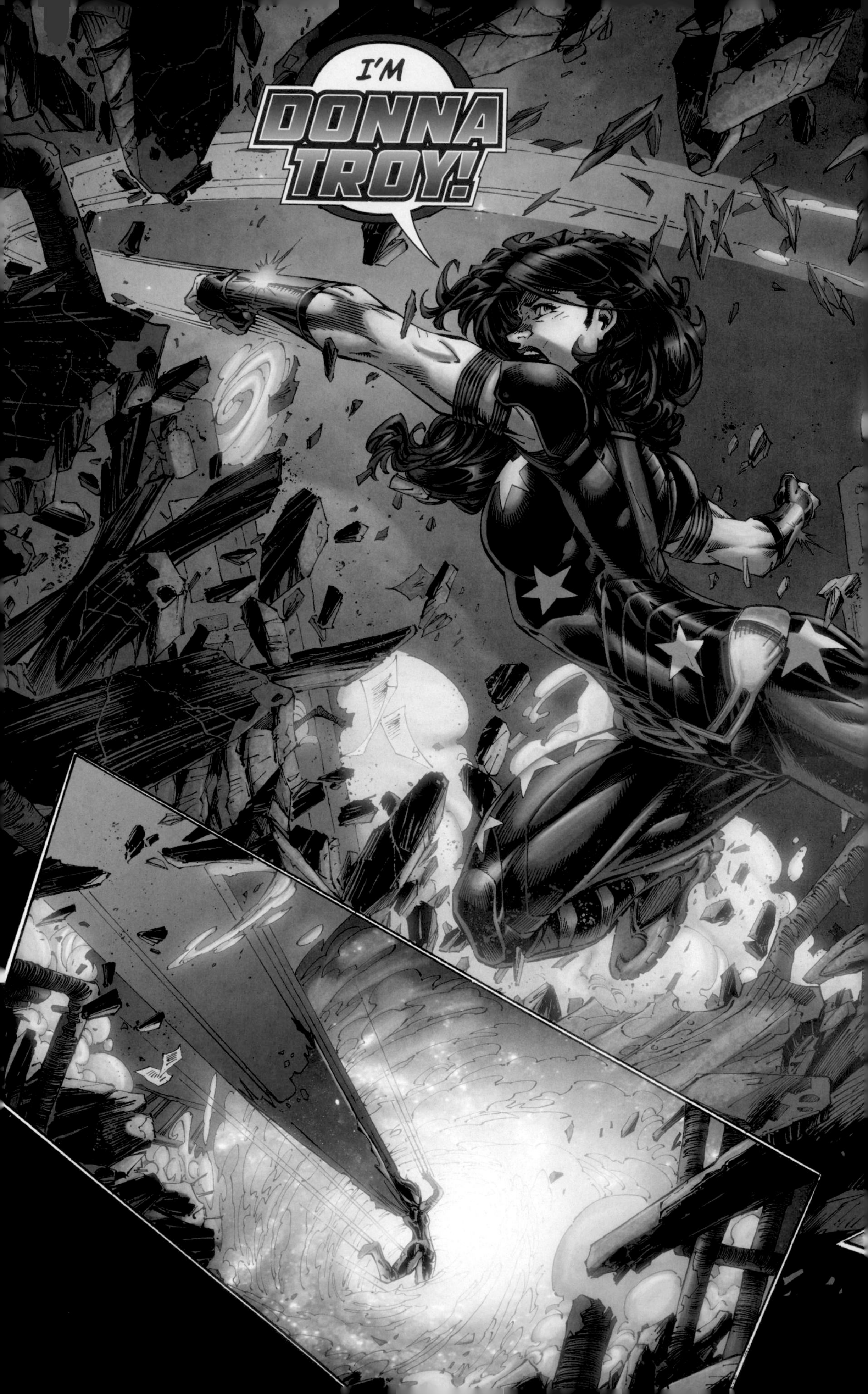
I'M DONNA TROY!

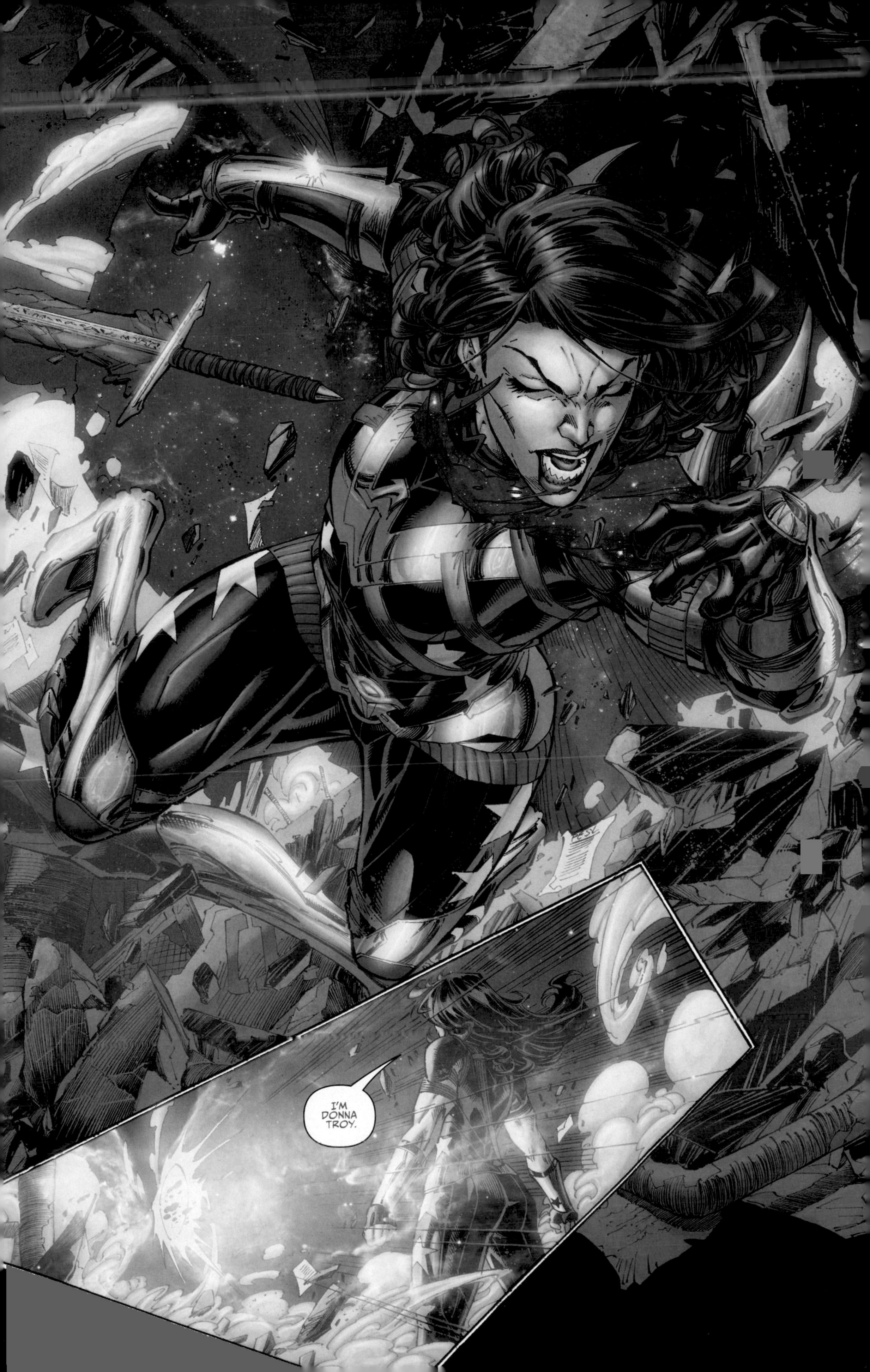
I'M DONNA TROY.

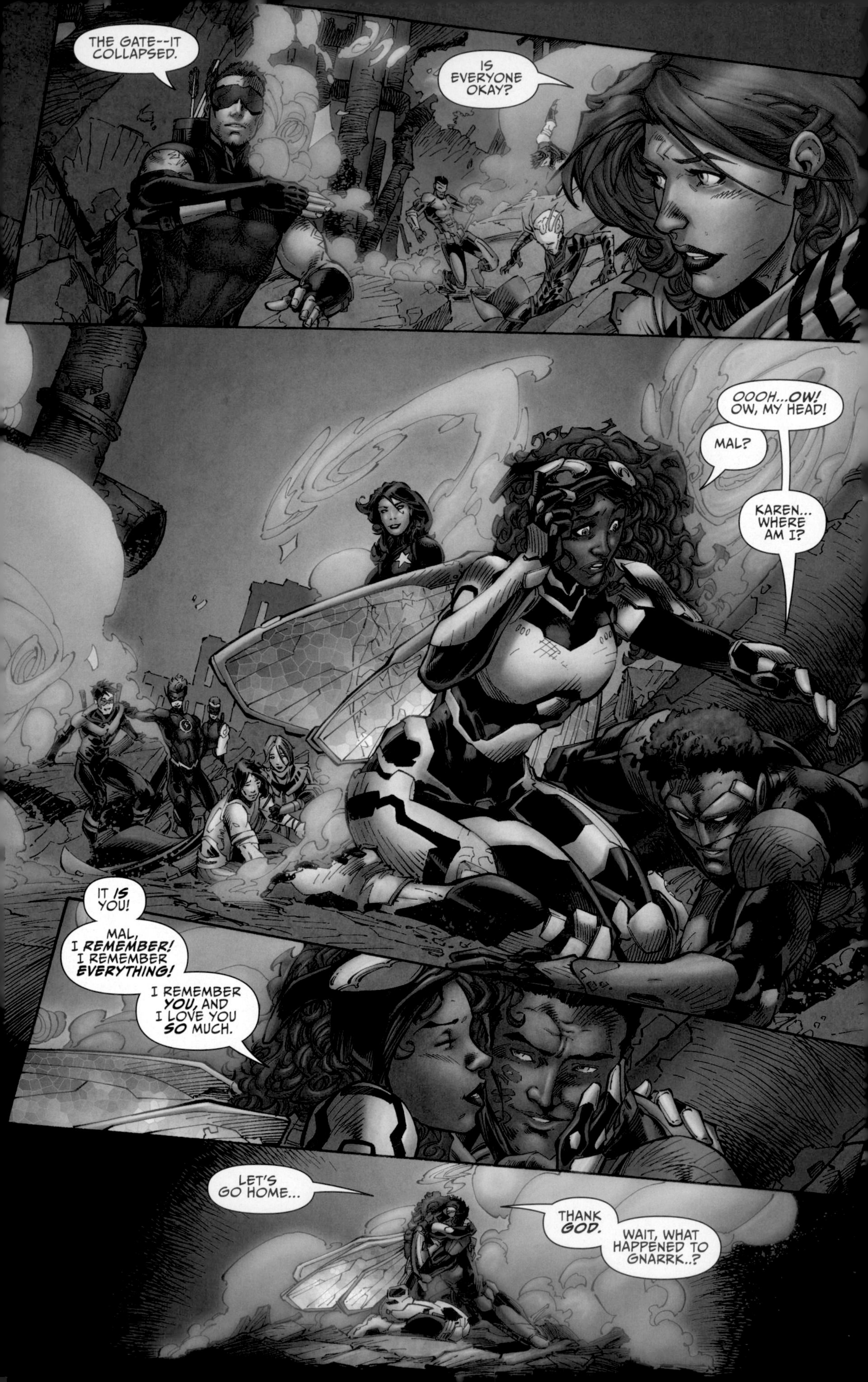
THE GATE--IT COLLAPSED.
IS EVERYONE OKAY?
OOOH...OW! OW, MY HEAD!
MAL?
KAREN... WHERE AM I?
IT IS YOU!
MAL, I REMEMBER! I REMEMBER EVERYTHING!
I REMEMBER YOU, AND I LOVE YOU SO MUCH.
LET'S GO HOME...
THANK GOD.
WAIT, WHAT HAPPENED TO GNARRK..?

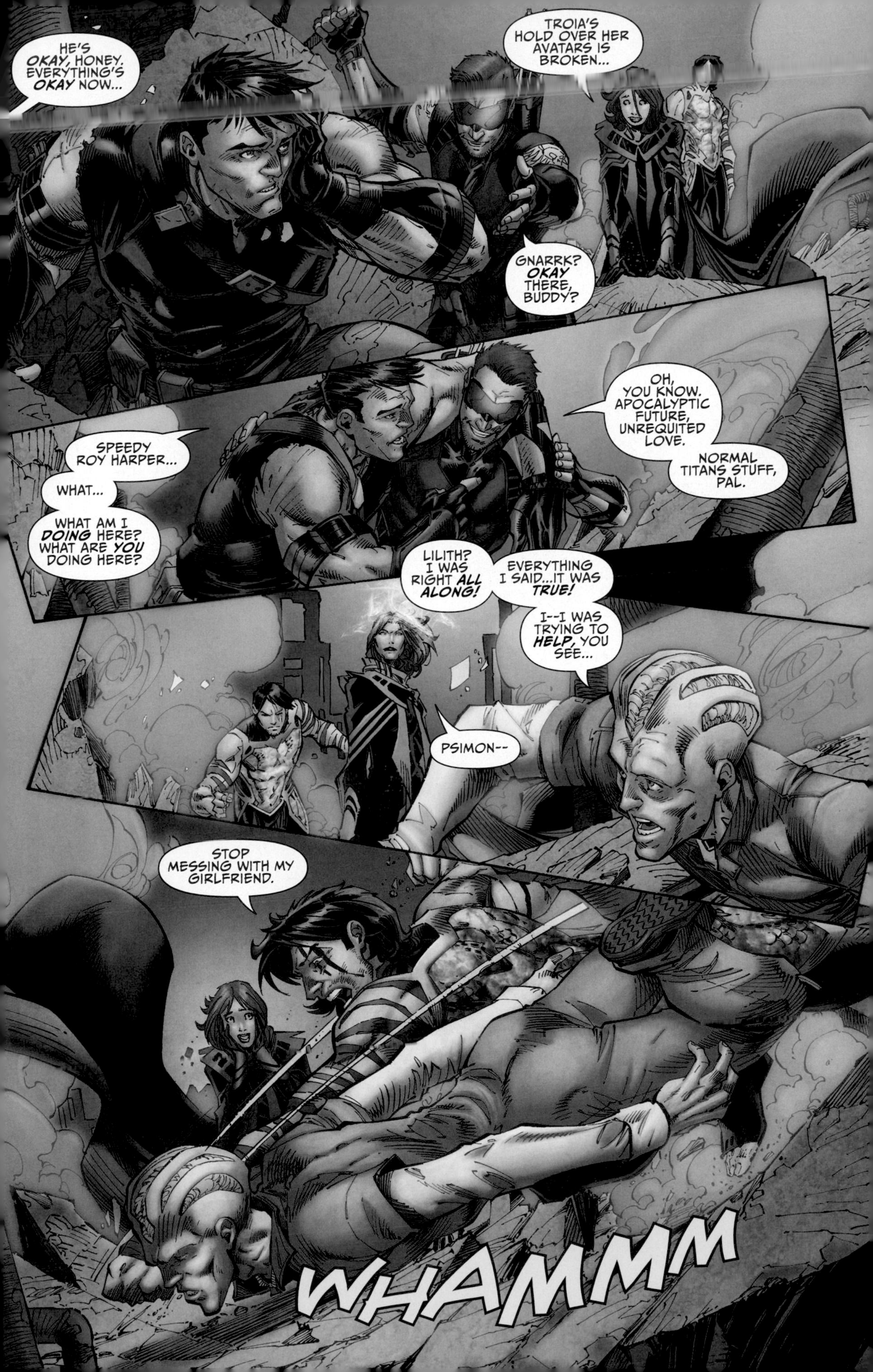
HE'S OKAY, HONEY. EVERYTHING'S OKAY NOW...
TROIA'S HOLD OVER HER AVATARS IS BROKEN...
GNARRK? OKAY THERE, BUDDY?
SPEEDY ROY HARPER...
WHAT...
WHAT AM I DOING HERE? WHAT ARE YOU DOING HERE?
OH, YOU KNOW. APOCALYPTIC FUTURE, UNREQUITED LOVE.
NORMAL TITANS STUFF, PAL.
LILITH? I WAS RIGHT ALL ALONG!
EVERYTHING I SAID...IT WAS TRUE!
I--I WAS TRYING TO HELP, YOU SEE...
PSIMON--
STOP MESSING WITH MY GIRLFRIEND.
WHAMMM

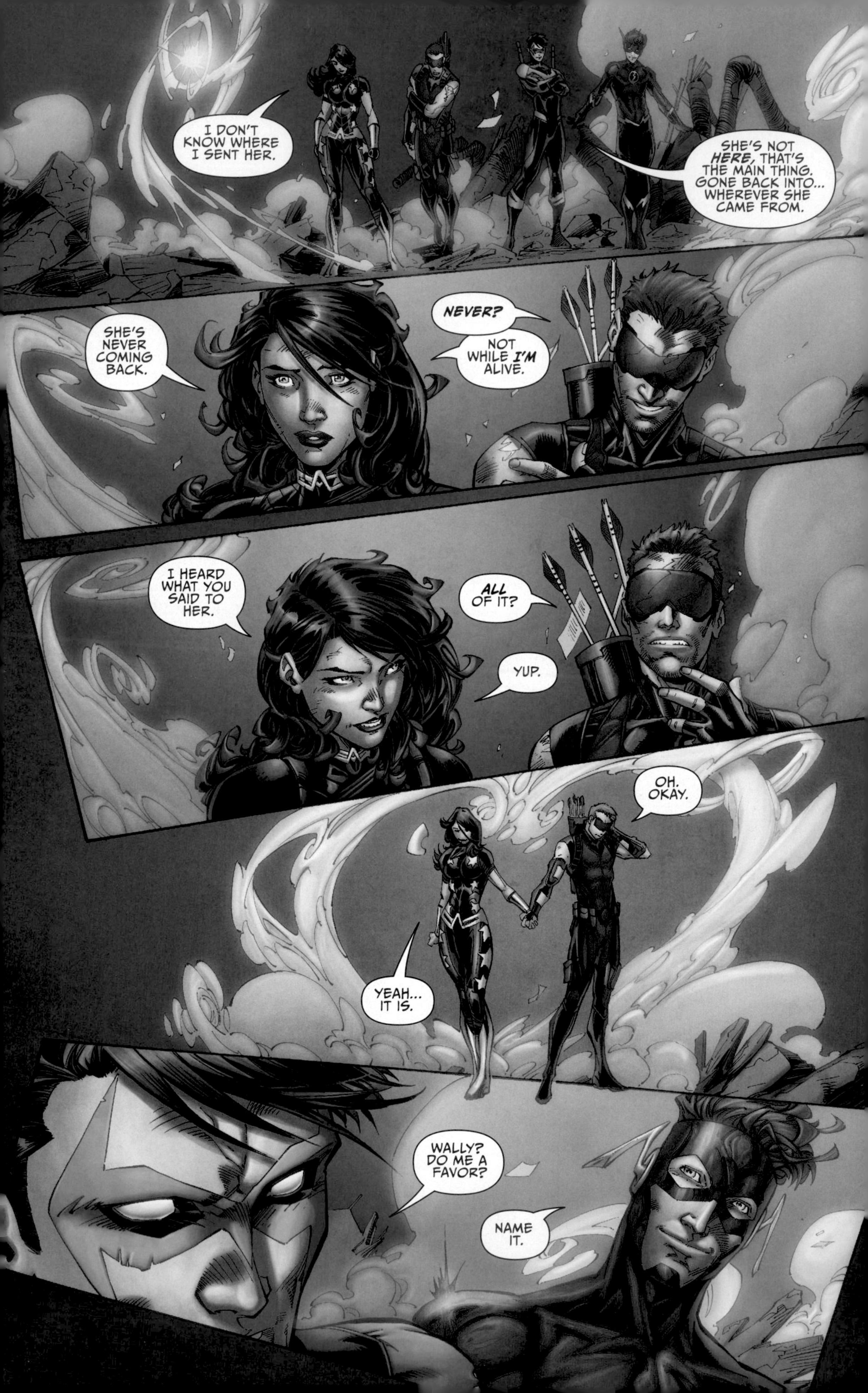
I DON'T KNOW WHERE I SENT HER.
SHE'S NOT *HERE*, THAT'S THE MAIN THING. GONE BACK INTO... WHEREVER SHE CAME FROM.
SHE'S NEVER COMING BACK.
NEVER?
NOT WHILE *I'M* ALIVE.
I HEARD WHAT YOU SAID TO HER.
ALL OF IT?
YUP.
OH. OKAY.
YEAH... IT IS.
WALLY? DO ME A FAVOR?
NAME IT.

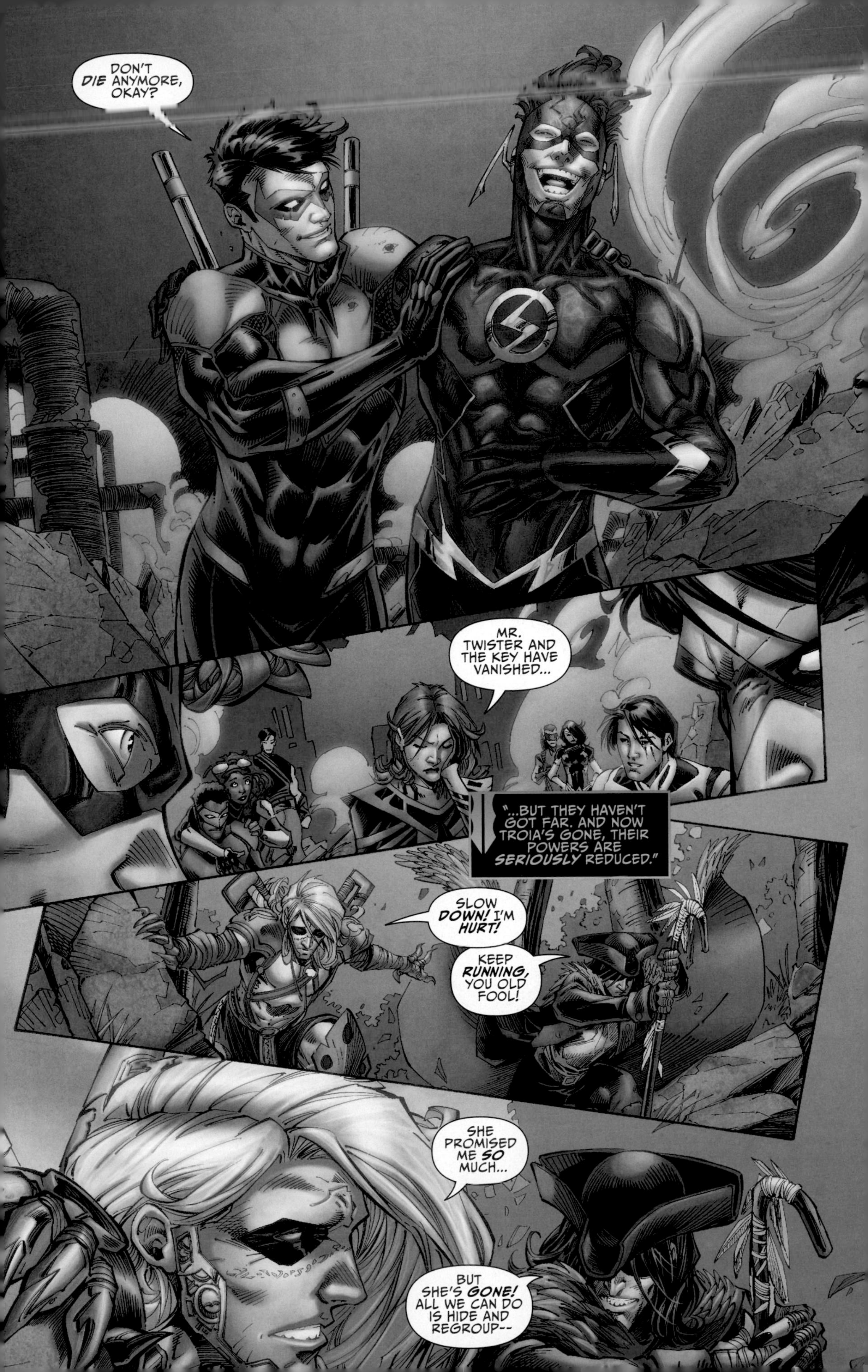
DON'T *DIE* ANYMORE, OKAY?
MR. TWISTER AND THE KEY HAVE VANISHED...
"...BUT THEY HAVEN'T GOT FAR. AND NOW TROIA'S GONE, THEIR POWERS ARE *SERIOUSLY* REDUCED."
SLOW *DOWN!* I'M *HURT!*
KEEP *RUNNING,* YOU OLD FOOL!
SHE PROMISED ME *SO* MUCH...
BUT SHE'S *GONE!* ALL WE CAN DO IS HIDE AND REGROUP--

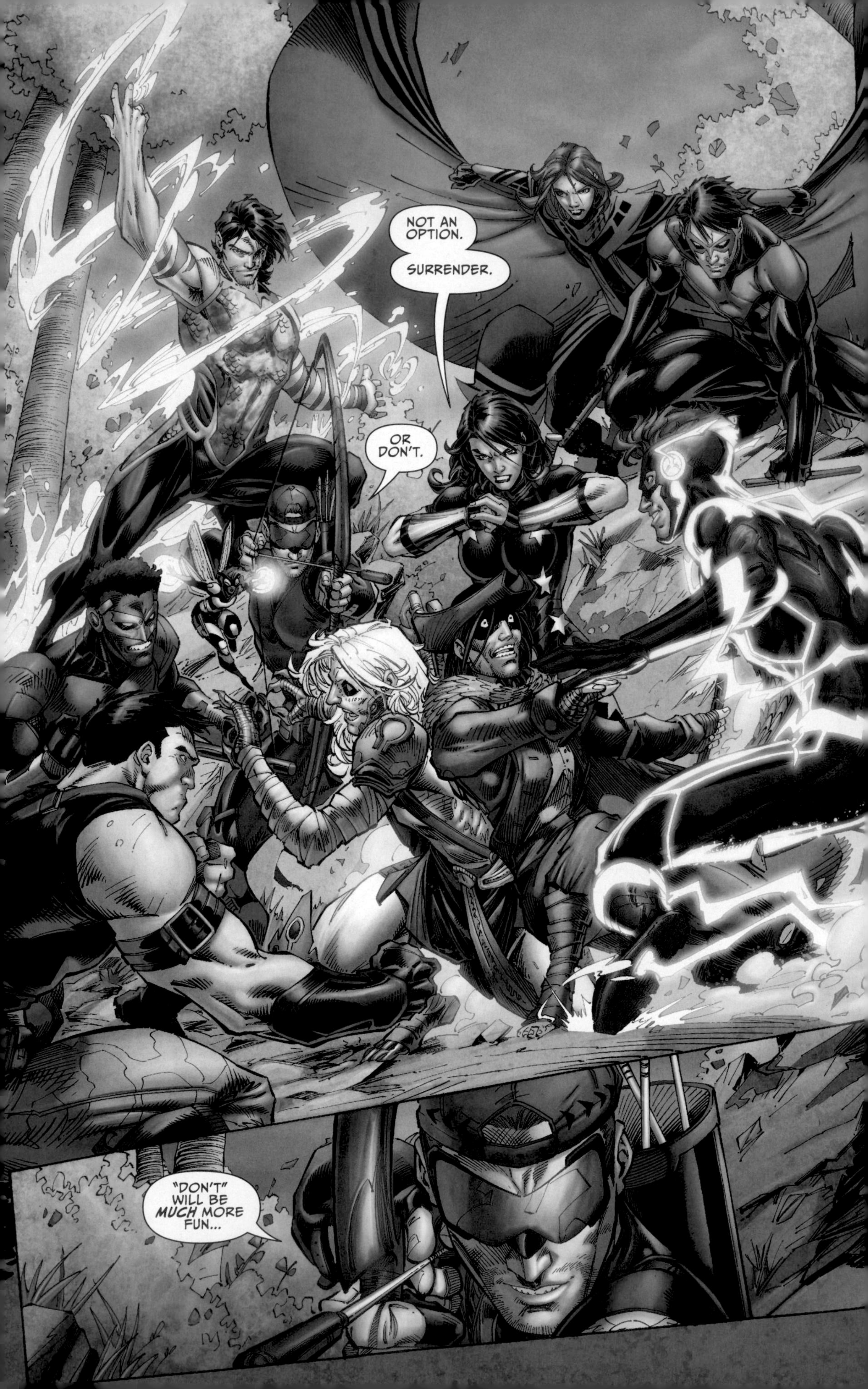
NOT AN OPTION.
SURRENDER.
OR DON'T.
"DON'T" WILL BE *MUCH* MORE FUN...

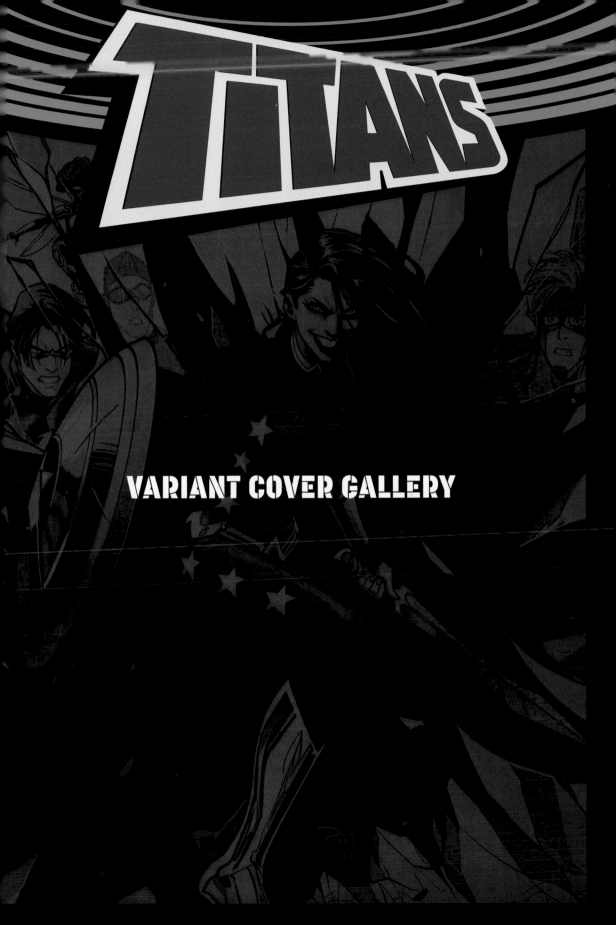

TITANS

VARIANT COVER GALLERY

TITANS #12 variant cover by DAN MORA

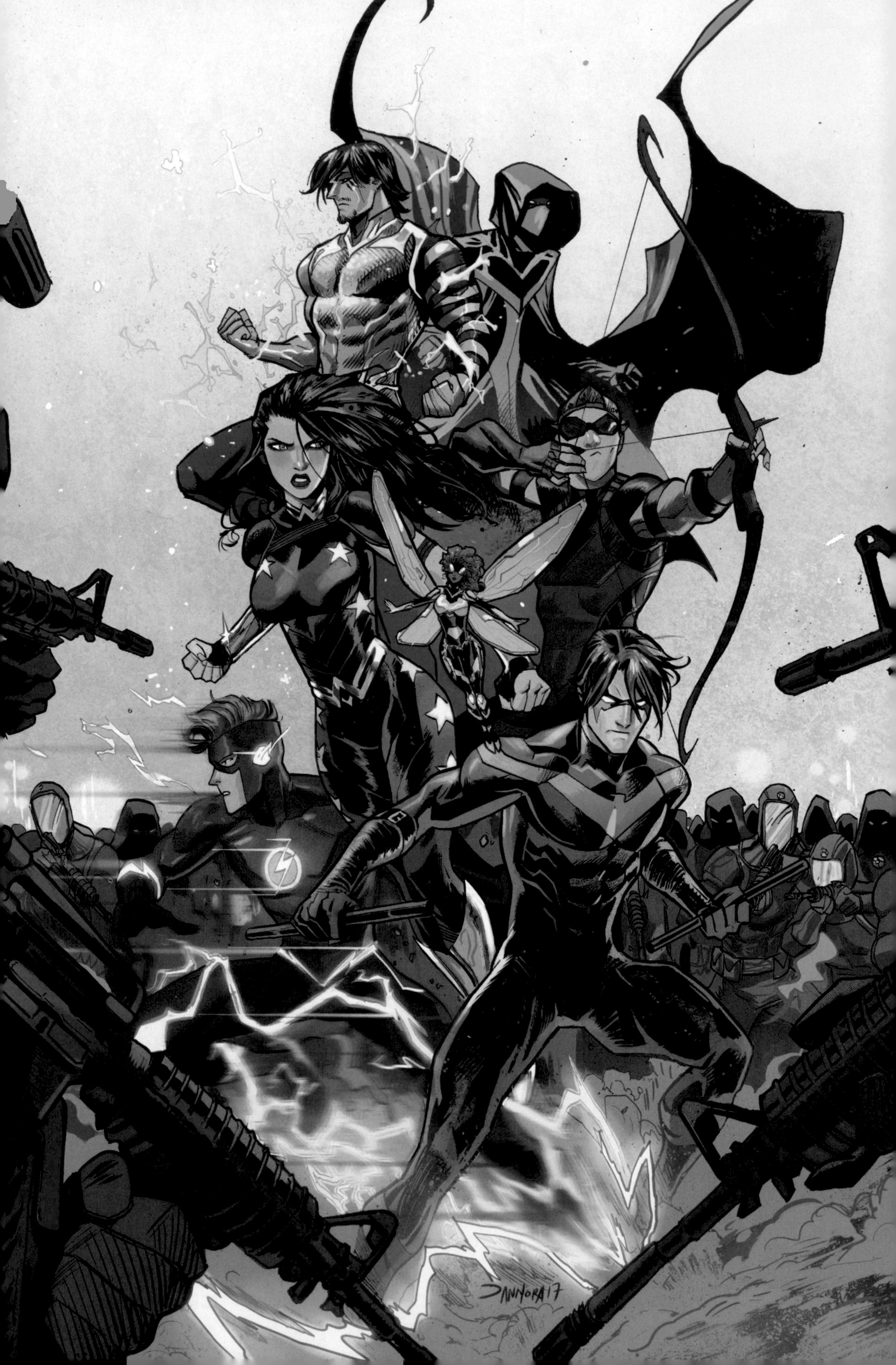

TITANS #13 variant cover by DAN MORA

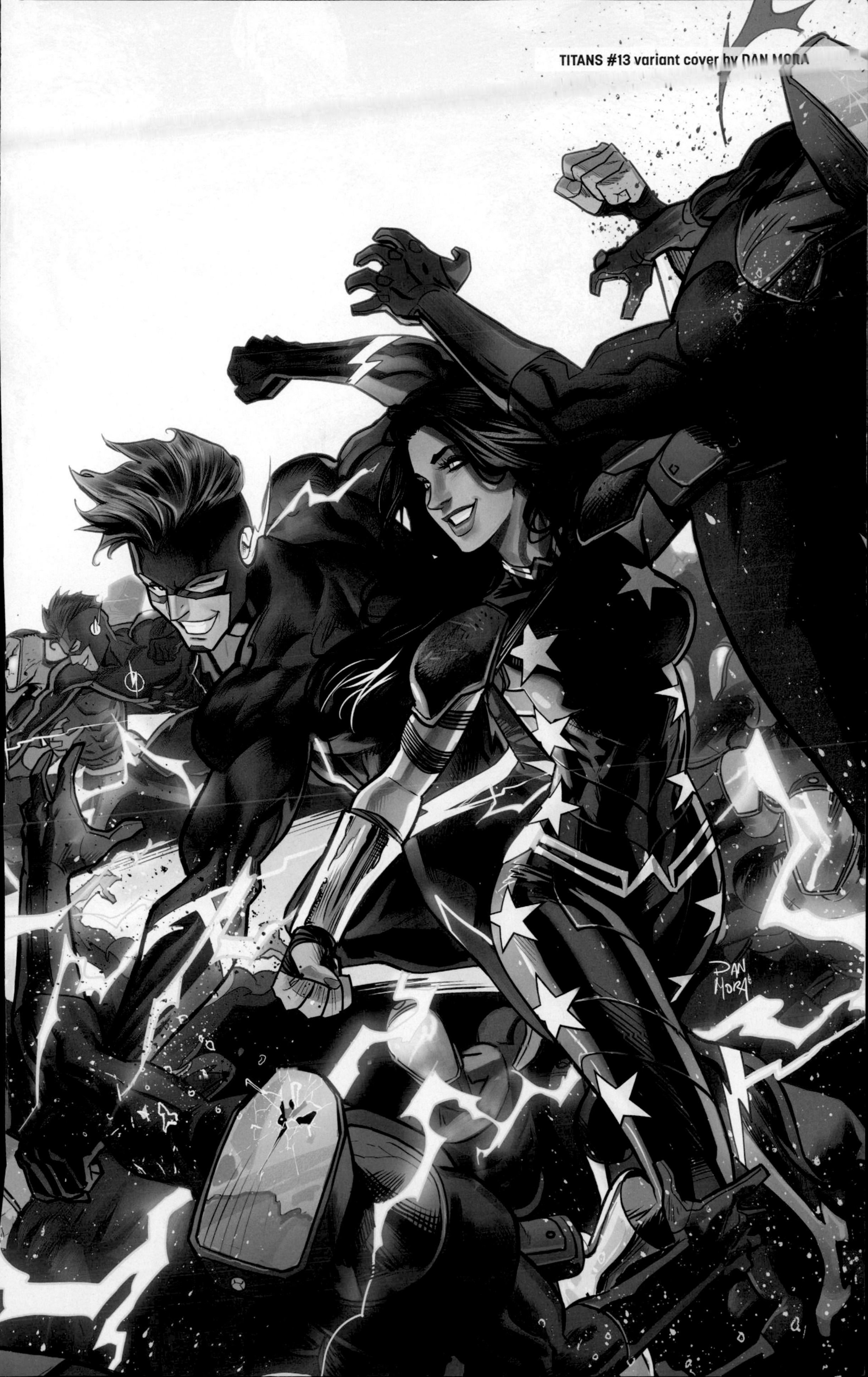
DAN MORA

TITANS #14 variant cover by DAN MORA

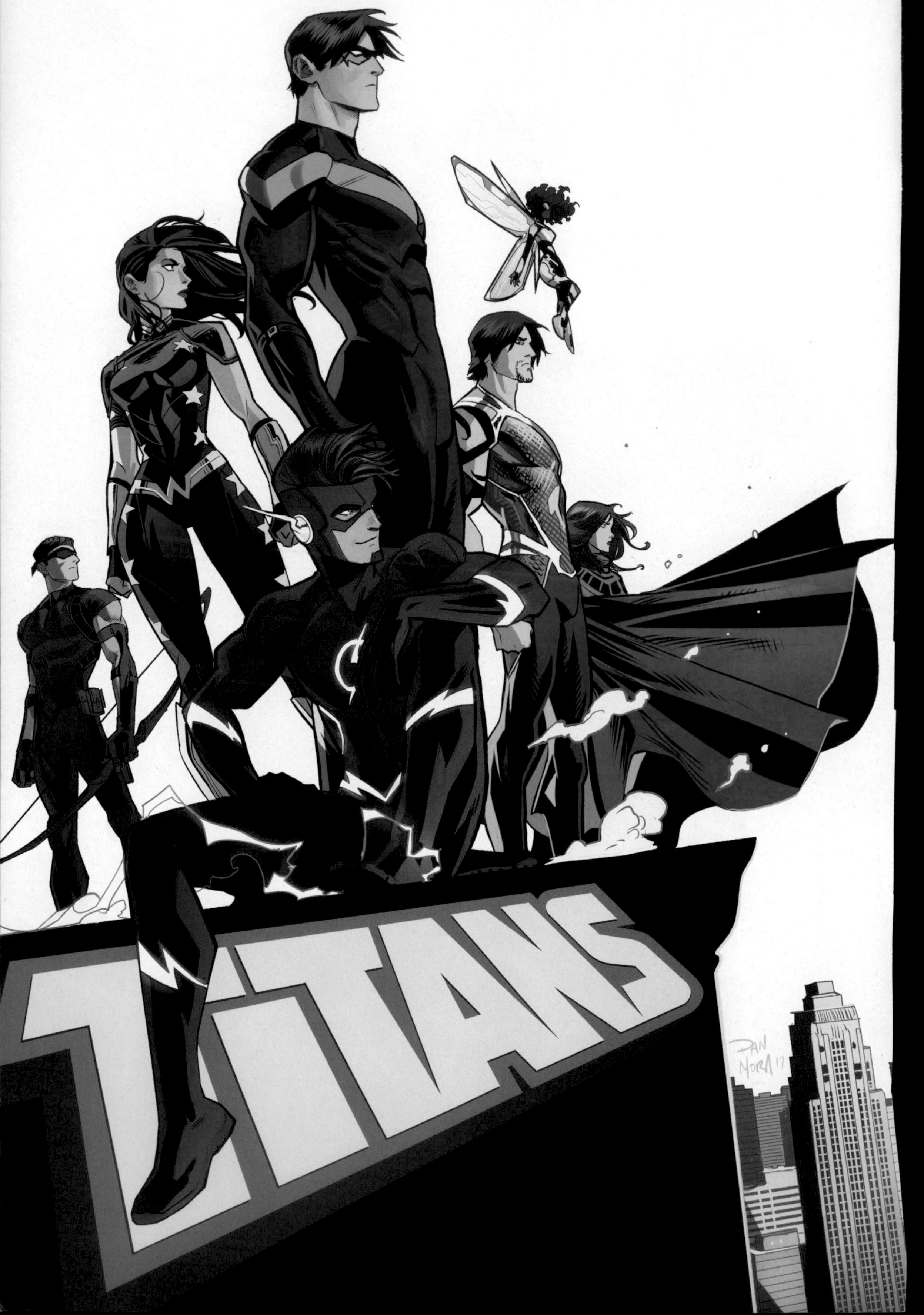
TITANS
DAN MORA '17

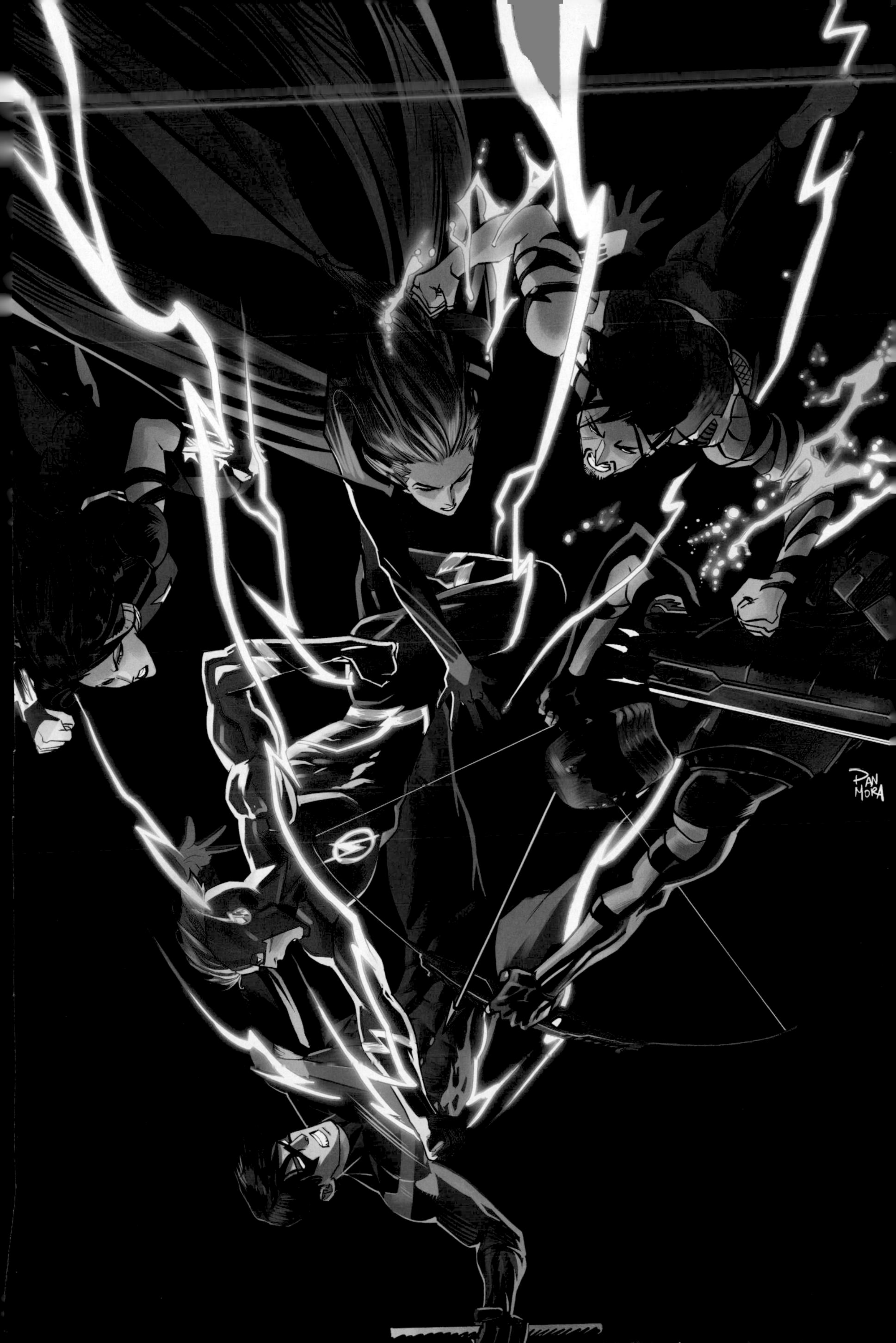
DAN
MORA

TITANS #15 variant cover by DAN MORA

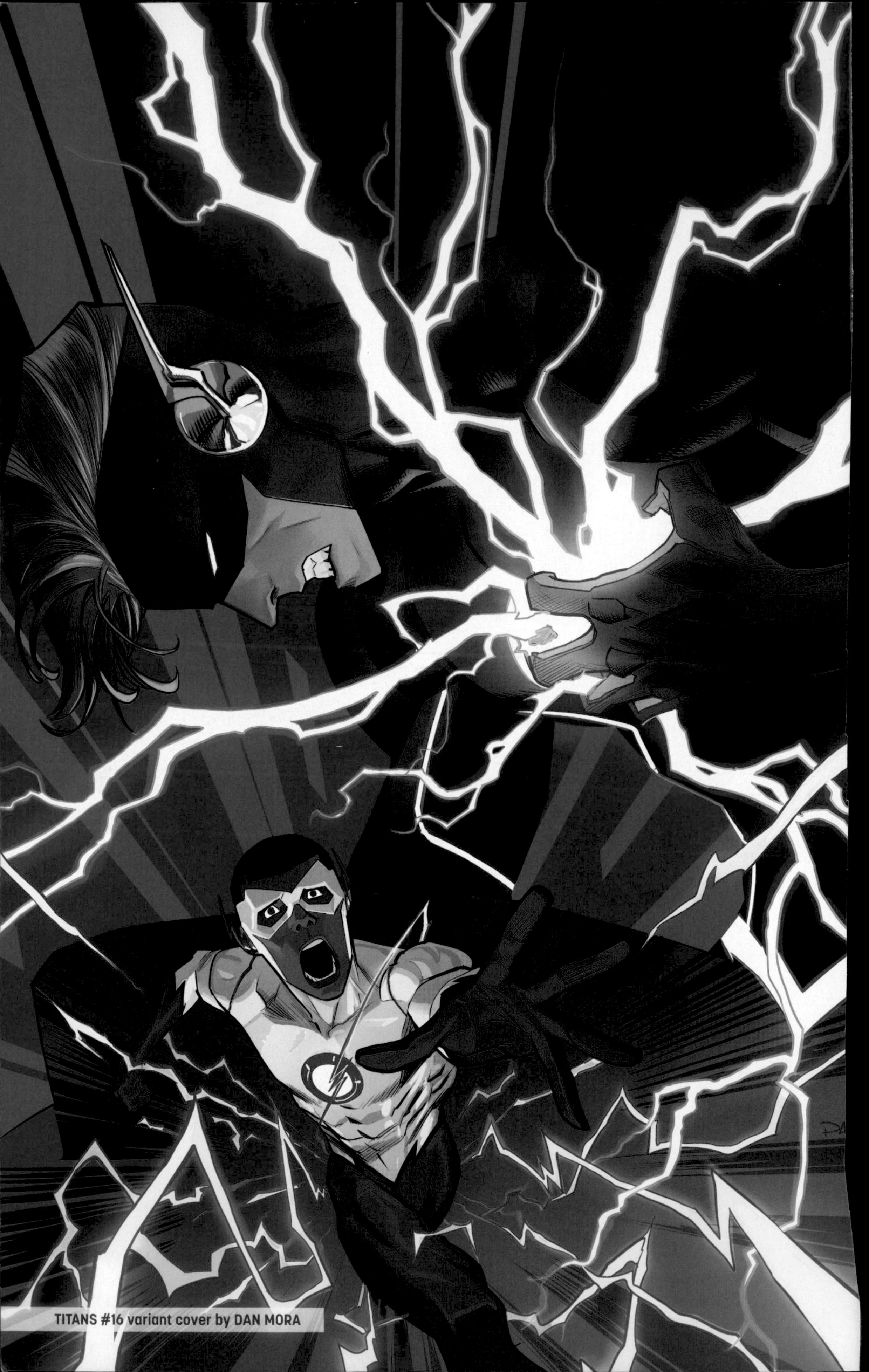

TITANS #16 variant cover by DAN MORA

TITANS #17 variant cover by DAN MORA

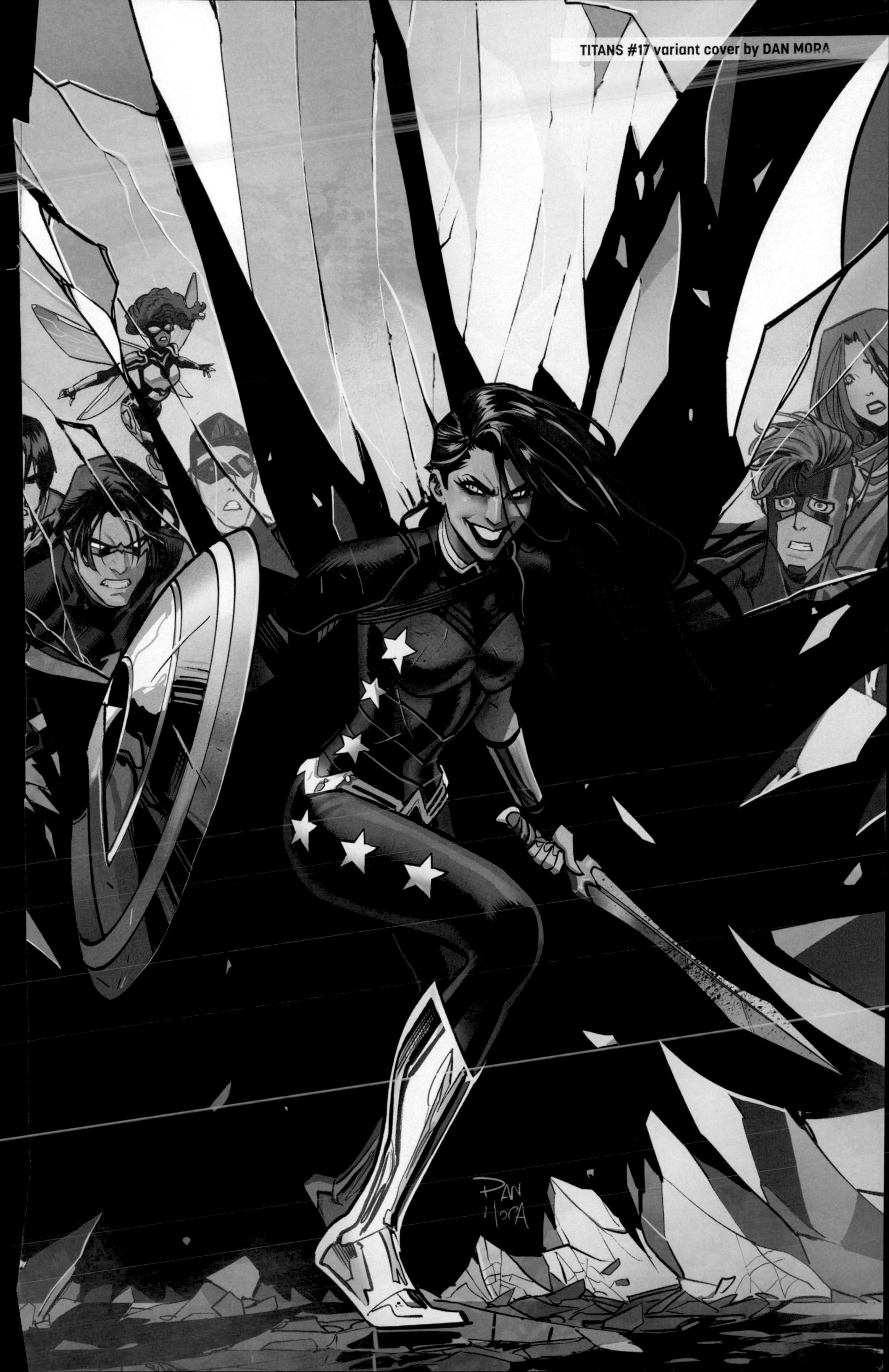
DAN MORA

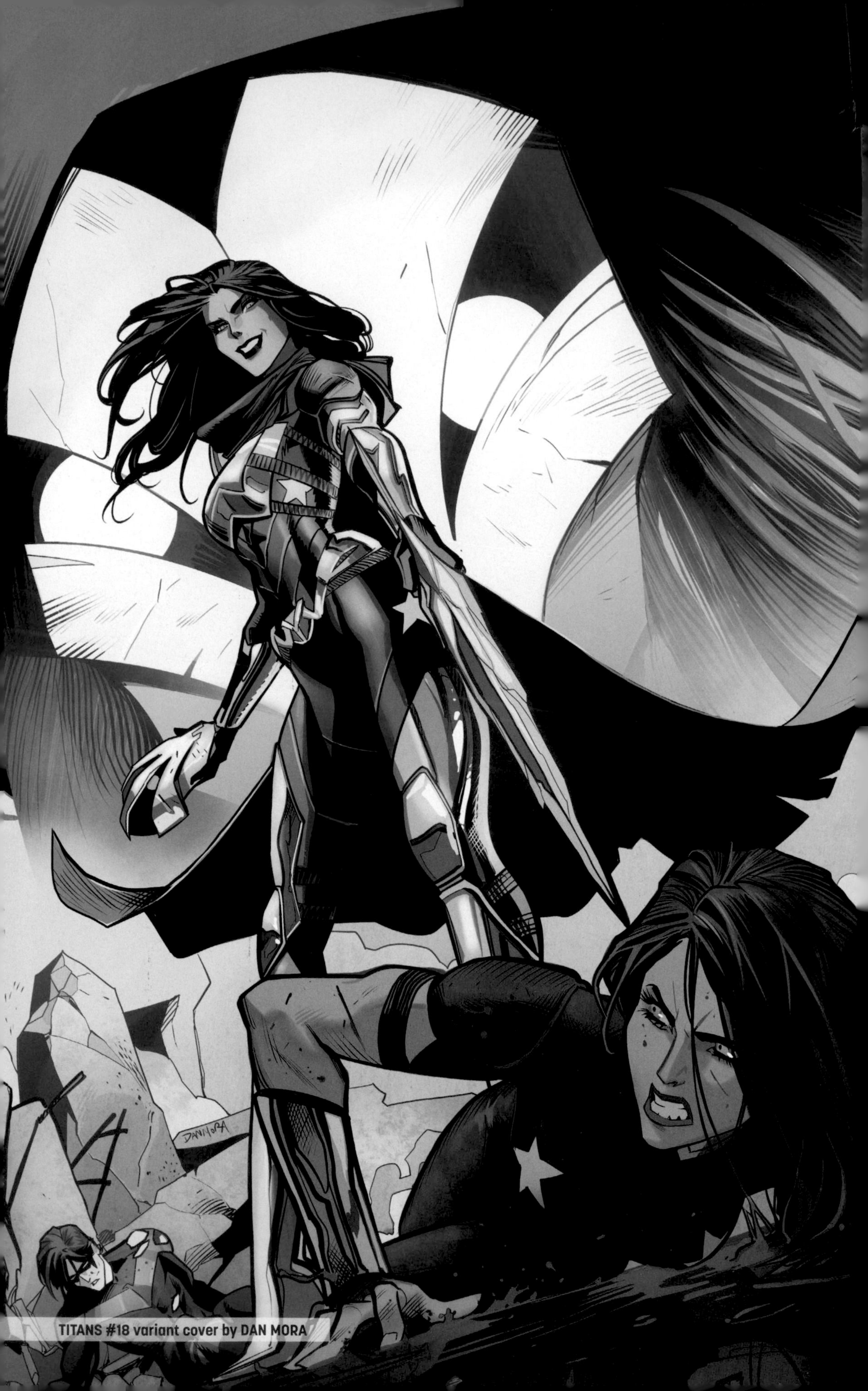

TITANS #18 variant cover by DAN MORA

"Stellar. A solid yarn that roots itself in Grayson's past, with gorgeous artwork by Barrows."
– IGN

"Dynamic."
– THE NEW YORK TIMES

THE NEW 52!
NIGHTWING
VOLUME 1
TRAPS AND
TRAPEZES
"I THINK A NEW GENERATION IS GOING TO FALL IN LOVE WITH NIGHTWING."
— MTV GEEK
KYLE HIGGINS EDDY BARROWS

NIGHTWING

VOL. 1: TRAPS AND TRAPEZES

KYLE HIGGINS
with EDDY BARROWS

THE NEW YORK TIMES BESTSELLING SERIES
THE NEW 52!
NIGHTWING
"NIGHT OF THE OWLS IS RAMPING UP AND IT IS AWESOME."
— IGN
VOLUME 2
NIGHT OF
THE OWLS
KYLE HIGGINS EDDY BARROWS

NIGHTWING
VOL. 2: NIGHT OF THE OWLS

THE #1 NEW YORK TIMES BEST-SELLING SERIES
NIGHTWING
THE NEW 52!
VOLUME 3
DEATH
OF THE
FAMILY
"THIS IS A BOOK YOU NEED TO READ."
— HUFFINGTON POST
AMUSE
KYLE HIGGINS EDDY BARROWS ANDRES GUINALDO

NIGHTWING
VOL. 3: DEATH OF THE FAMILY

READ THE ENTIRE EPI

NIGHTWING VOL
SECOND C

NIGHTWING VOL
SETTING S

"A new generation is goi
fall in love with Nightw
– MTV G

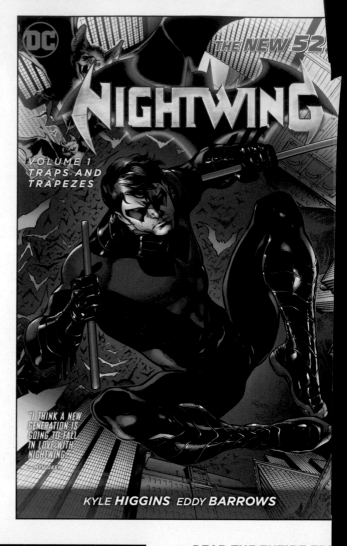